RELATIONS

RELATIONS

AN ANTHROPOLOGICAL ACCOUNT

Marilyn Strathern

Duke University Press   *Durham and London*   2020

© 2020 Duke University Press
All rights reserved
Printed in the United States of America on acid-free paper ∞
Designed by Courtney Leigh Baker
Typeset in Garamond Premier Pro and Knockout by
Tseng Information Systems, Inc.

Library of Congress Cataloging-in-Publication Data
Names: Strathern, Marilyn, author.
Title: Relations : an anthropological account / Marilyn Strathern.
Description: Durham : Duke University Press, 2020. |
Includes bibliographical references and index.
Identifiers: LCCN 2019036378 (print)
LCCN 2019036379 (ebook)
ISBN 9781478007845 (hardcover)
ISBN 9781478008354 (paperback)
ISBN 9781478009344 (ebook)
Subjects: LCSH: Interpersonal relations. | Interpersonal relations
and culture. | Ethnology — Methodology. | Anthropology —
Methodology. | English language — Discourse analysis.
Classification: LCC GN345 .S77 2020 (print) | LCC GN345 (ebook) |
DDC 302 — dc23
LC record available at https://lccn.loc.gov/2019036378
LC ebook record available at https://lccn.loc.gov/2019036379

Cover art and frontispiece: Joseph Wright of Derby, *An experiment
on a bird in the air pump* (1768). The National Gallery, London.

FOR MT, MCC

Contents

Preface · ix
Introductions: The Compulsion of Relations · 1

PART I

1. EXPERIMENTATIONS, ENGLISH AND OTHERWISE · 25
2. REGISTERS OF COMPARISON · 45
Coda to Part I: Comparing Persons Again · 69

PART II

3. EXPANSION AND CONTRACTION · 73
4. THE DISSIMILAR AND THE DIFFERENT · 97
Coda to Part II: Preparation · 117

PART III

5. ENLIGHTENMENT DRAMAS · 121
6. KINSHIP UNBOUND · 143
Coda to Part III: Visibility · 165

Conclusions: The Reinvention of
Relation at Moments of Knowledge-Making · 167

Notes · 191   References · 229
Index of Names and Places · 251   Index of Subjects · 259

Preface

Many more relations inhabit this book than those on which I remark. Ruminating on how paradigms shift and turn, some ten years ago Navaro (Navaro-Yashin 2009) concluded that ethnography leads one to write against that grain, namely against the way old conceptual apparatuses are forever discarded in favor of new ones. Ethnography instead invites trans- or multiparadigmatic writing. For when a conceptual apparatus is under scrutiny, one's inclination is to assume that it is being scrutinized in order precisely to discard, displace, or bypass it. That is not the case with relations, nor with the arena of their attention in the present work, sociocultural anthropology of the English-speaking variety. In fact I would not mind if much of what follows is received as a report on a state of affairs; the concept of the relation might then have been "ethnographically" conceived. To bring this about, we might say that the work had to be written precisely against the grain of that expectation about paradigms.

There are indeed many more relations in this book than those remarked. Among the unremarked is the sense of proportion with which disciplines marshal their subject matter. In mind is the order and range of detail that the reader will encounter in diverse materials presented here. By itself, detail may seem "out of" proportion (too much, too little). Yet the order of proposition hazarded by anthropologists is — more or less — taken for granted. They know what is meant by a case study or a particular example, or by a characterization of a mode of thought or set of values. There is, more or less, and embracing multiple purposes, an overall intention in common. In twentieth-century terms, the intention was imagined as elucidating the social or cultural character of phenomena, an imagination that endures latterly in vigorous attempts to make such terms appear anachronistic. The approach axiomatically assumes that the character in question must be grasped relationally, that is, analysis will rest in unraveling the relations involved. Such an assumption molds anthropological exposition, and this is the heart of the book. It is about descriptive (subsuming analytical) practices. I do not abandon my long-standing agnosticism as to the feelings, states of mind, or thoughts of the people mentioned here, but perhaps I make more explicit than usual my fascination with forms of expression and modes of argumentation, and the symbolic resources on which they draw. *Images* of thought, as Viveiros de Castro reiterates of concepts. They make the worlds through which we speak, no less.

I refer at many junctures to specific times and places, as I do, for example, to twentieth-century English. At times it is to comment on what seems unusual or unique. Indeed, expository convention often takes this to be the point of specificity (a first occurrence, an exclusive characteristic). However, an ethnographer might also wish to be particular about a concatenation of circumstances, apropos some twentieth-century English usage, say, without claiming that it never happened before the twentieth century or applies only to the English. After all, a phenomenon may be of "cultural" salience without conferring distinctiveness. This is frequently the case in what follows. I hope it will be clear which emphasis is meant. In addition, the materials are often doing double work; although I rarely draw attention to the connections, within many of the diverse examples are observations that support or supplement suppositions made elsewhere in the account. As to diversity of time and place, what are drawn from all those historical and geographical circumstances do not amount to independent data ready for further illumination by an already-made proposition concerning the concept of relation. Rather, with that concept being the object of scrutiny, they are intended as frameworks or contexts as though they were doing the work of analysis. It is thus that the air pump in Joseph Wright's eighteenth-century depiction of *An experiment on a bird in the air pump* (see the frontispiece) is, so to speak, the context for the bird's agitation and its dramatic effect on those around it. The cause, the slow withdrawal of air, points to the mechanical device as though its various elements offered an analysis or diagnosis of those relations. A timekeeper registers its effects.

My father (Eric Evans) always thought the householder with his hand on the watch might have been Erasmus Darwin, his two sons also present, although identifying the figures in the painting is a continuing matter of dispute. In other publications I have acknowledged my mother's inspiration; here, I acknowledge Eric's. He was nineteen when he bought a secondhand and much-annotated edition of Locke's *An essay concerning human understanding*, and at twenty-one he acquired a matching copy of *Essays, literary, moral, and political* by Hume, whose skepticism he so much admired. (That was about the age when Hume himself discovered those paradigm-changers, Descartes and Locke.) Eric might have been surprised that I have made so much of them since.

THIS BOOK BEGAN life as a collection of essays, in the main already published, and initially considered by Duke University Press as such. The essays' metamorphosis is due to the encouragement of the press; among other things, it has enabled me to correct some inaccuracies. With great warmth I thank Duke's commissioning editor, Gisela Fosado, who spurred me on, as well as Liz Smith and the editorial team. The cover design had an early beginning in Daniel Evans's conceptual work.

Since earlier versions of the chapters have thus appeared elsewhere, I must at the outset acknowledge these sources, while also making a general acknowledgment of those editors and convenors of collected works who, in all manner of ways, have been behind the present venture. The sources follow, in order of publication:

"Reading relations backwards" (Marett Memorial Lecture, Oxford). 2014. *Journal of the Royal Anthropological Institute* (n.s.) 20 (1): 3–19.
"Anthropological reasoning: Some threads of thought." 2015. Ed. S. Green. *HAU: Journal of Ethnographic Theory* 4 (3): 23–37.
"Being one, being multiple: A future for anthropological relations." 2015. In G. Mohácsi and A. Morita, eds., "Acting with nonhuman entities," special issue, *NatureCulture* 0.3: 122–157 (online).
"Connections, friends and their relations: An issue in knowledge-making." 2017. In P. Charbonnier, G. Salmon, and P. Skafish, eds., *Comparative metaphysics: Ontology after anthropology*, 61–83. London: Rowman and Littlefield.
"Naturalism and the invention of identity." 2017. Ed. C. Jensen and A. Morita. *Social Analysis* 61 (2): 15–30.
"Afterword: Becoming enlightened about relations." 2018. In N. Rapport and H. Wardle, eds., *An anthropology of the Enlightenment: Moral social relations then and today*, ASA Monograph Series, 171–188. London: Bloomsbury.
"Opening up relations." 2018. In M. de la Cadena and M. Blaser, eds.,

A world of many worlds, 23–52. Durham, NC: Duke University Press.

"Friendship and kinship: Comparatism and its theoretical possibilities in anthropology." 2019. In R. Gagné, S. Goldhill, and G. E. R. Lloyd, eds., *Regimes of comparatism: Frameworks of comparison in history, religion and anthropology*, 418–446. Leiden: Brill.

The chapters also draw on an additional essay:

"Relations." 2018. In F. Stein, S. Lazar, M. Candea, H. Diemberger, J. Robbins, A. Sanchez, and R. Stasch, eds., *The Cambridge encyclopedia of anthropology*. http://doi.org/10.29164/18relations.

The press's readers, who I now know were Susan McKinnon and Alberto Corsín Jiménez — they generously read the manuscript in both its forms — could not have been more discriminating or more helpful; I am grateful beyond measure for the detail and illumination of their comments. Parts of the book have been read to its profit by Debbora Battaglia and Jeanette Edwards. The whole work was tackled with considerable thoughtfulness by Peter Skafish and, with his historian's eye, Alan Strathern; I also benefited from their meticulous editorial scrutiny. I wish I could have taken greater advantage of all these readers' insights into what I was trying to do.

My thanks must also include colleagues whose hands had an emphatic imprint on the original essays: Karen Barad, Mario Biagioli, Mario Blaser, Marisol de la Cadena, Manuela Carneiro da Cunha, Janet Carsten, Natalie Zemon Davies, Gillian Feeley-Harnik, Sarah Green, Donna Haraway, Casper Bruun Jensen, José Kelly, James Leach, Geoffrey Lloyd, Gergely Mohácsi, Atsuro Morita, Elizabeth Roberts, Anne Salmond, Jonathan Sheehan, Anna Tsing, Eduardo Viveiros de Castro, and Kath Weston. And for many conversations and sharing of materials, I thank Olivier Allard, Françoise Barbira-Freedman, Barbara Bodenhorn, Louise Braddock, Philippe Descola, Susan Drucker-Brown, John Dunn, Debbie Epstein, Pat Fara, Don Gardner, John Hendry, Eric Hirsch, Martin Holbraad, Susan James, Jane Kenway, Bruno Latour, Ashley Lebner, Phyllis Mack, Jill Mann, Willard McCarty, Tom McLeish, Annemarie Mol, Morten Pedersen, Anthony Pickles, Anastasia Piliavsky, Alain Pottage, Paul Rabinow, Felix Ringel, Almut Schneider, Anthony Stavrianakis, Karen Sykes, Katherine Verdery, Aparecida Vilaça, and Robert Wilson, as I do several colleagues I first knew as doctoral students. They have all inhabited the writing, stretched the thinking, and generously participated — in agreement or otherwise — in this venture.

At the end of 2018, it is appropriate to recall Roy Wagner; as the volume took shape, he was a reader over my shoulder.

OTHER READERS WILL no doubt include those who find my painfully truncated deployment of a few conceptual markers to talk about "kinship," as an anthropological topic, thin in the extreme, but then I would put myself here, too. Conversely, many may find much in this account of relations tautologous. Tautology is usually deliberate on my part, as in the dictionaries that moderns write, in order to emphasize the expositional habit of describing something in terms of variants of itself. (For example, the notion that cultures can be compared; otherwise put, it is what can be compared in people's ways of doing things that is called culture.) Then there is the happenstance that at the moment when Duke had accepted the essays but before they had become the present text, Matei Candea sent me the manuscript of *Anthropological comparison*. To adopt his own phrase, it means that much of this book has already happened, that my moves have already been described. Although I allude to his work, this is not a response as such; however, that manuscript did have an effect on the writing insofar as it nudged me to make the pervasiveness of "similarity" as a relational trope even more explicit than it had been. Finally, over recent years several notable colleagues have contributed, through collections and journal issues, to critical interpretations of my work, including some of those whose work I once "supervised" but whom I haven't separately named. Engaging with them again would take reciprocity a step too far, but many are inspirational, and I cannot imagine they will not have breathed life into the present account. I express my thanks, indirectly, through a rehearsal of much that will already be familiar.

THE COMPULSION OF RELATIONS

Relations are ubiquitous in the accounts people give of their world, and no less in the observations or theories by which any kind of knowledge is made. Indeed, attempts to address the relation as a concept get quickly lost in the diffuseness of this highly abstract term. Seemingly, it has to be qualified to be useful, as when we speak of social relations or logical relations. Yet the term slips out of such restrictions in the kind of confident surmise, as frequently voiced, that there is something profound in pointing to a relational exercise or in uncovering relationality at the heart of people's concerns. To anyone interested in the way ideas are propagated, there is no point in wishing the ambiguities away. So while the subject of this book is all around, there might be something to be learned from bringing it, in part at least, into focus. The exercise might be particularly interesting to undertake for the kind of knowledge-making that does not simply seek out associations and dissociations across phenomena but imagines and describes them *as* relations, and indeed may use the epithet "relational" to claim a distinctive quality of analysis. This is especially true of the practices of (sociocultural) anthropology, and of what some would consider its principal means of existence.

"Now I see what anthropology is all about: it is about relations!" Lawrence Kalinoe's words spoken in Cambridge in 2000 rang with the clarity of a discovery. Only a short time into a joint research project with anthropologists and this lawyer from Port Moresby in Papua New Guinea had pretty effectively summed things up.[1] It was about then that the Melanesianist Gell asked what an anthropological approach to art might consist of, and he answered himself through a type of relation: if "anthropology has a specific subject-matter at all, that subject-matter is 'social relationships'" (1998: 4). However, this book is not concerned with a particular part of the world, although investigations in Papua New Guinea remain inspirational and have informed many past occasions on which I have explicitly dealt with relations, as well as furnishing some materials for this one. Nonetheless there is a decided particularity to my inquiry. I turn to the use of "relation" as it is configured in the English language.

The emphasis of this phrase is on configuring and use. My concern in this work is with the relation as an expository device or tool and I refer to its ideational capacity for such work by the shorthand, concept. Any focus on the term "relation" — or "relations" — draws attention to the obvious: that a single term may cover a variety of concepts. But adopting the view that, in Skafish's reprise (2014: 16), concepts "lead a virtual, self-consistent existence . . . [constituting] a space of their own in which it is their divergence and interconnections, not their degree of correspondence [with the world]," through which they provoke thought does invite one to think of the relation as a candidate. In any event, I treat it as though one could have just such a concept of it.

Usage is crucial to the present exercise. It is in paying attention to the way relation is used that we might come closest to something like an ethnographic account of it.[2] Any object that materialized in these terms would obviously be many-sided. Relation is at once one of anthropology's central tools of inquiry and a prime target of anthropological knowledge, while at the same time its theoretical invention as a scaffolding device precipitates its discovery as something that seemingly slips out from under explicit theorizing. Relations (in the plural) organize the sequencing of arguments and marshaling of ideas, quite as much as they weave through whatever material is to hand, sneaking up on one, springing surprises. Simultaneously confined and unruly: dog-leads wrapping themselves around every foothold; unherdable cats going off in every direction. At some moments, then, relations appear the only thing one can hold on to; at others, countless usages and applications render them conceptually elusive. It seems pointless to imagine gathering such a multitude under a single rubric, if not plain silly to be lured by the fact that so many circumstances meet in the one word (relation). But all this, precisely, is not in question. The word is an attractor: a term that engages other terms, a concept in a field of concepts, an idea that draws in values and disseminates feelings, a substantive from which adjectives (relational) and abstractions (relationality) can be made exactly as though everyone knew what was meant.

The account that follows attempts to elucidate the force that this attractor exerts in any attempt at exposition. Its magnetism shows equally in endless, pluralist, proliferations of application or of meaning *and* in the infinite differentiations, fractal or holistic, of versions of itself. This gives it the character of a duplex. Working with relations can turn out to be as trivial — because of their pervasiveness — as it is powerful — given their capacity to at once join and separate. Indeed, the relation can be a duplex in many registers.[3] That need not detain us now, except to add that for the purposes of this book the principal register concerns a kind of discourse, that of description, and within description, exposition: exposition's relation, we might say. Unqualified, the anthropology that is my principal expositional case is Anglophone. The substantive focus, then, is on how relations behave — how they are used — when English, and particularly the anthropologist's English, is the language of exposition. Overlaps, elisions, elusiveness, like Latour's hybrids, are not to be tidied away. One needs, rather, to be precise about the work such slippages do. Anthropological writing as usual, it could be said.

Relations start taking on the contours of an object of reflection insofar as they are seen to have certain correlations or co-relations, that is, are themselves held in place by relations evidently particular and specifiable. A brief introduction is in order.

An Introduction to Relations

Supposing sociocultural anthropology is indeed concerned with the elucidation of relations, then what is "anthropological" about them?[4] The relation has a definitive presence in anthropological work, including the positive tenor it generally carries, the privileged place it holds both in structures of argumentation and in what are understood as prime objects for study, and especially the way it is often introduced into discussion to signal a critical (in the sense of probing and questioning) move. Yet it is honored with no special, or specialist, definition. Indeed, Viveiros de Castro (2015: 16, emphasis omitted) observes that anthropology distinguishes itself (from other discourses on human sociality) "by maintaining only a vague initial idea of what a relation might be," precisely because its distinctive problematic consists less in determining which social relations constitute its object than in asking what its object constitutes as a social relation. My introduction to relations lays out certain situations in which relations are evidently constituted, some but not all of which will reappear later. For the introduction also serves another purpose. It will be seen, from the scope of what is laid out here, that the following chapters lean in one direction: their focus is on the effects of a specific line of Anglophone thinking. That skewing needs to be kept in sight.

The kind of description at which anthropology excels is expository; exposition entails setting forth information in a way that might encompass interpretation, explanation, and other analytical moves, but all with the aim of elucidation. Anthropological notions of analysis and theory, and above all that special trademark, the comparative method, take for granted that this implies showing relations between phenomena. Thus one may demonstrate the extent to which religious precepts uphold or challenge values promulgated by the state or hypothesize correlations between new technologies and changing senses of the self. That taken-for-granted status is built into the way scholarly narratives are organized. Most of the time it is indistinguishable from the perception that relations inhere in the object of inquiry, and the observer is drawing them out. The commitment of twentieth-century anthropology to holistic concepts of "society" and "culture" presented the world with what were above all sets of relations. People's actions, and their shared understandings, were to be described (analyzed, theorized) in the context of the diverse relations in which they were enmeshed. Anthropologists continue to show the logical or functional relations between entities they abstract, such as religion or the state, and create distinct fields of inquiry by showing the relational nexus of phenomena, such as gender understood as gender relations. They take it as self-evident that everywhere people, too, are drawn into relations with the things, beings, and entities that form their environment. Above all, the specific capacity of persons to relate to one another is taken as a fundamental truth of human existence. Social life is what goes on between them.

However, the Latin term *relatio*, from which "relation" came into English via Old French, did not connote that state of betweenness, and therein lies a tale — a veritable history about what gets to be articulated. Classically, relatio referred to what was carried back (to someone) as in a reply or report; indeed, it was a substantive for a motion (as in a proposal) or narration (creating a story). Medieval philosophers used relatio alongside *ad aliquid*, a concrete inclination "towards something," a disposition, directionality, order (Brower 2015). They drew from Aristotle's disquisition on categories: the idea that such an inclination was a property (or "accident") inherent in one entity in the way it pointed toward another.[5] Their reflections addressed common linguistic differences, as in the differentiation of absolute and relative terms, the latter arising from the comparison of things. An attendant concern about the way things bore on one another through, say, correspondence or disposition ("real relations"), with respect to the role of their own intellectual activity through, say, comparison ("relations of reason"), continued to bother European thinkers into early modern times. As for an articulation of how entities — such as intervals — might lie between other entities, Brower argues that it was less a matter of conceptualization (it would seem that the vernacular had no problem with the idea) than a matter of how relations could be represented in a formal system.[6] In any event, "relations between" was a relative latecomer to formal exposition. That this might have anything to do with the scientific revolution is a matter of speculation.[7] But possibly an emerging sense of a world that rested on explaining discrete phenomena by reference to the forces, logics, or structures that held them together had found in relations a new concept, or bundle of concepts, in an old term.

This position was not uncontested. If this is a development traceable in English, there were early modern continental thinkers who took relations in a different direction. Descombes (2014) rehearses Gottfried Leibniz's specific objections to the definition of relations proposed in 1690 by the English philosopher Locke.

Apropos the ideas that people form of relations, there were two parts to Locke's proposition. His assertion that the nature of relation "consists in the referring, or comparing two things, one to another; from which comparison, one or both comes to be denominated," rested on another, namely that there "can be no relation, but betwixt two things, considered as two things. There must always be in relation two ideas, or things, either in themselves really separate, or considered as distinct, and then a ground or occasion for their comparison" (1690: bk. 2, ch. 25, 5 and 6 [Nidditch 1975: 321, hereafter 1690: 2, 25, 5 and 6; 321]). The German thinker's famous riposte suggests that everything participates in a turning toward another: "There is no term which is so absolute or so detached that it does not involve relations and is not such that a complete analysis of it would lead to other things and indeed to all other things. Consequently we can say that 'relative terms' *explicitly* indicate the relationship which they contain" (from Leibniz, written in 1704; Descombes [2014: 204] reproduces his emphasis).[8] Caught up in a debate about the real and the unreal — or mental — status of phenomena as these thinkers were, Descombes spells out the implications of their arguments for two visions of social life: the empiricist view that social relations are exterior to individuals, and the idealist view that social relations are constitutive of individuals. The part of Locke's thesis relevant here — the suggestion that, as a mental exercise of comparison, relations are external to phenomena — diverges from that of his German commentator, which denies that there is any wholly extrinsic denomination because of the "real," in the above sense, connections among all things. One may start a description with a thing as though other things were extrinsic, but "complete analysis" will always reveal its relations with its surrounding milieu.

Although a distinction between external and internal relations was to have a very mixed future in philosophy, it has sometimes been taken in anthropology to reflect a truth about the priority to be given to the already-existing and thus discrete nature of entities, not in essence affected by their relations, as against the view that it is only through relations that entities come into being. These tenets become visible, for instance, in the way anthropologists organize the frameworks of their accounts and thus decide what they think needs expounding. From the perspective of modern anthropology, both positions can stimulate a stance of criticality.

First, "some descriptions of a thing by its [external] relations with its surrounding milieu have a real scope, [in] that they allow us to know the reality of that thing" (Descombes 2014: 204–205). Putting things into context — seeing the larger picture, showing the implications, effects, and outfalls (such as unintended consequences) between actions, events, structures, assumptions, and so forth — was always the aim of the traditional ethnographic monograph. Thus the reality of Zande witchcraft was to be grasped through a relational nexus that included princely politics, how kin are connected, and the logic of cause and effect (Evans-Pritchard [1937] 1950).[9] Here, too, lies the force of imagining merographic connections (M. Strathern 1992), a phrase that formalizes what is commonplace in English usage: the fact that nothing is simply part of a whole insofar as another view, another perspective, may redescribe it as part of something else. Religion and state (say) may be shown to relate to each other in this or that respect, while the analytical discreteness of each is retained by the fact that either may also be related to quite distinct segments of social life, as when mystical belief (or population statistics) is regarded as part of the one and not the other. Second, assuming relations are already everywhere furnishes anthropological discourse with a vocabulary by which to challenge the kinds of essentialist categorizations that imply the discreteness of phenomena. Lucien Lévy-Bruhl's concept of participation has drawn Sahlins's (2013: 33–34) attention: we take it for granted "that beings are given beforehand and afterwards participate in this or that relation; whereas, for Lévy-Bruhl, participations are already necessary for beings to be given and exist."[10] The political philosopher Ollman ([1971] 1976: 26) suggests that Karl Marx entertained a theory of "internal relations": things function because of their spatiotemporal ties with other things, and to conceive of things as relations interiorizes this interdependence.[11]

Descombes summarizes his own view of the problematizations here by observing that a theory of internal relations is untenable if it is presented as pertaining "between" individual entities: internal relations can link only relative beings as the parts of a whole.[12] It goes without saying that sensitivity to these conceptual usages underlines the interest anthropologists have shown, though all too rarely, in other vernacular counterparts to relations (notably, Corsín Jiménez and Willerslev 2007).

Conceptual Fields

Relations occupy conceptual fields along with other nouns, such as "terms" or "connections," whether applied to the apprehension of already identifiable phenomena being brought into (external) relations with one another or to phenomena (internally) constituted by relations. A relation-between imagined as composed of terms and relations — the relation only works with reference to something other, the "terms" it links — can be differentiated twice over. Thus, within the term, the conception of an entity's self-referential "identity" becomes modified when that entity is thought of "in respect to" another. This happens in the course of ethnographic application (for instance whether the magic one is thinking about refers to witchcraft or to oracles, all three substantives being summoned in the title of Evans-Pritchard's monograph). Within the relation, there may be reason to distinguish relation from relationship, or relation from connection, as we shall see in a moment.

These maneuvers, including imagining alternatives to the terms-plus-relation model, with its idiom of relations-between, have been deployed with critical intent. Recently translated works of Descola ([2005] 2013) and Viveiros de Castro ([2009] 2014) are exemplary here. Considering identification and relationship as fundamental axes of individual and collective behavior, Descola develops an intriguing theoretical possibility latent in the interplay between terms and relations: the very manner in which specific cosmologies privilege the one over the other. He thus offers a wide-ranging, "combinatory analysis of the modes of relations between existing entities" ([2005] 2013: xviii), which is how he explicitly introduces his emphasis on external relations among beings or things; his criticism of earlier models remains largely implicit. On the other hand, Viveiros de Castro deliberately writes against a formula that depends exclusively on "a connection or conjunction of terms."[13] Adopting Gilles Deleuze's vocabulary, he states ([2009] 2014: 170) "that the future of the master concept of anthropology — relation — depends on how much attention the discipline will end up lending to the concepts of difference and multiplicity, becoming and disjunctive synthesis." These alternative coordinates for thinking about relations explicitly challenge the presumption that the primary values to which relations lead are those of positive association, let alone binding ties or attachments.

They also challenge any seeming singularity of the concept. In an example to which we later return, relations are differentiated from "relationships." Moutu (2013) wishes to get away from an obsession with epistemological understandings of relations, insofar as, in the case of persons, they occlude the ontological character of relationships. A writer's relational practices (such as connection, association, resemblance, comparison) do not touch on the necessity and transcendence that, in his words, give relationships the character of an infinite being.[14] Thus there is nothing contingent, and everything necessary, about the way the Melanesian Iatmul pair older and younger brother together; insofar as each is also the other in another form, it is their *relationship* that (in his terms) transcends both the externality of their relating and their identification as similar beings. Such relating never ceases; this is partly because of its processual nature, which in some senses anticipates an observation from Pina-Cabral (below).

In other hands, it may seem equally crucial to split relation from "connection." (Here, differentiating epistemic relations from interpersonal relationships drops from view.) Although, following eighteenth-century English usage, anthropologists (author included, and in this book) often use "connection" as a synonym for "relation," the distinction yields further critical purchase.[15] Feldman (2011) argues for a difference between relations and connections as methodological constructs in the study of global processes. Unconnected actors (not in direct communication with one another) may nonetheless be related though "indirect social relations," mediated through some "variety of abstract mechanism," such as the surveillance systems, detention centers, and statistical operations that track a migrant's path (390). In other words, relations have an effect on—and pose problems for—actors far beyond the scope of their connections. Imagining an extraterrestrial perspective on the world, one invoking the potential of cross-world communication, invites inquiry into a different discrimination between connection and relation. Pondering instead how people can mistake connection for relation, Battaglia (2005: 26) contrasts relations with the envisioning of information networks so dense that they cover for the "work of relationality," singular acts of connection being fantasized as instances of social exchange. In her rendering, social relations and the work they entail are prematurely (like cart before horse) attributed to contact or encounter.

This phrase "social relations" is found frequently in twentieth-century British social anthropology. Sometimes it is used to distinguish relations of sociability (the tenor of interactions, transactions, obligations between persons) from relations of an institutional or systemic kind (economic, political, gender relations, as when Douglas [1970: xxv] talks of "relating" witchcraft beliefs to dominant aspects of social structure). On other occasions it summons the totality of social life, whether it is encompassed by the concept of society or, shorn of certain connotations of society, rendered as sociality. Such relations may be imagined in the first place as relations between persons, human implied. A seminal text is Radcliffe-Brown's 1940 address on social structure.

Radcliffe-Brown ([1940] 1952: 188–204) famously defined social structure as a network of actually existing relations. Thus he was at pains to differentiate a nonsocial entity, such as the "individual," from the entity that was (analytically speaking) a node in this network, the "person." In his vocabulary every human being was both: at once a "biological organism" and "a complex of social relationships." The person was a unit of social structure. A structural point of view, he said, requires studying how social phenomena such as religion or government have direct and indirect relations to social structure, here understood as "relations between persons and groups of persons." Pointing to kinship, an area anthropologists most readily cite as exemplifying internal relations, Radcliffe-Brown asserted that kinship structures consist of numbers of dyadic relations "as between a father and son, or a mother's brother and his sister's son."[16] These were the building blocks of society. His emphasis on the dyad, through which he focused on an interplay between two genealogical positions, puzzled later anthropologists for its privileging of genealogical thinking. Apropos kinship dyads, Bateson ([1936] 1958) had already introduced temporality in demonstrating the capacity of the dyad to substitute its junior for its senior entity, in ritual and across linear time. And Wagner (1977) would point to specific instances of analogic reckoning in which relational units might iterate other like units in different contexts without requiring an ego at their core.[17] Perhaps Radcliffe-Brown's intervention can be seen as clarifying a construction of persons as the terms to a relation.

Viewing social relations as the building blocks of society offered a critical purchase against what in retrospect seemed the random reporting of diverse customs, as exemplified in early twentieth-century accounts. Particular practices could be put into wider contexts, such contexts invariably consisting of the way relations were organized, a procedure that had long accompanied the analysis of kin terminologies. In mid-twentieth-century anthropology, this assumption about organization ("structure") fed the ability to correlate numerous dimensions of social life. Goody (1962) offered an extended example from West Africa with respect to descent group formation, inheritance, and funeral practices. West African mortuary institutions were concerned with the reallo-cation of rights and duties, after death, precisely insofar as a social person was defined through the mutual expectations that constituted his or her relation-ships.

Finding correlations between institutions within a society was accompanied by cross-cultural comparison between societies. Under the rubric of the latter, it was possible to compare institutions such as matriliny or witchcraft in terms of their local social configurations. Here, the notion of "relations between" at once facilitated the comparison of discrete phenomena, invariably along the axes of their similarities and dissimilarities, and produced as objects of study, "societies" and "cultures" in this mold, subsequently to be criticized in turn for the very presumption of discreteness. Comparison across discrete contexts—disjunctive comparison (Lazar 2012; see Gingrich and Fox 2002)—emerged as a later anthropological strategy. In any event, comparisons were leveraged against apparently arbitrary evaluations of what was or was not significant as an object of study.[18] (Any comparative move creates the potential of a critical outcome, insofar as bringing social or cultural phenomena into conjunction with one another shifts the observer's perspective.) As we heard, comparison was elemental in Locke's definition of a relation; for the medieval philosophers *comparatio* had apparently been more or less synonymous with *relatio*.

Needless to say, a reformulation of relations came to Lévi-Strauss's ([1945] 1963) assistance in his notable quarrel with Radcliffe-Brown, beginning in 1945. Take, for example, the visualization of descent groups. What to Radcliffe-Brownians may have appeared the interdependence of genealogically discrete kin groups upon one another, through marriage alliance and other relations, from a Lévi-Straussian perspective would have appeared like a description of external relations (not his term). Lévi-Strauss's own folding of affinity within the fundamental atom of kinship was instead a way of showing how such alli-ances were also presupposed (internally) by the total organization of relations. "Analysis can never consider the terms only but must, beyond the terms, ap-prehend their interrelations" (Lévi-Strauss [1973] 1978: 83). The whole is given before the parts, so one must begin with the whole, that is, with the relations among the parts.[19]

It is entirely possible to insist on linkages and the associational quality of the lives of collectives without explicit attention to the concept of relations; thus Latourian (2005) networks can intensify what is "social" at the expense of the "relational."[20] Indeed the ethnographic record affords numerous idioms for imagining the entailments or enrollments of all kinds of entities in one an-other's circumstances. Of course, the observer may gather these up as species of relations, regardless of whether a vernacular counterpart exists, just as anthropologists use the terms "culture" or "system" to describe social configurations that actors conceive otherwise or do not conceive at all. It then becomes a theoretical choice, if not a spectrum of possible combinations, to decide whether relations are articulated in all but name or are being articulated through the anthropologist's discerning apparatus. For where anthropologists do take it as a master concept — as in those English contexts where the invocation of relations is an invocation of the facility to "bring together" entities of any order — demonstrating relations is seen as probing beyond what is immediately accessible to observation. To reveal the relational dimension of this or that can also be empirical criticism of those cosmologies that cannot comprehend or else devalue the way phenomena entail one another.

Some Evaluations

It is no surprise that scholars in general, whose business is the narrational art of relating, deliberately pursue epistemological (or logical) relations; for anthropologists who are also ethnographers, this can appear consonant with a value placed on social relations in particular, echoed in their engagement with persons as interlocutors. A disciplinary disposition to uncover the significance of relations is thereby broader than the controversial use of cross-cultural ethnography to point up the identitarian bias built into the (Anglophone) anthropologist's native language. Emphasized by some present-day anthropologists more than others, exposing relationality is frequently understood as confronting assumptions about the intrinsic nature or self-identity of things. Controversy ensues when showing up such a bias is criticized in turn for the implication, from a "Western" perspective, that relations — including social relations — flourish in other, invariably "non-Western," places more heartily than at home.

When anthropologists talk about relations, it is persons who most often come first to mind, that is, beings inevitably enmeshed in a relational world, although these days persons may be other than human. This holds irrespective of whether, in any specific social configuration, people take relations as already there or else as endlessly needing to be created, repaired, or disavowed. In whatever manner people assume they are parts of the lives of others, they also put in relational work to uphold, deny, or reconfigure their relations with one another. It is this transformative, or transcendental, nature of interpersonal relations that leads Pina-Cabral (2017: 175–176), in his general address on the topic, to suggest that interpersonal relations are a bad analogy for the more general condition of being-in-relation. Rather, the former offer a special case to the extent that they are inevitably constituted through interaction and recognition, by contrast with relations that cannot grow in this way (his examples are sun and moon, fork and dish). With a faint echo of arguments in medieval philosophy about relations of reason and real relations, Pina-Cabral's criticism offers a perspective on vernacular usage.

In English, "relation" and its pair "relative" are also colloquial terms for kin. Idiomatically, this supports a tendency of relation to connote connection and attachment before it also embraces disconnection or detachment, just as familial ties are normatively imbued with positive rather than negative affect.[21] A cultural commentator might wonder about the extent to which such values bear on anthropological work practices, notably in the positive sense of accomplishment with which relations can be demonstrated; to accumulate relations — as in putting entities and beings of all kinds into contexts — is interpreted as an incremental activity. The commentator might also underscore the tendency of the English phrase "kin relations," so prevalent in anthropological discourse, to elide the analytical conceptualization of relations with the reciprocals or reflexivity implied in interaction between kinspersons. Inevitably, different argumentative positions emphasize relations as lying between kinsfolk as discrete persons, or as pointing to their mutual self-definition, or as some mix of the two. However, rather than regretting the apparent discord, or wishing to tidy it away, I suggest that such theoretical heterogeneity may strengthen rather than weaken the force of the concept. Any of these positions can be a source of critical thinking.

One argument for holding on to anthropologists' strong vocabulary of relations is that it joins the few languages we have, from the life sciences and elsewhere, for bringing home the lamentable blindness that has led to the present ecological mess. I refer to the limitations of what we are prepared to connect or countenance as relevant in the chains of being that link us all, as well as to the assumption that in an (ecological) context relations invariably signify interdependence. Yet that does not mean we can rest with present formulations of relating. Appeals to relations may reinforce rather than dispatch the underlying presumption of similarity between terms, as in terms to a relation. This may be highly relevant to activist dimensions of politics, whether remedial or revolutionary. For relations so conceived fail to challenge a prevailing orthodoxy in political action, namely the requirement that it proceed through demonstrating similarity or convergence of purpose ("common grounds," "joint interests") when parties reach decisions together. So conceived, this requirement cannot deal with those social expectations, to which of all disciplines anthropology has specialist access, namely those based on the collective work of difference and division (as we shall have occasion to note). "The relation," Haraway (2003:

24) observes, "is the smallest unit of analysis, and the relation is about significant otherness at every scale." Her conception of what heterogeneous relating entails is political in tenor.

A remark attributed to Bateson is that one cannot not relate.[22] Recent critical writing challenges how relationality, in a social or interpersonal sense, appears to suffuse anthropological accounts. Two examples serve.[23] Candea and colleagues (2015a) take up the positive affect attributed to relations as inevitably implying the desirability of close ties between people or mutuality of engagement. The work seeks to reevaluate detachment and disconnection in social life, analyzing strategies of separation and distancing—relations from another point of view—for their political and ethical interest. In a different vein, Holbraad and Pedersen (2017: ch. 6) ask what comes after the relation. They suggest that by intensifying it beyond recognition the anthropologist can develop examples of apparently "non-relational" ethnographic moments to sketch what a "post-relational" shift might look like. In the course of this, they uncover a renewed vernacular or indigenous (in their examples, Christian) interest in the individual, a connection-cutting entity, one that holds out the analytical potential of modifying the concept of relation itself. In becoming applicable to an introspective self-relation, it is no longer "owned by" social relations but is turned into something it was not before. A thread that continues to run through these usages is the overtly critical edge that being explicit about relations brings to debate.

A Critical Enterprise?

The accessibility of information, these days on hand from every side with such largesse, runs in hand with new forms of social accessibility—they are called social media, after all. An immediacy in people's interactions with one another is the virtue and allure of these instruments. Yet there is a long-standing position in social science, not least in anthropology, that appeals to the very opposite of immediacy. For all that it sounds similar, the notion of social mediation raises questions about the (social) relations entailed in particular events, and in turn about the role of (social) relations in anthropology's development of its critical capacity.

I speak of criticism both with respect to the scholarly exercise of scrutiny, including self-scrutiny and what is often called critique, and with respect to how such exercises may inform and be informed by political ends, even where such ends are not their primary goal. This is not to enter into debate over the politics of criticism (e.g., Bessire and Bond 2014). Rather, when we come to an appraisal at the end of the book, I shall suggest that the division Hage (2015: 84) would propose for (radical) political thought, between an "anti"-politics as a desire to oppose what exists and an "alter"-politics as a desire to create alternatives, may be folded into the primarily intellectual exercise of critical thought (albeit suspending his notion of what being radical entails). Exposition may go down anti or alter paths. This will underline with reference to anthropology what he shows of the social sciences as a whole, namely (and see Holbraad and Pedersen 2017: 288) that there is more than one critical mode. Other pluralities are already familiar. Consider how relations may appear either as a property of the regime being investigated or as a modeling that presupposes the relations at issue, which renders them attributes of the model. The outcome is an oscillation familiar in expository practice, and accommodations between viewpoints of this kind propelled much of twentieth-century comparative anthropology. Distinct positions turned out to be porous to one another: cultural particularities prone to echoing anthropologists' assumptions and their models prone to absorbing diverse cultural insights. At the same time, the oscillation underwrote a capacity for social criticism insofar as it made visible the mediating effects of specification or description itself, as through ethnographic example. This is the point at which (anthropological) practitioners become aware of their interpretive interventions.

If only by how it is known, nothing registered in thought or action is immediate in the sense of unmediated. The conditions of knowledge proliferate infinitely, and the portions anthropology examines never offer any claim to comprehensiveness. Yet it would be a pity if the self-evident nature of mediation renders it less than interesting. The discipline's capacity for social criticism is bound up with making known the mediating effects of the relations, thus identified, through which people live their lives. This is in no small part a matter of exposition. Anthropologists use varying epithets for relations to demarcate theoretical interests (politico-economic, ethnic, aesthetic, ecological, material) or analytic ones (moral, interpersonal, hierarchical, inclusive, cognitive). The term "relation" can qualify other terms or be implied in their joining, such as "property relation," "gender relations," or (relations between) nature and nurture. And then there are the relational connotations of method and practice, such as interpretation or comparison. Specifying the relation in question has expositional consequences.

Recognizing the work of mediation is as trivial and as powerful as describing relations. I return to Feldman (2011: 379), who would define (social) relations as themselves mediated by third parties or intervening agents of all kinds, by contrast with the "direct, immediate contact between people" he discerns in connections, a distinction that works forcefully for his material but depends on a specific reading of immediacy. Immediacy, argues Gershon (2010: 98–100, in a critique of Bolter and Grusin [1999]), has been claimed as one of the poles of a range along which communicational media are evaluated, the other being hypermediation. The first pole might have an explicit and often positive value, even though, as soon as someone deliberates upon which medium — texting or instant messaging, say — is best for a particular action, the visibility of the (transformative) mediator is already apparent. Her own observation is that people attend to different media depending on the context of their interactions. So it is the evaluation that needs scrutiny, the primacy put on enjoying or refusing an access that appears unmediated. This aspect of social media ideology is seemingly of a piece with that of zero-contract hours as a kind of unimpeded access to labor, instantly summonable convenience services and politicians' ability to tweet "the people," no less than with that of a scholar's illusion that description bypasses analysis or theory. To ask what relations have to be in place to mobilize the value put on such access turns relations into a tool of criticism.

Openness is part of their working potential. In his conceptualization of assemblages, Rabinow (2003, 2011) points to this openness with respect to a world already taken as given.[24] Assemblages, identifiable in problematizations of the forms and values of individual and collective existence (see Collier and Ong 2005: 4; Laidlaw 2014: 118), are made evident through new combinations of entities. Thus synthetic biology generates assemblages of organic entities as they are brought into the world. Things happen that did not happen before. "While [an entity's] properties are given and may be denumerable as a closed list, its capacities are not given . . . since there is no way to tell in advance in what way a given entity may affect or be affected by innumerable other entities" (DeLanda 2006: 10, quoted by Rabinow [2011: 123]). In Rabinow's (2011: 123) words: "Assemblages are composed of preexisting things that, when brought into relations with other preexisting things, open up different capacities not inherent in the original things but only come into existence in the relations established in the assemblage. . . . Thus an assemblage brings together entities in the world into a proximity in which they establish relations among and between themselves while remaining external to each other and thereby retain their original properties to a degree." Entities expose features previously unknown, then, as functions of relations with others, so that these features can never be exclusively properties of the entities themselves; relations open up the capacities of properties in unexpected ways and capacities come into existence through new relations.

Needless to say, the mediating effects of relations are supported by everyday expectations of modern scholarly (and academic) discourse: judging evidence, asking questions, uncovering assumptions, in short, creating problems. Problematizing issues expands the course of inquiry; it also widens what is demanded of expository skill. For identifying a problem brings up potentially countless remediations, opening the subject up to the relations that hold it in place and inevitably substituting new relations thereby.[25] It often takes the form of delegation from the study to the issue in hand (Salmon 2017). The challenge of relations is precisely how to turn a means of study into an object of study, in other words, how to also provide for them a critical account.

An Introduction to the Book

The reader might have expected something like this stance from an Anglophone anthropologist. Several of the strands encountered here will subsequently recur in the following pages, if only because of the characteristic versatility of relations and the manner in which they infuse and invigorate almost anything English speakers might wish to describe. To reiterate the observation in the preface, there may or may not be anything particularly "English" about such usage, while they are equally a particularity *of* English usage. To keep true to how such usages capture writer and reader alike, it is necessary to at once emphasize diverse inflections and indicate their inevitable presence as a condition of possibility for exposition itself. The compulsion of expositional relations joins with habitual assumptions about the connected or interfolded nature of existence.

The reality of relations is, in these several senses, never in doubt. At the end of the book I intend to recapture such a sense of reality by focusing on a thread running through anthropological exposition, namely, the critical potential that lies in making relations explicit. The six intervening chapters, however, also have aspirations of their own.

These can be expressed in terms now generally recognizable in anthropology (Riles 2006): by what means may relations be made into an ethnographic object? This is the point of being interested not in how the concept of relation should be defined but in how it is deployed. Accordingly, various references to anthropological works do not just carry this or that argument forward but also afford exemplars of particular usages. Since an exposition must engage substantive materials of some kind, I set up two narratives, both principal concerns of the discipline, although hardly exclusive to it. As I shortly explain, one narrative expounds changing notions of kinship, the other the lively art of comparison, and each has its own denouement. Finally the work as a whole could be read from a standpoint neither within nor outside anthropology, although it is prompted by an argument from elsewhere. This must be expounded first, as it is not part of the central narrative.

Intervention

In her elucidation of Niels Bohr's revolutionary descriptions of the nature of matter and light, Barad offers a formula for comprehending reports of phenomena: "Apparatuses do not simply detect differences that are already in place; rather they contribute to the production and reconfiguring of difference" (2007: 232). It follows that phenomena are not in this sense mediated through the instruments of observation; rather, they have no separate existence.[26] Bohr's experiments showed this: whether atomic entities such as electrons behaved as — appeared as — particles (a matter of position) or as waves (a matter of momentum) depended on the apparatus that was being used. Physicists had been preoccupied with the particle-wave duo. Like the oft-quoted riposte made by New Caledonians to the idea that Christianity had brought them the spirit ("We already knew the spirit existed. . . . What you've brought us is the body" [Leenhardt (1947) 1979: 164]), with his attention to apparatus Bohr seems to have brought them the body.

Under her flagship concept of "agential realism," Barad takes this forward to rework the very notion of phenomenon. "I suggest that Bohr's notion of a phenomenon be understood ontologically. In particular, I take the primary ontological unit to be phenomena, rather than independent objects with inherent boundaries and properties. In my agential realist elaboration, phenomena do not merely mark the epistemological inseparability of 'observer' and 'observed'; rather, phenomena are the ontological inseparability of intra-acting agencies" (Barad 2007: 333, emphasis omitted). Ontological entanglements, as she calls them, are primitive relations without preexisting relata. It is through intra-action that the boundaries and properties of phenomena become determinate and particular articulations of the world become meaningful. So "apparatuses are specific material configurations . . . of the world that play a role in the production of phenomena, . . . [apparatuses being] discursive practices . . . that are the material conditions for making meaning" (2007: 335). Material-discursive practices, causal intra-actions, do not imply human-based notions; indeed, she proposes these phrases in order to leave behind the notion of "concept" as too linguistic and not material enough in its connotations.

But I have work for the concept. I retain the notion precisely for its place as a device through which people organize their thoughts and give accounts of a world populated by other thinkers and speakers. Indeed, it is illuminating to envisage *the concept* as a piece of apparatus. Let me elaborate. Barad (2007:

340 ff.) explicitly distances her position from that of traditional epistemology entailing a conscious, knowing subject and its constructs (a figure prominent in the narrative of modernity that follows), and I do not retain the notion of concept to gainsay this. Indeed I would keep in mind her argument that, insofar as people are part of the world's ongoing (re)configurations, knowing must be treated as a part of being.[27] Prompted by but not in correlation with her model, I hazard that making an ethnographic object conjures up an anthropological entity to which something like her notion of phenomenon applies.[28] Thus the object will appear only in the presence of a specifying apparatus implying located intra-actions, as an "analytical context," to be introduced in a moment, might be. The notions produced through Barad's own conceptualizations gesture toward the special interest of relation with respect to *its* conceptualization. We might say it is at once a phenomenon produced by an apparatus (the concept), and works itself as a second-order apparatus, its own specifications producing phenomena of a particular kind (ideas linked in a narrative, for example); as the latter, it is as specific as Bohr's machine. Where she positions Bohr's innovations as the precursor for a social and philosophical analysis that can be amplified decades later, relations, as at once phenomenon and apparatus, have had a centuries-long history; they also bring forth a unique challenge to organizing an argument about them.

Outline

To organize an account of a concept — and an expository concept at that — as an ethnographic concern, it may be helpful to reverse certain customary orderings. This is said less to advertise a change in mode of writing than to invite the reader to take the substantive narratives that weave their way through the book in a special way. While composed of materials drawn from numerous situations in place and time, these are not being put into the position of an ethnographic base. Rather, their position is akin to an analytical framework: it is these very materials that specify the kind of relation at issue in this or that circumstance.

Those areas of the anthropological enterprise that practitioners call ethnographic are often staged to bring to the imagination assumptions and actions, including word usages, as though analysis were an outcome of them rather than also being a precursor. Yet it is widely appreciated that analytical frameworks (method and theorizing implied) invariably contextualize what gets reported in the first place — we can call them analytical contexts. So I am proposing to start at this end, and turn inside-out the usual relationship between concrete reports of social life and an otherwise abstract concept itself frequently presented as an analytic. Finding it in any event impossible to contemplate a single analytical field in which the relation's coordinates might be computed, even within the narrow range of anthropological usage, of which in turn I bite off the smallest slice, I instead focus on some of the relation's multiple happenings (and becomings) as they appear in this or that particular situation, text, or utterance. It is these latter that will govern or control the relation's appearance "analytically." Hopefully the relation will then emerge "ethnographically."

It would be impossible to gather the material at the same time: those situations, texts, and utterances need to be already described. I have taken material directly from a set of (my own) recent essays to yield a range of (albeit idiosyncratic) analytical contexts. In one regard, however, I have drawn on my previous depiction of anthropology's relation (M. Strathern 2005) as itself an analytic, and that shows in the duo of topics running as narratives through the six chapters. Kinship and comparison are iconic instances of the combined interpersonal and epistemic dimensions of anthropology's relation.

The first chapter, starting with relations at their most intractable, at once diffuse and highly abstract, turns to a habitual mode of concretization through the evocation of kin relations. It explores the descriptive deployment of "relations" or "relatives" as terms for kin, and the literalness with which the English language, by contrast with most of its European counterparts, has tied the notions together. The texts of certain early modern writers hint at particular conditions under which the very vacuousness of the implied concept might have acquired something of a social value. At the same time as old concepts of relation were being reinvented (extended, re-formed) for new circumstances, another concept was being refashioned: identity. Certain conceptualizations of personal identity and of reproductive substance appeared to implicate each other, expository language entwining the two, for instance, in the identity of lineal succession and the lineality of enduring identity.

In modern parlance, comparison becomes a specific kind of relation, rather than an alternative generic to relations as certain medieval philosophers may have used it. It presumes similarities and differences between phenomena whose own identity is prior to, in the sense of independent of, their being compared. Long embedded in the English language, the term "comparison" seems to have retained these contours, especially the emphasis on similitude or likeness. Chapter 2 follows some of the journeyings of this particular relation with respect, first, to certain vernacular usages as they apply to persons (such as comparisons between friends and kin) and the propositional recognition implied, and, second, to how the art of comparison has contributed to the self-consciousness with which anthropologists set about their work.

These two chapters compose the first part of the book. Connotations of relation (or relations) are thus historicized and culturalized, but at this point their organizing role in exposition is taken for granted. Part II emphasizes the work that the concept does when conscious appeal is made to it. Relations start bending and buckling under the expositional labor, the author making it obvious that — as well as reporting on others' usages — she, too, is putting relations to work. These chapters traverse similar grounds to those in part I, adding to a substantive narrative about knowledge-making and kin-making. Chapter 3 develops the self-consciousness or explicitness with which interpersonal connections are pursued. Its concerns include the interventionist nature of description and how that is then turned on relations, as in disputes over the apparently elemental definition (of relations) as a matter of comparing two things to one another. With an attempt from critical theory to summon a minimal account, minimalism being seemingly inferred from its counter-pole of expansion, it becomes obvious that any description of relations implies an intervention insofar as their further (expansive) specification is entailed.

The discussion of comparison dwelled on the notional duo, similarity and difference, at the heart of vernacular English understandings of relations. Chapter 4 redescribes these concepts through a selection of materials that invites the reader to reflect on the connotation of similarity in English, mindful of the way it slips into ideas of connection or correspondence, and through negation their opposites. Dissimilarity is thus the absence of similarity. Where it applies, the duo redescribed as similarity and dissimilarity releases the term "difference" for other usages. Perhaps most evident in this chapter, I am authorially positioning diverse materials as a kind of analytical frame, and the subsequent contextualization of the relations at issue is reflected in my own (expositional) usages.

Part III gives freer rein to certain inferences that suggest themselves, relations at this point including highly speculative ones. The reflective tenor of part II is thus followed by a mood closer to dramatization. This highlights certain expository moments in the formation of modern sociality. The crux is that, by contrast with many other cosmological regimes, the diminished status of kinship relations in naturalist cosmology (after Descola) remains perplexing. Chapter 5 dramatizes a philosophical contribution to the occlusion of such relations. The principal dramatis personae are Locke and Hume, and the plot is simple. Imagine a moment when a specific something did not happen: one might be able to record its aftereffects. And one can be pretty certain that the event in question did not start with Locke or end with Hume; it had been and went on not-happening. Suitably theatrical characters in respect of the popularity of their works, I have them play out on a small stage a specific failure of comparison; what was no doubt thoroughly conventional to philosophical disputation nonetheless closed certain directions down. The failure is underlined by a third figure, the botanist-painter Merian, with a seemingly alternative stance. The chapter has already rehearsed some of the issues of identity raised earlier, and she is a reminder that there was never only one view, that we can obviously recover quite divergent echoes from the past, and that the occlusion of kinship went hand-in-hand with the occlusion of women in certain kinds of publics. On the last observation, the recovery work that has been done over recent years, and in diverse disciplines (for which the historian Davis must stand as exemplar), is a reaction not least to women's invisibility apropos so many of the semipublic associations that encouraged scientific endeavor.

Drama continues in chapter 6, this time in terms of an inference drawn from some of the substantive materials on interpersonal relations. By now it is hoped that (the concept of) "interpersonal relations" will be carrying particular weight. The inference offers a response to Euro-American imaginings about the foreshortening of kin relations, both as social focus and theoretical object. In some respects counterintuitive (hence the need for drama), the response is a sober-enough suggestion about the conceptual limits of the phenomenon anthropological convention puts under the rubric of kinship. This play within a play engages with the role of such materials in understanding the relation, ethnographically speaking. It also assists further exploration of the carrying capacity of relations, what they bring with them, anticipating a return to the issue of their critical potential in the conclusions.

Despite everything that gets turned around in anthropological understandings, the relation persists. Indeed moderns might make the stronger claim that it is inevitably there at moments of knowledge-making. It is a constant ally in the formulation of understandings, although its users are not always aware of the directions it edges them toward. The issue for social criticism is to know what can be done with this particular impetus.

PART I

I. EXPERIMENTATIONS, ENGLISH AND OTHERWISE

Jostling with myriad other manifestations of the way phenomena emerge from what are, as the English terms have it, perceived as connections or links, the relation may also be imagined as an overarching or underlying concept that encompasses them all. Indeed, were one to take relation as a basic category of human understanding, the point would seem self-evident.[1] It especially applies to what we make known: any concept can be shown to have relational properties, and this reinforces the sense that knowledge brings things together. Yet even if everything that is known exists as a function of relations, the anthropologist might still be interested in when and how the relation becomes an object of attention. Consider its most intractable manifestation, as an abstraction whose sheer vacuity encourages its diffuseness.

Encountered in the relating of events, a reader ordinarily knows the work it does, pointing in a general way to the potential of interconnections that are otherwise specified in their particulars. It is intriguing, therefore, that among anthropological scholars — though by no means only them — it is precisely in its abstract form that relation often carries a positive value. By and large, it is a good thing to have found it! At the same time, the positive aura that is also attached to relation in the English vernacular gives it a tenor that comparative anthropologists venturing beyond the Anglophone world often have to discount. That positive, even benign, gloss may, of course, evaporate as soon as one starts specifying what kinds of relations are at issue: it is the abstract form that entices. Perhaps such a value is no stronger than that of any term with an approving or disapproving inflection ("mutuality" or "conflict," for instance). However, I suspect in the case of relation that its positive tenor is augmented by the role that relations play in modern knowledge-making. In general and unqualified, for again it may be completely different in its specifics, "knowledge" itself carries a similar aura of approval.

The two have long intertwined. When Marett, one of the early institutional founders of anthropology in Britain, referred to W. H. R. Rivers's "brilliant" commentary on social inquiry, he repeated that such inquiry's proper task was "the study of the correlation of social phenomena with other social phenomena" ([1912] 1936: 5). In a manner that has a satisfying ring to it, identifying correlations often brings an inquiry to conclusion. At the same time, relations recur as solutions to problems of exposition. The more the so-called bounded notions of society and culture are held up to criticism, the more relations, relationships, the relational, and relationality are evoked as prime movers (of sociality) in themselves. Quite aside from identifying relations in structures, systems of classification, co-variation, and so forth, the concept is applied with equal force to new objects of knowledge, emergent configurations, or co-constructions, and not only in a passive sense (everything is connected), but in the active sense of the observer-writer making phenomena appear, illuminating them, through the concept.

However, before we assume we know what we are talking about, let us begin with two objections to the way relation is often used in the abstract. They tell us there is something to inquire into.

I

Two Objections

The philosopher of science Stengers observes, in passing, that the modern English term "relation" (and she is thinking of an epistemic relation) lacks what the French *rapport* retains from its classical derivations, including the operation of comparison signified through reason and proportion. "Everything may be described as related, but not everything entertains 'rapports'" (2011: 48–49).[2] In preferring rapport to relation, Stengers wishes to further an argument about present-day scientific objectivity. "Experimental sciences are not objective," she writes, "because they would rely on measurement alone. In their case, objectivity is not the name for a method but for a positive achievement, for the creation of a rapport authorizing the definition of an object" (2011: 50), and thus agreement as to its nature. The labor of eighteenth-century chemists, who composed "exhaustive tables of affinities or rapports," is a case in point, and Stengers notes their starting position in Newton's 1704 *Opticks* and its mode of reasoning: "'[A] solution of iron in aqua fortis dissolves the cadmium which is put into it, and abandons the iron,' which means that 'the acid particles of the aqua fortis are more strongly attracted by cadmium rather than by iron.' Two chemical elements were thus compared in their 'rapport' to a third one with which both could be associated; the one with the stronger affinity for the third would displace the other from such an association" (Stengers 2011: 51). Abandonment, attraction, comparison, association, affinity: to an English speaker these are all types of relations, although for Stengers the term is insufficient to carry the creativity or actualization of an authorizing agreement. For her, relation lacks that positive tenor, such as was conveyed by Rabinow's experimental description of assemblages, where bringing entities into relation released capacities hitherto unknown. So what is it about Anglophone usage?

On the positive tenor of abstractions, mutuality is one of anthropology's (English-speaking) high-order conceptualizations of which there is a distinct cluster around the idea of kinship. Sahlins has concluded that kinship *is* a "mutuality of being": that is, "a manifold of intersubjective participations," a conjoint matter of interdependence, co-presence, and reciprocal belonging (2011a: 10). The conclusion follows comparative study across numerous social formations. Although Sahlins thus finds his evidence in all kinds of material, it is in considering "kinship" in the abstract that he evokes mutuality of being. He has notable predecessors here, not least Carsten in her substitution of "relatedness" as a placeholder for kinship, and Fortes's "axiom of amity."[3] When Schneider elucidated a code for conduct in American kinship, he characterized it as "enduring, diffuse solidarity," and while he eventually wanted to do away with kinship as an analytic, enduring and diffuse solidarity retained their value; indeed, that they were found across numerous American institutions was the problem for him.[4] Mutuality, amity, solidarity: the positive resonances are clear. Unqualified, kinship—like relation—is in English usage a motivated concept. Indeed, we might even come to perceive a particular relationship between the two.

Sahlins would be the first to say that mutuality is not the end of the story to be told about kinship. Yet perhaps, like relation, the positive tenor of mutuality, as it applies to these notions in the abstract (not necessarily in their specific applications), gives pause; maybe that is just a matter of English-language usage, but then maybe that is germane, too. For their capacity to carry value reinforces the observation that such notions are not reducible to individual instances of them: they have specific features *as* abstract forms. Let us refer to them as generics.

Now this is not to object to their infinite reach, the ubiquitous occurrence that troubled Schneider so, and certainly not to complain about lack of precision. The interesting issue is the extent to which such generics might be precise.

Sahlins is surely taking mutuality as a precise term for a diffuse phenomenon. And relation illustrates a precise feature that these generics share. For just as it is possible to recognize the workings of mutuality of being or solidarity while at the same time not knowing what kinds of beings are mutually entailed or who responds to the call of solidarity, one can show how relations have properties or effects without having to specify exactly what is related. Take Stengers's observation about Newton: it was possible to demonstrate attraction while not yet knowing the properties of what was being attracted or to show an affinity between entities before knowledge of what they ("particles") were. The agreement would become their property, the "object" now capable of description; any redescription (testing) of the rapports would then focus on revealing again the power of the attraction, and so forth. Through a different language, similar issues were discussed by Newton's contemporary, Locke. In a short chapter entitled "Of Relation," Locke discusses how relations have their effects without necessarily specifying what is related. He then vitalizes the abstract formulation through various concrete examples, among them, "those who have far different ideas of a man, may yet agree in the notion of a father" (1690: 2, 25, 4; 320).

It is this last move to which Pina-Cabral objects. In dwelling on a theory of personal ontogeny, he makes clear his objection to anthropological sociocentrism, that is, to using social relations as a prototype for all relations. "Relations that involve personal ontogeny are a bad analogy for the more generic condition of being relational in world. . . . Persons are not only particular, they are also possessed of an immanent transcendence" (2017: 176) not relevant to other entities. The nature of relations concerning persons with one another is always changing with respect to the social interactions they generate; for persons, being-in-world is inevitably being-with-others, another way of saying that interactions have their own, transcendental, effects. This leads him to criticize the long line of "Anglo-American philosophers" who treated "all relations as being akin to paternal filiation," succumbing to the sociocentric trap of seeing every relation as propositionally instituted in the way kin relations are (2017: 176). By "propositionally instituting a relation . . . , I place it within another field of relatedness; I transform it into . . . a feature of the scaffolding of mind" (2017: 179, emphasis omitted). Insofar as ontogenetically constituted relations between persons inevitably entail recognition (have a distinct propositional status), which affects people's presence and action, they are quite unlike relations or affordances pertaining between hosts of other things unaffected by whether they are recognized or not. Hence it is a logical scandal to find an exemplar of all forms of relations in those of filiation and paternity.

We may put the two objections together. The first tells us that there is something about the exposition of interaction that seems missing from the thin English-language usage of relation, while the second helps define the interest of this book in, exactly, the phenomenon of vernacular usage. The first thus gives me a reason for attending to that thinness, and in that attention to thicken it, or at least ask where thickness might lie. The second allows me to distinguish the anthropological aims of this exercise in elucidating prevailing usages — and indeed obsessions, such as the weight placed on acts of recognition — from the equally anthropological aims of Pina-Cabral directed to new conceptualizations of, in his phrase, the human condition.

Central to the latter's position is a desire to overcome the kind of reduction that treats all relations as forms of knowledge, that is, as "ideas in the mind of propositionally reflexive persons" (2017: 173). I concur. But that should not occlude the investigation of moments — and the European Enlightenment was conceivably one of them — that seem to have set in train a conflation of (references to) social relations and knowledge relations, or more accurately renewed what had always been a possibility. One milieu in which this possibility was actualized was indeed a propositional world, that of exposition, whether it was philosopher-scientists who were holding forth or people pondering on their connections. Attending to the relations people appear to be making, including cross-overs and mixes, is anthropological business, too. Grasping in turn the nature of anthropologists' own practices and preoccupations, at moments at which they are trying to describe and explain things, in short being expositors, also tells them more than perhaps they thought they knew.[5] I propose to ask just what may be learned when (say) filiation becomes exemplary of other kinds of relations.

II

What Kind of Kinship?

The very clarity of certain concepts appears to compel Locke to elaborate his discussion. Indeed, he tells us that his exploration is in aid of clarifying the workings of the mind,[6] as when the mind comes to know things by comparison with other things; one effect is that knowledge derived from acts of comparison acquires characteristics of its own. This is where his examples from kinship come in.

The ideas which relative words stand for, are often clearer and more distinct than of those substances to which they do belong. The notion we have of a father or brother is a great deal clearer and more distinct than that we have of a man [that is, an individual human being].[7] . . . [Thus] comparing two men, in reference to the one common parent, it is very easy to frame the ideas of brothers, without yet having the perfect idea of a man. . . . [So] to have a clear conception of that which is the foundation of the relation . . . may be done without having a perfect and clear idea of the thing it is attributed to. (1690: 2, 25, 8; 322–323)

Locke refers both to a class of "natural relations," including "father and son, brothers, cousin-germans, etc., which have their relations by one community of blood, wherein they partake in several degrees," and to the linguistic conventions that designate different kin (Pina-Cabral's propositions) so that "by distinct names [kin terms] these relations should be observed, and marked out in mankind" (1690: 2, 28, 2; 349), and, thus distinguished, carry duties and obligations. In drawing examples among others from relations between kin, he elucidated relations between ideas (the idea of a brother is evident from ideas concerning ancestry).

What do we know of English kinship at the time? Whatever it was, it is not going to be one thing.[8] Seventeenth-century England witnessed numerous political and theological divergences, not to speak of constitutional experiments, with philosophers reflecting on the legitimacy of government and the sanctity of kings. How to think about this as an epoch, often called "early modern," is a continuing source of historical controversy. Among well-known disputes has been that over the form of family and household relations, with some asserting, in the words of one historian, that "the family in early modern England was just emerging from its 'traditional' state, [while] revisionist historians used the same categories [of exposition] to emphasize that the family in sixteenth- and seventeenth-century England was in fact already 'modern'" (Tadmor 2001: 9). Obviously I am agnostic here, whatever the outcome of tracking a route through differently positioned interpretations.

Gathering momentum in the seventeenth century, Perry (2004: 40) suggests, was the drift of a formerly "bilateral, cognatic kin system to a lineage system defined predominantly through the marriage of first-born sons . . . [with] the consequence of disinheriting daughters."[9] Men's emerging preoccupation with capital accumulation eroded both the wealth and the autonomy that women of property-owning families had once enjoyed (Erickson 1993).[10] With this drift, women's power came less from their roles as daughters and sisters than from those of wives and mothers. Changes in household composition showed in how people extended themselves through the labors of their servants, and in what it meant that servants were wage-workers (Steedman 2009). And as anthropologists have done before her, Tadmor argues that, while in the seventeenth (as well as eighteenth) century the English household/family was characteristically "nuclear," it does not mean that there was no nexus of connections between households (2001: 18). We might wonder what was changing there, too.

Tadmor's own interest is the way people spoke about family and kinship, and she offers a detailed account of language usage, tracing key words as they occur in diaries or literature. She is perhaps best known for elucidating a principal connotation of "family" as commonly embracing everyone living in a household: parents, children, and diverse dependents such as servants and apprentices. Co-residence implied submission to the authority of the household head, which existed alongside contractual arrangements. Diverse terms were used for kin living elsewhere, with the core vocabulary of consanguineal terms incorporating affines of all kinds; these existed alongside generics such as "kin" or "kindred," and "friends" as a term embracing kin and non-kin (Tadmor 2001: 123, 130). The generic terms are interesting, in Tadmor's view, since they at once suggest an inclusiveness to which indigent kin might appeal and an opacity about the degree of connection involved, equally affording grounds on which help might be refused.

It was at this time that into the pool of generic terms dropped "relations" and "relatives." Apart from a reference in the sixteenth century, recorded kinship connotations of "relation" and "relative" stem from the seventeenth.[11] By the eighteenth century, with which Tadmor is mainly concerned, relation is thoroughly embedded as a generic noun for kin. In commenting on the plurality of terms for kinsfolk, she observes that usages stem back to different roots and occur in different registers (2001: 154–155). And something that happens to be well recorded in seventeenth-century writings is the explicitness that developed over language use.[12]

The language in question was English, and its relationship to Latin. With vernacularization on all sides came scope for extensions of meanings and applications to changing situations. Obviously it is not just the appearance of a word that is significant: words may undergo periods of popularization or "discursive lift-off" (Withington 2010: 234).[13] For instance, the term "society" was not just recast: it acquired new connotations consonant with fresh attention to the public sphere as an "extra-familial space"—that is, as "a kind of social interaction lying somewhere between the realms of 'the family' and 'state'" (2010: 14, 13).[14] "Relation" had long existed in the vernacular, at least since the fourteenth century, with the sense of correspondence or association; it implied a concept of logical or epistemic operations, as in making a comparison or the recital of a narrative. Was the very concept of relation subsequently affected by new appropriations from the Latin, and was it to have discursive lift-off in other fields as well? What were the circumstances of its introduction into the sphere of the interpersonal ties of kinship? We could inquire what was happening (first) in kinship practices that made new usages plausible, and what was happening (second) to make new usages plausible for those concerned with words.

Apropos kinship practices, the stability of the core (consanguineal) English kin terms over many centuries is used to support arguments about the antiquity of family arrangements.[15] Of course, modern commentators would allow changes in patterns of use, but the terms were remarkably constant. However, there was in the seventeenth century an arena where novel terms flourished, and we know what it was. When it came to thinking of kinsfolk generically, "relations" (and "relatives") was added to the repertoire. And somewhat later the move happened all over again with "connection." Over the seventeenth century, apparently, "connection" appeared as a new term for the linking together of words and ideas or "being related by a bond of interdependence, causality, logical sequence, coherence" (in the twentieth-century phrasing of the *Oxford English Dictionary* editors, with a reference to 1613). It was then to gain popularity in the eighteenth century as a key, though not exclusive, term for relations with kin of all kinds. Did new concepts come with these new terms?

Tadmor observes that there was hardly a term for kinsfolk, specific or generic, that could not also be used of persons in non-kinship contexts (2001: 157, 164). The precise significance of generics, such as "relations" and "friends" (and later "connections") for kin ties, was that they combined recognition—acknowledging the kinship of this or that person, that is, choosing to know them—without specifying degree, without, in short, specifying the nature of the tie, and thus the kinship properties embodied in those who were related. With its emphasis "not on the actual degree of the relationship, but on its recognition . . . the term 'relation' conveys the idea that an individual has kin, rather than any specific information about the structure of the kinship relationship" (Tadmor 2001: 125, 127). Nonidentifying generics were used of intimate kin such as parents or children as well as of distant people whom one may not have heard of before they were on the doorstep. A diarist, Abigail Gawthern, reported just that of "a Mr Wallace we found in the house who said he was a relation" (quoted by Tadmor 2001: 124).[16] Tadmor adds, "The umbrella-term 'relation' was evidently useful enough in this case to demand recognition and to enable Mr. Wallace to make a financial claim on his distant kin." In short, one might allow that a person was a kinsman without exactly knowing how the connection was traced.[17]

While all this gave some flexibility to the way people defined the interpersonal networks within which they moved, as Tadmor suggests, it suggests to me that drawing on a notion of relation could also have served as a commentary on the value of linkage as such. These terms seem to have worked as generalized invocations, at once capable of precise effects (the power of recognition, or the reverse) while not having to summon the embodiment of the relation in the specific persons through whom it was traced. Was there a sense, too, in which the relation's template, the epistemic or logical relation, already an abstraction, was also changing?[18]

One response is to point to what was happening for those concerned with words. Cast back to the popularization of the term "society," and an emergent public sphere ("a mode of collectivism best described as voluntary and purposeful association" [Withington 2010: 13, emphasis omitted]). This offered a new verbal context for thinking about relations. An older view that preindustrial English society was based on the family is challenged by those who would emphasize the "associational ethos" of the early modern period. There was, from this latter perspective, a widening spectrum of social interaction rooted in the basic value of association, a web of interdependent "associations" (in Withington's phrase) that constituted what the writer of the first printed text to deploy "society" on its title page, in 1576, called civil society. This particular writer imagines that web as bringing together diverse associations, based on country, town, private corporation, friendship (in a non-kinship sense), and "kindred" (Withington 2010: 103). We might wonder about the connotations of kindred, then. If we take "society" as pointing to a widening ethos of association, is there another way of (our) imagining a public sphere then interposing itself between family and state? Perhaps the conceptualization of kinship ties ("the societie of kindred") was being caught up in a similar change of direction. Relations: we need look no further for the appropriateness of a highly generic term for kinsfolk, one that could summon relationship through another abstract concept, association.

Other Assemblies

The epistemic template of relation may have been changing in other ways, too. "An assembly of several People in one Place, on purpose to assist each other in business . . . a particular tie between some Persons, either for interest, out of friendship, or to live a Regular life . . . a Company of them joined together in the study of some Art or Science" (cited in Withington 2010: 108): these were components for a definition of "society" in a mid-seventeenth-century work called *The new world of words* (Phillips 1658; see also Phillips 1696). Note the reference to science. For there was, of course, a whole other domain of self-consciousness about language, stimulated by questions of identification, verification, and recognition, explicitly addressed to how things are made known. Shapin puts it bluntly: "The seventeenth century witnessed some self-conscious and large-scale attempts to change belief, and ways of securing belief, about the natural world" (1996: 5). Our present sense of radical change having been afoot comes, he says, from people at the time. Part of it, as Haraway (1997) tells the tale, was not only creating a disinterested objectivity but also establishing who counted as a credible witness; she at once excavates and builds on Shapin's work (e.g., Shapin 1994), to show how that question (who counted) molded ideas about gendered persons. The positioning of men and women in the new knowledge-experiments of natural philosophy was to have enduring effect.

From those of his writings we have briefly touched on, we might surmise that Locke was putting into the language of comparison the kinds of notions, long familiar from astronomical and other practices of plotting coordinates, that later commentators would call correlations. At the beginning of the seventeenth century, Galileo Galilei was staking everything on his detection of exactly such.[19] Whether of the surface of the moon or the appearance of sunspots, it was respective positionings generated by observations made at different times that yielded evidence of what existed. In the case of Jupiter's satellites, which he dedicated to his Medici patrons, Galileo did not need to know what he was looking at through his telescope: tracking over time the changing positions of the entities with respect to one another, and to the planet, was enough to show that there was a phenomenon to be observed (Biagioli 2006).[20]

Seventeenth-century philosophers were reflecting not only on government and sovereignty but also on the character of knowledge and human understanding, bound up with knowledge-experiments that conceived nature as requiring explanation, and explanation requiring verification. From the multitude of techniques through which early modern scientists/natural philosophers described their world, the earlier fragment citing Newton must do proxy for ways in which a significant dimension of their work, at once its means and end, was experimenting with relations. At the same time, description becomes a new object. Arguably, it would seem, terms for concepts were becoming subject to trial, at least indirectly, in that what came to stick must have found "an agreement" with circumstance or debating point.[21] The English concept of "affinity," which for Stengers seems the closest equivalent to the French rapport, implies a kind of relation; that underwent change, too, although on an opposite path from both "relation" and "connection." Affinity started out with reference to kinship, marriage, and companionship, to have become by the seventeenth century a term including the logic of causal connection and structural resemblance.[22] If a leached-out, generic apprehension of "relations" allowed movement between abstract demonstration, which could be invested with proof through measurement and correlation, and a generalized notion that drew on nonspecific ideas about interpersonal connections applicable to human affairs, then "affinity" shows that it was a movement that could go in either direction. Conscious or otherwise, this was experimentation with language.

From a present perspective, ambiguity abounds in Locke's usages. He may or may not have had in mind that, when he was using examples from kinship to illustrate the concept of relations, his neighbors and consociates were beginning to use the term when speaking of kinsfolk. In discussing comparative and relative terms there was in any case a long philosophical tradition of referring to kin (Wilson 2016).[23] Another sense in which he might not have had to think is discerned by the political theorist Dunn (1969: 21) at all those places in Locke's exposition where he "scarcely needed to use his mind to set out the theme, with the whole array of traditional English values to say it for him." That said, ambiguity can be a source of information about the kinds of relations between words and/or between concepts in which an anthropologist might be interested, much as in another context Balibar ([1998] 2013: 97–98) refers to Locke's word play (places where, to develop his thesis, Locke would draw on all the semantic and syntactical resources that the English language offered him). And terms do not change in isolation; they are invariably in some kind of "relation" with others, and that applies as much to relation itself.

Light may be thrown on changes in usage, then, by what else was happening. I turn to two concurrent sets of uses, first concerning "friend," and then at more length concerning "identity." Both lay out materials that will be helpful to later discussion.

III

Friends

The particular way in which "relation," with its connotations of bringing things together or referring one thing to another, lodged itself in the sphere of kin ties makes something akin between the new learning and the new kinship. English kin terms only go on looking "traditional" if one ignores what was happening to generics. This raises a question to be asked, ethnographically, currently, of vernacular English usage: why do we assume kinship to be about relations?

The question is, of course, almost unaskable, especially by social anthropologists, for many would surely entwine it all over again with their apprehension of relations as a basic category not just of thought but also of mutuality of being. The assumption that these go together implies a veritable bundle of concepts, not least in reference to narratives of kinship (underlined by Crook's [2007] experimental exception). Indeed, in one sense it will take the rest of the book to come to a conclusion; in another, however, the preceding discussion has given us a tool to start working with. For even if we cannot approach a phenomenon directly, we might be able to detect a distinctiveness in its effects, as in Newton's comparison of the relative affinities of chemical particles or Galileo's corrugated moon surface observed in the changing shadows it cast. If the phenomenon is imagining (describing, narrating) kin ties as relations, are there any effects of its verbal explicitness to which we can point? Some indirect evidence comes from the relationship of ideas about kinship to other generic nouns for kin *before* "relations" came along.

A salient term that was still in the seventeenth century being used to refer to kinsfolk, though by no means exclusively, was the generic "friend." "Inclusiveness and opacity were also among [its] main characteristics" (Tadmor 2001: 129). If we are to believe the historian Bray's (2003) account, the new ideas about civil society, which eventually displaced a notion of society in the older sense of company, also displaced references to the mutual corporeality on which friendship and kinship were in previous centuries both based.[24] Friendship could be celebrated as a conjugal bond, notably in the brotherhood sworn between men before witnesses at the church gate, the place where betrothals between men and women were also sworn, while in death friends might be laid to rest side by side, as spouses were, closeness being evinced in the way friends gave their bodies to each other. These images made concrete the kinship between those so sworn (they were "wed" thereby). Conversely, "the good of kinship lay in the friendship (the 'society' [as in companionship]) that it could create between individuals and groups, who might otherwise be at enmity" (Bray 2003: 214). In this it had a significant political role, of which an important element was public display of bodily intimacy.[25] Contemporary English usage allows us to deploy "companionship" to refer to the kinds of connotations that "society" once held. While, as Withington documents, "company" underwent changes in connotation (2010: 113), it retained a sense of conviviality or sociability (Anglo-Saxon "fellowship") that the more abstract "society" was to sketch more faintly.

There was to be something of a revolution in expressions of affect; recall the new conjugality by which women became defined principally as mothers and wives rather than daughters and sisters. During the course of the seventeenth century, older practices of friendship came under suspicion, eventually to be capped (in the mid-eighteenth century) through explicit legislation that forbad the formation of marriage by mutual agreement before witnesses, as the medieval church had once sanctioned (Bray 2003: 215). Apropos marriage, "friendship was no longer to be created in relations that overlapped with it and were akin to it"; rather, an emergent "'rational' ethics require[d] the moral basis of friendship to reside in an undifferentiated benevolence" (2003: 217, 213). We know that another otherwise undifferentiated concept, and in the abstract with benevolent connotations, had, of course, become the new generic for kinsfolk.[26] Here, in its co-evolution with ideas about friendship, conceivably lies some of the thickness of the concepts that were being bundled together as relation(s).

Identity

Among the linguistic innovations of the seventeenth century, one term that gained currency was "identity." It became applied to the self-sameness of persons as much as of phenomena in general, something of an irony for those philosophers who, drawing examples from familiar experience, found one's self to be the most unstable of entities. They argued over whether someone, understood as a self, could be a permanent subject, given all the variations in time, states of consciousness, and so forth, of which people were aware in themselves. The issue was not invented by early modern writers, but they could draw on a current vocabulary for it. This put persons into a wider field of inquiry concerning the identity of things.

Under debate was "the riddle of identity" (Porter 2000: 166). Personal identity or the self, Locke declared, "is not determined by identity or diversity of substance, which it cannot be sure of, but only by identity of consciousness" or understanding (1690: 2, 27, 23; 345).[27] It was a matter of discerning the intrinsic qualities that made the self. (There were others who found the same instability in consciousness that Locke did in substance, arguing, for example, that perception was discontinuous and divisible.)[28] The political philosopher Taylor reflects on Locke's "unprecedentedly radical form of self-objectification ... [enabling us] to see ourselves as objects of far-reaching reformation.... To take this stance is to identify oneself with the power to objectify and remake, and by this act to distance oneself from all the particular features which are objects of potential change [such as substance].... This power reposes in consciousness" (1989: 171–172). In the "person," then, Locke is dealing with a thinking, intelligent being (his phrase), a forensic entity who can be held to account. When by contrast he comes to talk of the permanent sameness of "man" (the individual living organism, or human being in later parlance), the identity of man is not differently conceived from that of plants or animals.[29] "For in them the variation of great parcels of matter alters not the identity. . . . [A] plant which has . . . an organization of parts in one coherent body, partaking of one common life, it continues to be the same plant, as long as it partakes of the same life" (1690: 2, 27, 3–4; 330–331).[30] Apropos the objectification to which Taylor refers, different questions are thus being asked of plants, animals, and man, on the one hand, and of the person, on the other. Although, Locke says, we "know that, in the ordinary way of speaking, the same person, and the same man, stand for one and the same thing" (2, 27, 15; 340), he reveals a radical divergence in how the identity of the former and the identity of the latter are formed.

An anthropologist might remark that the discussion about personal identity and living organisms makes no mention of kinship. The philosopher neither depicted persons and selves as kin nor pondered on the procreation and nurture of man as a reproductive being, and neither figure was held in place by kin ties with others. Instead, "person" had what we might today call quasi-theological or moral characteristics ("consciousness") while "man" had natural ones ("life," "an organization of parts").[31] Discussion about identity, whether of persons or of human beings, was thus held apart from a discussion about the formation of (social or other) relations.[32] That positions relations as a matter of "external" linkage. For the reader is invited to imagine a being whose relations — including those of kinship — lie outside its essential nature. We shall have cause to return to this.

And what aspects of kinship might the anthropologist have expected here? As in the case of the associational implications of relations, certain ideas about kinspersons, families, and interpersonal connections were apparently traveling along the same route as, and enrolled the self-same concepts of, identities external to one another. So one might wish to take the very implication of rendering relations external both to the individual organic being and to the conscious person or self *as* an emergent modeling of kinship.

If the notion of an entity with (external) relations to others echoes some of the ways people of the time were coming to think about kin ties, this was hardly restricted to England. Across Europe, the "passage from the Middle Ages to the early modern period" witnessed developing "family strategies," for instance in the "patrilineal and similarly exclusive conceptions of kin organization [that] acquired an almost constitutional status" (Sabean and Teuscher 2007: 15). As we have seen for the English, these included the shift (as it has been put) from kin connections based on extensive collateral relations to an emphasis on lineal descent and property accumulation through men. While these changes clearly concerned those with property, they were not confined to such considerations. Davis (1978) describes family strategies in sixteenth- and seventeenth-century France and elsewhere that hailed from a wide social spectrum but invariably involved a consciousness of family history, family futures, and the transmission of patrimony. She observes (1986) that, like families, individuals were acquiring a distinct sense of their life histories. Whether for those of much or little means, the "individuality" of people and families might sharpen certain identities at the expense of others. "Women," Duhamelle (2007: 133–134) states, "were gradually excluded from participating in the circulation of wealth between lineages as their shares in family goods were progressively diminished," culminating in a decision in 1653 to abolish their inheritance claims in favor of "a new self-representation [of the family] that enhanced male descent." Aspects of this account of German nobility (the Rhenish imperial knighthood) could as well have been written of ordinary folk in England. In 1670, the English parliament intervened in the administration of probate (settling the inheritance of a deceased's estate), with the effect of undermining women's entitlement to personal property. Erickson (1993: 230) adds that an "overt identification of 'the individual' with the male individual" was evident "in the burgeoning number of publications on political and property theory."

Eighteenth-century Europe realigned sentiment and alliance with new patterns of social and familial endogamy. Although, according to some historians of Europe (Sabean and Teuscher 2007: 16; also see Sabean 2007; Johnson et al. 2013), such patterns displaced those structures of inheritance and succession that had led them to talk of patrilines and agnatic lineages, the realignments brought with them new claims for family definition. Ideas of exclusiveness were continuing to evolve. If this, too, is identity in the making, as Davis (1978: 87; also 1986) argues for early modern family life, the resultant familial alliances seem to be enacting further forms of external relations between units. Whether between lineages, families, or conjugal households, the discreteness of those units appeared increasingly emphasized.

In all this, a momentary turn to procreative idioms of blood, away from those of flesh, had enabled "lines" of blood to be identified.[33] Here one might wonder at the role of reproductive material in imagining external relations. The connotation of corporeal entities as belonging to a physical world implied their being identified, and thus fixed, in relation to one another, and this went for procreative elements, too. Drawing on materials from Italy, one historian directly addresses a developing theory of bodily transmission: "Blood was identified as the substance that transmitted qualities from one generation to the next" (Delille 2013: 130). It also circulated. In seventeenth-century Europe at large, "each consanguineal link could be a conduit of blood, and each alliance, a sharing of blood. . . . [So] a group of males, an agnatic line, a house . . . could express the marriage of one member with another house as a mingling of blood: [such] an alliance could only be thought of . . . through a language of flows, channels, conduits, coursings, and circulations" (Sabean 2013: 145). Blood was an old metaphor for kinship; that heritage was being conferred by "nature," with blood guaranteeing the transmission of qualities, is arguably what was new (Delille 2013: 127, 130).[34] "Families or lineages were natural beings whose social personality rested on a foundation which today we would term biological" (2013: 132). Blood was not alone — semen and milk had similar properties. The specific interest in blood is that it replaced, in Delille's words, the medieval notion that generation was the result of fleshly contact.[35] External relations between (individual) familial units or bloodlines being visualized in terms of circulations of blood (through marriage) were concurrent with such units acquiring distinct identities.

Delille's references to what was conceived as natural appear deliberate, for the theory of which he makes mention is, as he puts it, a "naturalist theory." If relations were also co-evolving with ideas about identity, from a present-day perspective they were emerging as epistemological grounds for recognizing a rather special state of affairs. I refer (after Descola [2005] 2013; Latour 2013a, 2013b) to the cosmology of self-acknowledged naturalists and moderns.[36]

Naturalist Premises

Attributing such developments to a distinct cosmology is stimulated by Descola's *Beyond nature and culture* ([2005] 2013). "Naturalism" is one of four experiential regimes by which people identify and make relations with what is around them, "identification" and "relating" being, in his thesis, basic modalities in the structuring of individual and collective inferences about the world. He puts forward a preliminary specification of external relations. "Relationships are thus here understood not in a logical or mathematical sense (i.e., as intellectual operations that make it possible to establish an internal link between two concepts) but rather as the external links between beings and things that are detectable in typical behavior patterns and may be partially translatable into concrete social norms" (113). While identification involves a relation insofar as "it is based on judgments of inherence and attribution" (of specific properties), that relation remains intrinsic to the object identified, and when he talks generally of relations his concern is rather with "the connections that this object has with something other than itself" (114). Clearly, relating and identifying are not restricted to naturalism (and apply across the several regimes or ontologies described by Descola), but in naturalism their positions are closest to those that much anthropology has traditionally occupied.

In this naturalist world, entities can at once be defined through their intrinsic properties and ordered or classified through their relations with external others. When Descola ([2005] 2013: 239) says that naturalism privileges terms over relations, he means to point to what is generally taken for granted as a sense of the prior existence of things. That would not, of course, say anything about the precariousness of ordering and its relational effects (Law 1994: 23), only perhaps that, beyond philosophical and critical reflection, moderns are effective in hiding the precarity. Arguably it is just such precariousness that kinship arrangements sometimes reveal. A supposedly natural order of kinship may be resting on a schema of external relations, yet the latter's externalizing and differentiating effect — as in encouraging the expansion of connections — could also lead, by overinsistence on that effect, to ambiguity about closeness and distance. Take practices of familial alliance.

The eighteenth-century middle-class stress on alliances between families through marriage seemingly gathered momentum alongside the (social) class-consciousness of desirable investment in same-status matches. This contributed to a fresh focus on conjugality, insofar as "marriage-as-alliance . . . expressly put the interest of the new [conjugal] unit above the interests of either of the spouses' natal families" (Perry 2004: 231).[37] One may thus wonder whether the pleasures and perils of close marriage typical of (upper) middle-class England over the ensuing century were not a hypertrophied outcome of the value placed on seeking "good connections." For diverse reasons and variably according to social strata, from the late eighteenth and into the nineteenth century marriages among close kin became widespread across Europe (Sabean and Teuscher 2007: 21–22). High rates of cousin marriage reflected repeated unions between families, within and across the generations, and the English bourgeoisie were no exception. Kuper's (2009) study pinpoints what was often expressed as desirable intimacy, the closeness of natal family members being assimilated to the closeness of affinally related ones. This was a time when unions between cousins or brothers- and sisters-in-law were as common among doctors, lawyers, and clergymen as they were in business, notably among elite Quakers prominent in banking, not to mention intellectual and scientific circles. Marriage repeated "between families" seems to have merged into a sense of marriage "within the family" (2009: 27). Hence an ideal marital arrangement in the Victorian novel included adoption "into the family [of] someone who is almost a member of the family already" (Sanders 2001, cited by Kuper [2009: 17]).

Now experiments in plant and animal husbandry had led to a scientific literature on the effects of selective breeding, and "debates about the value of creating healthy stock by introducing new hybrid strains, or the opposite — increasing quality and quantity by 'breeding in and in' — became more widely known" (Davidoff 2012: 239). That similar effects could be observed in human populations came to color later nineteenth-century concerns about heredity and the substance of connections between kin. Where the capacious concept of nature embraced biology, it presented reproduction as a physiological phenomenon, and protagonists argued over the consequences of close unions on the physiology of offspring. Literary scholars have "noted that the legitimate desire for a cousin sometimes appears [in writings of the time] as a stand-in for forbidden attraction to a brother or sister" (2012: 239). Forbidden though it might be, the extravagant sentiment that close family members could display for one another — and the amorous language in which they spoke — seemed on a continuum with conjugal feeling. The latter part of the century saw vigorous public debate on whether the incest taboo was "a law of nature" or whether marriage restrictions were rather "the fruit of civilization" (Kuper 2009: 101; in America, see McKinnon 2013: 54–56). Anthropologists came on the scene at this point, talking about primitive kinship and the evolution of society.

Debate did not end there. What is suggestive is the shape given it by those early modern developments in ideas about relations and identities. Vilaça (2013: 364) offers an arresting correlation between an emerging notion of the (human) individual and the differentiation of (human) culture and (non-human) nature as discrete domains.[38] An obvious entailment of imagining that there is an external relation between nature and culture is the separation of the terms (nature, culture) of what may otherwise be — and in the eyes of many today should only be — imagined as an internal relation of mutual implication. This impasse has been attributed to acts of purification, the sundering apart of impenetrable entanglements.[39] However, the entailment also seems to have had an outcome less remarked upon. When "individuals" and the "identity" of phenomena become prominent, as they are in common parlance, so, too, do externalizing "relations." Colloquially put, it is as though there were at once more individuals and more relations around! For relations so conceived at once hold things apart and hold them in place, that is, sustain their identities. I take this to be a cosmological premise (of naturalism), and one that seems to have been at stake in anxieties over the "confusions" of close marriages.

We can express the premise more formally by further generalizing the contrast between internal and external relations, and I take my cue from Jensen (2012) and Morita (2014).[40] The contrast implies differentiating between the relativity of internal relations (relations and relata being mutually defining) and the contingency of external relations (of things already existing). To this we may simply add that the very differentiation holds these two axes together. This is not insignificant in Anglophone kin reckoning.

Consider again the conventional understanding that kin terms, and the kin positions implied, present examples of internal relations, relation being contained in the terms themselves. For all that is the case, we could as well speak of kin relations linking persons as more or less self-contained beings, external to one another insofar as such relations are contingent on the character of what is being related. Classificatory schemes in general commonly define entities according to intrinsic properties that enable the classifier to assess their similarities and differences. The external relation between them keeps the separateness of the terms in play. There seem parallels here, on the one hand with talking about kinspersons (relations/relatives) with respect to a generic supposition of mutuality and, on the other, with relations/relatives as interpersonal connections regarded as extensions or additions beyond or outside the self.

To step out of frame for a moment, I turn to Amazonia, a region that has become a locus classicus of debates about ontologies. Viveiros de Castro lays out, as one of the fundamentals of thought in the "modern West," its contrast between overtly relational and other kinds of substantives: "Kinship terms are relational pointers; they belong to the class of nouns that define something in terms of its relations to something else. . . . Concepts like fish or tree, on the other hand, are proper, self-contained substantives: they are applied to an object by virtue of its intrinsic properties" (2004a: 472). Such self-contained substantives appear in stark contrast to those of Amerindian perspectivism, where entities ("substances") "named by substantives like *fish*, *snake*, *hammock*, or *beer* are somehow used as if they were relational pointers, something halfway between a noun and a pronoun. . . . [Western naturalists might say] [y]ou are a father only because there is another person whose father you are. Fatherhood is a relation, while fishiness is a[n] intrinsic property of fish. In Amerindian perspectivism, however, something is a fish only by virtue of someone else whose fish it is" (2004a: 472–473, original emphasis). He invites us to imagine that all Amerindian substances are of this sort. "Suppose that, as siblings are those who have the same parents, conspecifics are those that have the same fish, the same snake, the same hammock, and so forth. No wonder, then, that animals are so often conceived, in Amazonia, as affinely related to humans. Blood is to humans as manioc beer is to jaguars in exactly the way that my sister is the wife of my brother-in-law" (473). There might be a relational inflection to [Western] naturalists' sibling and in-law relations, then, but not to the way they think of blood or beer (the one is held in place by an internal relation, the other by an external one). And here Viveiros de Castro's description touches on identity.

The relativity of naturalist kinship does not, in truth, seem all pervasive. While kin terminology remains an example of relative thinking, when the terms are deployed with respect to kinspersons, they are often used as if kinspersons, too, were "proper, self-contained substantives." That is just how naturalists think of blood or beer. In the way they treat one another, kinsfolk are not principally sustained as relatives through, for example, the permutations of their positionings with other relatives. Rather, as Schneider (1968) pointed out long ago for American kinship, they have first to be sustained as (individual) persons, as a mother, uncle, cousin, each with his or her own intrinsic and characteristic mode of behavior or quality of relating. Externality further resides in the distinctiveness of the "different" entities being related—in short, in perceptions of the fishiness of fish or of the maternity of the mother, the fatherly qualities of the father. These are acts of self-referencing. To return to the close unions of the nineteenth century, relationally speaking much seemed to turn on knowledge of appropriate ("natural" or self-referential) ways of acting; hence what became important was the appropriate behavior ascribed to (the nature of) each person's position. Brother and sister, husband and wife: there was no elaboration of relations to hold kinspersons in place, through, for example, systematic play on analogies across different kin positions.[41] Rather, the identity of kinsfolk—in personal conduct, in considerations of duty or obligation—relied heavily on discrimination between different affective registers of sentiment and closeness. Exceptions proved the rule: parallel intimacies to some appeared to others as dubious conflations.

However intense people's kinship lives, of which the nineteenth century has afforded a brief flavor, they may be consigned nonetheless to a rather restricted domain of action. Thus while kin relations in some experiential regimes are the very exemplars of cosmological process, in naturalism they are repeatedly pushed to one side. This brings us to schemas of comparison, to which the next chapter turns and in which friendship will figure more prominently. Whether cosmology is at issue (as in "naturalism") or something closer to culture (as in "Euro-American") will depend on the task in hand.

2. REGISTERS OF COMPARISON

Its diffuseness does not mean that the concept of relation is innocent of history or ideology or whatever will reveal its worldliness.[1] I ponder on this through materials where the reader's likely familiarity with them will perhaps allow something of a larger enterprise to be seen in a small part. Comparisons between kinship and friendship, such as we have already encountered, are frequent in the English vernacular. While exposition will entail further inquiry into interpersonal relations, the focus of this chapter is on comparison, on the epistemic relation. In common usage, "comparison" can both include the alignment of similarities and differences or be distinguished as focused on similarities by contrast with "contrast." Comparison and contrast thus point to each other. Comparing or contrasting ideas about family and friends may show up an ambiguity in the terms through the very attempt to reduce it. Brought together, the two terms otherwise tend to cross over and slide around each other. For their part, sociologists as well as anthropologists may affirm the affinity of kinship and friendship by glossing them as "personal relations." This appears to specify a type of relation, yet it is one that, by contrast with many other relations (including those of kinship), announces itself as basically formless; it seems to summon no more than a general associational ethos between individuals. Before noting how such an ethos may be discerned in vernacular usage, an initial comment is in order.

Having spent some time in the past problematizing comparison, if not actually doing away with it, naming it here allows me to be explicit on a point that also concerns its avatar, relation. I am not speaking in my own words, except insofar as they are words of scrutiny, but rather describing how comparison, and relation, works in English/Euro-American.[2] (Of course I speak English/

Euro-American, too, and am not excluding all of myself when referring to such usage.) The point is that I am not here interested in making an argument about comparison; I am very interested in how comparison is used in argumentation.

I

An Associational Ethos

When people draw on kinship idioms to refer to occasional meetings with erstwhile strangers, comparison may be implied. It is a feature to be found in the English literary association the Henry Williamson Society, which gathers together enthusiasts for this deceased author. Society members sometimes refer to their annual meetings as "family" gatherings.[3] That they are not acquainted along any other axis, Reed (2011) claims, does not detract from the quality of their relationships. This rests on a comparison of experiences, and the special kind of shared knowledge that results, above all, from how the first encounter with Williamson's books had been a life-changing moment. Readers report being taken over by this writer crashing into the living room, displacing the reality of ordinary domestic relations. The Society itself has a clear organizational purpose: to afford enthusiasts, unable to communicate their feelings about the author to those near them, the luxury of being with others in the know. Such an associational ethos has long been an unremarkable manifestation of social life, made explicit in the countless societies within society calling themselves "societies," in the sense that became popular in seventeenth- and eighteenth-century English.[4]

Society enthusiasts find themselves "occupying or occupied by another consciousness and so looking at the world from a perspective that is not their own" (Reed 2011: 10). They feel they know the author personally. This duplication of consciousness works at a distance, in their temporal separation from Henry, as well as through the intermittency of their gatherings. Such exercises of the imagination are elicited by the practice of solitary reading; readerly enthusiasm comes to isolate them from those who are otherwise close, including family: "Kin, colleagues, friends or neighbours may appear . . . like strangers" (10). Where strangers are like kin, kin can appear strangers. Estrangement seems manifest in the failure to communicate, a common experience in dedication to a cause where the most familiar persons appear not to understand. What Weston (2018) finds in writers of the Scottish Enlightenment, a specific evocation of sympathy as action at a distance, could almost describe the intimacy that his devotees claim with Henry and the bonds they activate among themselves. Weston is interrogating contemporary presumptions that, to the contrary, equate closeness with proximity and with feelings of both sympathy and empathy, but perhaps it is these that also come into play in the reversal of relations between kin and strangers on which Reed reports. It is not just that kin, friend, acquaintance, stranger all seem at times interchangeable. The frisson for Henry's associates surely rests on an unexpected sense of how to think about intimacy or what to expect from proximity. This throws into relief the regular ordering of interpersonal relations through vernacular comparisons based on formulating closeness and distance.

It is a peculiarity of the way interpersonal relations are generally depicted in English that distance is often taken as a matter of degree, leading to a sliding scale in the extent to which persons admit others as near to or far from themselves. It was precisely this circumspectness that, in taking over their consciousness, Henry took away from his readers. Measures of closeness and distance can coordinate almost any dimension of social life, including assumptions about increasing and decreasing knowledge in the form of knowledge of the self and acknowledgment of others. Such measures also organize rather simple notions of security and enmity, as in the idea that strangers are more distant than friends and accordingly more likely to be hostile or that people one does not know are more threatening than those one does (as in fearing aliens and fearing that aliens will think the same). The map we may suppose in people's heads at such moments outlines a kind of sociogeographic field of ever-widening concentric rings, within which all manner of others can be placed.[5]

Relations imagined as connections between persons draw on both connotations of distance: the one that summons a presence through the exercise of imagination and the one that rests axiomatically on perceived degrees of proximity.[6] The connotations may work together. Perhaps some of the frisson, mystery even, that surrounds the concept of "friend" is the sense of a closeness that works equally "at" (stimulated by, a function of) or "over" (bridging or obviating) a distance. While friendship brings a general assumption of close connection, its purported characteristics range from mutual interest to disinterestedness, and strangers, acquaintances, and kin may be as easily turned into friends as they are held distinct from them. Insofar as the uses to which English speakers put these terms indicate something of the form in which their social world appears, their implicit knowledge of the appropriate social context invariably sorts out the relevant connotation. The long-term question for our purposes is how to characterize the amorphous character of that which, precisely, requires such sorting out.

Pondering explicitly on interpersonal relations and the effect of distance (both connotations coming into play), Biagioli (2006) offers a comparison across two moments in time. Springing from what was afterward called the scientific revolution, they concern credibility: the manner in which Galileo was credited with having made astronomical observations and how more than fifty years later the Royal Society of London established its reputation. It turns out to be a comparison of comparisons.

When Galileo was staking everything on his detection of what we would call relations (see chapter 1), these were essentially comparisons of the respective positionings of phenomena. Another comparison also raised its head: that between astronomy and what was known of the astronomer. At a critical period in the development of his telescope, Biagioli argues (2006: 14–15), "distance and limited information" emerged as a condition for the construction of Galileo's personal credibility. In 1610 he was jockeying for Medici patronage for his investigation of Jupiter's satellites. Keen in turn for an enlargement of renown, the family allowed him to use their name for the "Medician stars." They were in Florence, he in Padua. They pressed him for a demonstration, but finally acceded to their name being used in advance of receiving the instruments that would enable them to see what Galileo saw. Now Galileo had already sent the first printed account of his discoveries to an acquaintance, the Medici ambassador in Prague, asking if he would solicit the Imperial Mathematician Johannes Kepler's opinion. (Had he been nearby, Kepler would have realized that Galileo had not yet received patronly endorsement.) Kepler, who represented Galileo as a longtime friend, had no access to a suitable telescope either; and when he enthusiastically confirmed the discoveries, it was without having seen the stars for himself. (Some thought the spatial distance from which he wrote gave a disinterested cast to his support.) Biagioli pinpoints the role that partial knowledge played in building up reputation. This world of patronage entailed sustaining links between individuals "known" to one another who vouchsafed one another's credibility. The link, a guarantee of trust in the person, sometimes meant taking other kinds of knowledge on trust, too.

The partial nature of knowledge at a distance also operated in the "kind of corporate infrastructures typical of scientific academies," as the transition from patronage to the institution-based frameworks of early modern natural philosophy shows (Biagioli 2006: 45). After its establishment in 1662, the Royal Society rapidly found itself the object of voluminous correspondence from scholars and amateurs across Europe. Its secretary realized that in sending the

Society accounts of diverse experiments, attaching themselves to its endeavor, these correspondents were also furnishing it with the very signs of scientific activity. He set up a journal: while few people came to meetings and there was often a dearth of local experiments to report, the journal could be a carrier of this external interest and thereby broadcast a message about the Society's success. "In exchange for the sense of partaking in a prestigious enterprise — a belief that could be sustained through partial perspectives produced by distance — the correspondents sent their reports and observations to London, effectively providing the Society with a blood infusion" (2006: 49).

In comparing the aspirations of the Royal Society with those of the Medici patrons, Biagioli argues that the Society was promoting a socio-epistemological framework for natural philosophy, not a set of specific claims or theories.[7] So instead of the customized dedication of spectacular but occasional discoveries, "the Society set up a system of credit that was based on the steady flow of generic communications" (2006: 73). Geographical remoteness allowed the number of correspondents to grow without increasing personal interactions with members in London. This filter had implications for personal endorsement. Although correspondents needed to be introduced by people already known to the Society, they did not need to be gentlemen and could contribute without becoming members. Yet the same comparison that lay at the root of Galileo's efforts resurfaces: the relation of phenomena observed to the observer's status. If the reliability of a knowledge claim was inseparable from the social qualifications of the person making it, how could the Society gain credit through reports from nongentlemen? "Correspondence did not do away with problems of credibility but reframed them within an epistolary etiquette that was necessarily different from the bodily etiquettes that regulated short-distance, face-to-face interactions among English gentlemen or Continental courtiers" (2006: 69). Correspondents sustained the Royal Society's authority to turn reports into public knowledge. The Society had found a mode of communication that simultaneously reflected the value of interpersonal relations, and put value on their disembodied version, in circulating information whose character was from its point of view, as Biagioli aptly puts it, generic. Imaginatively incorporated into the Society thereby, correspondents were operating both "at" and "over" a distance.

During the course of the English seventeenth century, associational life was acquiring its own etiquette; caught up in a new sense of purposeful association, as we have seen, the abstract connotations of "society" also refabricated older concepts such as that of "company."[8] Participation was filtered: societies were known by the kinds of men (gender was invariably the first filter) they included and excluded, and had their own canons of appropriate behavior. "Early modern 'societies' and 'companies' ranged from informal interactions (like men 'making merry' in an alehouse) to formal corporations (like the Royal Society or East India Company) with varieties of social networks and institutions in between. . . . [W]hile this spectrum of associational forms clearly made for an increasingly diverse range of groupings and activities, the concept of purposeful association remained remarkably stable" (Withington 2010: 176; also see Dear 2001). Moreover the purpose at the center of the association would give many such entities a life that lodged in the company at large and not just at moments of meeting; that is, association — as in the present-day literary society — worked at a distance, too.

Perhaps the distance across which such interpersonal relations could be effective gave friendship some of its dimensions, even as the vehicles for these relations were changing. Galileo could call on a remote "friend" (such as Kepler) but not on the same protocols for disembodied ("generic") information encouraged by the Royal Society.[9] The latter's communications were seemingly part of an emerging associational life that afforded friends, acquaintances, and onetime strangers a purpose for thinking of themselves together. The generic idea of being in association is at once as diffuse as and no vaguer than that of relation.

Biagioli's exposition entails a comparison of comparisons (Lloyd 2015: 29). We know that the relationship (comparison) between an investigation and the authority it commanded was of lively concern to thinkers of the period (Shapin and Schaffer [1985] 2011; Shapin 1994), and Biagioli is contrasting different ways in which this was handled. One of them presaged the phasing out of that indigenous concern, as we shall see in the next chapter. Anthropologists often find themselves dealing with relations between relations as comparisons of comparisons (for an example, Descola 2001: 109; see Candea 2019). This is no more evident than in the arena of kinship and friendship, where we turn first to mainly vernacular usages and then to mainly anthropological ones.

II

The Personal and Impersonal

The last few years have seen a steady rise in the United Kingdom among those who, whether as living or deceased donors, have contributed to organ transplantation.[10] For a long while, the paradigmatic transplant concerned organs from deceased persons, allocated on a need basis to strangers, as blood donation was primarily conceived between strangers (Whitfield 2013). A recent phenomenon is the increase in the proportion of living donors (of kidney, liver, and, rarely, lung). The accompanying language is illuminating. While a small number come forward for what are officially designated "non-directed," "altruistic," or "stranger" transplants, the majority of living transfers are "directed" to people known to the donor. The latter is translated as meaning "family and friends."[11] An observer might say that the language of altruism that is so clear in the case of stranger donation becomes ambiguous when parties are known to one another; indeed, it may seem nonsense to disentangle self-interest from other-interest. Insofar as a relative is part of your family, you are simultaneously helping the relative for yourself, or for kin closer to the recipient than you are. Precisely the same could be said of friends. One guarantee of continuing relations is that reciprocities are plural and open-ended, and in these respects there is no difference between friends and relatives.[12] That in the case of friends the connection coexists with these reciprocities, whereas kin relations are based on other factors as well, does not erase the similarity.

This short exposition lifts the curtain on many issues involved in English-speaking understandings of kinship and friendship and their place in diverse interpersonal relations. Sentiments may be ascribed to kin and friends alike. At the same time, facilitated by the medical substitutability of body parts, organ donation draws on a foundational naturalism, one that divides the diversity of social life from a continuum of human physiology and invites in the stranger. Common feelings that people recognize in one another, whether or not phrased in terms of a generalized humanity, assume similarities in a substratum of shared biology or psychology. People may naturalize concepts such as individual consciousness or expressions of aggression or sympathy toward others, even while distinguishing between their (individual) freedom of choice in seeking out friends and the givenness of the relatives to whom they are irreversibly connected. Such considerations are among the many leading to comparisons between impersonal and personal relations, and what they purportedly say about where interests lie. Anyone may be moved to help; personal knowledge is amplified by a general sense of how associates in close relationships behave.

Whereas kin and friends may be considered together or apart depending on circumstance, on one specific axis — the particularistic or personal nature of association — they may be distinguished from a generalized field of impersonal relations. In their overview of a voluminous range of writings on friendship, Beer and Gardner (2015: 426) comment that, as with kin, friends not only enjoy one another's goodwill but crucially know the basis for their interaction, and each "knows that the other knows it." This contrasts with the impersonal relations of "mere" acquaintances. That said, in the very comparison with personal relations, the concept of impersonal relations acquires its edge as not mere at all.

People can move meaningfully between being impersonal and personal with one another, and in English the notion of an acquaintance may indicate someone who behaves as a bit of both (Morgan 2009). The historical sociologist Silver (1990: 1476, after Georg Simmel) observes that persons are substitutable for one another in impersonal relations, by comparison with their nonsubstitutability in personal ones, prototypically between friends. It is interesting that the prototype is friendship, for kin positions would introduce ambiguities insofar as the grounds for comparison rest on differentiating the uniqueness of persons as individuals from roles (as of kinship) anyone can assume. Further ambiguity awaits. As a technical phrase, "stranger donation" refers to a living organ donor giving to a common pool, and thus in "no relation" with any potential recipient. It is a kind of collaboration between strangers, an impersonal one by contrast with collaborations between people acting out existing personal ties. The logic of the situation invites reflection back on what is happening when kin and friends are donors. Insofar as the paradigmatic organ transplant has always been transfer between strangers, perhaps we can reverse dominant vernacular usage and — in the way they act — redescribe donor kin and friends *as* "strangers." This would imagine them as impersonal if nonanonymous participants in today's intimate publics, such as geographer and social theorist Amin (2012: 16, 30–31) discerns in the society of strangers. A politics of care could be decentered from ideas of interpersonal or associational orientations alike.[13]

Silver turns to a more ancient society of strangers, with its own particular contouring of self-interest and disinterest.[14] It was "acquaintances" and "neutral strangers," "authentically indifferent co-citizens," who peopled the then-new "strangership" of commercial society imagined by writers of the Scottish Enlightenment (1990: 1482–1483). In European history at large, the development of impersonal relations is regarded as the trademark of modernity. The familiar story dwells on a specific sphere of civil society where self-interest could flourish, impersonal relations being identified with the development of market transactions between notional strangers, explicitly removed from the restrictions of preexisting bonds once held to engage kin and friend alike. With their own ethics, envisioned as the civilities of commerce, the interests at stake were not disguised. At the same time, Silver (1990: 1486) notably adds, these writers imagined this sphere precipitating its opposite, a separate domain of "personal and civic friendship." The friendship that had formerly, and firmly, indicated common interests began to acquire the connotations of disinterested fellow-feeling. As to what counted as personal, what new sense did it acquire when private friendship became its prototype? Early modern cogitations on interpersonal relations might be germane to appreciating both modern and Enlightenment preoccupations, and, with the latter, some of the then-changing contours of kinship.

Comparing Persons

Of diverse changes in kinship practices identified as early modern, I have speculated on whether an associational ethos was not also part of a certain generic conceptualization of kin relations. Chapter 1 observed that connotations of friendship were simultaneously undergoing metamorphosis. Up and into the seventeenth century, friend could be used of kin and non-kin alike; when it lost that kinship referent, friendship was also shorn of many of the corporeal connotations it earlier carried. "Kinship and friendship [had] turned on the same axis" (Bray 2003: 214; see Tadmor 2001: 212). The virtue of kinship, which once lay in the friendship that it could create, was also perhaps displaced by a new accent on personal relations of the kind that Silver describes. "Relations" became a habitual marker of kinspersons as "friends" ceased to be.

An overlay that seventeenth-century English seemingly introduced was an emphasis on friendship as a matter of knowledge in the sense of recognition. It was always the case, with respect to kin, that out of "people to whom an individual is deemed related . . . [are those] whom an individual chooses to acknowledge as kin at any particular moment"—and to underline the antiquity here, this comes from an account of post-Roman, early medieval, Europe (Smith 2005: 84). Indeed, the Old English term *freond* for "kin" is interpreted by the same writer as pointing to the kinship that made a practical difference. Interests were aligned: out of all one's kinsmen, friends were those who could be relied on (2005: 97–98).[15] Was anything changing in the way such recognition took on the characteristics of knowledge deliberately activated? Conceptualizing knowledge (knowing that you know) introduces further layers: you may know several people, near or far, but you also take care to "know" those who matter. In some seventeenth-century milieux, one could conceivably talk of a fresh tenor to recognition. Where practices of accreditation in knowledge claims, scientific or otherwise, allowed new inflections to knowing the world around you, ever-differentiating permutations of social class created fresh occasions for filtering potential interactions, and thus for social inclusion and exclusion. Personal relations, by comparison with impersonal ones, were those you recognized.

Connections amplified personal relations. Tadmor (2001: 161) refers to the eighteenth-century significance of "connections" for seeking employment and gaining preferment, not least because of the element of choice in recognition. The generic forms certainly offered possibilities for modulating the range of those one did or did not wish to acknowledge. Among the diarists on whom Tadmor draws is William Stout of Lancaster (after Marshall 1967). A "remote relation" is someone he takes on as an apprentice; the phrase "near relation" describes a nephew, while "next relation" is used of a man who inherited from his cousin. One diary entry of 1703 describes a child brought up by "some of his mother's relations," while another about the same time refers to someone who left his estate to his half-brother "without any respect to his father's brother or relations" (Tadmor 2001: 124, emphasis omitted). "Stout's main point in making this [latter] utterance was to describe a case of wrongful inheritance, rather than to list all the possible kin who did not benefit from this man's estate. In the same way, when Stout referred to the child . . . [it] was not to describe the exact living arrangements, but to place the child in the context of a broader story about his mother's imprudence and the family's downfall" (2001: 126–127). The generic lent itself, then, to pronouncing broad judgments on the fortunes of different branches of a family or circle of connections. In turn, "having relations" pointed to an individual's general web of kinship ties, as Tadmor puts it, and thus their attachment to a range of others, as when another diarist used the shorthand "relations" for the intimate persons who gathered at his wife's deathbed.

Persons may be compared, then, through the withholding or awarding of recognition. Discrimination on that basis had the potential to relegate a more distant sphere of personal connections to something approaching the impersonal. For where kin were specifically demarcated by the term "relation," they were *also* being rendered like everyone else of one's circle. In that the speaker did not have to specify degree, reckoned through steps of parentage and descent, the connection was generalized. It was suggested earlier that when Galileo summoned his absent friend, he was evoking corporeal ties. Kin terms in English facilitated similar imaginings, summoning the specifics of connection (even if applied generally), "cousin" being a notable example, as well as of friendliness in acquaintance; a corporeal connection could be imagined regardless of distance. Was "relation," by contrast, more evocative of a kind of knowing or acknowledgment, especially of a kind that could be accredited remotely, as in the Royal Society's reports? With relation, kin might be recognized on the assumption that there was bound to be some link between them, but Tadmor's argument is that you did not have to specify that degree in order to "know" the person. It was enough to be in association, and to talk of close and distant relatives. As in all interpersonal relations, this sliding scale could be adjusted to substantively different circumstances, including those introduced by wealth or class. Making way for other kinds of social discriminations, the substantive content (their degree) of particular kin connections could be left undefined.

Whom one recognized as kin was a question central to an anthropologically famous mid-twentieth-century study undertaken in a middle-class sector of North London (Firth et al. 1969). It exemplifies how we might grasp comparisons between persons, and particularly between kin and friends. For setting out to investigate kinship, the anthropologists found themselves talking about friendship. Their study does not just play out, in another time and space, some of the issues in knowledge-making we have been discussing, but also shows the investigators engaged in the same game.

While Firth and his colleagues were clearly secure in their own usage of terms for kinship, what jumps out from their account is that they left the description of friendship largely up to their Londoners. The ethnographers go into detail on the variable ways in which people decided whether particular categories of persons counted as kin ("family," "relatives," "relations"). On the one hand, a single woman referred to "family" as those who are close to you, citing brothers and sisters, but it was also a term of moral responsibility and could be extended to aunts, uncles, cousins. On the other hand, there was a "secondary lot," and she spoke of someone connected to her as "not a relation, only by marriage"; here the investigator confidently writes, "For this woman affines [in-laws] were definitely not included in the definition of 'family'" (1969: 91). The authors alluded to what was then an old debate in Anglophone anthropology (about whether affines should be included with consanguines as kin), but the point is that, within the scope of their analysis, blood kin and in-laws obviously belonged to a single conceptual universe. However, when it came to friends, not only was there no such precedent in anthropological debate, there was barely any attempt to develop an analytical position.[16]

The trouble was, an interviewee observed, the inquiry was "all about relatives and nothing about friends" (Firth et al. 1969: 114). People themselves frequently brought friends into their responses to questions about relatives. Talking of a brother's widow, one said, "No! She's not a relative, she's a friend." The speaker's husband put it the other way round: his wife's brother was so close that, "yes, he was a relative . . . [and as for] his widow — we've just accepted her as a friend, as a relative . . . who's welcome in the house" (97). When people juxtaposed relatives and friends, comparison invariably concerned the quality and strength of ongoing ties. There were degrees of inclusion. One could be friendly with someone without being a friend, or a friend might be "almost one of the family"; indeed as someone said, "a close friend becomes a relative" (116). The anthropologists commented on the choice that people exercised both over who counted as kin and who counted as friend, adding, however, that this came out of the material — it was not something people stressed. Instead people *spoke* about the categorical contrasts that set relatives apart from friends.[17] Choice was seen to attach to friends, not relatives — "You can't choose 'em, you've got 'em" (114). Tensions with kin were set against being able to relax with friends. Someone whose affection and sense of duty meant he kept up with parents and sisters never invited them to his house where friends were regularly entertained ("This is my castle and I do not want relatives in it").

Degrees of inclusion have influenced sociological as well as anthropological accounts of personal networks: indeed, we might call it a vernacular framework. Speaking generally of social relations — in which every individual is embedded — as a network, the anthropologist Boissevain (1974: 25, 47; see also Boissevain and Mitchell 1973) draws zones of intimacy as circles emanating out from a central ego. Thirty years later sociologists Spencer and Pahl (2006: 52) use a similar schema, concentric rings, in discussions with British interviewees about how they would plot people on a "personal community map."[18] This particular inquiry into the connections that people found important put friend-based and family-based networks alongside those based on neighborhood, partner, or profession. However, people's struggles over whom to include or exclude as "family" vacillated (like the North Londoners') between whether categorical or effective relations were at stake. Down to the same adage apropos being able to choose friends but not kin, individual designations of friends and family nonetheless overlapped, with this or that person "more friend-like," "more family-like" (2006: 114).

The comparisons these indigenous moderns make between individuals within their personal networks betray a consistently affective overlay to the categories they use. This is especially clear when — faced with a researcher's questions — they have to make choices in the abstract, and at issue is closeness and distance. Closeness has resonances of affective, and the effective expression of, attachment. Thinking of an individual friend as "family" may make the friend closer, while thinking of a relative as a "friend" may make the relative closer. Stressing contrast or opposition between friends and family conversely evokes detachment. Comparisons can also be expressed in terms of who is a "real" or "true" friend or relative, which bears on a local theory of sorts, namely that concepts have core meanings extendible beyond their original connotations, or can be applied as metaphors or similes (friend-*like*, family-*like*).

If pressed, many moderns would no doubt regard the terminology of paternal relations in a church, or of fraternal ones in a trade union, as figures of speech.[19]

An implicit framework for making comparisons, seemingly laid down in certain early modern practices, appears clearly outlined in these latter-day usages. (1) Comparison appears as a matter of degree, whether the degree turns on distance, social and otherwise, or — with affective or evaluative resonance — on how far persons "really" fit a category, and thus live up to expectations. (2) Comparison allows a distribution of characteristics or attributes across designations for persons, the characteristics simultaneously having their own values, such as value placed on the given or the chosen, and deriving from conventions associated with specific roles, such as friends are friendly, in-laws awkward. (3) Above all, comparison includes people in and excludes them from specific categories (regardless of whether the categories overlap, are context-dependent, and so forth); a category is self-evidently composed of entities that share similar features (the criterion of inclusion), by contrast with entities that are differentiated (a criterion for exclusion). Categorization can proceed without remark, but it can also entail self-consciousness in the way people think about the implications of comparing kin and friends.

In short, these modern connotations of comparison emerge with contours prefigured in earlier concerns about knowledge. Describing this epistemic relation thus serves as a bridgehead to explicit anthropological comparisons of friends and kin (Firth and his colleagues stumbled into the field inadvertently); some anthropological accounts seem like veritable echo chambers of this vernacular framework.

III

Comparisons of Comparisons — 1

In common usage the connotations of "kin" and "friend" are clearly situational, as we have just seen, giving rise to overlapping possibilities. So what are English-speaking (-writing) anthropologists going to make of kin and friends elsewhere? While expositions of kinship may have little to say about friendship, anthropological attention to friendship invariably deals with kinship. Across social formations, this becomes a veritable comparison of comparisons. Three edited collections give us a foothold for discussion, the first (Leyton 1974a) produced in the wake of the then-new social network analysis, followed by Bell and Coleman (1999) criticizing the notion that global transformations were creating a ubiquitous understanding of friendship, and most recently Guichard and colleagues (2014), whose agenda is to resituate friendship apropos kinship.[20] Beer and Gardner point to a voiced fear that kinship studies might engulf the sphere of friendship, so that empirically distinct ways of being friends become lost to comparative analysis.[21]

Resonating with the positive connotations of closeness already encountered, some anthropologists stress that the very concept of friendship implies an idealized form of itself ("true" friendship) (e.g., Paine 1999). Thus Carrier (1999: 21) forthrightly defines friendship as a relation "based on spontaneous and unconstrained sentiment or affection," and immediately sets up a contrast: "After all, if the relationship is constrained we confront something very different from what we call 'friendship,' something [more] like bureaucratic relationships, kinship relationships or patron-client relationships." His "we" occupies the specific vantage point of "Western thought," so he is problematizing this concept of friendship through a comparative move. Like Paine (1999: 39), Carrier argues that we cannot understand conceptions of friendship without understanding conceptions of self and person. Not only is there a history to Western usage, and diversity between segments of the population, there is also evidence of very differently constituted "social selves" in other regimes, where people's notions of self mean they are unlikely to think of friendship "in the modern Western sense" (1999: 35). The possibilities range from the shock of an anthropologist returning to her native Brazil to hear everyone calling all kinds of people "friends" when it had such a narrow social usage in the England from which she had come (Rezende 1999), to a study of networks in China where fewer than 7 percent of named people were described as friends by contrast with a reported almost 70 percent in the United States (Smart 1999: 119).[22]

Nonetheless, in pursuit of kinship and friendship across diverse locales, a recurrent set of contrasting attributes orients anthropological comparison: formal/informal, public/private, immutable/variable, involuntary/elective, specialized/unspecialized, constrained/free from constraint, and so forth. The contrasts hold implications for social action; they also imply theoretical sensitivity to what is relevant to social analysis. Thus kinship may be presented as "central" to friendship's "peripheral" location, or a matter of "societal" as opposed to "personal" relations.

A complaint about such models motivates Guichard's collection on sub-Saharan Africa. If friendship outside "Western" countries is still understudied, that is because of the "premise that the room left for friendship to flourish as an extra-kin relationship is inversely proportional to the importance of kinship as a factor structuring community" (2014: 1). Far from staking out a distinct terrain for friendship, she wants to bring kinship back in. Studying the one apart from the other, she argues, ignores the extent to which friendship is so often an ideal model for relations between kin, as it ignores just how friendship is frequently transformed into kinship (for example, through marriage alliances). Among the contributors to the same book, Werbner (2014: 143) concludes, apropos urban Gaborone in Botswana, that "both the urban friendship circle and boon-companionship mesh durably with kinship, and do not displace it, or take any load or emotional charge from it." However, compared to kinship, such friendship is narrowly defined along gender and class lines and restricted to same-generation associates.[23] Warms (2014: 120), speaking of merchants in Mali, argues that in modern African cities "kinship and friendship may reinforce one another." There need be no inverse relationship between the demands of kin and friend; that notion has only become "commonsensical in our own society" (120) because of the modernist myth — a self-conscious "vision of Western society," in Warms's phrase — that as people leave "tight knit" village communities bound by formal ties of kinship they make informal, voluntary associations in town.

In the anthropological effort to make "friend" work as an analytical category alongside "kin," there seems no case that does not have a range of ethnographic variations. People may agree on a line between friends and acquaintances, but you cannot use the terms in present-day Finland as you would in England (Abrahams 1999). In rural Lesotho half a century ago (Wallman 1974), while you would be aware of the prevalence of kin terms for all manner of local and political relations, when kin help one another in everyday affairs they are not necessarily doing so *as* kinsmen; kinship may be significant, irrelevant, or avoided for the task in hand. Nonetheless what for much of the twentieth century made the anthropological accounts comparable was the knowledge that such variation was no more nor less than any cross-societal or cross-cultural comparison was bound to yield. Comparison, elaborating on local attributions of dispositions and habits to this or that kind of person, assumed that there was a systemic description to be given of the society or culture in question. One sign of the systemic was that such a description axiomatically accounted for internal variation: insofar as the whole could be framed comparatively, so, too, could each detail or part.

This possibility was underlined by anthropological disagreement as to what that whole might be. The positions adopted in the 1970s by Paine (1974a, [1969] 1974b), who worked with largely European materials, and by Schwimmer (1974), on Oceania, are instructive. Drawing on the (vernacular) middle-class culture "of our own society," Paine argues that friendship is a phenomenon restricted to certain social configurations characterized by autonomy, unpredictability, and terminality in which the intimate and the private play important roles. It is "a sociological and cultural device [in the management of interpersonal relations] in respect to which there exist different alternatives" in other societies ([1969] 1974b: 119). Taking issue with this, Schwimmer (1974: 49) focuses on the potential universality of a "type of association which is initiated by mutual attraction and which is maintained by the exchange of intrinsic benefits." Across Oceania, such "friendship" may seem at first sight residual to affective relations between kin, but the theoretical justification for paying it attention is whether "our analysis is able to reveal in it a structural principle" (51). In effect, both anthropologists reiterate a founding assumption of comparative endeavor: exploring these interrelations was the means and ends of social inquiry.

Degree of fit, distribution of characteristics, categorization on the basis of similarity and difference—the debates offer a parallel with those vernacular (English) connotations of comparison elucidated in the conduct of Firth's London study. To these connotations, twentieth-century anthropologists added a further crucial dimension. What above all organizes the elements of a comparison are models of social or cultural life; being explicit about this organization is the anthropologist's principal self-conscious move. Hence models can compete with one another over what should be reckoned (say) a structural matter. When Paine ([1969] 1974b: 120) appropriates a comment on ritual kinship and applies it to friendship—in many situations, friendship "avoids being implicated in the internal dimensions of the kinship structure, for it involves no structural issues (Pitt-Rivers 1968: 412)"—he intends "social structure" in the Anglophone sense. When Schwimmer (1974: 51) uncovers a whole friendship universe and its internal categorizations as a result of structural analysis, he intends something closer to the Francophone inflection of "structuralism." However, this comparison was never labeled as such. Rather, the explicit relationship between these two analytical procedures invariably appears as ethnographic expertise: which argument seems to make best sense (closest fit) of the particular data each has to hand. Whether models of organization or the organization of models, in these twentieth-century materials at least, organization there always is. The goal is a systemic account.

Detecting parallels between the coherence of anthropological analysis and the coherence of the anthropologist's subject matter became increasingly subject to critical reflection over the latter part of the twentieth century. It augmented self-consciousness about knowledge-making, which the very idea of an analytical vocabulary had always entailed.

Paine and Schwimmer seem equally captivated by Aristotle's *Nicomachean ethics*. By no means the first or last anthropologists to have commented on its discussion of "the distinctive friendship of kinship" (notably Sahlins 2008: 45–46; 2013: 20; and, via Thomas Aquinas, Fortes 1969: 239n), each takes up Aristotle's contrast between ties combining pleasantness and usefulness with the goodness of perfect friendship and those showing only some of these components. They then diverge. Paine (1974a) pursues the moral content of these concepts as a measure against which to assess modern anthropological writings on friendship. Matters of enduring concern since the beginning of social science, equality, solidarity, and instrumentalism in people's relations with one another all come to the fore. Schwimmer (1974) goes for the overarching term *philia*. Focusing on this Greek concept of friendship that embraces both kin and non-kin, he adopts it as an analytical category. Yet this deliberate departure from English word usage opens up rather than closes down need for further exposition.

One sign of the 1970s interest in friendship was a semipopular account written by Brain (1976). Opening up to a general English readership the varieties of relations in which people express love for one another, manifested above all in friendship, it is with intent to surprise that he discusses "kinship and marriage" in the Papua New Guinea highlands. Referring to the Kuma of the Middle Wahgi Valley, Brain speaks of how special the brother-in-law relation is to male friendship—men explain they marry women in order to have the women's brothers as their friends. Indeed, the "relationship between brothers-in-law is the only one in which friendships can develop in a way which renders personal devotion . . . crucial in determining the actions of one man towards another" (1976: 172). Emphasizing the easygoing nature of this tie, he observes that unrelated friends call each other — compare themselves with — "brothers-in-law."

A comparison with the Bangwa of the African Cameroon mobilizes *their* comparison between a husband's relations with his spouse's legal guardian (marriage lord) and those he enjoys with her brothers and other in-laws. Brothers-in-law are notably relaxed with one another, free of the suspicions of witchcraft or sorcery that affect so many other relations. Bangwa can marry ("fairly close") patrilineal kin, converting them into affines; yet insofar as affines are sought after as a "means of making new friendships" (Brain 1976: 174), replicating marriages between people already so linked is then forbidden. This protocol reverses both the Kuma preference, which is to concentrate marriages between friendly clans who are also military allies (Reay 1959a), and those of their highlands neighbors where intermarrying clans are either out-and-out enemies to one another or else are sometimes friendly, sometimes hostile. (When enemies are affines, enmity operates largely at clan level, the personal relations of in-laws being notionally protected.) Note the shift in the anthropologists' comparisons. No longer comparing "friends" with "family" or "kin," they are now differentiating kinds of kin relations from one another.

Schwimmer (1974: 51) does just this in his observations on philia. The purpose of the analytical category is to illuminate structural principles governing the recognition of friendship. Drawing on his work in lowland Papua New Guinea, he describes how Orokaiva institutionalize friendship through reference to three modalities (modes of interaction) in *kin* relations. These can be compared as: (1) cooperative alliance, centered on sibling and parental bonds; (2) competitive group exchange, especially with affines and maternal kin; (3) and the interdependence found between spouses or between cross-cousins (cousins linked through opposite-sex siblings). Within each modality, same or similar terms occur for both kin and non-kin friends. Thus structured, friends are distinguished according to the same criteria as kin are; as a consequence different categories of friends cannot be reduced to one another. Where Bangwa suggest that friendship differentiates kinds of kin, here Orokaiva inform us that kin can differentiate kinds of friends. In turn, Schwimmer's focus on friends affects what he had previously taken for granted as a kin universe. Friendship now "becomes a dynamic dimension of kinship" (1974: 57), and he speaks of a philia universe.

Applicable to any consideration of kinship and friendship, such a universe turns on permutations of identification and differentiation, yielding four organizational possibilities, in which the distribution of designations becomes a matter for empirical inquiry.[24] Thus there may be complete overlap between designations of kin and friend or no overlap at all. In twisting his language with that Greek term, Schwimmer tells us he was deliberately making use of an unfamiliar concept. He needed to name what he took as "a universal type of association," one characterized by the exchange of benefits arising largely out of the association itself. Yet what enables Schwimmer to make various comparisons across societies contains an interesting assumption. His Orokaivan example of philia relations is structured by those three modalities of interaction (alliance, exchange, or interdependence); rather more than the mutual alignments that Beer and Gardner (2015) see intrinsic to friendship in Aristotle's sense, for Orokaiva—and for Papua New Guinea at large—a whole cosmology is inscribed in "the exchange of benefits." Brain might say that Kuma brothers-in-law can show devotion not based on material interests, but that would leave out the critical exchange on which their very relation is (materially) based: the marriage of the woman who faces the one as sister and the other as wife.[25]

If comparison encourages expository neologisms, such as philia relations, it also circumscribes other descriptions. In a Papua New Guinean context, introducing the Euro-American comparison of kin and friends in terms of interest and disinterest would yield little. It is pointless to expect an absence of material interest. Relations of all kinds are made material — it is the equivalent of being recognized. The influence that persons have on one another may be mediated (through gifts, say) or unmediated (a capacity to effect health or harm), but it makes no sense to imagine the materiality of that influence as a matter of choice.[26] The woman between the two men, and the substantial consequences flowing from this, is reason enough why the Kuma brother-in-law relationship is an interested one, regardless of how it is implemented. In Schwimmer's view, it is the imperative nature of kinship bonds that makes them appropriate expressions of mutuality for certain kinds of unrelated friends.

Exposition demands looking again at the concept of exchange. Men's difference from each other is an outcome of the relations linking them; otherwise put, they interact by virtue of the distinctions between them. What brothers-in-law exchange is the perspective each has on the wife/sister: she divides the men. One view is thus acknowledged in the other, a nonreversible relation between specific partners, which may for Kuma and their neighbors be explicitly transformed into the reversible ceremonial positions of givers and receivers of wealth. A woman, too, turns in two directions: in the Papua New Guinea highlands (there are other versions), the husband elicits her productive and reproductive capacities for his and his son's clan, not for that of her father and brother. Without those two sets of kin — conjugal and natal — being held in an ongoing interchange, a woman's capacity for social action is diminished. It is here that degrees of expectation become highly relevant, judgments are made about the satisfaction with which male affines conduct their affairs, and the health of the woman and her progeny become a vital measure of the state of their relations.

It is hard to resist the conclusion from this Papua New Guinean (and Cameroonian) excursus that people are "comparing" certain relations with other relations. Yet what is captured in the observer's notion of comparison? Schwimmer's linguistic intervention reminds us how anthropologists may have to navigate the language of exposition. The materials, from Melanesia at least, make some rather less obvious points, which are worth spelling out.

Degree of fit, distribution of characteristics, categorization on the basis of similarity and difference: I suggested that these elements of twentieth-century anthropological models of comparison ran alongside certain vernacular (English-speaking) practices. They do so together with the additional self-consciousness of investigating the roles played by society or culture, and (so it was noted) their rendering as specific structures or systems. With the vernacular connection, it is not too far-fetched to ask if there might be counterparts to these elements in the comparison of relations suggested by aspects of (say) Melanesian kinship, especially given the tenor of marriage exchange.[27]

For here we seem to be dealing with a calculus of sorts. Relations give perspectives on other relations. Where a wife is marked as a brother-in-law's sister, my relation with her (man-speaking) is like your relation with her, though the terms to the relation (spouse/sibling) are different; my relation is unlike yours, though the woman is the same woman. At least, that is how one might write out a comparison of such relations in English, rendering similarity and difference the crucial operators. Yet, in Melanesian (so to speak), the two sets of relations (spouses/in-laws) are neither merged into each other nor opposed, and their parallelism is of a rather particular kind. Between the men, each side of a reciprocal relationship already incorporates the corresponding perspective. The above statement would need rewriting: "My relation with her is [defined by/divided from] your relation with her." This is not readily encompassed by a vocabulary that turns on similarity and difference. Let us break this observation down through the elements of comparison already laid out.

First, although what we might call degree of relating is found in greater or lesser extent in the way particular brothers-in-law deal with one another, the relation as such is not made present to such and such degree through individual personal enactments. Rather it is regarded as held — whether in place or in abeyance — by all the relations around, for example through the (marriage) exchange that has already reconfigured their kin networks. This bears, second, on the distribution of characteristics. Marriages, like deaths, are critical moments in the rearrangement of, well, anthropologists might say social life, but their interlocutors might say flows of procreative potential or some such. While these kin categories can provide the anthropologist with schemas of social classification based on attributes and characteristics, what is probably at issue for the parties themselves will be something closer to capacity or efficacy such as is manifest in well-being. From this comes the third point. These categories are about the vital influence persons have on one another. To conceptualize a (non-kin) friend as a brother-in-law is to acknowledge the material consequences of the relationship for each other's fortunes. Otherwise put, the relationship has brother-in-law-ish outcomes: it is the relation that is the value-bearing entity. In sum, English speakers could indeed find counterparts to various elements of their concept of comparison, while at the same time these counterparts add up to nothing like the comparison of similarities and differences as they know it. The final question is whether there is any counterpart to the anthropologist's self-conscious organization (structural, systemic) of items laid out to be compared. This requires lengthier treatment.

When Schwimmer refers to Orokaivan brothers-in-law belonging to a mode of kin relating through which people also conceptualize friends, he detects a formality in the allocation of friendship relations. Apart from the extent to which they engage in competitive, reciprocating partnerships, these brothers-in-law work under the constraints that all affinal transactions entail. Other relations in the philia system, cooperative alliance and unions based on interdependence, also demand the observance of etiquette. Insofar as these relations are bound up with specific modes of interaction, then perhaps acting out such specificities constitutes something like a meta-discursive commentary, and thus self-conscious reflection, on what relations mean to people.

The most important form of Orokaivan hereditary friendship, that of "cooperative alliance" (it has a special term), includes sharing between siblings. It may draw in previously unrelated persons such as the in-married wives of a village. Not connected among themselves before arriving there, women will establish specific bonds with one another, creating occasions for visits and gifting between villages. In turn, men who establish hereditary friendships based on cooperative alliance call each other brother; if they do not live nearby, they nonetheless conduct their gift giving not with the expectations of reciprocating partners but in the idiom of sharing. Again, it is the relation that stamps its value on the transaction. Thus a host shares with his brother when the latter comes to visit; on the obligatory return visit, the erstwhile guest now shares in likewise manner. Staged interchanges are signifying events (Stasch 2009: 17), making explicit the displacement or substitution of people's perspective on others, sequenced through time and space.

Reflective as one might understand such formal categorizations to be, acknowledging the effects persons have on one another, one can still ask whether this explicitness implies anything like the self-consciousness of an anthropological comparison. To look for counterparts to meta-discourse, Euro-American observers would no doubt investigate indigenous knowledge practices and their accessibility to the thinking self. But suppose they were trying to describe a world where nothing present announces what it otherwise ("really") is, and where the idea that you learn by looking would strike people as extraordinary, for you wait on what the future will tell — an inscrutability as true of your state of relations with kin and friends as of anything else.[28] Between an enactment and the interpretation of it, time must lapse; past events, including how persons impinge upon one another, are "known" through their subsequent effects. (Your previous hospitality to friends is measured by, exchanged with, their hospitality to yourself.) Nothing passive is implied about waiting on the future (Rollason 2014): Melanesians spend much time trying to bring revelation forward, whether one is talking of now-abandoned practices of divination or of the speeding up of exchanges, as Pickles (2014) has described for the highlands town of Goroka through the medium of card games. Players regard the games as engaging different speeds, slow and fast, and he argues that they offer an analytical device for reflection on social change (where "fast" relations tend to overtake the "slow"). Ceremonial exchanges and card games alike "encourage people to think analytically and reflectively about their past and future efforts" (2014: 278).[29]

Perhaps the kind of self-consciousness at issue may be addressed through another twist to language. In discussing how Melanesian ethnographers have often recorded the personal hospitality they have received, Wagner (2012; also see 2001) observes that hospitality is invariably impersonated in such narratives but not "expersonated." Too narrowly rendered, it is not given a larger concretivity in how those narratives are organized. The former term is familiar enough; the latter demands, precisely, exposition. In ordinary usage, impersonation exaggerates or neglects particular features of its subject in copying ("abstracting") it, while the extraordinary term expersonation "registers more concrete particularity than is found in the original. . . . Hence an impersonation involves all those actions in which a subject mimes him- or herself as an individual character or personality, whereas an expersonation is something like a professional monograph, in which the author's selfness is devoted to a totally objective personality profile in which they imitate the predilections of others" (2012: S162). While he gives several examples, I keep with this initial "Euro-American" one of the monograph. Jumping off from *that* enables critical purchase on the concept of self-consciousness.

If self-consciousness, as moderns commonly understand it, is a version of the quintessential impersonation of a subject as a self, then it entails self-reflection, this being a form of (self-)objectification through imagining one's self among or from the perspective of others. A Melanesian moment of expersonation affords a counterpart of sorts to that impersonated self-consciousness, although it need not turn on any prior determination of what is "inside" or "outside" a person.[30]

The moment in question locates persons through an encompassing field of diverse and specific interchanges. An expersonated "self"-consciousness inheres in the way the relations are acted out. Others are in this sense known reflexively, that is, through what happens to the self. Thus Stasch (2009: 102, 170) talks of the "reflexive sensibility" about or toward social relations — whether as matters of attraction or repulsion — on which the Korowai of West Papua frequently dwell. Perhaps those Orokaivan forms of interaction could be described as expersonating the selves of the brothers or brothers-in-law or in-married wives as they appear over the span of multiple relationships. Certainly we may ponder the explicit emphasis, to that extent "self"-conscious, that such people give to the appropriate acting out of relational imperatives. Impersonation, by contrast, might appropriately describe the embodiment of life-force or ancestral power (imitating/being one's own ancestor).

A common feature of anthropologists' engagement with their materials is that concepts imported for one purpose may be exported with new resonances for another. It would not seem unreasonable to lift, from the discussion of the perspectives that Melanesian kin relations give one another, the idea that each pole incorporates the other's perspective and apply the idea to the reciprocities of Anglophone kin reckoning; it would, however, be necessary to add that this is not what English usage dwells on. However, I see a promising export in the concept of expersonation, retaining its original conjunction with the impersonation of a subject as a self. What began with Wagner's homely example can be augmented with something learned from this Melanesian moment.

Consider again how, over the English seventeenth and eighteenth centuries, a freshly minted axis of comparison between kin and friends comes into circulation: self-interest and disinterest, and its interplay with what is or is not instrumentalized.[31] Enlightenment writers contrasted a burgeoning commercial society with a precommercial society that could offer no possibility of disinterested relations. "The Scots' theoretical project required an enlarged domain of indifferent persons available for market exchanges and contractual engagements," specifically separate from what "was unoriginal at the time and later became a cliché: the individual together with close family and friends in the innermost of concentric circles" (Silver 1990: 1491). Cliché though it might be, we can give this self-description of the modern self a twist. Suppose what is being described is none other than the condition under which aspects of the person appear expersonated, namely as a ubiquitous field of commerce, among whose anonymous dealers individuals are generically motivated by self-interest or instrumentalism. Conversely the impersonated self is recognizable in private lives, in which personalized sentiment is played out in a "self-less" and in that sense disinterested way between consociates, leading to those accounts of friendship that insist there is nothing comparable in societies untouched by modernity. In short, the friend (modern-style) becomes an apt impersonation of "personal" ties. Or, to restore the vernacular, friendship "serves as a prototype of the larger category of personal relations" (1990: 1475). Conceivably, that is what some of Firth's Londoners assumed the anthropologists were investigating.

Under these conditions, "interpersonal relations" emerge as a distinct sphere of social life, in form a bit like a philia universe.[32] It is divided between the personal and impersonal — the existence of a dispassionate bureaucracy allows friendship to flourish without institutionalization (Paine [1969] 1974b: 137). At work is what Schwimmer might identify as a structural principle: personal relations take an oppositional form precisely with respect to impersonal ones. As we have heard, "[only] with impersonal markets in products and services does a parallel system of personal relations emerge whose ethic excludes exchange and utility" (Silver 1990: 1494). In Beer and Gardner's (2015: 425) view, a scholarly triptych centers the comparative exposition of friendship between two wings: "Key features of friendship (its 'private nature,' 'voluntarism' and 'individualism') mean that it has in large part been constituted by its juxtaposition with, on the one hand, the affective but 'obligatory' relations of the kin domain, and, on the other, those impersonal relations that constitute the broader institutional order of modernity."

Coda to Part I

COMPARING PERSONS AGAIN

Through giving a few contours to comparison, as an epistemic relation, some of the material on interpersonal relations that preoccupied the opening chapter has been thickened in the second, at least insofar as (properties of) persons can be imagined as compared with one another. Comparing kin and friends turned first on resonances between English vernacular usage and a habitual style of comparative endeavor found in anthropology (comparing comparisons), and then introduced material from old Melanesia. In elucidating that material, the otherwise unremarkable supposition that comparison turns on similarity and difference ran up against certain equivocations, suggesting it might sometimes be appropriate to suspend the very notion of "comparing" relations. In the light of Melanesian usage, deploying the concept of analogy for all those ways in which relations are used to talk about (other) relations might mean separating analogy from comparison. But that will bring us right up against the English language. We shall see what happens in part II.

Rather as Angkaiyakmin youths take the half-knowledge they glean from their elders and splice it with something learned elsewhere (Crook 2007: 26–27), I have borrowed half of an analytical pair, impersonation and expersonation, to make another pair, expersonation and self-consciousness.[1] Expersonation works only as a comparative, in the sense of a cross-cultural, device; it has nonetheless been helpful in bringing the narrative back to vernacular English understandings of persons. One strand of discussion in the first chapter concerned the identity of selves and the external character of their relations. This is not far in the background of those writers for whom (the impetus for) making friends exemplifies a particular kind of (self-consciously) modern self.[2]

Relations imagined as connections "between" persons also support the individuality of each. Contrasts and comparisons seem to ride with ease on the back of that betweenness.

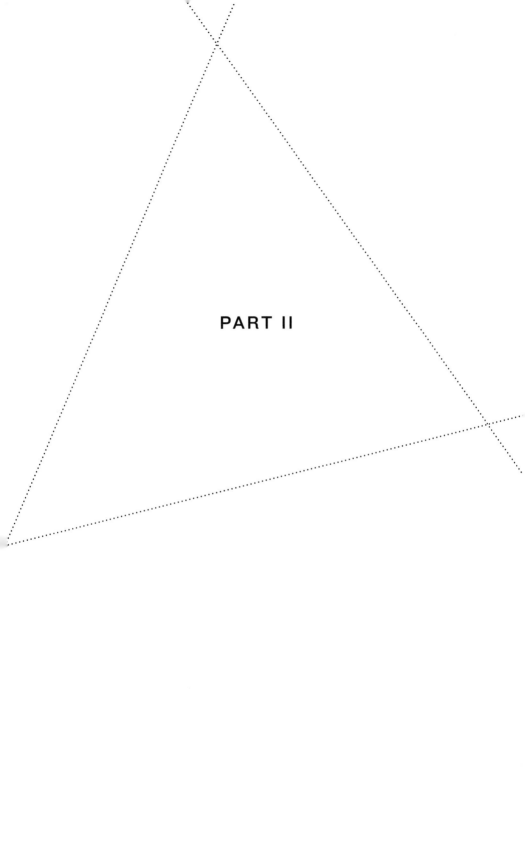

PART II

3. EXPANSION AND CONTRACTION

Description seems such a mundane activity for the text-based scholar that it is interesting to come across it as a focus of attention in other fields. In pondering on the present, neo-baroque state of anthropological knowledge-making, Corsín Jiménez's (2013) account of its strabismic double vision turns to Alpers's work on realism in seventeenth-century Dutch painting.[1] The art historian called her book *The art of describing* (1983). We quickly learn she meant description in a special sense—a technique of making the observer disappear by dislocating the eye from a single viewpoint.[2] "The mobile eye [of Dutch composition] cuts the world two ways: it multiplies with one eye what it divides with the other, and in doing so opens up a space for a third form of vision: a 'seeing double' that is more than one and less than many" (2013: 54). Among several scopic regimes of modernity (after Jay 1988), it is one—and Corsín Jiménez draws attention to the connection—that might have been shared with microscopists and optical experimenters of the time. The world seen microscopically both multiplies the innumerable small elements within a larger body and in enlargement divides a part from the whole (my paraphrasing of Alpers). Painter and microscopist alike treated the eye as taking in the world. "A split eye signals the birth of . . . an aesthetic 'which consisted in making something visible, in being a pure apparition that made *appearance appear*, from a position just on its edges' (Buci-Glucksmann [1984] 1994: 60)" (Corsín Jiménez 2013: 55–56, my emphasis).

In the register of academic knowledge-making, description is intimately bound up with exposition, whether regarded as a base line from which explanation or other conceptual work proceeds or as the very goal of laying things out. Exposition entails iteration—making appearances appear—by virtue of the way it draws attention to itself. Chapter 2 touched on the routine self-consciousness with which anthropologists organize materials and develop models; languages of expertise create themselves in turn as objects of knowledge. It is no surprise that the anthropologist's relationship to other people's knowledge, expert or vernacular, is always at issue. Then, of course, and I keep it running through the book, there is the issue of his or her own vernacular.

Where anthropologists dwell on the language of analysis, they do so partly to resist explosion into particularisms, partly to steer a path between common-sense understandings and what is turned into technical discourse. Under the pressure of practicability and public communication, they may play down the alterity of their language; under other circumstances, they may exaggerate it. Twisting or de-forming one's words is a means of bringing to the fore the narratives—perhaps meta-narratives—of those whose worlds are being summoned. Schwimmer and Wagner deliberately diverge from usage customary in analytical vocabulary and the vernacular alike. One consequence is a kind of self-splitting. We shall be following certain entailments of that.

The previous discussion of comparison trails an interesting problematic. To various elements of the comparative method—adumbrated as degree of fit, distribution of characteristics, categorization on the basis of similarity and difference, plus models of social life—one can find various approximations beyond a Euro-American orbit. There may be situations where approximation, and thus extent of similarity to what is already known, is of little help. Nonetheless, as far as such elements are concerned, it has been possible to show parallels of sorts, an "other" version, such as is coaxed to appear through the negation of each point. Thus we saw that distinctions may be made within a series of attributes without implying a sliding scale of degree; characteristics may not of themselves appear to be value-bearing entities; difference need not turn on questions of category-exclusion; to attend to social as opposed to some other kind of life can miss the point. Such step-by-step negation mirrors the original set of propositions, outlining a counterpart comparative maneuver. Then that instant of comparison may itself slide away. The apparent mirror image does not necessarily entail elements *organized* in the same manner. In fact, all that holds them may be their phantom counterpart in the first, that is, the way the original fitted together. Put otherwise, the anthropologist's comparative enterprise is found not only in its elements but also in the relations that compose them. An ever-expanding goal: the quest for a counterpart must now include a counterpart to those original organizing relations.

That relations organize expositions of all kinds is a notion hardly needing exemplification. Nonetheless, the organizational expansiveness of the relation is worth underlining, as is the kind of agency implied. To then inquire whether there might be anything elemental about the concept of relation itself will raise the further, intriguing, notion of imagining it as a contraction of such possibilities.

I

Relating Relations

With the logical or epistemic sense familiar to English speakers, relating includes the narration of a story. While any story becomes a narrative of connections, of relating relations, a philosophical or scientific exposition puts particular weight on verifying the connections being claimed. The question of how one knows what one knows was obviously a concern of Enlightenment thinkers; with scientific experiments, it was, as we have heard, partly resolved through verifying the standing of witnesses, as so many mirrors to knowledge. This relating is readily intelligible in today's parlance; then, it had been accompanied by another, now-antiquated, use of "relation" as a substantive. The term widely referred to a type of story, best translated as a report, which had standing as a narrative that was believable. The genre carried its own agency, authority.

Known to historians as *relazione* (*relazioni*, from the prototype, Venetian diplomatic reports), a relation in this sense became increasingly common across Europe in the sixteenth and seventeenth centuries, most famously for anthropologists including reports sent back by Jesuit missionaries from New France.[3] It was to a large extent overtaken by subsequent conventions of writing (such as that encouraged by the Royal Society's *Philosophical transactions*) and fell into disuse. In their heyday, relazioni served among other things as devices to bridge the known and unknown through the authentication of the author presenting his (and invariably his) observations. This was the crucial (personal) relation that supported the very notion of a relazione. By no means every relation of occurrences counted; according to Cohen and Warkentin (2011: 9), relazioni were set apart from treatises, meditations, and essays precisely in the way that the author cited "the authority of experience in establishing a relation of trust between author and reader." What subsequently overtook this form of relation was the transfer of trust from the teller to the tools of investigation. Cohen and Warkentin call this Descartes's victory: rely on the method, not the investigator. Natural philosophers turned their description of the connections by which they knew things along a path since well trod, rejecting the acquisition of knowledge through authority in favor of acquisition through methods of reasoning.

Inevitably such methods brought witnesses, on hand or remote, within the orbit of the experimenters themselves, a kind of expansion of the self. And does another set of relations emerge? Is self-consciousness about method, and the expert language entailed, akin to what came to be reconceived or reinvented in terms of a splitting of the self?[4]

In his discussion of the Enlightenment formulation of the self as a rational entity through being divided into two, a management theorist takes up a proposition from the eighteenth-century philosopher Hume: "The self becomes ethical by considering how one's actions are viewed by an 'impartial spectator'" (Hoskin 1996: 271). Hoskin draws a line running through Hume from Thomas Hobbes, a century before, to Hume's contemporary, Adam Smith.

> Where Hobbes had looked out, through his perspectival window, onto the foolish and selfish selves in the thought-world beyond, Hume had attempted to construct a sort of reverse viewing, from the thoughtworld beyond, back on to the self who views. Hume's formulation of the impartial spectator paints a picture wherein I become ethical by looking through my window on the world and seeing there some moral Other, the impartial spectator, whose surveillance of me ensures that I develop moral sentiments. On this reading, what Smith achieves is a step beyond this, by discovering on the far side of the "window" a mirror self, the self that examines, which stands in for and replaces the Other as judge of self. (271)

The splitting—a strabismic doubling—implies relating parts of the self to one another.

Hoskin's historical trajectory looks forward to new forms of description: the description of performance to which measurements could be given, equally applicable to eighteenth-century university examinations and nineteenth-century financial auditing. The ethical self was the rational, self-examining self. At various times anthropologists have seemingly rehearsed all three positions (Hobbes, Hume, Smith), whether following notions of the privileged observer, of the relativity of the familiar and unfamiliar, or of discovering the self in the other or the other in the self. These give expression to concerns over the accuracy or appropriateness of the social knowledge so gained and, vis-à-vis fellow academics, the relation of method to subject matter, including the extent to which anthropological knowledge necessarily includes relations established with diverse interlocutors. What holds firm is the (relation of) differentiation of method from what is under study: alterity is conserved insofar as the purpose of developing an anthropological language remains distinctive.[5]

Method may be variously externalized (guidelines for proceeding) or internalized (dispositions arising from skilled practice), but present-day anthropologists are particularly lively to their own relationship to method at moments of intervention. Consider Green's (2014) interest in the conditions of possibility of the world anthropology inhabits, and the clues to that indicated by what counts as (agentive) interventions in it. One example lies in anthropologists' descriptions of professionals who see their very job as intervening in people's lives. Where this includes describing what is happening, then it seems that description itself is possiblized as intervention.[6] An ethnographer (Lea 2008) who worked with a community of health professionals in Australia's Northern Territory voices something akin to this postulate.

Medicine has always been an arena in which interventions are deliberately designed to have effective outcomes. Given the endemic ill health of the indigenous population, Territory Health Services address an ever-deteriorating situation with ever more effort at intervening. Their own rubric (health service) holds together a mass of diverse relations, in turn organized by a vernacular notion of organization (organizing organization, we might say [Law 1994]). They pursue ever-expanding protocols of coordination, proliferating schemes for "collaboration, cooperation, networking, team-building, [and] information sharing" (Lea 2008: 63). Yet the greater the organization to which the administration aspires, the greater fragmentation it sees.[7] This despair underwrites a bureaucratic project. People delivering care want to do their best by the systems that also systematize them — intervention through organizational means implies making the organization work.[8]

One means is self-description. The organization keeps detailed track of itself; auditing procedures address not only the outcomes for health but also the officials' organizational effectiveness as service providers. Implementation plans are rolled out with performance indicators, alongside annual reports, data summaries, target reviews, workshop recommendations, and so on. An inordinate amount of time, many complain, is taken up with (precisely) describing what is happening. Yet describing bureaucratic performance is seen as a precondition to changing things.[9] At the end of every day of their exhausting induction "in the field," new recruits are presented with evaluation sheets. Regardless of any external monitoring, and devoted to improving the program, the organizers beg for feedback from those whom they have been inducting on the way they have carried out their job (of induction).

This is the world in which the anthropologist also lives. Lea does not mince her words about the liberal rationalism that brings bureaucrats and anthropologists into proximity; rather than chiding bureaucratized perceptions for their limitations, anthropologists might want "to comprehend the cultural habits we share with their formulators" (2008: 234). Significant in Lea's albeit controversial rehearsal of this stance is her emphasis on the tools of description. "We" anthropologists "are ensnared by the same belief in the power of representation to bring the misconceptions of others to correcting light" (234). The distance between the Australian ethnographer and the Northern Territory health bureaucrat provokes a sympathetic alignment of their descriptive endeavors. To spell this out is itself something of an intervention on the ethnographer's part — certainly in conventional understandings of the relations involved. Thus Lea's monograph concludes that, for all the problems there are, "it can be liberating to gain some sense of the lived-in, externally driven and consensual limits on our own agency," and of the actors' faith that sustains "the power of description to amend conceptualizations of how the world 'really is' and with that improved perception to somehow yield a better outcome" (237).[10]

Insofar as exposition makes explicit an interpretive relation with its object of description, it bears on notions of self-scrutiny: the relation divides understanding from what is about to be understood. We could say such ideas themselves intervene to make visible or heighten consciousness about this activity, and thereby expand it, as in cultivating awareness of the effect conceptual tools and methods have in shaping inquiry. At the same time there is nothing new in saying that exposition is also an entanglement of descriptions from many hands. Anything available to description is already described, a kind of precondition of anthropological knowledge-making.[11] So I shall thread this self-consciousness through a local context — bureaucratic medical services — to make other (already-existing) descriptions evident. I shall also take from the past. Relating relations: if that reduplication echoes certain times in painterly and experimental optics whose descriptive effect could be explained more generally as making appearance itself appear, it also echoes early modern philosophical musings on human nature with their project of understanding understanding.[12] Appearance as an object of viewing, understanding as an object of reflection, like auditing that draws on both, perhaps in the quest for social knowledge, these tell of more than a predictable reflexivity. It is through specific local and historical ideas of eye and mind, and through equally specific genres of reporting and evaluation, that moments of relating become themselves objects of description.

The notion of description as intervention can be followed through a set of organizing (at once scholarly and vernacular) relations that in salient respects mirror those of method and object of inquiry, namely society vis-à-vis nature. It goes without saying that they signify a naturalist cosmology. The ever-expanding nature-society (or nature-culture) dyad seems forever subject to fresh criticism and reformulation, and forever to regain its influence. Certainly concepts springing from it (the dyad) have long been the carriers of anthropological exposition. The specific relations to be described depend on their locale.

An Organizing Relation: Nature and Society

Suppose you are in a place where it is far from clear what the ontological status of people's descriptions of themselves might be. Suppose people think it is possible to change your "race" or "body," as seems true in parts of South America. Euro-Americans would not be surprised if the anthropological description of those particular "descriptions" becomes entangled in the language of nature and society (nature and culture). In the interventions I am thinking of, such a language pulls at two threads. On the one hand, ideas about a natural world and its progressive modernization underlie the efforts of the health practitioners who treat these people; on the other, disciplinary theorizing on nature and society becomes a critical tool for the ethnographers on the spot.

Take the bodily change implied by the process of "becoming white." Becoming white is becoming *criollo* or *creole*, to take as reference points Venezuelan whites in Amazonia (Kelly 2011) and Ecuadorian whites in the Andes (Roberts 2012). In various ways these whites would describe themselves as moderns. All those activities requiring organizational effort that characterize bureaucracies are also projects of a self-conscious global modernity. In the Venezuelan Amazon, they are found in the travails of young doctors on field assignments, undergoing training in a state-provided health service. (Kelly refers to the doctors' ideologies as "Western" or "Euro-American.") The Ecuadorian Andes, however, offer a modernization associated with technological development through the private fertility clinic. The two ethnographers describing these moderns either link people's efforts to ideas about nature and society, or make a contrast with those who hold such ideas. For both situations, medical care is taken by recipients or clients as signs of their own increasing ability to enact whiteness; through receiving care, they become "white people." This in turn looks like a case of indigenous redescription.

In their civilizing mission, Venezuelan doctors—whites, criollos—working among Yanomami Indians "make bodies" in the sense of changing what they regard as indigenous lifestyles, and "make society" thereby. "[One] component of the civilizing project is about making society . . . because for criollos, society was missing and needed to be made" (Kelly 2011: 97). Again, "doctors see Yanomami as part of nature: [above all] disorganized" and "the more disorganized Yanomami appear, the more doctors strive to organize" (137, sentences transposed). It is the conceptual organization of the criollo nature-society axis that leads Kelly to distinguish what Yanomami and criollo each take for granted, that is, the relation between what is assumed as given and what is regarded as made through human intervention. In this respect, criollos participate in the general Euro-American understanding of this relation, one that renders society existing as a civilizing, developmental project with respect to nature. For Yanomami, the reverse holds. Social conventions that criollos understand as fabricated are taken by Yanomami as innate to or immanent in how they live. However, Kelly (2011: 98, 222–223) is at pains to point out that neither the understandings nor the misunderstandings each has of the other match up.[13] Nor should we jump to any easy conclusion about what is involved in Yanomami "redescribing" themselves.

The kind of care Yanomami would like to elicit from the doctors—despite staff being stationed for very brief periods—is the care of kinship. In the comment about what criollos thought was missing, I missed a phrase: "[One] component of the [doctors'] civilizing project is about making society, *not kin*" (2011: 97, my emphasis); making kin is a Yanomami aspiration. Like race (whiteness), kinship is to be made. In the case of criollos, outsiders must be domesticated into the status of potential in-laws (affines) who will mediate between Yanomami and the outside world (with its knowledge and goods, not restricted to medical care). Much as criollos would change them, Yanomami are trying to change criollos—not to make them Yanomami, but to turn them into potential in-laws (there is no intermarriage; this is a generic designation), thus keeping up the flow of services, knowledge, and trade goods that only criollos can bring. At this point, the descriptive intervention of the anthropologist becomes apparent. In Kelly's view, if there were an indigenous analogue of nature it would be affinity. He writes, "Doctors and Yanomami enter each other's worlds as forms of the innate," innate being subsequently glossed as potential affinity (for Yanomami) and nature (for criollos) (2011: 137, 225). The expository consequences of this intervention are evident. We come to understand that affinity inscribes an innate axis in a world of social convention, and it is the latter that Yanomami take for granted.[14]

It is the quality of affinal relations that makes sense of the apparent continuum in becoming white. Yanomami describe one another in terms of those who are more and those who are less white. However, rather than a scale implying degree, any specific point along this continuum juxtaposes positions that are radically "other" to each other. Otherness is not diminished by the continuum; instead, people assume different positions on it, being now white, now Yanomami. This is not seen by the medical staff, who would themselves understand "becoming criollo" as an evolutionary or developmental process. For them, becoming/being white could even indicate transcendent values generated by the inevitability of modernization, which they represent even while it is beyond their efforts to fully implement. The role of the organizing nature-society relation is clear; Kelly supposes its Yanomami counterpart as the relational condition of alterity. Prior to and beyond human agency, there will and must always be others. Yanomami are not so much redescribing themselves as distributing themselves at different moments in time and place across already existing descriptions.

Roberts shifts the axis of analysis. She sustains a running contrast with attitudes ultimately derived from the European Enlightenment, as are found in twentieth- and twenty-first-century Euro-American accounts of assisted conception (e.g., 2012: 94–95, 114). Among them are concepts entailed in a once firmly held nature-culture paradigm whose starting point was that nature, to which "the body" belongs, is a more or less immutable given. Where Kelly summons the relation between nature and society to illuminate the way ideas held by Venezuelan doctors are entwined with those of anthropological discourse, Roberts effects a separation. The (nature-culture) relation that organizes anthropological accounts of assisted conception, in North America (say), does not hold across the Ecuadorian clinics.

Many (not all) Ecuadorian clinicians share with their clientele, according to Roberts, approaches likely to have roots in religious categories based on pre-biological determinations of lineage, precursors to the present-day concept of race.[15] The continuing assumption is that, "in Ecuador, people can change their race" (2012: 114). Here is another descriptive intervention on the anthropologist's part. The consequence is the weight to be put, in her words, on the multiplicity and plasticity of being. Phrases such as "people can change their race" describe neither logical confusion nor social construction but rather the ever-present possibility of ontological transformation. These people are participating in Ecuador's nation-making through a national whitening project, the continuation of earlier "whitening interventions" (Roberts 2013: 568). Especially in the case of the poor or clients of Indian background, simply to be the object of such attention is transformative. Under the care of whites (as doctors and clinical staff categorically are), clients become white. "Through IVF," Roberts (2012: 75) observes, "women can become whiter reproducers . . . [by] being cared for the way whiter women are cared for."[16] A grounding assumption about the malleability of bodies produces redescriptions very different from those the ethnographer can accomplish.

In the context of her account, the epithet "assisted" before "assisted reproduction" takes on unexpected resonances. In this Catholic country, whose church frowns on fertility procedures, God is everywhere, and an immediate, not distant, presence. God's giving of life is constantly brought home, this presence harnessed by the clinics. The scientific techniques that assist the procedure are also the means through which clinical personnel assist God; Roberts observes that clinicians do not perceive themselves as "playing God" but rather as being "God's helpers." Hierarchically speaking, patients are in turn assisted. For many, assistance is less about modifying the materials of fertility (IVF, egg or sperm donation, embryo freezing) than about the patronage bestowed on them. Generally speaking, "private medical clinics are similar to haciendas in that the relations are paternalistic (not consumer oriented)" (2012: 57).[17] Patronage is acted out in the clinic through the social activity entailed in attending to patients' health and comfort, a relationship of dependence being actively sought by Ecuadorian women. "Assistance, not autonomy, is the very basis of existence" (212). The clinic demonstrates that the patient is worthy of care and of the patron's notice.

Is this the kind of pre-Enlightenment world that early modern philosophers might have recognized? A significant axis, which Roberts takes as a departure from Enlightenment ideas, concerns God's intervention in everyday life, as in enabling people to have children. A noninterventionist God is another proposition altogether, making way for an expanded notion of nature's agency. In discussing the world-changing import of the contraction (my term) of one source of intervention being displaced by the expansion of another, Roberts (2012: 13) quotes Hume to the effect that a miracle (as some might regard divine intervention) would be a violation of the laws of nature. The same philosopher who was caught up in ideas about self-scrutiny was of his time in being committed to elucidating human nature. Ecuadorian concepts afford a lens through which to revisit the Enlightenment.

Hume argued (against Hobbes) that natural leanings are less to be curbed than cultivated.[18] We have already noted that one contemporary means of cultivation in the (social) world at large was the expansive cultivation of connections. Arguably, connections — referring to persons also known as kin, familial or otherwise, or more generally one's associates — first stood alongside and then displaced earlier perceptions of patronage. Patronage, as today between Ecuadorian clinical staff and clients, described the quality of a specific tie between persons known to one another; connection, by contrast, was one of those terms of unspecified and expansive possibility, from which you might acknowledge this associate or refuse that. For the propertied and aspiring middling classes of the English-speaking eighteenth century, it is almost as though acquiring good connections was like becoming white.

Nonetheless, there were crucial differences. Enlightenment notions of refinement and cultivation were constantly tethered back to a view that one should not move too far from nature (your own nature or the workings of nature in general). A relation existed here, quite as much as the relation between the two selves, in that cultivation ("society") and nature also entailed — and expanded — each other. Further, and specifically, the eighteenth-century idea of desirable connections mobilized the concept of affinity through connotations of similarity. Similarity underlay both a dominant use of "connection" to refer to alliances between families through marriage and the likeness found among same-status kin or associates. By contrast, Ecuadorian patron and client were differentiated not just by social standing but also in the way their relation was organized, that is, hierarchically. For their part, Yanomami affines evoke alterity, not self-sameness, and point to transactions that made one "more white" (those interventions along a continuum where any juncture might be a radical break). If, in what was taken for granted in relation to criollos, the Yanomami analogue of nature was indeed affinity, then affinity had a quite different location in the kinship universe from that imagined by English speakers.[19] English affinity, the term by derivation connoting "on the borders" or "bordering on" and thus neighboring or near to others, gives the viewpoint of the speaker as an ego in a center looking outward. Indeed here there is, in this respect, no ontological difference between the radiating spheres of affinity and of consanguinity.[20]

Recall the two-way passage of affinity and connection (see chapter 1). On the one hand, the early modern concept of "affinity" moved from delineating kin relations by marriage to include epistemically understood resemblances or rapports, perhaps thereby endorsing an abstract stress on sympathy or on likeness. On the other hand, "connection" expanded from its epistemic usage in the seventeenth century to, in the eighteenth, embracing kin as well, although by no means exclusively. If these are diverse outlines of a newly visible attention to knowledge about persons and their spheres of interaction, they came with injunctions about the social consequences of acknowledging people's relatedness.[21] Such relations pointed to (the act of) relating as itself an object that could be described.

Generic English-language concepts for interpersonal ties invited calculations as to nearness to and distance from the speaker. We could conclude that they turned such calculations into interventions in a social world. To solicit or deny a (social, kinship) connection produced or created difference or sameness anew (either up or down). Assertion or denial of recognition carried social effects.[22] The same might be said, epistemically speaking, of deliberate interpretation or choice of descriptive language. Whatever was named, discovered, or written about mirrored back the author's location (position, standing, viewpoint) in the universe. Intervention had a duplicating effect.

II

Of No Great Import

There is "only one impossible relation: the absence of relation" (Viveiros de Castro 2003: 11). Tracking something of the proliferating character of relations through the elements they organize, as we have been doing, implies that there is nothing apparently elemental that cannot be further reducible (divided, multiplied) through further relations. (In organizing mode, it is irrelevant whether the relations might otherwise be distinguished as external or internal.) Yet this has not prevented definitions—Locke's is in the introduction—that suggest there might be an irreducible or elemental form of relation "itself." As a prelude to hazarding that there is "no difference" between expansion and contraction when it comes to relations, I begin with one attempt to give relation a minimal or irreducible form.

A relation, Gasché (1999: 9) suggests, entails an event anterior to itself insofar as "there is no relation . . . without a prior opening of the possibility of the being-toward-another by which the subject is allowed to arrive 'in' the place of the other." It is a "threshold" that communicates between "domains." Departing from an earlier tradition of philosophical discourse that takes the relation to be a diminished entity, he calls it an "elemental" or "minimal" thing. Indeed he argues it is hardly a "thing," insofar as relation is at work before the identity of things can be discerned. From Gasché's antiformalist perspective, it follows that this minimal thing is not categorically unified, and in this sense is hardly a concept. Not of little import after all; or rather import it has, even though it seems characterless. Against the reach of vernacular usage, always there in the background, the implications are profound. Gasché thus finds himself talking about a kind of consciousness (a relation to the self) that is not self-conscious (it is not reflexive), and thus of a self that is not a reflex of a self-other, subject-object, divide. Repetitive action is an example of a nonreflexive mode of self-reference. Formidable problems of exposition ensue: "Nothing could be more resistant to the habits of language than the expression of such a relation" (48). His general argument is that the anterior event, the minimal thing that he also calls relation, which produces the world as differentiated *re-*

lata (entities, terms), has to be other than relation as it exists as a subject in philosophy, though philosophy may be a locale for perceiving it.

These comments come from an introduction to a body of essays on Nietzsche, Heidegger, Derrida, and diverse companions, decapitated for my own purposes (leaving the body of the text largely untouched). Far from claiming everything for philosophy, this critical theorist and scholar of comparative literature indicates other possibilities for reflection on the minimal thing. He mentions literature, theology, the natural sciences, and one might add to his list anthropology. Among many candidates for what might count as minimal, in the sense of elemental, about the relation are two on which anthropology touches.

Gasché seems to be saying that the relation is minimal insofar as it is a thing that is not yet a thing, that is, has not yet been captured by a concept (not his phrase). And when it is, I infer, it is captured by disciplines in diverse ways. He talks of knots. There can be no one minimal thing (grammatical form regardless), only multiple "shapes that, rather than being modalities of one basic concept of relation, are irreducible, even though they imply and gesture towards one another" (Gasché 1999: 11). Rethinking the notion of relation must resist the lure of formal or categorical unification and deliberately tie the clusters of traits that make up relation into knots that, with a momentary plurality, allow themselves to be undone again. In an image reminiscent of scholastic debates of medieval Europe, he describes relation's "being-toward-another" and of traits stretching from the place of the subject to the place of another. This gives the opening where he himself does not venture, namely into Anglophone anthropology. Indeed, the latter's claims to insight might seem too obvious. Is it not in persons that Gasché would find irreducible direction toward others? Yet Gasché himself would not, insofar as the supposition lies beyond the line of critical thought from which he comes.

First, anthropology might find a place for the elemental relation in what were once called "social relations." Almost as though it were of their inventing, social anthropologists emphasize the supposition—shared, of course, broadly beyond the discipline—that consocation is intrinsic to human existence and its flourishing, making the relation the very condition of possibility for sociality itself.[23] Anthropology's concept of sociality acts out the idea of relations as an organizing matrix, whether of social institutions or of persons. In recent years the former has contracted as an expositional focus of relations, the latter expanded. The person and its associations proliferate, these days consocation being limited neither to the human nor to the animate. Distancing themselves from too-human connotations of society, anthropologists and their companion scholars reach into other languages, such as those of symbiosis, or adopt lexicons neutral as to the kind of animation implied, as in the case of "collective."[24] If no one denies that persons, human or not, are always in the company of others, and cannot be in existence otherwise, the interest of this kind of English-speaking anthropology in persons and relations reinvigorates the concept of sociality. As a precondition, the relation appears irreducible.

Second, the same seems to apply to the splitting (or duplication) of the self. In the case of human persons, it requires only a short step to conceptualize relations in terms of meaningful communication, and thus invite questions about consciousness, intentionality, and all the apparatus by which the wider Euro-American vernacular supports notions of the thinking, feeling subject. Entertaining the idea of the person as a conscious self and the source of thought is the knot we have already been untying and retying. Given that Gasché's minimal thing becomes something else when it is conceptualized as relation, at the very expository moment it is brought into discourse it acquires attributes as an object of discourse. In that the relation's discursive origin is in thought, *as* an object of thought its "other" appears to be the (thinking) self that is the source of thought (the notions are externalized with respect to each other). A similar "cluster of traits," also encountered in many humanities disciplines, reveals an interplay of "self" and "other" as a dynamic said to drive much of human interaction. Some would say that this is where the elemental relation irreducibly lies. For Euro-American metaphysics and vernacular alike, the cosmological import of a self-other divide makes it a prime candidate. Needless to say, the reflexivity implied entails specific forms of relating insofar as, unsurprisingly, it endorses "the modern concept of being as a self-present subjectivity" (1999: 58, capitalization ignored).

In both cases, the knot that appears to hold steady the relation as a minimal thing has already slipped into an order of specification that belongs to its becoming manifest as a concept. Now Green's (2014: 2) invitation to think about interventions was woven with the same metaphor (the knot), and in her case this is precisely what she intended conceptualization to carry: what keeps materials "ethnographic" is that their knotting cannot be unraveled all at once. The knot itself has become a "thing," above all evident for the anthropologist when the manner in which it ties notions together, their momentary organization, *impedes* cross-cultural description.[25]

Take the cluster of notions that assume social life is woven like a fabric, linking and connecting everyone as selves to others, when ethnographically speaking it may be people's separation from one another that is deliberately brought about through social interaction (Candea et al. 2015a). Close to my own interests are the modalities of gift exchange, such as characterize parts of Melanesia, with the imagination of division and detachment implied.[26] There are other kinds of separation and encompassment (Scott 2007), not to speak of Amazonian predation and familiarization (Fausto [2001] 2012b), alongside ownership or "alter-ship" (Brightman, Fausto, and Grotti 2016; Costa 2017). It is easy to say that such detachments are also forms of relations, but what disappears from view is any simple self-other dynamic. Rather, in terms of the grounds they offer for a relational exposition, self-other relations might be better described as analogous to those of (say) giver-receiver or predator-prey. Indeed, in the hands of the anthropological comparativist, such grounds can equally become the means for the productive "undoing" of one set of relations by another, for example, of one ethnographic instance seen through another's contours. Thus the comparative move means that, by contrast with its primordial place in the vernacular, the doubled self-other appears more like Green's knot than Gasché's, no longer elemental. Its ubiquity seemingly contracts under specification, in a way surely not envisaged of the minimal thing.

One social arena appearing in this chapter is that of academic disciplines and their interdisciplinary traffic, not only medicine but also strands within critical theory and anthropology. Apropos the latter, particular anthropological traditions may come into focus (as "Anglophone," for example) for their occluding effect on others, and on other disciplinary traditions—contraction from one perspective, expansion from another. But while many phenomena come to seem enlarged or diminished in relation to others, quantification is inappropriate when it comes to relations themselves. There is no quantitative outcome from expansion and contraction, and that applies equally to relation as a minimal thing or to relation as an already specified concept. If, as Gasché (1999: 10) puts it, the former has a "multiplying power" that "secures the difference of things," then every conceptual specification that contracts or particularizes the latter's operation is also a multiplication of its manifestations.

It is largely with concepts of relation that we shall proceed. It is possible to dequantify the images of expansion and contraction by foregrounding relating as an act, and to speak rather of (the action of) the lifting or placing of restriction. Recent discussions of interdisciplinarity disclose a relational practice in the use of concepts that is unrestricted in its reach.

Restrictions

To reflections on the alterity of languages of expositions with respect to their objects and vernacular sources, we can add their concourse with one another. Now philosophizing, as an alter-world of Euro-American thought, has like any branch of scholarship invariably been in tussle with ordinary linguistic usage. If this is analogous to the anthropologists' tussle with their own vernacular origins in Euro-American "culture," there is a necessary distance from commonsense and everyday usage, as the Enlightenment savants observed. In anthropology's case, to the extent that its conceptualizations are distinguishable from those of philosophy through the "relations with the ethnographic materials that give rise to them" (Holbraad 2017: 153), ethnographic descriptions are particularly vulnerable to the double charge of ignoring commonsense and (not least among anthropologists themselves) peddling exoticism. While nothing is intrinsically exotic, "everything and anything is potentially in an exotic relation," Kapferer (2013: 815) asserts, and in his view (a deterritorialized) engagement with the exotic is a powerfully anthropological mode of inquiry. What is in effect the exoticism of study may be mistaken for the exoticism of, and thus in Salmon's (2017) phrase be delegated to, what is being studied. We may expect a similar delegation to occur between disciplines that can come to seem exotic in relation to one another.

I was drawn to Gasché for his relation to the methods and interests of critical theory only to find, within the few pages of his introduction, echoes of the way anthropologists — in particular currents of discourse — organize their material. Gasché offers: relation to the other precedes identity; relation secures the difference of things; relation to the self can escape the dialectics of self and other; entities may all be in the position of others among one another. These come from lines of thinking openly acknowledged in some anthropological practices, occluded by others. It is not hard to pluck parallels from certain Melanesian- or Amazonian-inspired descriptions: value put on relationships rather than on the individual or on wholeness (Robbins 2004); difference preceding and encompassing identity (Viveiros de Castro 2001); an orientation toward becoming other (Kelly 2011; Vilaça 2016); strangeness integral to relatedness (Stasch 2009); relationship defined by division (Schram 2015) — in short, identity presupposing relation; relation creating difference; relation to another without conjuring that of self and other. Following the relations at work in these theoretical dovetailings and crossovers may lead down several routes. There is no simple disciplinary nexus here; the anthropology is of a particular kind with its own antecedents, and the philosophy is being interpreted by a critical-literary theorist.

Restriction through specification (my phrase) is the answer that three North American sociologists, Camic, Gross, and Lamont (2011), give to what they perceive as the complex field of permeable, overlapping working practices by which social knowledge in general is formulated. "Field" is not quite right: their image is the "vast expanses of the dense forest in which the making of social knowledge occurs" (1). "At site after site, heterogeneous social knowledge practices occur in tandem, layered upon one another, looping around and through each other, interweaving and branching, sometimes pulling in the same directions, sometimes in contrary directions" (25). Such practices cannot be circumscribed within traditional disciplinary enclosures, nor even within academia. Together they appear multiplex, polymorphous, an "intricate spider web . . . in which social scientists and humanists, as well as other social researchers and experts, routinely participate as they produce, evaluate, and use social knowledge" (25). Such scholars are at once open to disparate currents and heterogeneous contingencies and engage in them; intervention divides and multiplies their positions further. Nevertheless the authors see clarity in a major restriction or limit that frames their task, and hope in further delimitation.

A prime mover of their exercise springs from the relation of "social knowledge" to the "natural knowledge" of science, the stated goal being to appraise similarities and differences between the two. Their complaint is that, unlike natural science, adequate attention has not been paid to the diverse ways of working that comprise social knowledge. Only when the deficit has been addressed will researchers be able to track the "members of this fertile species, studying its branches [its constituent disciplines] in relation to one another, and examining the similarities and differences in the practices by which the various branches produce, evaluate, and apply the types of social knowledge with which they deal" (Camic et al. 2011: 13, emphasis omitted). Only specification will enable one to grasp what is distinctive about that, hence the need to compare its diverse parts (knowledge-making across the humanities and social sciences) with one another. For now this remains an ideal. Offered in the meanwhile is a series of questions to encourage empirical study. The authors regard the complexity they have uncovered as both a reminder that there is nothing monolithic about the creation of social knowledge and an invitation to awaiting riches.

It would be a mistake to think that in the imagined heyday of disciplinary self-definition relations were less complex. Commenting on the traditional organization of anthropology in the United States, Lederman (2005: 54–55) notes a pronounced "family resemblance" between the divisions that separate subfields of US anthropology at large — cultural and biological anthropology, archaeology, linguistics — and those that split these subfields within. The fundamental division is between positivist (objectivist) and interpretivist (contextualizing) ways of knowing. In fact, Lederman (2005: 50) remarks that "disagreements about the subfields are part of a rift that is not confined to anthropology, not even to academic discourse. This fault line . . . runs through American culture." In short, these divisions keep their form across different scales, dividing whole disciplinary domains from one another, and academic from other forms of enterprise. What separates (physical) sciences and (literary) humanities separates elements within social science, within anthropology, and within subfields of anthropology. The distinction reproduces positions that coalesce around a set of two values, the effect being that the values are maintained in relation with one another.[27] There is no limit to its (the distinction's) application. If the complexity and density of interaction is a problem, we have moved from an expository solution based on restrictive relations to one that also summons unrestricted relations.

A sociological observer, struck by the pervasiveness of a quantitative/qualitative divide between preferred methods (Abbott 2001: 60), similarly notes that what holds within is also evinced without, citing, for example, sociology's relationship with economics. Then again, within what is usually defined as a quantitative community lies an opposition between quantitative and qualitative versions, and so on.[28] Such modeling of the relations within and between disciplines and subdisciplines reveals the model's fractality. Coining the term "fractal distinction," Abbott analyzes the way a distinction repeats its own patterning as geometric fractals do. Not in his language, but what emerges from his account is the relational character of fractal distinctions, the same relation repeated over and again, generating similar structures at multiple scales of organization. Out of all the entanglements of cross-cutting possibilities, it is this relational character that conserves a sense of clarity at every juncture.

> Most of us would say that the distinction of history from sociology reflects the distinction of narrative from causal analysis. But with each discipline the fractal distinction is repeated, producing [both] . . . mainstream history versus social science history and . . . historical sociology versus mainstream sociology. But social science history is closer to . . . mainstream . . . sociology than to . . . history, and historical sociology [is closer] to . . . mainstream . . . history than to . . . sociology. That is, we cannot assume that the dichotomy of narrativism versus causalism simply produces a linear scale from pure narrativism to pure causalism, because the second-level distinctions produce in this case groups that have moved past each other on the scale. (2001: 14)

Lateral divergences and convergences are far from segmentary alignments of similarities and differences.

Here the relation in question (the fractal distinction) is restricted in its concrete manifestation, as in that between positivism and interpretivism, but any such manifestation may be replicated in an unrestricted way, interminably. Insofar as it holds its terms steady, the relation can be reenacted at countless local sites and still be recognizable. Indeed, each replay proliferates more local sites. (For practitioners, such iterations generate new energy for innovation out of old positions.) Unrestricted in its application, it appears irreducible.

III

Flow and Overflow

Comparisons seem to work most obviously when they show the "kinship" of phenomena, in the sense of reckoning similarity by degree, that is, through the correspondence of distinct features that enables one to compute how similar or different this is to or from that. I revert to the vernacular renderings, and those anthropological ones closest to them, elucidated in the preceding chapter; let us call them conventional. As a tool for restricting or specifying relations, conventional comparison gives specific form to the entities so related. At the same time it is acknowledged that no amount of specification will stop the flow of knowledge that spills over, requiring and generating new perspectives, as the moderns' forest of social knowledge practices shows. This gives food for thought with respect to comparisons of kinship and friendship. The scholar's motivation in restricting the application of the two terms (kin, friend) comes from hope for analytical rigor, just as people use them of one another with evaluative or judgmental intent. But can we talk of "unrestricted comparison"? I suggest that what in English is a contradiction in terms is also an insight or entry into appreciating the effects of an interminably reproducible (and in this sense unrestricted) concept of relation.

In observing that there is only one kind of relationship, that which is created in the act of relating, Wagner (2011: 161) alludes to an earlier essay on kinship where he writes that relating is a disposition "formless and characterless in itself" (1977: 640). I stay for a moment with that famous essay, for it affords an alternative to the awkwardness of (the phrase) unrestricted comparison. Certain readings of analogy illustrate the potential.

The concept of analogy is not as exotic as it might appear. Imagine it as a moment in the contraction and expansion of relations. One of Wagner's abiding formulations lies in the interrelation of literal and figurative modes of apprehension on which, he argues, symbolic thought depends. The liveliness of his formulation is exhibited in his ever-changing terminology for this dialectic, condensed as two poles, each the limiting condition of the other: the literal refers entities to one another, keeping them distinct thereby, while the figurative pole is found in what he variously calls metaphor, perceptual image or analogy. In relation to the point-by-point, contracted "microcosm" of referential coding (coordination of diverse elements), Wagner posits the perceptual image as an all-encompassing, self-referential, expansive "macrocosm" (filling the frame of perception) (1986: 24–25). The same distinction may also apply within the field/forest of analogy. "Analogic flow" across a multitude of relations, within what he calls the larger frames of culture, lies in the potential of relating to spill over the actualization of specific analogies formed through selection and differentiation.

Such usage sidesteps other readings of analogy, as, for example, implied in Descola's description of entities participating in one another.[29] Reminiscent of Abbott's fractal distinction with its unrestricted iteration, Descola refers to "analogism" as "a mode of identification that divides up the whole collection of existing beings into a multiplicity of essences, forms, and substances . . . so that it becomes possible to recompose the system of initial contrasts into a dense network of analogies that link together the intrinsic properties of the entities that are distinguished in it" ([2005] 2013: 201). It follows that analogy becomes "thinkable only if the terms that it compares are initially distinct," comparison implying "the ability to detect similarities" out of "differences infinitely multiplied" (202).[30] Per contra, Wagner's exposition of referential coding, applicable to distinct entities, is presented simply as the other side of an analogical, frame-filling counterpart. The one cannot be envisaged without the other, although different socio-symbolic regimes may dispose of the pair differently.[31] Thus to imagine that all "human relationships are analogous to one another [can serve] . . . as a foil to the traditional anthropological assumption of the innateness of kin differentiation" (1977: 623).

In that a foregrounded figure occludes, or in the long run obviates, what is already present, Wagner's analogy implies a displacement of perceptual space.[32] Does this further imply a kind of comparison? Before we return to the issue in the next chapter, something can be said with notions of restriction in mind. Conventional formulations of comparison rest on the literal feature-by-feature clarification of already-existing identities. They are restricted, in other words by prior conceptions of similarity or difference, with the basis for comparison presupposing an operational axis of similarity ("comparability"). Yet to formulate the question on this basis is already to formulate it comparatively: is analogy similar to comparison? Let us conclude the chapter with a possible analogic formulation that would resist (being ascribed to) this kind of comparison.

Here there need be no restriction to the capacity for creating equivalence: "unrestricted analogy" is not the oxymoron that unrestricted comparison is.

Corsín Jiménez (2011) muses on today's networked economy of knowledge and on the prerequisite, and expectation, that knowledge must forever flow, by adapting the proposition that all human relationships are analogous to one another. "Let us [instead] begin with the proposition that all forms of knowledge are analogous" (141). In Wagner's reference to kinship, specifying distinct degrees of kin connection delineates a restricted or "controlled flow" of analogy, while its opposite is uncontrolled flow or "total, unrestricted analogy," in behavioral terms (as he puts it) complete familiarity and lack of constraint. The Euro-American knowledge economy of moderns and naturalists understands restricted knowledge as property, its counterpart being "total unrestricted access to the knowledge commons" (Corsín Jiménez 2011: 152). Like relating, knowing is, we may add, itself formless. The parallel is made possible by a transformation into analogical relations of the habitual homologies of certain naturalist — whether vernacular, or anthropological — categories.

Wagner's inspiration comes from the Daribi of Papua New Guinea where the flow of exchange relations, mythical sequences, and other acts at once brings together and keeps distinct different loci of relationship; one effect is to locate kin positions through other kin positions (for example, a "mother" is another kind of "father"). However, such understanding of the grounding nature of relating is distracted by the Euro-American, or in his terms "Western," proclivity to link people in kin relations with their appropriate nature vis-à-vis society and biology, notably as a matter of social or natural kinds (a "mother" is distinguished by the nature of her "maternal solicitude"). Wagner highlights this second, identitarian, perception of relatedness as at the root of conventional anthropological approaches to kinship analysis, especially in its mobilization of homological equivalences. He then transforms a (Euro-American) homological series of kin positions into an analogical one. Through this transformation, Wagner argues that kinship (via the work of differentiation and specification) is in essence restriction and the opposite of such restriction lies precisely in relations of complete or total "unrestricted familiarity" (1977: 639). However, I propose keeping for a moment with the Euro-American configuration, and its initial coordinates in nature and culture. These coordinates would seem to generate a very particular mode of restricted or controlled relating (via differences taken as given in nature; similarities revealed through people's agency in relating things). But there is more implied.

Like the economists' externality, what overflows in the Euro-American knowledge economy is the endless possibility of a kind of knowing, which "self-detaches (spills over) itself" and "in doing so contributes to the largesse of public knowledge" (Corsín Jiménez 2011: 152). If we were seeking something akin to "total, unrestricted access" in knowledge-making, the question is what overflows in the case of vernacular, and conventional, understandings of Euro-American and English kinship. Are there relations here we might better conceive through an analogical mode? Consider again the natural (social) basis on which Euro-Americans think kin relations are built. What might be the substantive enactment of unconstrained solicitude when it is precipitated by a homological control of kin equations through the notion of natural (social) kinds? To recall the close of chapter 1, we can say that mothers are persons who show distinctively maternal solicitude, just as fathers show paternal solicitude, and so on. First and foremost, such kinship thinking takes natural (social) kinds of relatives to be personified, and individualized, in such beings. Suppose, keeping true to naturalist epistemology, we take the person conceptualized as an individuated being with relations attached, and subject that to analogical transformation. Simple to the point of seeming self-evident, persons would be to their relations what any entity is to its supports or contexts.

By this route we also arrive at interpersonal relations and the unconstrained relating they imply. The sentiment or solicitude ("familiarity") of kinship outreaches the restrictions of kin relating. When in unrestricted form such familiarity pervades interpersonal relations at large, then the solicitude of kinsfolk in turn becomes the kind of solicitude found among friends as well. In this naturalist regime, all that differentiates friendship from the kinship that entwines in and out of it are the restricted controls of naturally (socially) defined kinship kinds. Interpersonal relations as such escape this confinement. And the analogy with persons is open as to the entities to which relations (supports or contexts) adhere. So there is no reason not to add friends and friendly solicitude to Wagner's list of analogical equivalents, or to add interpersonal relations to Corsín Jiménez's delineation of the knowledge commons. Yet just as the commons may emerge as a form of (anti)property, so interpersonal relations becomes a sphere in itself. In its own terms the sphere knows no bounds, being recognizable as much in idealizations of friendship as in the "pure relationships" of the Late Modern Age, or even in assumptions about a generalized humanity supported by reference to common biology or natural continua of lived experience.[33]

The anthropologist might conclude that, from this perspective, unrestricted "interpersonal relations" are as well understood as "kinship" as not. They point to a sphere of unconstrained relationality. So both the flow of knowledge and the flow of solicitude may be analogized as a *flow of relations*. The conclusion is there in the words of these two thinkers (Wagner [1977: 624]: kinship as incorporating "the essence of human solicitude that we call 'relating'"; Corsín Jiménez [2011: 142]: the organization of knowledge as "an analogical economy of relations"). The subject of restricted and unrestricted flow appears as relating "itself." Perhaps, too, we can simultaneously appreciate the role of relating in producing the very grounds for imposing restrictions (as in the delineation of categories, the specification of concepts), as well as its appearance as a vacuous generality, difficult if not impossible to grasp. When restriction is through control of relations, the unrestricted is—irreducibly—"pure" relational flow.

In these transformations, differentiating and equating work as modes of acting rather than as the properties of things. Neither restricted nor unrestricted relating maps in any axiomatic manner onto a world whose elements are already understood in terms of their similarities and differences. Yet to let go of similarity and difference as the properties of things is to let go of one of the linchpins of modern Anglophone notions of comparison and thereby of relations as such.[34]

4. THE DISSIMILAR AND THE DIFFERENT

The ambition of this chapter is to lay grounds for probing into notions of similarity in the imagining of relations. Consider what until now has been respected as a fusion in English: the running together of seeing "similarities" and making "connections." The fusion contributes to a general default position: whatever the entities that are being joined or co-constituted, they exist in a relation of (positive) mutuality, which is also — if only in the implied comparison — a point of likeness.[1] The probe may help resolve a conundrum. Where concepts of similarity and difference as the properties of things are indeed salient, as in conventional English usage, the anthropological puzzle is how to best render them *in* English. For the indigenous formulation may not suffice; indeed, the concepts may require a strategic deployment of vocabulary. So what terms are at our disposal?

Negation is a simple form of restriction. Connection and similarity have negative word forms (disconnection, dissimilarity), which as oppositive concepts often carry a negative tenor. Similarity, along with sameness or likeness, possesses a further antithesis in "difference."[2] This pulls similarity apart from connection, whose direct antithesis (disconnection) connotes a relatively uncomplicated surmise about the absence of or withdrawal from some (reason for a) tie.[3] Difference, however, persists as altogether a more complicated concept.[4] It does not just point to the substantive state of being unlike but also nods toward its interventionist verbal form (differ, differentiate) — making a distinction, having an effect, recording a change, being discriminating — where not only similarity but also the notions of agreement and identity are antonyms. Given that agentive force, connotations of difference in this strong sense have "different" possibilities from the weaker, more passive register of unlikeness. As an expository aid, it can carry its own tenor, such as that of dis-junctive synthesis, which is not restricted by any sense of negation.[5] I propose to use it where one might wish to insist on alterity or divergence, while also keeping in mind the (differentiating) restrictions we have been discussing. The advantage of giving this very ordinary term such conceptual status lies in its potential *removal from* dissimilarity. In turn, dissimilarity (unlikeness), moving in to take up the passive sense of difference, is thereby exposed as the negative of similarity, and thus its dependent.[6] Another way to put it perhaps is to say that, where natural difference is taken for granted, the (social, cultural) work of relating — finding points of similarity — at once endorses that innate difference and throws up a synthetic (socially or culturally defined) contrast to similarity, which I am calling dissimilarity. In any event, this twist of mine, to cover dif-ference with dissimilarity, where that seems to be meant, is intended to make explicit a bias in English usage, namely the way similarity is widely understood as a property of, and a value inherent in, relations. Difference, meanwhile, is freed from such an evaluative nexus.

The words matter. It is helpful to keep with chapter 3's concerns over knowl-edge, and with comparable materials, for some preliminary observations about English-speaking expressions of similarity and dissimilarity before elaborating on certain conditions under which difference appears. These lay some ground for returning to the issue of comparison and analogy, an opening of sorts into part III and its address to a particular style of kinship thinking. Deploying the duo, similarity and dissimilarity, is my interpolation from now on.

I

Premises of Similarity

One manifestation of similarity, nuanced by concomitant dissimilarities, has been powerfully evident in the neoliberal equivalence of cultures. I take a mo-ment from more than fifteen years ago, when neoliberalism was running high. It concerned UK policy making with respect to dealing with overseas requests for the return of human remains housed in public institutions. Very telling is a crucial interplay between similarity and dissimilarity in the hands of the policy makers.

The national Working Group on Human Remains in Museum Collections (DCMS 2003) defined its principal interlocutors as scientific experts and in-digenous peoples.[7] Its task was drawing up guidelines to assist UK legislation for the tenure and repatriation of body parts — from skeletons to samples of tissue and hair — being held mainly in museums. Scientific or research interest was justified by the information the remains could yield, including their relationship to other collections. It was feared that knowledge would be lost with repatriation, knowledge that only experts could extract and relate to other sources of information. Statements from interested people in Australia, as well as from New Zealand and North America, were put side by side with the research view. Indigenous Australian submissions talked about kinship. That the claimant Australians were "related" to their ancestors while overseas scientists were not had implications for relations between the parties. To the former, there was nothing more they needed by way of information about themselves in order to press their claims; entitlement was proved through narrative, dance, and song. This knowledge was effective only when used by those in the right relationship: its effectiveness could not be enhanced through acquiring someone else's "knowledge." (You are not a descendant of someone else's ancestor.) Enhancing knowledge was, of course, the principal card held by the researchers.

The Working Group bent over backward to be open to cultural sensitivities (recognizing "cultures" as equivalent), in its lights with compassion and respect. However, its further premise was that when people say things about themselves they are imparting information, and this was taken as a baseline of similarity across the parties. Should demands compete, then interchanges can be moderated and positions defended as they are in a debate. Debate, deliberate exposure to dissimilar positions, in this Euro-American view, fruitfully opens up information about the nature of the world. Even more so, "sharing" and "exchanging" information can be regarded as routes to reaching agreement, implying similarity of intention. The Working Group's politics anticipated such an agreement: cross-cultural understanding was the idiom in which it apprehended its task, and cultural dissimilarity could be managed like any other dissimilarity of viewpoint.[8] Either side might attempt to persuade the other; a compromise or balance of viewpoints would inform the Working Group's recommendations.[9] Ultimately these positions were framed as comparable with one another.

Politics on the part of activists taking the claimants' position evoked an environment from which debate looked alien.[10] A contrast between the two sides could not be reduced to a contrast of viewpoint, nor to the idea that through information-sharing indigenous peoples would appreciate the context from which the scientists were operating and shift their own views accordingly. The claimants' representatives repeatedly refused to acknowledge that ancestors were scientific specimens. Those taking the research position had suggested that in return for handing over material, they could extract information from it first, such information being subsequently as available to the claimants as to anyone. Either claimants might allow UK museums to retain portions of the materials for (say) future DNA investigation, or else, while taking back the remains, they might nonetheless be willing to make arrangements to secure future access for scientific inquiry. To some claimants, both offers were offensive.[11] Their spokespersons regarded the confrontation between them and what they took to be the museums' or researchers' entrenched view not in terms of "knowing" at all; if anything it was in terms of "being," specifically how the two parties existed with the remains/ancestors. There was no premise of similarity here.

On the face of it was an obvious contrast between the relational potential the researchers saw (gaining more knowledge) and relations between persons (ancestors and descendants), although apart from their own interests scientists and researchers could empathize with a relational perspective of an interpersonal kind. Yet to describe the relations in this manner, whether familiar to the Working Group's thinking or a gloss that an anthropologist might make, is to already enact a specific relation vis-à-vis the Indigenous Australian position. The description indeed implies a relation between perspectives as it is understood in the English vernacular, namely a social relation between separate (dissimilar) parties that is simultaneously an epistemic relation between viewpoints. That empathy, trying to feel what another feels (Weston 2018: 16), is also endorsing a relation across domains of knowledge. Crook (2007: 10) puts it forcefully when he refers to the Euro-American habit "of eliding the solidity of a social relationship with the solidity of knowledge — and then taking one as a measure of the other."[12]

Here is a difference that is not one of dissimilarity. For if the claimants' representatives regarded themselves, in a strong sense, as different *kinds of people* (my phrase) from researchers, their being could not be posed in terms of such a relation between viewpoints. Their words sounded like this: "We went to the Natural History Museum [in London] to see our ancestors and we were told that we cannot see them. For us it is like going to see somebody in hospital. To us the people in museums are not dead, they are living"; "How can research possibly compare? We're tired of other people interpreting us to ourselves" (DCMS 2003: 55, emphasis omitted). The idea that one might put oneself in another's shoes, including with the purpose of gaining information, comes close to being nonsense.

I have expanded this rather homely exposition precisely in order to bring it home. It clearly shows the workings of what, and especially in relation to Indigenous Australians, Povinelli (2002; see Weiner 2006) has described as a neoliberal politics of recognition. On the institution's side, the careful pitting of viewpoints has neoliberalism written all over it. As though on another side, others have used the language of divergent worlds. Referring to Verran's (1998) description of Indigenous Australian worlds belonging to stories of—about, through, with, in—landscapes, Law writes (2004: 135, emphasis omitted) that "we [Euro-Americans] are not a part of these worlds. . . . [W]e do not exist to those worlds. Just as they do not exist to us." Emphasizing the fact that, even if in dialogue a term (such as landscape) is apparently shared, anthropologists know that objects of knowledge for the ethnographer may have little correspondence in the vernacular under study, de la Cadena (2010: 350–351) pushes us to consider the truism in terms of cosmopolitics. Intersecting at unpredictable junctures are worlds each of which recognizes its own environment. Cosmopolitics ("relations among divergent worlds": de la Cadena 2015: 28) may turn on dimensions simply not in one another's sight. As Vilaça (2016: 119) says, difference is not always evident. A difference one cannot see is altogether other from dissimilarity; its effects are in what happens.

Demands from the South Pacific

Activating relations of sharing or exchange between holders of knowledge is often proposed as a solution to perceived inequalities. Thus "knowledge exchange" was an idiom through which, on one academic occasion, Pacific Islanders voiced their claims to overseas researchers. The way they did it illuminates a productive difference. Yet, arguably, the difference was doubly concealed, both through a language of similarity of interest and through a divergent deployment of the key concept, relations. Let me somewhat speculatively pursue apprehensions of difference (as distinct from dissimilarity) in situations near to my own and colleagues' hearts in the Pacific.

When difference is invisible, as in access to exotic power, people may strive to register its effects through dramatic action, as anthropologists have understood Melanesian millenarianism in the form of cargo cults. But difference may also remain unarticulated, as I infer might have been Pacific Island diplomacy on this occasion. In 2012 the European Consortium for Pacific Studies (ECOPAS) established a network of research institutions from Europe and the Pacific to collaborate in developing long-term strategies for social science and humanities research on climate change (Crook and Rudiak-Gould 2018). Its origins lay in a previous moment, when a roundtable of Pacific Island scholars urged their colleagues—predominantly (sociocultural) anthropologists—"to recognize the responsibilities to Oceanic peoples, to the Academy and to Civil Society that come with the exchange of expert knowledge."[13] Frustration was expressed that, for all their interchanges, unmet obligations still lay on the researchers' side, as did the need to remedy what often seemed a one-way flow of information. The speakers wanted their colleagues to act. The formation of ECOPAS was a direct political response.

This brought about a productive and creative alignment: the newly articulated division between Pacific Island scholars and overseas experts created a new kind of relationship between them. The former spoke of responsibilities to the academy as much as European scholars acknowledged those who had been party to their research. Admittedly what Islanders took for granted Europeans needed to be told, but they were open to relational obligations and no doubt glad that personal relations with Island scholars could be a sign of relations with many others. Pacific Island scholars had their own academic and research-interested view on the matter; deficit could be made up precisely through focusing on knowledge. Hence ECOPAS was to endorse "knowledge exchange"—just what had seemed impossible to the UK museum researchers—as one of its work packages.[14] The common coinage of that anticipated exchange was conjured in the participants' seemingly similar interests. However, I speculate that there was more to the initial division beyond the obvious dissimilarities that participants brought to the table. Neither dissimilarity nor similarity canceled out a persisting difference. Pacific Islanders had nothing to gain by simply assimilating their social position to that of the European academics, nor by overcoming how different their circumstances, and the origins of them, were. Moreover, for their part, they did not need to do either in order to act; on the contrary, a quite radical divergence may have been an obvious premise of the exchange.

Another source of difference could also have been concealed. Given the agreement that researchers had to acknowledge the obligations activated by their (personal) relations, one might ask what was to count as relations. It would not be surprising if the European researchers read this acknowledgment as an ethical position that gave moral authority to stimulating further flows of knowledge. The ethics would be consonant with the importance Euro-Americans give to cultivating interpersonal relations, as we saw in the Working Group's expression of compassion and respect, a potential domain of right-acting that could afford a legitimate basis upon which to acquire things from others.[15] Yet such understandings were unlikely to be commensurate with the implications Pacific Islanders give to the differentiation of relations. We should inquire for a start into the way knowledge is bound up with what counts as relations. Stengers's argument concerning divergence allows an opening here.

In the world to which the politics of research belongs, relations are key to comprehension. Pushed to it, many scholars would take the ontological position that relational descriptions of the world are made possible by *its* inherently relational properties. Denial therefore becomes arresting. When Stengers (2011: 59) admonishes that divergence "is not relational. It is constitutive," relational here refers to the domaining of knowledge into so many discrete entities connected through interchanges across (disciplinary) practices.[16] This is the Euro-American world as it appears much of the time, so that, in bureaucratese, boundaries delimit dissimilar kinds of expert knowledge, and as we saw in chapter 3 the need to create or produce relations between them is constantly stressed. By contrast, divergence (Stengers says) is not "between" practices — a practice does not define itself in terms of its divergence from others, for each "produces itself." Insofar as divergence is constitutive, then, it allows no domaining; practices appearing to juxtapose one another are not divisions of the same world, do not occupy the same environment. Her "ecology of practices" introduces a different kind of relation: "I use ecology, as a transversal category, to help define relational heterogeneity . . . situations that relate heterogeneous protagonists," each on its own behalf (2011: 59; cf. [1997] 2010b: 197).

If there was a difference, in this sense of divergence, of relational registers in the agreement about knowledge exchange, perhaps it was hidden in the very appeal from the Pacific Islanders to which the European scholars responded. The reproach at once brought to light and resolved a potential impasse for everyone; divergence was instantiated and concealed at this moment of agreement between them. To dilate: the agreement was over a means to knowledge, that is, acknowledging relations. At the same time, relations that some of those present — among Islanders, say — might take as prior to any exchange or interchange (the relational dispositions they took for granted), others — among their European counterparts — might imagine as having to be put creatively in place (in their needing to be told or in setting up an institutional mechanism). Such a positional divergence differentiates the premises on which action is taken forward. Only other contexts would tell if the difference was of any moment or not.

One context in which differentiation emerges as work to be done comes from an anthropologist's explicit interpretation of the concept of knowledge. Reite people (Madang Province, Papua New Guinea) value knowledge in the form of potent stories that affect the landscape as they do persons. Narration is not marked out as an intellectual activity. "Differences are between *kinds of people* with different control over knowledge," Leach (2009: 181, my emphasis) observes, "not between intellectual and other forms of activity."[17] People would only talk of knowledge that they themselves owned, an owner being liable for the effects of anything passed on to another. "Expressing knowledge amounts to claiming inclusion in the relationships (including those to land and spirits) that generated the knowledge. One cannot 'know' something without it being a part of one's make-up, and as such, something that connects one to others" (2009: 182). Leach suggests that this kind of transmission between persons is analogous to English speakers' concept of "kinship."[18] It is a kinship rooted in a place; land underwrites the social relationships it nurtures, and knowledge springs from particular landscapes. As the substance that links people in close relations (see also Bamford 2009), knowledge is thus a means of those relations coming into being.

If knowledge makes kinship, that in turn inflects its transfer at ceremonial events. Reite people exchange not knowledge but its products — the wealth and food that a place produces. These are given to recipients from other places, primarily in-laws and maternal kin, acknowledging thereby the debt of their nurturing contributions. The gifts make two kinds of persons: affinal kin are related in a manner quite distinct from what binds people of a single place together. The division is productive, not a difference in the apprehension of relations (as I inferred between Pacific Island and other scholars) but in the relations people enact. Persons enjoy the products of others' knowledge without controlling its source, for that continues to belong to those of the place from which it comes.[19] Such ideas about attachment and detachment would be bound to shape the very concept of knowledge exchange.

Leach (2012: 255) reflects on a contrast with two deep-seated Euro-American assumptions: first, that knowledge can be detached from those who produce it, to be circulated (as information) without reference to them; second, that its effect is not dependent on such persons, but on its correlation with apparently independently occurring phenomena (only some knowledge will be recognized and accorded expositional status, the rest being erroneous belief, inappropriate personification, and so forth).[20] The two assumptions can take on a political cast when the work of detachment is concealed in an apprehension of knowledge as (free-floating) items of information, as accompanied some arguments defending museum retention of remains.[21] The Reite riposte might be that diverse local knowledges cannot be put together as though they were dissimilar perspectives on the same reality; rather, one has to respect the divergent ways in which people are constituted in their relations.

In the spirit of knowledge exchange, Leach coauthored a book on local plants with Porer Nombo from Reite, juxtaposing descriptions in Tok Pisin (Neo-Melanesian "pidgin") and English with Reite plant names (Nombo and Leach 2010). Interestingly, questions were to be raised less about the presence of foreign knowledge or the exposure of indigenous knowledge to outsiders than about the presentation of the plants. A book launch at a university in Papua New Guinea aroused intense interest in reattaching the specimen photographs to the Reite author. There was a barrage of questions over where exactly the plants had come from, who had an interest in them, and whether Nombo was responsible for their use in his village.[22] The politics of attachment, one of ECOPAS's concerns with the exchange of knowledge, shows up the politics of detachment. For the view of Nombo's Papua New Guinean interlocutors could not diverge further from the notion of knowledge distilled in a (detachable) representation of the world. Nombo himself talked of "knowledge as remembering, as acting, as thinking on an experience or moment of transmission between persons. It is clear that what he describes is acting in and on [personal] relations" (Leach 2012: 264). Otherwise said, such relations are revealed to have differentiating effects.

II

Relations and "Relations"

This describes the first of three Anglophone attempts, through deliberate intervention, to differentiate (in the strong or positive sense) the relational language at the anthropologist's disposal.

Deforming one's terminology, as chapter 3 illustrated, may signal an effort to sensitize the connotations of a vocabulary that thus becomes internally divided. Carneiro da Cunha (2009) does so with the concept of culture. Her complaint is the way anthropologists slide in and out of diverse usages. Inflecting a distinction between "culture" (in quotation marks) and culture (unmarked), she describes how "culture" travels the world, often imported to profound political effect into people's delineation of themselves. At the same time, this explicit "culture" coexists with an implicit culture. The latter is evident as a matter of endemic internal logic. The coexistence of the two concepts, between which public discourse — indigenous or metropolitan — forever weaves in and out, gives rise to misunderstandings over (say) the nature of knowledge. Her words now have a familiar ring: it is not that the context of the concepts necessarily differ, she says, "rather that they are not in the same universe of discourse" (2009: 13). For Carneiro da Cunha's principal concern is with a contrast between the public interethnic logic of "culture," "a collective regime imposed on what was previously a network of differential rights," and the internal logic of culture, precisely that differentiated network, also in a strong sense, which has room for all kinds of divisions within (2009: 80–81).[23] The former comprise visible dissimilarities (cultures inevitably distinct from one another); the latter's constitutive divergences can be hard to see.

Internal differentiations deal with visibility in different ways. Consider certain kinds of doubt; I borrow a term that arises whenever Euro-Americans question how they know, although the issue is not — in this case — handled as a matter of knowledge. With Carneiro da Cunha's device of inflection, and just for this instance, I shall divide "relations" from relations. The division registers an internal (cosmological) divergence.

A pioneering scholar of the Papua New Guinea Highlands, Reay (1959a) once described the display of aggression that Kuma men (introduced in chapter 2) would mount in the course of a fertility-promoting pig ceremonial. Their spear dance, a stylized brandishing of weapons against unseen enemies, directed aggression outside the clan community. Ceremonies also occasioned internal attacks, more like games or sporting contests, protagonists being rival subclans or, spectacularly, men versus women. A mock battle that Reay (1959b) witnessed in 1955 began with the men and women of a settlement grouping at opposite ends of the ceremonial ground, stinging nettles in their hands, rushing forward to brush the skin of their opponents, then retreating to hurl soft ash and lumps of mud at a distance. Apropos Carneiro da Cunha's divisions internal to culture, diverse differences were thus being enacted. Aggression, mediated by weapons and decorations, was displayed against traditional enemies, normally remote, always attackable, and certainly not present on this occasion. Between men and women, familiar to one another, body contact was much closer to being unmediated: nettles, ash, and mud created corporeal intimacy. Reay contrasted the two types of ritual conflict. In the games, "the drama lies in the conflict itself"; in the stylized war display, drama is supplied by the ornamentation and dance movements, for the "spear dance dramatizes readiness for conflict rather than conflict itself" (1959b: 295, 291). Whereas the games would stop at the first serious injury, warfare could result in deaths. I intervene in this account to suggest that we take dramatizing readiness and dramatizing conflict as different Kuma efforts to divide people from one another.

Assertion of clan solidarity in the spear dance tested the strength of preexisting "relations," as in the categorical designation of traditional enmity; sustaining such antagonism was said to be a condition of the clansmen's own future strength. In this, the dance had something of a divinatory effect in its impact on them. The conviction of performance comes close to Holbraad's (2012: 220) "inventive definition," an announcement providing a newly conceived baseline for future action, and thus an inauguration of it. With the future in mind, dramatizing aggression took the categorical knowledge of preexisting "relations" as a newly enacted premise for the fertility to come. Reenactment was required or the world would not be thereby renewed. "Relations" with the enemy already existed; it was the clan (the dancers) who had to be remade.[24]

While the nettle games had rules, here Kuma men and women acted out a state of affairs that had no resolution: confrontation ended when the participants stopped. The "relation" between men and women was remade in their absolute separation. However, what was also brought into being, this time an unmarked relation, was the delineation of a confrontation whose outcome was decidedly unpredictable. Setting into motion conflict between the sexes, this relation subverted the certainty of the categories—it left wide open how "men" and "women" would appear in the course of (re)enactment. I would interpret this as existential indeterminacy as to what kinds of creatures were being made manifest. No one knew quite how others would behave, and thus what one would show of oneself. It entailed less a new premise for action than an experimental probing of what the effects of conflictual interchange might be. Hovering over the men and women was a question about how their relating would make visible what men and women (otherwise) were.

Both performances sprang from doubt. A difference lay between making explicit preexisting "relations" as a premise for acting, where uncertainty concerned the effectiveness of the clan's claims to its internal, ancestrally supported properties of strength and fertility, and uncovering previously implicit relations, where something like indeterminacy attached to the very properties a gendered being would evince. In short, "relations" bring their defining features into new positions of stability, while relations seem to leave open the existential status of the features themselves. In the latter, the relation is evident (in conflict) but who knows where it will lead, for that will appear only in the outcome. To ask how radical the divisions are here, between clans or between men and women, is to put the very comparison between Reay's two forms of ritual conflict to task. Conflict divides the actors. Where in English one might think of clans as similar political entities, or men and women as dissimilar persons, the Kuma clan is being invoked (against others) through the uniqueness of its own (ancestral) power, while "women" gathering at one end of the ceremonial ground elicit the appearance of "men" at the other, neither themselves nor not-themselves. The dynamic of doubt seems to have consequences that go off in different directions. The one tips into overt reinforcements of solidarity and enmity, the other draws back into possibilities for conjugal intimacy, which customarily following the games have been in the background all along.

A Pacific Island scholar might comment on the artificiality of this analytical exercise, at least if what appears to the reader is a domaining of the two enactments of doubt. Indeed, the English-language device I have been using ("relations" and relations) is misleading if it implies only their comparability. These conflicts diverge from each other, insofar as each is productive of itself. Criticism put forward by Moutu (2013), who worked with Iatmul people, from the Sepik River area, has a place here.

Relations and Relationships

Moutu voices a disagreement concerning the Anglophone duplex on which I have frequently drawn, namely the interplay of epistemic (logical, conceptual) and interpersonal relations. Working through his criticism will highlight the fusion of connection and similarity with which this chapter began. Moutu proceeds through detaching relations from relationships.

"Contra Strathern [2005], I argue that what distinguishes 'relationships' ontologically from the epistemological forms of relational practices—such as connection, association, resemblance, comparison, etc.—is necessity and transcendence, which give 'relationships' the character of an infinite being" (Moutu 2013: 202). Anthropology's epistemic understanding of relationality occludes the ontological character of relationships. Such relationships implicate persons, a designation covering a range of phenomena. The Iatmul archetype of a person embodies a pair of brothers, that is, it is the pair that is the complete person.[25] Thought of together, as elder and younger, this duplex engenders a "pattern of thought" that organizes certain dispositions (such as being slow and fast) and, applying to men and women alike, organizes the perception of all kinds of relations across the generations or between the ritual moieties who initiate one another's youth. Thus the grandfather who reappears in his grandson is elder brother to younger brother. Brotherhood is necessarily oriented toward a certain kind of becoming; the one brother is always becoming the other. As Moutu formulates it, the ontology of brotherhood exists as an "internal necessity" to the very conceptualization of relationship.[26] His formulation summons Viveiros de Castro's comparison of canonical relations between certain indigenous peoples of Amazonia and Brazilians (along with other Western peoples) from a Euro-Christian background (chapter 1). For the latter, "brotherhood is in itself the general form of relation" (2004b: 18), where the Amazonian form would be the affinity of brothers-in-law. While brothers-in-law are linked by the difference that divides them, brotherhood speaks to partners in a relation being connected through what unites them, insofar as each is "in the same relation to a third term" (2004b: 18, emphasis omitted). This kind of brotherhood is not at all what Moutu is describing for the Melanesian Iatmul. Elder divided from younger, Iatmul brothers are more like Amazonian brothers-in-law than they are like Euro-Christian brothers. More radically, they relate as life and death to each other, and infinitely. The one is always overtaking the other, and thus relationship never ceases.

This forces us to think of those Euro-Christian brothers subsisting in the same relation to a common term. For English *usage* makes it possible to leave the third term aside: two entities or beings can appear connected simply through the similarity of one to the other. (The shortcut can always be given its longer version, in that there is always a third reference point to connecting entities.) A derivative of that vernacular usage is the counter-possibility of conceiving terms connected by a relation of dissimilarity. Note that the phraseology is not good English, which would be inclined toward a substantive alignment in which terms were not connected by but distinguished or contrasted by their dissimilarity. Needless to add, something stronger than dissimilarity seems warranted in the description of the Iatmul elder-and-younger-brother pair.

The Iatmul orientation toward certain kinds of becoming demonstrates (to the anthropologist) relationship in an unusual form. Always-becoming works as a kind of differentiation in that being in one state anticipates being in the other. The other is not a later stage of growth or evolutionary development but rather an alternative, an alter made episodically present. And it would be cutting off understanding too soon to imagine the one as simply the negation of the other. The Iatmul divide between elder and younger, life and death, exemplifies potential transformation. This "infinity" of relationship also entails a reversible visibility of phenomena. For the difference of each (brother) from the other is underlaid by an expectation that something is other than what it appears to be or, more appositely, than what it is now. Even more so than for Kuma men and women in ritual conflict, such transformations do not seem reducible to the discriminating effects of (what Euro-American exposition would find in) similarity and dissimilarity.

Pondering on how to fulfill the aspirations of Papua New Guinea's founding constitution for the post-Independence adoption of customary law into the country's underlying law, elsewhere Moutu (2014) poses a version of the problematic equivalence of cultures raised by Carneiro da Cunha. The need to encourage new formulations of the country's underlying law comes from an effort to maintain the distinctiveness of the postcolonial legal system from that of its colonial predecessors. Its means seem to lie in making connections through comparisons or parallels between one culture's kind of law and another's. So legal work is carried out, as it is anywhere, in the lawyer's endeavor to turn everyday usage (custom) into something that would yield generally applicable precepts (law). Precisely in order to differentiate it from colonial or imposed law, customary law thus appears as a social form comparable to "law" itself. In effect, the practice of such a comparison leads to an "excess of similarity" (the phrase is Demian's [2014]) between the two.[27] If, per contra, "different" comparative procedures are required, if it is a division (from the colonial past) that the Papua New Guinean legal reformers try to sustain against the background of the obvious similarities of modern judicial processes, then the reformers might be prompted to start not with the similarities but with the social divergences implied in their positions. Moutu might have drawn on his own contrast between (epistemic) relations and (the ontological implication of) relationships. However, he does something that is in retrospect particularly germane to the present discussion.

There is a conundrum, he notes, intrinsic to the fundamental concept of legal precedence—yesterday's precedent in today's decisions and today's in tomorrow's—in which one case is compared against another in terms of its similarities, just as customary law is measured up against (the rest of) law. Moutu writes if "precedence subsists on a method that employs similarity then how can a concept of similarity make our *Underlying Law [Act]* different" (2014: 6)?[28] There could not be a clearer critique of the conceptual impasse that comes from trying to activate difference through ideas of relating saturated with the connectives of similarity.[29]

Non-relations

Unlike similarity and connection, negatives for relation have an oddity to them, that is, the concept is not easily defined in antithesis.[30] Its very form thus lends itself to the logical propositions that one cannot not relate or that the only impossible relation is to imagine its absence. This does not stop English speakers creating a hybrid negative; with the idea that anything can be negated, they can speak of non-relations.

Non-relations occur in popular usage where the activation of a relation parsed as a connection between entities may be denied or rejected; this move is assisted no doubt by its kinship avatar (it is colloquial to deny kinship to persons because they are "not relations"). However, the concept may also appear in deliberate provocations to commonsense understandings, as in the connotations of Stengers's "non-relational" divergence. The concern with knowledge that has reappeared in this chapter is not irrelevant to such provocations. For naturalists and moderns, relating appears at once necessary to and transcendent of knowledge-making. There are countless ways in which one may be in doubt or "not know" things, but insofar as knowledge is implied in what is brought to consciousness, a mindful being cannot not be in a state of knowing. There is, in this sense, no knowledge that does not relate relations. Two deliberate efforts to sidestep such a position offer a final comment on how scholars may differentiate the relational language at their disposal: one effort is inspired by a Spanish philosopher and the other by an American biologist and feminist critic.

Corsín Jiménez and Willerslev offer "an indigenous re-description of the Euro-American concept of the relation" (2007: 537). A certain presence accompanies Yukaghir hunters of Siberia, in the form of a shadow-force, an immaterial twin that appears simultaneously with the perceived person. All physical entities have this hidden side: things "are never just themselves, but always something else as well" (528). The economic relations of sharing and the economic relations of (hierarchical) exchange shadow each other in this sense. So there is a radical difference between hunters' relations, now toward their kin and now toward their Russian sponsors (sources of fuel and ammunition), with the possibility of each kind of interaction becoming the other, a reversibility especially apparent in somewhat parallel relations with spirits. An elk hunter is always on two missions, visible and invisible; the hunter can seduce the elk because his shadow spirit has already seduced the elk's spirit. The hunter's shadow spirit, it is said, "moves in and out of these two hunts, turning the visible and the invisible inside out, and recasting the shadows of both worlds as it . . . sneaks between their limits" (536). Given that every being casts such a shadow, Corsín Jiménez and Willerslev perceive the shadow working like the general category of "concept." Its conviction rests not on a relational definition but on a specific effect, as one might say Reite knowledge is known through its effects, here its capacity for self-displacement. In other words, it appears analogous to a concept not because one can lay out the relation of one entity with other entities but from the way the concept creates its own space for expression, pointing to an idea of entity or being that is always something else. The shadow is an alternative in the same shape or outline as the being in question, yet is not it. As they promised, this is not a description of the concept of relation but a Yukaghir redescription.

Inspiration came from a Spanish thinker's unconventional argument. Corsín Jiménez and Willerslev (2007: 537–538) look to the work of Eugenio Trías, who characterized traditional philosophy as de-limitative, outlining the conditions under which a concept has a purchase, rather than seeing how concepts work by pursuing them to *their* limits. (A philosophy of the shadow is not just a Siberian conceit.) Between the Yukaghir alternatives of economic engagement, an anticipated reversibility sustains relatively stable pairings of states of being/becoming. This particular instance of reverse visibility is described by these authors (537) as "non-relational": no explicit relation pertains between the two states, as comparison would provide, only the existential given of one position being occupied rather than another. As for the difference between Yukaghir and Euro-American reasonings, they turn it into an intersection. Out of the energy that the authors derive from Trías's work on concepts, and out of their controlled equivocation with respect to Yukaghir ideas, they make an explicit analogy between the shadow (as a form) and the (concept of) relation.

What lies in the anthropologists' hands is, as always, their expositional ambition. Corsín Jiménez and Willerslev have themselves created a veritable shadow to relations in as near to a non-relational manner that it is possible to get. A strategic example from within Euro-American discourse offers another displacement, where relationality of one kind is denied for another to appear.

I refer to Haraway's astonishingly prescient "cyborg manifesto" ([1985] 1991), which we might describe as the shadow of a world taken (conceptually) to its limits. This is the familiar world of entities imagined "relationally," acting as parts of a whole, negotiating overlapping identities, devising programs to erase contradiction and seeking virtue in unification. It is the single world of domains, contexts, and perspectival viewpoints that Luhmann (1990) analyzed in terms of multiple autopoietic systems. But, as I see it, through using different modalities of relations, Haraway effects something closer to a Yukaghir redescription. Thus she presents her principal actor, the cyborg, as an image or a myth, refusing to match its reality with the realism of "social analysis" (though there is much social analysis in the manifesto). Cyborgs dissolve the domaining sustained by dualisms, boundaries, and the politics of domination, including the domination of women alongside all those constituted as others. Cyborgs do not reinstate sisterhood; that would be a form of brotherhood in the Euro-Christian sense. They do not point to the perfection of relational interconnectedness; that would reinvent a communion that "overcomes" dualisms and aspires to connect up all the divisions of a one world ([1985] 1991: 176). Relations are doing something quite different in this piece. One might even say they are "non-relations" with respect to the (relational) world one thinks one knows.

The cyborg was summoned at a specific political moment in scientific-feminist history, to capture among other things the then-emergent feedback loops of communication technopolitics and the microchip revolution. It is as though Haraway had taken Luhmann's complex systems and subsystems, each creating their own environments, but refused them autopoiesis—the power of myth is to allow such refusals. Self-reference loses its force when the cyborg self "is a kind of a disassembled and reassembled, postmodern collective and personal self" ([1985] 1991: 163).[31] To the contrary, when their reproduction is already "mixed," systems are already made up of other systems. The cyborg manifesto is at once an ironic comment on organicism as a misplaced image of holism and a foreshadowing of the profoundly already-related skeins of symbiosis on which Haraway (2003) was to write another manifesto. Contacts involving beings that continue to diverge can be imagined as intersections or, in Stengers's (2011: 60) phrase, connecting-events, just as cyborgs are "needy for connection" (Haraway [1985] 1991: 151).[32] Far from "relating" discrete domains of life, the cyborg's relations were never knowable as distinct from it. It is all relation in that sense. Haraway (1997: 37) subsequently observed, "The technical and the political are like the abstract and the concrete, the foreground and the background, the text and the context . . . questions of pattern, not of ontological difference. The terms pass into each other; they are shifting sedimentations of the one fundamental thing about the world — relationality."

Yukaghir hunter relations give us a way of imagining cyborg relations, yet are not them (thus Haraway's world is not hinged with a reversible alternative). What I take from the manifesto is that it was never sufficient to imagine that cyborgs were in conflict with or in disagreement with the world they redescribed. Rather, they displaced it. To revert momentarily to the Kuma device, instead of setting out specific kinds of "relation" to that world, in being all relation cyborgs were already it. Residing as its shadow, where cyborgs lived was at once not that world and more like it than the world understood or knew of itself. And descriptions of the world through cyborgs were able to displace other descriptions precisely because cyborgs were already in existence. Perhaps these, too, are contours of non-relational shapes.

I have tried to allow varieties of conceptualizations to breathe in their own (conceptual) environments. If we were interested only in recuperating relations of "difference," there would have been no need for the repetition of contexts. But what I hope also springs out from these attempts to differentiate relational discourse is a pervasive (English) background parlance of similarity and dissimilarity. This creates a platform from which to propose a further analytical context for the exposition of comparison and analogy.

III

Difference and (Dis)similarity in Analogical Mode

A romance well known in Middle English, which circulated in various versions in the thirteenth and fourteenth centuries, tells of two male children, identical in appearance, who swear eternal friendship (Mann 2008).[33] Both marry, the first to do so giving one of a pair of identical gold cups to the other. At a crucial moment when the latter sacrifices his future for his friend, the two change places and back again, but finally end up apart, rich man and leprous beggar. Yet the beggar never relinquishes his cup, and the pair is reunited when each discovers what is in the other's possession. An angel tells them the disease will be cured if the beggar is bathed in the blood of his friend's children, and the rich man's wife agrees for the sake of the friendship. However, the slain children come to life, all live happily ever after, and when the friends die on the same day they are entombed together. The tale refers to general suppositions of the time (leprosy could be cured by bathing in the blood of children), to chivalric and legal institutions (blood brotherhood), and to social practices (sworn brothers laid side by side in one grave).[34] Allusions to Christ, the slain son whose blood healed humankind, abound.

The reader hardly needs reminding how variegated comparisons between friends and kin can turn out to be. Among many examples of passionate friendships, for Brain (1976: 30–31) this medieval story, "Amis and Amiloun," stresses the unity of two friends.[35] Yet how curious to extract "friendship" from everything else, not least from the other relations through which their bond is stressed. The friends are brothers who are not brothers, to be buried like spouses when they are not spouses. What comparisons are these? Where has the distinction between friend and kin gone? Why the identity between two cups filled with wine as a "visual surrogate for the identical bodily appearance of the two friends and the ties of blood brotherhood" (Mann 2008: 155)? As for the widespread equation of spilt blood with the blood of Christ, alongside the reference to resurrection or miraculous rebirth is "the subtle pressure to read the wine as blood [that] gives the cups a Eucharistic quality, and so links them to the healing bath of [the children's] blood" (155).[36] My own queries sound intrusive, and so they should. The comparative question about distinguishing kin and friend is misleading; as we know, this was an era when friend was among the generics used for kin at large (as well as for non-kin). When in the late seventeenth and early eighteenth centuries friendship began to be conceptually and verbally divorced from kinship, certain assumptions by which one set of relations was described through another set—as inhered in the triangulation of friends, brothers, spouses—ceased to be tenable. Such usage was either assimilated to literary devices as in metaphor, widespread and unexceptional (treating friends as brothers), or regarded as inadmissible practice, both startling and dubious (treating same-sex friends as spouses). However, I turn the intrusiveness in another direction. The short answer to the question about comparison is that this is not *comparison* as moderns know it.

In the equivalence of friends/brothers/spouses, the story would seem to offer an abundance of similarities. Apart from play with and denial of resemblance, the presence and absence of likeness, and the twinning of identical forms, relations turn on where and when persons or substances are located and how entities come to occupy one another's places. Thus in placing the two cups together when wine from one is poured into the other, or in laying friends side by side, each appears as (to borrow Mann's term) a surrogate of the other. Perhaps it is the place-changing of Amis and Amiloun, in time, in space, that above all separates them and makes obvious their mutual surrogacy. This sounds like the analogical process of substitution described at the end of the previous chapter, which left in the air its relation to the concept of comparison. I now return to it.

At the end of an exposition on how relations may at once expand and contract descriptive possibilities, I made a move to detach analogy from comparison. In the present chapter, a move to detach difference from dissimilarity has taken center stage. In both cases the intention is to highlight certain presumptions about current analytical/vernacular usages. (These moves are not meant to be normative, though they address definitions that might already have that import.)

Now the common definition of analogy in English implies the connecting of otherwise dissimilar entities through a relation of similarity perceived between them, their agreement or correspondence thereby demonstrated. The entities are dissimilar in some respect; the relation instantiates similarity; similarities and dissimilarities become combined. However, suppose the act of relating were that of differentiation. Notwithstanding the fact that negative analogies (contrasts) are conceivable in English, or that classification by division has ancient antecedents (Lloyd 1966; 2015), differentiation in the strong sense does not turn on computing preexisting similarities and dissimilarities. The point can be further exemplified by the now-familiar Kuma. Men at once substitute for one another, as co-members of a clan, and divide themselves off from members of other clans through exogamy, a division repeated at every marriage: sisters and brothers are differentiated from husbands and wives. Clan unity implies absence of differentiation, and emphasizing unity does not change anything — men instead celebrate unity by differentiating themselves from absent enemies. What by contrast relates brothers-in-law is precisely their difference, that disjunction created at marriage. Their interaction springs from the analogy between the relations by which each differentiates himself from both wife and sister, but "differently" (with respect to the women concerned) from that of his counterpart. This existential imperative, requiring repeated differentiation, yields a form of analogy potentially alien for English speakers.

Differentiation overcomes not similarities, which then combine with dissimilarities, but indifference, convergence, lack of differentiation.

So what about the abundance of apparent similarity in "Amis and Amiloun"? When one thinks about it further, it seems equally alien. Indeed, I wonder whether the resemblances and likenesses being stated, displaced, and reinstated do not amount to a presumption of similarity whose negative or antithesis is not quite our familiar dissimilarity. Rather, antithesis seems to lie between a concealed as opposed to a (miraculously) revealed similarity. Revelation is through signs, the detection of a similar entity in another form or another place.[37] Similarity is not a ground to discerning dissimilarity, such as one might find in variations that have a common reference point in natural behavior or in the inclusiveness of taxonomic ordering. On the contrary, might one dare suggest, the medieval romance recounts moments of concealed or denied likeness between the sworn brothers. The pair can and should be openly realigned, with each substitutable for the other, which is indeed the culmination of the narrative. As we heard, while friends are distinct from brothers/spouses/cups, the discrete terms pointing to the particularities of things, they can be made to resemble one another by the way they are placed or localized in the unfolding narration. Analogy building on relations of resemblance turns the particularities into a chain of equivalences. In this configuring of transformations, one can thus act on potential resemblance — create a relation out of it — whereas to act on the discrete particularities themselves would simply add more and more particulars, which does not change anything.

The point of rehearsing these divergent versions of analogy — prompted by Melanesian clanship, a medieval tale — is to highlight a third position, the one from which either seems strange. This is exactly the place where we began, the notion of analogy in present-day English parlance. Here analogies are seemingly dominated by an *interplay between* "dissimilarity" and "similarity" (under the latter, I subsume what English may discriminate as both the same and the similar [see note 2 for this chapter]). Comparison itself offers an identical interplay, and indeed analogy and comparison may be taken, in either direction, each as an instance of the other.[38] It is in this third context that — for naturalists and moderns — comparison works with reference to a common ground (or "third term"), similarity being implied in the reason for bringing entities together. At the same time, we have already noted that English speakers may equally well avoid reference to what is held in common and plunge into direct comparisons of similarities and dissimilarities. Vernacular usage thus renders these two terms analogous (qua similar) to each other.

Coda to Part II

PREPARATION

In a scintillating and much cited couple of pages, Foucault ([1966] 1970: 54–55) delineated the profound consequence for Western thought that sprang from supposing an order of comparison based on identity and difference. Such analysis came to life, in the latter part of the seventeenth century, in lieu of an old hierarchy of analogies. The new order displaced resemblance as the "fundamental category of knowledge." Henceforth "every resemblance must be subjected to proof by comparison," which turned on the discovery of its identity and of its particular series of differences. In English, somewhat ambiguously, the term "identity" is at once used for the self-sameness or uniqueness of entities (as encountered in chapter 1) and allowed to travel "between" entities by reason of their similarity or what they share as the same.[1] Among other things, the external relations by which an entity is individualized may also serve as relations of differentiation. Foucault's text at this point almost seems to imply — it is not, I think, his intention — that uncovering the differences that secure an identity will then lead to the making of connections. A Wagnerian commentator could have added that insofar as such connections are no longer to be discovered, they must be accomplished through method and system.

Foucault continues thus: "The activity of the mind . . . will therefore no longer consist in drawing things together, in setting out on a quest for everything that might reveal some sort of kinship [*une parenté*], attraction, or secretly shared nature within them, but, on the contrary, in discriminating, that is, in establishing their identities, then [in establishing] the inevitability of the connections with all the successive degrees of a [taxonomic] series" (55, emphasis omitted).[2] This European phenomenon, no doubt diversely enacted in diverse vernaculars, was among other things enacted in (changing) English apprehensions of the relation. And here similarity seemingly acquired a privileged value not only through the notion of connection but also through being simultaneously entailed in identity and in the dissimilarities of a discriminating analysis.[3] Such an evaluation is no less true in perceptions of kinship, literally speaking, to which part III again turns.

In readiness for that, we need to reenter the universe of naturalists and moderns where "difference" is the vernacular counterpart to similarity, and we might want a brief reminder of the cast this gives to analogy. It was to overcome certain contradictions in the oneness of continuity and the multiplicity of particularities that Locke praised the intellectual act of comparing things through relations of "identity and diversity" (1690: 2, 27, 2; 329). Now identity and alterity, similarity and difference, analogy and contrast are all relational pivots of Candea's (2019) exposition of anthropological comparison. While he allows that there may be positive or negative analogies, the latter involving relations of difference (his term), his main argument on the point brings together analogies, which "point out similarities between different things, relations or forms," and contrasts, which "point out differences between things, relations or forms" already in some sense commensurable (2019: 215–216). Analogies do not require perfect identity, to keep with his words, any more than contrasts require perfect difference (questions, we may say, of degree and fit): they replicate within what the combination of both renders obvious. Comparison is that combination, visibly holding similarity and difference together. "The distinctiveness of *comparatio* . . . lies precisely in the way it conjoins analogies and contrasts" (205, original italics). In anthropological hands comparison is also much more, he observes, but the distinction between — and comparability of — similarity and difference in this sense gleams through his account, like light falling on the moving wheels of an argument-engine. Any particular resolution can always be resolved into further similarity and difference. I take this as a report from the field.

Similarity says it all. Where (the term) "difference" summons the concept of dissimilarity, the latter will continue to be the term I use. "Similarity" encloses the relation between them. For, as Candea observes, albeit in the idiom I am suspending, "sameness" (similarity) is always holding "difference" (dissimilarity) at bay.

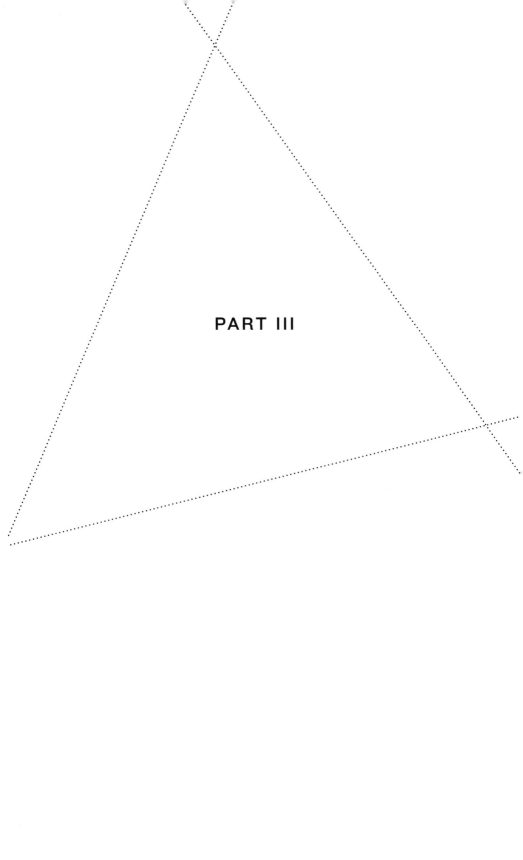

PART III

5. ENLIGHTENMENT DRAMAS

Someone who might have appreciated a discrimination between dissimilarity and difference was the renowned German artist and naturalist Maria Sibylla Merian. As a reminder of possibilities quite other than those pursued by some near contemporaries, to which I turn here, her exploration of what were in effect relations (my term) offers a seventeenth-century counterfactual to the course of certain events. Its potential for divergence from them is, however, the better apprehended as an afterthought to those events; Merian is initially introduced in the context of further reflection on the abstract quality of relations.

It is time to respond to a question posed a while ago by Carsten's rethinking of personhood and kinship. She called for an appreciation of Western people's "everyday sense of relationality" (2004: 107). The question is how the world ever made such an appeal to the appreciation of relations necessary. What was being emphasized and what was overlooked? She suggests that discussions of the person emphasizing "the notion of an abstract and legally defined entity, the bounded individual with rights over property . . . [have] obscured the most obvious contexts in which relationality as an aspect of personhood is expressed," namely kinship (107). In other words, it is the relationality of kins-*persons* (the linguistic relationality of kin designations never being in doubt) that is overlooked. Carsten refers to these relations as intrinsic to the person. In the context of such a common, everyday sense of relationality, then, why does so much effort have to be poured into giving it life within various discourses, scholarly and otherwise?

The role that the scientific revolution or the Scottish Enlightenment might have played, and whether or not this is particularly an English speaker's problem, is a further issue thrown up by the present book. Clearly things were happening elsewhere of which developments in England were but one version, and its spokesmen (to put it like that) but players on a wider stage. Israel's (2001: 515) reference to the Anglomania that swept Europe in the 1730s and 1740s, when Locke along with Bacon and Newton were "almost everywhere eulogized and lionized," insinuates their longer eclipse by the radical potentials of European intellectual life at large. The intellectually safe Locke, in his view, contributed little and late to the European Enlightenment. Yet ideas flow with language regardless of their caliber. The entwining of kinship ties and relations that we met in Locke's exposition may have been an incidental matter of rhetorical convention, while at the same time, and seemingly peculiar to linguistic idioms in English, a similar entwining was being concretized in the adoption of relations and relatives as substantives for kinsfolk. It may repay us to look more closely at Locke's usages, as well as at Hume's subsequent recasting of them.

As it turns out, it will be necessary to talk about something that did not happen — in fact by the time it did not take place, it probably could never have. Yet, after Munn (1990), as an "event" it will have had something of a future, its reverberations available for reflection; we might even sense an aftereffect, the jolt of realizing that something had never been there. I thus invent a second counterfactual, in this case from the perspective of the kinds of twenty- and twenty-first-century discourses on persons and relations to which Carsten refers. While what-could-have-been does not entail any specific premonition of it (evidence of it being a contemporary issue), that subsequent jolt is another matter. I shall make a little drama out of it.

I

Varieties of the Abstract

Almost in the genre of anthropological arrivals (Firth thus began *We, the Tikopia* in 1936), the historian Davis has us meet Merian at the point in 1699 when she is boarding a boat in Amsterdam bound for two years in the Dutch colony in Suriname. Already in her fifties (her adult daughter was with her), and already reputed to be a skilled painter, "she was also a knowing observer of the habits of caterpillars, flies, spiders, and other such creatures" (Davis 1995: 140). She had published on the bodily transformation of caterpillars, which she bred as well as depicted, and was seeking out their tropical counterparts. It was not unusual for naturalists to go to distant places, although it was unusual to have no official sponsorship. Merian returned home with many specimens and drawings, and her double volume on the insects of Suriname secured her position among Amsterdam scientists.

The sugar planters of Suriname were bemused. "People ridiculed me for seeking anything other than sugar," said Merian (Davis 1995: 173). But then, as Davis drily remarks, resident Africans and Amerindians assisted her more than European planters, and Merian drew on the knowledge ("testimony") of both slaves and Arawak/Carib "Indians." European naturalists rarely mentioned the servants who assisted their research; Merian tells of the conversations they had. She was clearly ready to acknowledge other sources of observation, although to conclude that she was deliberately giving her account a relational texture introduces a present-day sensibility. A converse anachronism to present-day ears is her reference to assistants as slaves and servants. At that time in Europe servants would be regarded as extensions of the persons of their masters and mistresses (Steedman 2009: 19), so the multiple hands we might today perceive in Merian's intricate drawings could as well, as it was perceived then, be all parts of Merian's hand. Nonetheless Davis (1995: 190) emphasizes that her "scientific style and conversational exchange encouraged ethnographic writing indifferent to the civilized/savage boundary," a marked divergence from the then-burgeoning travel literature.

Merian's 1705 *Metamorphosis of the insects of Suriname* has been described as belonging to a new form of planetary European consciousness (Davis 1995: 180–181, quoting Pratt [1992: 31]), as, one by one, plant "life forms were to be drawn out of the tangled threads of their life surroundings and rewoven into European-based patterns of global unity and order ... [and] into the language of the system." Abstracted, in other words, through observation, naming, and formalized classification. At the same time, and this is Davis's own point, Merian's ecological awareness left space for Suriname insects and plants to flourish "in local terms and relations," through "nature's connections" (Davis 1995: 154). Merian had deployed this narrative strategy before, leading the reader from the familiar to the strange and back again; what she now took to a further level was her interest in the life cycle.[1] The preface to the new book stated that what had been missing in overseas collections—from the Americas, Africa, the Pacific, as specimens had come to Amsterdam through Dutch traders—were precisely the origins and transformations of the insects. "The beautiful specimens were stilled, wrenched from context, lacking process" (167) ("context" and "process" are Davis's vocabulary). Tearing a creature from its habitat is a compelling image of abstraction as a mode of rendering information useful to the comparison of general forms. However, Merian wanted to do for South America what she had done earlier when, across copious copperplates, she depicted insects from life. Their immediate environment was present, as in the many pictures organized around a flowering or fruiting plant showing the leaves on which caterpillars fed and where eggs were laid. The metamorphosis of these beings was her concern. Her illustrations followed no recognized classificatory order; the observer was instead directed to look within each life, and appreciate how the process was repeated, insect after insect.

Metamorphosis was thus brought to the imagination. That one mode of being emerged from another could not have been more concretely depicted. Her focus on process and context, as modern parlance puts it, also entailed inferring connections: "Her insects and plants were telling a life story . . . to evoke a particular and interconnected process of change" (1995: 149).[2] Davis's interpolation of connection is apt insofar as in the English of the time "connection" indicated a bond of interdependence or coherence in the linking together of ideas. That could be made visible in the presentation of a principle stated abstractly. Smith's summary observation on philosophy came to deploy it thus: "Philosophy is the science of the connecting principles of nature"; it introduces order into chaos "by representing the invisible chains which bind together . . . disjointed objects" (quoted in Porter 2000: 150).[3]

In making order out of a discordant chaos, as one might have taken the disjointed appearance of creeping caterpillar and fluttering moth, such philosophy was concerned with principles of coherence. Abstractions presented to the imagination can in turn acquire concrete form. To the extent that an abstract principle makes an appearance, as in Smith's binding chains, that which is inferred from observation comes to have its own "observable" characteristics. If this is the story of Baroque sensibilities in art and science (making appearances appear), it is also the story of the Enlightenment savant concerned with the nature of (that is, understanding) understanding.

Let us look, then, toward an English-speaking corner of Merian's world, to certain intellectual alliances encouraged by natural philosophy, where the seventeenth-century scientific revolution so-called was arguably a precursor to the Scottish Enlightenment of the eighteenth. (Notably, the Scottish Enlightenment distinguished itself from its European cousins by a self-consciously scientific cast.) English linguistic idiom was the medium of Scottish philosophizing, not apparently without some comment (Herman 2001). In any event, the term "relation" was in use, broadly speaking, as a synonym for connection or for association in the sense of linkage. Hume's *Treatise of human nature* ([1739–1740] 2000), described as *Being an attempt to introduce the experimental method of reasoning into moral subjects*, begins with what we need to know of the workings of the mind in order to know how we know anything. His thesis famously turned on what he took as a ubiquitous facility, the connection or association of ideas, and with typifying different kinds of relations created thereby. Indeed, relations were crucial to Hume's engagement in a long-standing debate about the particularity of ideas. The idea of relation, too, was in the process being "figmented" (Ingold 2013: 737).

Hume's discussion touches on the vexed depiction of ideas with regard to their general character. "'Tis evident, that in forming most of our general ideas . . . we abstract from every particular degree of quantity and quality, and that an object ceases not to be of any particular species" (1739–1740: bk. 1, ch. 1, 7; Norton and Norton 2000: 17 [hereafter 1739–40: 1, 1, 7; 17]). Evident as this process might be, he set it against the impossibility of forming an idea, as in the idea of an object, without also summoning some particular impression of it. Consequently, although ideas may be general in their representation, they are invariably particular in themselves. Hume instances "figure" as a general term that is brought to the imagination by circles, squares, triangles, and so forth, the mind running over several discrete examples without resting on any one. It is the very capacity to connect ideas that allows the sense of generality. "A particular idea becomes general by being annex'd to a general term; that is, to a term, which from a customary conjunction has a relation to many other particular ideas, and readily recals them in the imagination" (1, 1, 7; 20).

Insofar as Hume is here engaging with Locke, who used the idea of a triangle to argue to the contrary (namely that it is possible, with some contrivance, to think of a triangle without thinking of it in any particular form) (Norton and Norton 2000: 432), this point and counterpoint beckon the anthropologist toward the relativity of the epithets "abstract" and "concrete" and the concepts with which they dance. Each has its own force. In truth, either may be deployed in figmenting relations.

Varieties of the Concrete

Introducing a third edition of *Elements of social organization* ([1951] 1961), Firth pondered on anthropologists' efforts at understanding. How do they know what they know? Describing how they set about reaching their primary objective, "correct observation," at once throws up a problem of method. The problem is acute when it comes to social relations. Social anthropologists might be said to study society, Firth said, but that is not what they observe. "They do not even observe social relationships; they infer them" ([1951] 1961: 22, emphases omitted). Rather than observe, anthropologists — especially through experience as fieldworkers — abstract types of social relations out of continuous and ever-changing flows of activity. Need for abstraction is evident if social relations are to be seen as the building blocks of social structure, along with the (largely unremarked) epistemic connections implied as when he writes of "the relations between economic and moral standards" (138). Content with abstraction when it comes to imagining society and relations, Firth nonetheless finds himself obliged to oppose the abstract to the concrete: the "more one thinks of the structure of a society in abstract terms, as a group of relations or of ideal patterns, the more necessary it is to think *separately* of social organization in terms of concrete activity" (35–36, my emphasis).

It could almost have been as a rejoinder to Firth that his younger contemporary, Fortes, offered a very different observation about relations to chew on.

> Textbooks always remind us that social relations are abstractions, since they are not directly visible or tangible, as individuals and activities are, but have to be established by inference. . . . "Siblingship" is manifested in [i.e., inferred from] kinship words, in eating customs, in incest taboos[,] . . . etc. But let us turn the matter inside out. We can then say that in order to be at the disposal of [i.e., brought to the imagination of] those who engage in them, social relations must become discernible, objectified. They must be bodied forth in material objects and places, in words, acts, ideas, attitudes, rules and sanctions. . . . Ego knows that he is B's sibling and acts accordingly. . . . He signifies his engagement in the relationship by the nomenclature he uses towards and about B, by his attitudes, claims, and conduct. . . . It is distinctive custom that makes a social relation signifiable by those who participate in it and cognizable by those who are external to it. (Fortes 1969: 60–61)

To be concrete is what is needed—listing all the ways in which a phenomenon can be made to appear. The reader can give another turn to his specific example. In drawing attention to relations between siblings, Fortes is offering a concrete instantiation of siblingship, siblingship in turn being offered as a concrete instantiation of (social) relations. For other mid-twentieth-century anthropologists, when relations were conceived as parts of a system, "relations" acquired concreteness even as "system" emerged as the new abstraction.

That Fortes is working through an exposition on kinship is not incidental, although an evocation of kin ties does not have to be restricted to "social" relations.[4] The long history of evoking kin ties in order to illustrate the character of relations in general has been noted apropos Locke's usages. When fifty years later Hume was dilating on the nature of understanding, and on the troubled notion of an idea, he made the same move. This is Hume talking of the connections and associations of ideas, and the especially powerful relation of cause and effect, in the way the imagination runs from one idea to another: "Two objects are connected together in the imagination, not only when the one is immediately resembling, contiguous to, or the cause of the other, but also when there is interpos'd betwixt them a third object, which bears to both of them any of these relations. . . . Cousins in the fourth degree are connected by causation, if I may be allow'd to use that term; but not so closely as brothers, much less as child and parent" (1, 1, 4; 13, emphasis omitted).

Kinship thickens his discourse again when he describes attraction or resemblance by asserting the affect they carry. He has been writing on how objects or circumstances arouse emotions, and draws readily on interpersonal relations (my phrase) in this regard. "Whoever is united to us by any connexion is always sure of a share of our love, proportion'd to the connexion, without enquiring into his other qualities. Thus the relation of blood produces the strongest tie the mind is capable of in the love of parents to their children, and a lesser degree of the same affection, as the relation lessens. Nor has consanguinity alone this effect, but any other relation without exception" (2, 2, 4; 228). Hume then runs through various acquaintances, for otherwise than by degree he does not differentiate the emotions insofar as they flow toward anyone who is an object of attention. At the same time, in the manner in which he represents this knowledge, the concepts of connection and relation seem to be concretized by the discussion of kinspersons. What kinds of kin are they?

In his illustrative conjunction of relations and kin, blood ties ("relations of blood") exemplify relations depending on cause and effect, which may be "esteem'd near or remote, according to the number of connecting causes [ancestors] interpos'd betwixt the persons" (1, 1, 4; 13). As to contiguity and resemblance, in the sentiment felt toward kin, ideas run together with impressions.[5] The conditions for human flourishing include sensibilities informed by people's inclinations and feelings toward others, and moderns would seem to be in a thoroughly recognizable world. Importantly, Hume's general address was to persons as moral agents, where acquaintances and friends are as significant as kin. At one point he writes of the "easy sympathy and correspondent emotions" that preeminently characterize "relation, acquaintance, and resemblance" (2, 2, 4; 229). In part what appears recognizable about this modern world is precisely the kinship in this milieu.

Although Hume refers to specific relationships—fourth cousins, for instance—he was using blood ties to illustrate an abstract quality, namely degrees of intensity in relating (going out of his way to observe that, contrary to common parlance of the day, distance is itself a relation). If we infer that he apprehends bilateral kin reckoning in terms of circles of kin at ever more close or remote degrees of distance, that was, of course, a model Europeans had long encoded in the kinds of rules and sanctions Fortes might have had in mind, such as marriage prohibitions concerning consanguines and affines (see, for example, Goody 1983). What seems modern about this rendering is a particular emphasis given to three interrelated components. First, emanations of sentiment and feeling are not just calibrated to proportions of kinship distance, but also characterize connections of acquaintance and friendship. Hume seems to be evoking a wider, generic sphere of interpersonal relations to which kinship happens to belong. Second, connection itself becomes a calibrator of degree. As he said, whoever is united to one by a connection is loved "proportion'd to the connexion." In this sense a connection in and of itself is sufficient to carry affect, and does not have to be further specified.[6] It is almost as though it had a concrete presence as such. Third, and we return to similarity and dissimilarity, there is an underlying presumption of similarity in the mutual accord implied. Logically speaking, "resemblance" is only one dimension in the connections being made; rhetorically speaking, Hume is bringing that connecting to life through social vignettes of ideas and impressions flourishing in companionable and emotionally positive conversation, just as (in this view) people drawn to associate together find that what they like in one another is not unrelated to the likeness they perceive between themselves.

Hume's narrative thus has an interesting effect. While examples from kinship may make concrete otherwise abstract notions of relations, thinking of kinship simply in terms of a close or distant connection seemingly flattens or generalizes ("abstracts") the connotations that summoning blood ties might otherwise carry. The same effect is true of the term "relation" itself; we are where we have been before (chapter 1), but in a further register. Hume pairs (and sometimes elides) relation and acquaintance. "There is another phaenomenon," he writes (2, 2, 4; 228, emphasis omitted), "viz. that acquaintance, without any kind of relation [that is, 'blood relationship'], [also] gives rise to love and kindness. . . . These two phaenomena of the effects of relation and acquaintance will give mutual light to each other, and may be both explain'd from the same principle."[7] In English, acquaintance—like relation—refers simultaneously to a connection between persons, and to those persons so connected, as when one names one's acquaintances. Once again, generic forms allow attachment of moral regard for others without the terms having to specify the nature of the tie or indicating anything further about the parties' identities.

In this regard, and echoing a similar surmise in chapter 3 apropos consanguines and affines, we could almost say that no ontological difference interposes itself between kinsfolk and acquaintances. It is alongside such an Anglophone possibility that I pursue Carsten's plea to appreciate people's everyday sense of (kin-focused) relationality. The issue was what kind of world makes it necessary to draw this everyday sense to anthropologists' attention. Perhaps the answer lies partly in what did not occur as well as in what did, or in what was made possible by the occlusion of other possibilities. All explanations suggest counterfactuals (Hawthorn 1991), but I am suggesting something specifically detectable in its aftereffects. This is the moment, then, to make good the promise of relating something that never happened. The time would belong to the latter part of the seventeenth century; insofar as that nonevent endures as an aftereffect, we could be witnessing its reverberations today — yet perhaps we already have a glimpse in Hume's writings a mere half century on.

II

Familiar by Degrees

Hume was hardly alone among writers of the Scottish Enlightenment to dwell on the power of the relation in (human) understanding and in (philosophical) narrative, although through his interest in the connection of ideas he seems to have displayed particular scholarly affection for it. Indeed, to a latter-day reader, it is striking how affect-laden some of his terms appear. The language of attraction that had served natural philosophers witnessing the effects of materials upon one another could be equally deployed to indicate the morality of interpersonal sentiment in the formation of human nature. When Hume entitles a chapter section "Of the love of relations," he draws together all the benign principles of association by which people understand familiarity, resemblance or likeness, and the "sympathy, which always arises betwixt similar characters [qualities]": the very conception of such a nexus is *itself* "peculiarly agreeable, and makes us have an affectionate regard for every thing that produces it, when the proper object of kindness and good-will" (2, 2, 4; 229). This is where relations of blood come in, and his remark that the same is true of any relation without exception (see above). The observation continues: "We love our countrymen, our neighbours, those of the same trade . . . [and] [e]very one of these relations is esteem'd some tie, and gives a title to a share of our affection" (2, 2, 4; 228). Whoever are united through a connection, recognizing that connection leads to claim or entitlement.

In the same chapter we read what could almost be Fortes on the need for concretization, except that by "custom" Hume indicates something closer to habituation than convention. The philosopher is discussing what he calls the "double relation" of impression and idea that arises from sheer durability, as found in associating with acquaintances and relations. "For as the company of strangers is agreeable to us for a short time, by enlivening our thought; so the company of our relations and acquaintance must be peculiarly agreeable, because it has this effect in a greater degree, and is of more durable influence" (2, 2, 4; 228, emphasis omitted).[8] He continues: "Custom also, or acquaintance . . . strengthens the conception of any object. . . . And as reasoning and education concur only in producing a lively and strong idea of any object; so is this [durability] the only particular, which is common to relation and acquaintance. This must, therefore, be the influencing quality, by which they produce all their common effects; and love or kindness being one of these effects, it must be from the force and liveliness of conception [idea formation], that the passion is deriv'd" (2, 2, 4; 229).

The language flows between interpersonal relations and a generic sense of relatedness: "Whatever is related to us is conceiv'd in a lively manner by the easy transition from ourselves to the related object" (2, 2, 4; 228–229) could cover either. And, among persons, we are reminded that relations may refer both to those with a common causation in blood ties and to anyone connected through common sentiment. This gives a two-fold intimation of the drama I want to unfold.

On the one hand lies Hume's delineation of nonspecific sentiments, of the kind that had by the 1740s been cultivated for some time in public life and was expressed in societies or consociations formed on the basis of common interests. Hume himself states that "people associate together according to their particular tempers and dispositions, . . . [and may] remark this resemblance between themselves and others" (2, 2, 4; 229). He then draws back into an epistemological observation: for where "they remark the resemblance, it operates after the manner of a relation, by producing a connexion of ideas" (2, 2, 4; 229). Both the ideational formation and the sentiment one has for others are matters of human nature. Displayed here are all the ingredients of that generalized notion of the person whose alliances and affinities are determined by degrees of similarity to and dissimilarity from others.

On the other hand lies the evocation of kinship that had initially provided Hume with a concrete illustration of relations. Compelling one would think for its specificity, it becomes instead swept up in this nonspecific field of generalized human sentiment, with its differentiations attuned to relative closeness and distance. When his discourse on persons' interactions with one another includes talking about kin, it is rarely to introduce an ethics of kinship based on any kind of distinctiveness, let alone attention to particular reckonings of connections.[9] Such distinctiveness is amply evident in other eighteenth-century writings, through genres such as novel or theater, but for this writer it is seemingly off stage. Hume refers to ties between father and son because they afford a good illustration of proximate relations. The particular and potentially thick example is applied with the thinness of a generality, at least insofar as the principal entailment is that fond feelings can be experienced with greater or lesser intensity.

Without making too much of it, we may note that Hume rarely draws on the terms "kin" or "kindred." Yet he would have found in them a description of the kind of human nature he was delineating. Since Anglo-Saxon usage they had long been generics not only for family and blood relations but also for a "natural" group of which an entity or being is a member (a "kind"), or for a class of persons, and thus for persons allied through nature or character. In the sixteenth and seventeenth centuries kindred became a general term for an affinity with respect to resemblance or agreement, as when entities sharing some particular characteristic were described as akin to one another. Such a generic idea would seem to have answered so many of his purposes. Maybe Hume was not thinking of kinship as an arena of relations to be specifically demarcated. Maybe he wanted to avoid specifying the feelings that kinsfolk have toward one another in any way that presupposed kinsmen/women were dissimilar from close acquaintances. Maybe his focus on human nature would have been blurred by the notion of anything qualitatively distinct about interpersonal connections among kinfolk. For where kin ties *were* thought to be qualitatively unique, they posed problems his contemporaries were still concerned to shake off.

To those for whom the European Enlightenment was continuing the liberating process of freeing public life from patronage and patriarchy, and freeing (male) persons from the bondage of family ties, making an address to a publicly lived life beyond the sphere of family matters must have seemed unremarkable.[10] Concomitantly, the inclusion of references to relatives in the passages I have cited would have been equally unremarkable in the circles within which Hume moved. Kinship conventions entertained a certain understanding of personal ties, which at once valued a generalized or public sympathy for others, and classed diverse relatives (kinsfolk) through their connections in terms of consociation, social recognition, and permitted or desired familiarity. That said, at certain moments Hume's thought experiments delve more concretely into specifics. Comparing what happens to a relation between child and parent, according to whether it is the father or the mother who marries for a second time, is thus used to illustrate how the reciprocal flow of relations between objects may or may not be affected by their independent relations with third parties (2, 2, 5; 230–231). Yet he seemingly has no use for notions of kin or kindred as a distinct focus of attention. Although sometimes qualified by "blood," and he also talks of "ties of blood," he widely draws on that more diffuse generic, "relations."

However, insofar as Hume's writings betray the reverberations of a drama, then they are also a curtain opener for a scene already enacted. The script had been written fifty years before, and we have already been spectators ourselves, early on in this book.

What Never Happened

To the extent that Hume's work was building (by no means without criticism) on that of Locke, let me treat the latter as a predecessor. It is at this door that I wish to lay what never happened.

Locke's discussion of what he called personal identity sets the scene.[11] The reader will recall that he brings this concept to the imagination through delimiting other identities: thus the self is determined not by the identity of substance but by that of consciousness, "whereby I am my self to my self" (1690: 2, 27, 24; 345). As with Hume, Locke's "person" or self is one who reflects on its own being.[12] We also saw that this being could not be constituted more differently from that of the individual organism, the "man" (human being) whose continuing identity inheres in its life. One of Locke's examples was the oak tree: "An oak, growing from a plant to a great tree, and then lopp'd, is still the same oak" (1690: 2, 27, 3; 330). The tree changes in substance over time, yet through the continuity of its life remains the same tree. Like plants, like animals. As far as fixing their identity applies, a person is thus differentiated from all kinds of organisms (plants, animals, man). It is worth repeating his observation that although in ordinary parlance person and man stand for the same thing, his (philosophical) inquiry into the matter has revealed something otherwise. Distinct foundations for identity distinguish man from person.

Here is the jolt! Today's reader is drawn into the discussion about personal identity and living organisms without noticing that there is not a single reference to kinship. Taking this discussion alone, I doubt the thought would even arise. Yet kinship is present elsewhere in the same work, and that prompts attention to the absence.[13] Locke drew in kin ties in order to make visible an otherwise abstract conception of relations; when it came to selves or human beings, his attention appears to have been elsewhere.

The counterfactual question is whether Locke, and contemporary and subsequent debate, could have taken his understanding in different directions had he presented these entities—selves (persons) or human beings (man)—as kin, their effects on one another inevitably implied. For this attribute of kinship could have been the imaginative link, the train of association, that brought relations to mind. Thus the thinking self might have summoned a multiplicity of such selves in dialogue with others. Conversely, if understanding relations is not intrinsic to the dual concepts of person or man, are we to conclude that kinship, being entwined with questions about relations as it is, finds itself irrelevant to these formulations of identity, too? As it stands, determinations of the nature of personal or organic identity could take place without any figuration of relations. We do not have to decide if it was a matter of oversight or omission or whatever might have implied an anterior idea of it. It is simply what did not happen.

Of course, I am being theatrical. Our program notes might say that Locke never intended relations generally to carry the kind of interpersonal or intersubjective dimensions that seemingly creep into his illustrations, and that anyway—in his chapter on identity and diversity—exposition is specifically addressed to how ideas are formed. Attention might then be drawn to another actor. For any premonition of such relations is upstaged, preempted, by a relation already present: it is embedded in his initial concept. Locke's (1690: 2, 27, 1; 328) starting point is that, philosophically speaking, identity is itself a relation, springing from comparing a being or entity as it exists in any particular time or place with respect to its enduring self.[14] The figure seemingly leaves no room for other relations to appear. If anything this underlines the unfolding plot. It points to what did happen.[15]

Now although Locke's *Essay* introduced kinship (among other examples) to concretize what can be inferred about relations, we have seen that human beings and persons are concretized through life and consciousness. These constellations of ideas do not touch each other—separate argumentative treatment, separate subject matter. Other kinds of relations appear extrinsic to the self; the self as such is defined through a specific relation of identity bridging aspects (of the one self) otherwise distinct from one another.

Recall that the general act of relating rests on an intervening comparison consisting of an external link between prior terms. To recover Locke's words from the introduction: "There must always be in relation two ideas, or things, either in themselves really separate, or considered as distinct, and then a ground or occasion for their comparison" (1690: 2, 25, 6; 321). What he puts in an epistemic register could equally be rehearsed in an interpersonal one.[16] Descombes ([1996] 2014: 213) observes of Locke's illustration of a conjugal relation, that "this relation amounts to a comparison that the mind makes between two individuals . . . [whose] relation is thus exterior to their reality as individuals." Let us pause on the notion of exteriority. For Locke, it is principally that the intellectual act of comparison deploys relations extraneous to what is being compared.[17] To the latter-day reader relations may well seem "extraneous" in another sense, that is, rendered irrelevant to certain subject matters. I wrote of relations appearing extrinsic to the self; if Locke's comparisons are always superadded to preexisting entities, exposition directed to elucidating the essence of a subject do not have to engage them. Then there is some of the evidence he uses. In the conjugal example, Locke is drawing on a well-established trope for relative terms, namely, "when I give Caius the name husband I intimate some other person" (1690: 2, 25, 1; 318).[18] The same correlative was often used to show the kind of relation whose terms (here Caius and Sempronia) are unaffected by the addition or subtraction (the image is mine) of relation. By precisely the same token, and to opposite effect our reader might observe, the very social relation established through marriage (or conversely dissolved) is being presented as though it were indeed like an addition to or subtraction from the person.[19] Caius the husband is not (just) Caius. Husband and wife, Locke says, seem so nearly to belong to one another. This can also entail a perception of exteriority, but relations now appear as attachments to the person — and, indeed, as dispensable or not. And here the curtain suddenly goes up on another tableau.

Or, rather, it goes up on an earlier speculation. I suggested that rendering relations "external" both to the self-conscious person and to the individual organic being models a particular kind of kinship-thinking apparently emerging in Locke's time. To return to the sketch in chapter 1, Sabean and Teuscher had argued that what was to take off in the eighteenth century, and across Europe at large, albeit in fits and starts and thus often coexisting with the old, were new apprehensions of familial ties and alliances. Early modern "structures stressing descent, inheritance, and succession, patrilines, agnatic lineages, and clans, paternal authority, house discipline, and exogamy gradually gave way to patterns centered around alliance, sentiment, interlocking networks of kindred, and social and familial endogamy" (2007: 16). It was possible for the concrete image of a lineal entity with (external) relations attached to morph into that of a family (now meaning conjugal family) looking outward to (cultivated, class-laden) "connections" that could also be enfolded within. In this sense, what did happen was, of course, already happening.

Our program notes might also say that insofar as he was following expositional conventions of the time there was nothing unusual about Locke's usages. But that is exactly why one does not otherwise notice anything. While the writings of Locke — along with Hume — were but moments in a cascade, the preeminence they have been given in defining modern thought (English-speaking), not to speak of their considerable popularity for subsequent generations, gives edge to this drama of expository possibilities.[20] They provided their innumerable readers with an enduring framework for pondering certain questions. Together they show us something that did not occur, a link never made and, whether unremarked or avoided, a certain dissociation of ideas about persons and relations. If selfhood is to be apprehended in consciousness, just as life has its own continuity, each points to itself and their consequent identity gives each a sense of concreteness. It is relations that can come to appear abstract, insofar as they have to be the subject of intellectual work to be visible at all; in such a line of thought, relations become an observer's inferences.[21] What was it Firth said? The more one thinks of a society in abstract terms, the more it is necessary to summon the idea of social organization as concrete activity, for him one that points to itself through people's organizational actions.

And what was it that Fortes said? That relations have to be bodied forth. How interesting that when, decades after Locke's essay, Hume gives his own sense of concreteness to epistemic relations it is specifically through summoning generic qualities of association, including the familiarity of resemblance that operates in the very act of making connections. In his account, relations acquire a kind of animation, not to speak of abundancy in the "easy transition of ideas." Indeed the concreteness that relating itself seemingly comes to bear is one reason for his particular illumination of the notion of identity. He evokes a familiar image, but uses it to make a distinctive point. "An oak, that grows from a small plant to a large tree, is still the same oak; tho' there be not one particle of matter, or figure of its parts the same"; for the tree is held together by the relation perceived between its different moments, "so strong a relation" that despite total change "we still attribute identity to [it]" (1, 4, 6; 168). In other words, it is the — mindful — facility to relate that gives rise to *illusions* ("attributions") of continuity or identity.[22] The illusion is a direct register of the force of the relation. Needless to add, happy in dispensing with a coherent sense of his own person, Hume's skeptical discussion of selfhood has nothing to do with interpersonal relations, let alone kinship.

III

Interchangeability

The aftereffects of what never happened may have been quite profound for latter-day formulations of individual and society. Questions about the identity of persons or human beings separate from questions about relations: we could see much of twentieth-century Anglophone social-critical thought as making up for what seemed a relational deficit in vernacular understandings of the self-contained individual.[23] And if indeed kinship, being entwined with questions about relations, finds itself extraneous to these understandings, too, this has surely bedeviled English-language attempts to get to grips with some of the materials with which anthropologists (in particular, not exclusively) deal. The appeal to remember everyday relationality is part of anthropology's intermittent resistance, at times even insisting on the significance of kin relations as though this were a disciplinary vision making up for a deficit from other quarters. Within anthropology, too, failure to pay attention to kinship relations in discussions of self and personal identity renders invisible the kind of intersubjective self-creation that, for example, Toren's (1990, 2009) theorizing of personal ontogeny has consistently had to bring to her colleagues' notice.

Nonetheless, the other side of what did not happen is what did: the character of the (kins)person in the making. In the milieu to which the Scottish Enlightenment addressed itself, people could talk about kinship in a way (it was not the only way) indistinguishable from general observations of human nature. When the focus was on the quality of sentiment, persons were seemingly interchangeable with one another, a classic attribute of impersonal relations — an engagement of selves otherwise separate from their diverse, distinctive relationships.[24] Someone whose identity is secured through consciousness has relations aplenty, not least in the manner of an external world internalized as objects of thought. Such relations can become a source of intense ethical reflection, as Hume's writings make abundantly clear, and from this emerges the particular kind of moral person that Hoskin has described (chapter 3). It is one who reaches outward toward others, whoever they are, they being undifferentiated among themselves apart from the discrimination implied in recognizing others like oneself.[25] Recall the concomitant nexus of concepts: degrees of similarity and dissimilarity indicate closeness and distance, such that similarity shows itself as the basis of solidarity and common feeling while dissimilarity leads to strangeness and estrangement.

We might find other Enlightenment dramas, then, in what happens to impersonal relations. Bureaucracy is one of many locations where the same plot could be restaged, albeit with concerns other than the workings of the mind, given that it has become an iconic field of normative "indifference."[26] I take a cue from a twenty-first-century reenactment of the contrast between man (human being) and person, as it is found in the international legal and bioethical literature on organ transplantation. Its concerns appear split between the functioning body as a "biomedical whole-parts aggregate" and "the thinking, reflexive person" whose autonomy is important in consent protocols (Jacob 2012: 160). The drama is in who has to be brought onstage in order to make the accompanying bureaucratic process work. There could not be a clearer revelation of everyday relationality, and people's expressed need to attend to what they perceive as insufficiently relational.

For many years—things have changed somewhat since then—much work was needed to put to one side the social (including kinship) origins of bodily organs; as healthy, usable body parts, their origins were reascribed to the technologies and practices of professional expertise. Medically speaking, the interchangeability of organs was crucial to the whole enterprise.[27] In Canada and the United States, as well as Europe, it was imperative for medical suitability to be considered separately from whatever other connotations an organ may have carried (Waldby and Mitchell 2006).[28] In deceased donations, for instance, it was regarded as essential to the physical and mental health of patients that their thoughts did not dwell on the dead donor. The surprise has been the extent to which many relatives of organ donors and recipients react to the anonymity of transplant protocols. For some, the keeping of social origins matters a great deal, so that the material of the bodily organ becomes connective tissue. Among the kinds of equations these practices generate are those that seize on the connection; it is a move that reverses—or rather reverts to the vernacular—those possibilities for strangerhood described in chapter 2. So what is always true of nonanonymous, living donations between relatives or friends can be extended to embrace strangers in deceased donations (e.g., Kaufman et al. 2009; Sharp 2006). Imagining part of their departed relative continuing to live in another person has led to instances where deceased donors' kinsfolk have gone to great effort to identify the recipient, while families of both donors and recipients report feeling that their bond creates a connection. Whether or not these new bonds are regarded as substitutes for the "real thing," one kind of relation is replacing another. In short, we could say that these families are restoring something of the relational context that had been excised in the process of organ extraction.

Unanticipated as this was by early advocates of transplant surgery, the restored "kinship" rests on a familiar notion of ties being carried by biological substance, generating a disposition of care to promote mutual well-being. Interpersonal, if not personal, intimacy is valued. In other situations, value may be placed on the impersonal, as a sociolegal scholar undertaking ethnographic research has found (Jacob 2012). Those twin views of the biomedical aggregate and the autonomous person between them neglect an important actor. This is a subject—donor or recipient—of transplant procedure, the documented person who has to be imagined relationally. According to Jacob's exposition, a documented person is what certain bureaucratic processes demand.

Suppose, instead of the families of organ donors and recipients making up a social deficit, donors and recipients invent families for themselves. Against a backcloth of international medical protocols, this is the drama Jacob describes for living organ donations. The inventors are Israelis seeking access to kidney transplant agencies prepared to match potential recipients with willing donors. The script is an ethnographic window on practices and assumptions about to change, for the study was done just before new Israeli legislation made various forms of payment for organs illegal. With payment still in the picture, the then-professional consensus was that organ donations were acceptable on grounds of altruism only; certification of donations therefore required considerable legal and bureaucratic oversight. A matched pair could qualify as ethically suitable if the donation were shown to be between kin. After all, between kin lay "the naturalness of family duty and altruism" (Jacob 2012: 83). Once biological compatibility was established, the potential donor and recipient would together present their case to various committees, including an account of how they were related. As a matchmaking intermediary described it, "We sit together, we talk, we try to find a story, make a connection. . . . We invent a story, a cousin, an uncle, etc. . . . from nothing" (69). Kinship before the transplant, rather than after; although built up from some of the realities of the pair's lives, this kind of relation was not expected to endure beyond a need for the requisite paperwork.

The naturalness of family duty and altruism was an assumption on the part of the transplant regulators; they thought that kinship connections produced a propensity to donate and receive organs. However, distinctive of Israeli procedures at this time was a bureaucratic discourse on kinship.[29] Pretransplant kinship was not just the creation of the pair and their intermediaries but of the whole administrative process that controlled transplant procedures. "Kinship can evolve as a tool: for example, if the concept of kin may be played with tactically by the welfare state and its bureaucrats as a tool to allocate (or not) benefits, it can surely be maneuvered, in response, by people who wish to adapt to the state's definitions of kinship. Kinship can thus have a distinct bureaucratic and legal existence" (Jacob 2012: 6). Transplant relatedness emerges from this analysis as a set of scripts privileged by administrative apparatus. Such relatedness has its own character as a contingent kinship that exists on an ad hoc, instrumentalized basis for a specific purpose with limited temporality. At the same time, Jacob insists, this kin relation is not a substitute for the "real thing" (65).[30] It in itself evinces and enacts kinship values. "What gets to be performed before the committee," she writes (81), "is essentially the relation itself." The narratives give it uniqueness and specificity; the suitability of the transplant becomes persuasive by its idiosyncratic relation to the persons seeking approval. We can add that the documented relations between donor and recipient remain "impersonal" — there is no other depth to their involvement with each other, and on either side the actors are interchangeable with others but for the contract between them. The relational deficit (my phrase) that the transplant professionals imagine, in requiring altruism be made manifest, disappears when the parties become noninterchangeable through their (qualitatively) unique relationship. The parties oblige by narratives of engagement, and creating kinship is the means.

If there is indeed a perceived deficit, it is not simply "found" in circumstances such as this, but is also part of a framework for critical appraisal, in Jacob's case of the global literature on transplantation. This shines equally through an account of certain antecedents to industrial interchangeability, which was to become the very mark of the impersonal. Tsing's epithet for qualitatively unique relationships is that they are nonscalable. Hers is a proto-Enlightenment plot.

Scalability points to processes, typical of industrial production, that allow infinite expansion in the size of activities without transforming their object or product. Such scalability, Tsing says (2012: 507), "is not an ordinary feature of nature," and making projects scalable requires work, including work that extracts projects from relationships seemingly beyond their design. "Ordinarily, things that expand change as they take on new materials and relationships . . . [so why] have people called expansion 'growth' as if it were a biological process?" (506, sentences transposed). Her concern is the historical moment that made expansion seem an inevitable adjunct of human development. Her neologism is "nonscalability" — it is time, she says, to have a theory of it. Inventing the negative is not meant to introduce a normative evaluation but rather to render the scalable specific to certain enterprises and thus to denaturalize its inevitability. What is interesting is the role she gives to relations, for the critical thrust of her argument is to point to their inherent nonscalability. Her view bears comparison with that of Rabinow (introductions): "Because relationships are encounters across difference, they have a quality of indeterminacy. Relationships are transformative, and one is not sure of the outcome" (510). Such theorization could not itself proceed without relational finesse, that is, putting concepts in the company of one another.

Tsing (2012) takes us back before Locke and Hume. Scalability (the concept, not the term) came into being with European colonial plantations between the fifteenth and seventeenth centuries, including the sugar plantations of the Caribbean. The success of sugar production lay in planters experimenting with types of cane and soil in order to facilitate the interchangeability of forms;

the varieties of sugarcane propagated were genetic isolates without interspecies ties, that is, with "no history of either companion species or disease relations" (511); the "same" crop could be grown anywhere suitable. To do this, "one must create *terra nullius*, nature without entangling claims" (513, original italics). If this meant rendering the landscape uniform for a uniform crop, it also meant erasing the land's social features, the claims, demons, ownerships (Harvey and Knox 2010) of those already there. Thus, too, were the cane workers encompassed. "As cane workers in the New World, enslaved Africans had great advantage from the growers' perspective: slaves had no local social relations and thus no easy place to run. Like the cane itself, they had been transplanted; and now they were isolated. They were on their way to becoming self-contained" (Tsing 2012: 512). Ingenious, indeed, this new era of expansion without transformation. It reinforced, thus laying new grounds for, the notion of pluralism as an amassing of units (see Mol 2002).[31] Future factories were to model themselves on the early plantations. As with sugar cane, so with organs: expansionists need accurate specifications of the transplant's identity for its embedding to succeed.

Doubled by their own relational interventions, both writers appear to be remedying a relational deficit. The deficit is created by the value being placed on interchangeability, one that also applies to the impersonal. As an inventive twist on the interchangeability of organs and attempts to meet demand by increasing supply (making them scalable), Jacob pinpoints the moment at which transplant partners are relationally reconceived in bureaucratic kinship. As far as the supposedly self-contained cane workers are concerned, there is nothing to be taken for granted; Tsing observes that they are specifically defined through jobs rendered interchangeable by the time frame of milling engineered into the cane. These materials speak of circumstances familiar to moderns and naturalists.

Metamorphosis

Circumstances could have been different. Indeed, in crucial respects they *were* different for those who followed lines of European philosophizing that took the interpenetration of phenomena for granted. For some of them no doubt, the very notion of a relational deficit, the need to re-embed phenomena (wrenched from context) within their constitutive relations, would have seemed bizarre. The conclusion returns briefly to this alter-lineage. In the meanwhile, I extrapolate from an illustration to hand. It is my initial counterfactual, this time referring to something that happened, although I do not trace what future lives it may already have had.[32] Merian's own concept of metamorphosis must be counted as part of the then-contemporary interest in identity.

The sources of the Scottish Enlightenment have been called as much Dutch as English, and it was the naturalists and collectors of Amsterdam who welcomed Merian's return from her investigative travels. Hers was an era of amassing and recording specimens of natural history, harbingers for later interest in human curiosities. The most notable English collector of the time placed Merian's two volumes on Suriname where visitors could look through them, at the top of the stairs in Montagu House, predecessor of the British Museum (Sloan 2003: 19). Like her earlier investigations, these resonated with other endeavors. Just as philosophers of the day tried to make causal chains out of ideas, and worried (or did not worry) about identity and the continuity (or otherwise) of substance, so, too, the lives of caterpillars, pupae, and moths. To see what we now easily call their life-stages, she had to depict the causal chain that made these creatures part of a self-same being. Davis comments on the role of the event in Merian's vision. The illustrations were based on observation, and observations were verifiable insofar as they were encoded in occurrences recorded at geographic locales or periods of the year. Conversely, putting temporally distinct moments together, her pictorial recording of larvae feeding, or a bush in flower, made an event of each observational moment. I labor the point in that one historian (Dear 2001: 139; cf. Shapin 1994: 197) of the scientific revolution emphasizes the event in the new styles of reporting adopted by the Royal Society, a genre whose purpose was to narrate an occurrence located in place and time. Yet let us look again, and consider what else Merian was putting together on one page.

An illustration of the life cycle of a (Surinamese) frog certainly brings several events together.[33] It depicts a frog releasing eggs, tadpoles at diverse stages, and the plants on which they lie or under which they shelter in a watery environment; the plants attract insects and the frog's dinner is painted in one corner. This is an image of species interdependence. However, what is striking, in a thoroughly conventional way, is that if you look at each of the animals you see quite distinct forms; elsewhere she draws the different-looking stages of plants as well. The distinct forms thus "related" by the unfolding of life are possible intimations of development, progress, and the discrimination into lower and higher forms of life that other schemas of classification were to bring. That aside, I draw out an altogether more simple point. As plain as could be, Merian shows that resemblance and similarity are not the only markers of intimate relationships. Quite radically different forms can metamorphose into one another.

So very close are Locke's and Hume's oak trees, which show how (continuity of) identity subsists in (the continuity of) the same life. Yet the echoes with Merian's demonstration of the life cycle thereafter dissipate. It was the nonobviousness of organic or personal identity on which Locke and Hume dwelled. It was not something one observed without specifying the relation between each moment of existence (although to make relations the focus in the way Hume did was to throw doubt onto the phenomenon). With an organism, their emphasis was on being able to account for an apparent sameness over its life span *regardless* of its growth (in Tsing's sense), that is, regardless of its changes in matter or substance, and thus of the material form in which it exists. It is precisely those material forms that Merian's pictures thrust before the viewer.

In the case of frogs and butterflies, present-day familiarity with the idea of metamorphosis, and the commonness of her examples, may make it hard to see Merian's innovation. At the same time, it would be an anachronism to take her juxtapositions of distinct forms as pointing to the kinds of relations of alterity on which some of today's anthropologists ponder in certain kinship calculations or regimes of knowledge. Nonetheless, her illustrations draw attention to unlikely manifestations of life. In the world of her fellow naturalists, this was the time when comparative and other classificatory principles were being formalized with respect to similarity and dissimilarity.[34] If the relations she drew between these life forms were startling then, startling to a latter-day eye is the realization that a premise about degrees of similarity would be supremely inadequate for understanding them. You could not infer the relations between these forms on the grounds of the likeness and unlikeness of their attributes. Merian offers an alternative source of illumination, inviting a sidelong glance at this particular premise.

6. KINSHIP UNBOUND

It was for a long time put down to the ethnocentric vision of early European settlers in Australia that they could only see the appearance of the countryside, where trees often grew without underbrush, as park-like. Their drawings and descriptions seemed images brought from home. Yet if woodland and grassland had been deliberately managed by controlled firing, encouraging new shoots in order to attract game, the cultured resonances of the park were perhaps indicating something not otherwise visible. As a historian, Gammage (2011) has reconstructed areas of the ancient Australian landscape that now appear as no less than elements of a vast managed estate.[1] His evidence includes diverse traces borne by still-standing trees, their present-day shape formed in response to no-longer-present neighbors or to now-absent open land. Extant vegetation becomes an outline of, something peripheral to, what had once been. Aboriginal land as a continuous estate was simply too big for European settlers to visualize.

A relational deficit, an association of concepts that did not happen, something missing: this is like contouring a space left by relations no longer present. Where the missing bit is seen in kinship terms, a relational remedy may well summon recognizably Euro-American notions of families and relatives. On another scale, the "obscurity of kinship in modernity" (Lambek 2013b: 244) paraphrases an occlusion of relational thinking also remarked on by critics of Anglophone thought. The early modern "thinning" of specific designations of kin by the generic, relation, seems to belong here. At the same time, everything we read in Hume suggests that relations themselves do not just acquire something of an independent presence but become animated through their countless associations, and that rather than too few there might be too many (after Green 2005). Here, in open view, that English designation of kin actually "thickens" the concept of relation.[2] I wonder if this strabismic optic does not show what it is to be at once in and out of sight.

The references to something that might have been present are partly tongue in cheek. As McKinnon (2013) reminds us, the idea that kinship belongs to some prior stage of development or to some primordial condition is intrinsic to the well-known story of modernization, also rehearsed in the supposition that enactments of kinship were much more prevalent in the past than now.[3] Yet in Gammage's tale of ancient woodlands, told from today's present, it was the settlers of the time who did not see the landscape before them for what it was. The missing-kinship puzzle is an odd kind of nostalgia (Battaglia 1995). Perhaps those references are also about contemporary oscillations in the visibility of kinship.

For there is a further puzzle, which is the oft-remarked obscuring of kin relations that occurred in anthropological exposition in the latter part of the twentieth century. The puzzle in English-speaking anthropology was the shrinking of kin connections as a matter of theoretical significance, regardless of the apparent truncation of certain familial relations.[4] That theoretical shrinkage subsequently stimulated an energetic counterresponse. Those North American families who once had to struggle to put transplant donations in a relational context today find themselves in a much more normative position, an analogy for the anthropological place of kinship studies in the twenty-first century. Topics once shorn of any kinship dimension have seemingly recovered it, and burgeoning discussion finds kin relations — previously unseen — now rooted in and growing in all kinds of locales.[5] That said, we might ask what anthropologists these days are making visible as "kinship."

And is there something it is still difficult to see? Are we looking at a kinship that does not look like kinship? Did it become too big to be visible? Perhaps we can take the response to what I have dubbed Carsten's question in another direction.

|

An Immodest Proposition

Suppose there were a blockage, at once vernacular and anthropological, to seeing the very scope of Euro-American kinship because a great chunk of it is called by another name. This is my proposition for friendship. (Why the epithet Euro-American must remain until the conclusion.) The proposition is developed via two expositional routes.

There are many ways of imagining kinship/friendship. The first route brings us to something of a vernacular sense of what keeps, or fails to keep, the pair in orbit round each other. The second, signaling social science discourse and a view that takes the concept of society as its reference point, shows — under different exercises of social construction — how the one may eclipse the other. The expositions are spelled out in the following section through materials that are in time both before and after what we have learned from the previous chapter, and especially from Hume. A preliminary run (of the two routes) is given in the rest of this section, a nod of sorts toward how these issues have played out in the more recent past.

The first begins with those early twenty-first-century figures, Facebook's "friends." The alluring immediacy that some people may always have found in the notion of personal relations is reinforced through a positive equation between being friends and the accessibility afforded by online communication. Such friends are not just compared with nonfriends. In an era of Facebook, and irrespective of friending's often impersonal connotations, Miller (2017) observes that people the world over make comparisons between friendship and kinship. Where once friends might be drawn into a kind of fictive kinship, Facebook's friending terminology subsumes kin under friends, a kind of fictive friendship he suggests. It rests on a crucial tension. As their great-grandparents and grandparents did (we heard them in chapter 2), the English talk today, though they are now also talking in a global idiom, of the contrast between being able to choose your friends but not your kin.[6]

Miller points to a divergence between anthropological and vernacular usage. While "contemporary anthropologists prefer to regard both kinship and friendship as part and parcel of a much more general anthropology of relationality" (2017: 380), the vernacular contrast works as an ideology, emphasizing an opposition between obligation on the one hand and an idealization of intimacy, authenticity, and liberal choice on the other. In retrospect it seems inevitable that when children's use of Facebook is burdened by parental insistence that they stay in contact with relatives that way, the overworking of relations frequently puts them off. A comparative view of social media indicates (Miller 2016; Miller et al. 2016) that it is the ideology that feeds Facebook rather than simply the other way round. The discernibly distinct ideological dimensions of kinship on the one hand and friendship on the other are found across very diverse vernacular locations; yet the contrast is invariably loaded by the ascriptions of modernity that people give to new forms of friending. A study of an English village surprised Miller in this regard, by both the reach of such usage and its ready acceptance among older people.

In turn, homegrown contrasts receive fresh impetus; it is the repeated distinctions, like so many fractal iterations, that help drive the adoption of friend as an idiom for kin (as in parenting and grandparenting relationships). Miller's own argument, that kinship and friendship are "ideological tropes that stand as idioms for much wider values" (2017: 381), ranges over a field of concepts engaging a tension recognizably Euro-American, writ large in terms of constraint and liberty, society and individual, duty and affect. To adopt Robbins's (2016: 774) language, when such ideas are turned into values (both the concepts and the antithesis between them) an anthropologist might consider them holding a transcendent place in people's thinking. Although Robbins's concern is religious configurations, through which people reveal to themselves what is not ordinarily accessible, there is also much about the everyday that is not ordinarily accessible.[7] Where everyday distinctions between kin and friends are also axes of a cosmological order, each needs to keep circling round the other.[8] Indeed, the pairing (the relation) of kinship and friendship, and of the values invested in them, brings to mind the personified dynamic of the Iatmul elder brother/younger brother duo: the one oriented toward or "becoming" the other already contains the other thereby. Such a dynamic would inform enactments of friendship and kinship as much as their idealization. Miller shows that, as they are worked out ("in practice"), friendship operates far from the ideal of voluntarism while, far from being dispatched as oppressive, kinship may be realigned to contemporary ideals of authenticity. Finally, in the way in which the idioms are organized, their analogical work (including what is recognized as "metaphorical") — kinship as friendship, friendship as kinship — keeps the two sets of values that he identified in orbit or in tandem, that is, in relational tension with each other. Related thus, the value distinctions may conversely keep kinship/friendship in tandem.[9]

Anthropological and sociological exposition, the second route, turns on the prominence accorded to particular constructs. Thus the theoretical linking of friendship and kinship, as Schwimmer proposed, can be flatly abjured as a conceptual possibility; from historical sociology, Silver (1989: 279n) at once notes Schwimmer's anthropological argument and nonetheless insists that friendship and kinship are "utterly distinct." Indeed. (The next section relates a stand-off within anthropology.) Initially sketched here is the perspective implied in such controversy, namely the perspective from society, and who speaks for it.

Think what happens when "kinship," detached so to speak from its invisible pair friendship, is hitched to "society," and society is studied as social structure. One result is a terrain of the kind created by British social anthropology — though not by it alone — in its discovery and invention of kinship systems across the world. There was, as seemed apt of so many places, an overwhelmingly societal (structural) dimension to kinship that could not be replicated in northern Europe or America. This expansion and contraction of kinship space clearly rested on the expositional position that the concept of society held in social science theory. The inevitable followed. In twentieth-century theorizing, social structure subsumed kinship; a simultaneous orientation to the polities and cosmologies of diverse other places peripheralized interest in Euro-American kinship as such. To be brutal about the latter, where was its societal or structural dimension? Society's transcendental place in the theorizing of the time seems only emphasized by the way English speakers tend to treat kinship as a matter of personal relations, and such relations appear mundane. Hence kinship scaled with reference to underlying or overarching structural concepts, such as "state" or "economy," diminishes understandings focused on families and their relatives. This is precisely the vision that the anthropological study of kinship over the last thirty years has done much to challenge, whether attending to governmentality, intercontinental networks, or the science of substance, or to the values given to blood, intimacy, regeneration, and so forth. In this regard, I subsequently turn to some of the contributions to *Vital relations* edited by McKinnon and Cannell (2013b); they encourage one to think further about what counts (in Euro-American) as transcendental.

Now anthropology never quite hitched friendship to society in the same way (hence the equivocations of chapter 2). As far as Euro-American sociality was concerned, society might eclipse kinship, but far from friendship being doubly eclipsed it seems to have been with sighs of relief that various writers felt they could slip out from under the restrictions of social structure altogether. Interpersonal relations had their own (social) reality. Boissevain (1974: 4) was explicit: the networks of shifting alliances, cliques, factions, and coalitions that turn on interpersonal relationships, as they impressed themselves on him in Sicily, "are the basic stuff of social life. Nevertheless I found it difficult and often impossible to reconcile these observations and experiences with the model of society which . . . I had been trained to employ." And for many anthropologists that absence fed into the way in which the one (kinship/friendship) might trivialize the other (friendship/kinship). The distinction was construed alongside an expectation of a structuring framework, and the framework became the reference point for evaluation and thus of discerning or deciding what was or was not of "societal" dimension. This was an enduring issue in theorizing kinship and friendship together. At its extreme, it was as though they could not be part of the same social field.

But from what perspective is anything laid out as a field? Suppose there were social forms of networks that were *self*-occluding. The very figure of a network could be tracing the spread of a relational field only part of which appears fully visible at any one time. Such a partiality appears in Riles's (2000) study of activist networks mobilized for meeting global goals. Relating persons, organizations, and action plans, frequently concretized in the form of lines linking points, makes visible what they called networking. Their personal relations are generally taken as quite distinct, belonging in effect to a domain on their own. Yet, as they are worked through, the manner in which activists' networks both do and do not overlap with activists' spheres of personal relations leads Riles to the perception that networks and personal relationships are the same form seen twice. She elucidates just how this "figure that, seen twice, appears to turn inside out and thus to generate a sense of reality or dimensionality, [so that] each serves as the inside or outside of the other" (69). Personal identities "outside" networking become from that viewpoint superficial, just as network relations "outside" personal linkages appear to be obsessed with protocol. If friendship and kinship might also be seen as inside and outside each other, perhaps we should look to the similarly trivializing and thus occluding effect that either may in fact have on the other. In this glimpse into what is not otherwise seen, the inside-out of Riles's networks is internal to the pair; the theoretical move allows one to imagine kinship and friendship as versions of each other. It is as though either alone exists in an apparently half-specified, half-visible, and thus incomplete state. Yet insofar as each gestures toward the contours of the other, perhaps each intimates the other as its own missing side.

Taking this double route to imagining the paired life of kinship/friendship, too large to see as it is, has also left much behind. The same expositional strategy can be amplified through two sets of historical materials. I shall keep close to the modes in which relations are being described; the hope is that by keeping close we may yet see more than immediately appears in them.

II

Vernacular Vehicles

Attending to the seventeenth century at large, a specialist in English literature considers the recurrent analogy between family and state, at a time when "analogy was a fundamental early modern form of reasoning" (Ng 2007: 13).[10] She relegates Locke to an epilogue on its eighteenth-century afterlife. Familial metaphor might be the language of political debate, yet insofar as the early modern family "did not conform to a single model, the family metaphor in the period did not have a single meaning" (12). It proved a powerful resource for contemporary criticism, and was itself criticized, metaphorical usage as a figure of speech being subject to the scrutiny of rhetoricians.[11] Metaphor was defined as an application of one thing to something it does not "naturally" or "literally" denote (hence the possibility of regarding such a conjoining as "only a metaphor").[12] I use what was regarded as a vehicle for conveying ideas as a vehicle for myself: a vernacular English metaphor for one of the ways in which friendship/kinship keeps other values in relational tension, and keeps itself thus.

Seventeenth-century descriptions of metaphors were one thing, their usage another; if ideas can be carried back and forth, then a metaphor could go both ways. Nonetheless it is historically significant that it was the family that seems to have been the primary metaphorical vehicle, for in the end it was the familial side of the equation that was to drop from sight. In brief, the family (including household, marital, and diverse kin relations) variously offered models of political life, monarchy, government, management, commonwealth, and so forth, addressing thereby certain orderings of people's relations: the nature of people's care for one another in relation to the embodiment of authority and power in a figurehead. Ng's argument is that so much was encompassed by the kinship configuration that it underpinned a sprawling and constantly changing arena of debate, one in which (I add) diverse values could be aligned and realigned. Metaphors from family relations often led to contradictory claims. Because of all the issues that might be drawn from them, they formed the ground for multiple communities of discourse with varied and opposing points of view. Familial idioms provided ammunition as much for ideas of fraternity between equals as they did for defense of kingly patriarchy, and if marriage evoked union it also evoked adultery (as Milton spoke of the church's relations with the state, that is, with the world rather than with God). Yet the apparent persistence of the basic analogical relation meant it could answer almost any deployment of the values being questioned, while keeping those issues of government, authority, and well-being in relational tension.

Disputatious use of figurative language, a source of illumination and betrayal alike, had long generated its own arguments among experts on rhetoric (Dawson 2007: 68). Sixteenth-century tract writers, including those addressing themselves to the condition of marriage and household government and, through pursuing diverse allegories, the condition of the church, were using a language that was indeed open to criticism. An understanding that scripture conveyed figurative meanings was explicit in Puritan tracts. One such writer (William Gouge) talked of words having both "a literall and a mysticall sense," as in the biblical passage stating that man and wife are one flesh; the mystical union of Christ and church is summoned to show how closely man and wife are bound (Ray 2002: 27).[13] Objection was also made that words were unlike the entities to which they were being applied. Concern about the "ornaments" and "abuses" of language, in the opinion of the rhetorician George Puttenham, came from the "doublenesse" of figures of speech. "For what else is your Metaphor but an inversion of sense of transport?," he declaims; the meaning of one word put upon another is "a kinde of wresting of single words from his owne right signification, to another not so naturall, but yet of some affinitie or convenience with it" (quoted in 2002: 17). With the vehicle regarded thus, in the end what was used metaphorically could be replaced by other metaphors.

If the basic analogy took the form of a correspondence between terms in which family was the vehicle, it is clear that seventeenth-century arguments about the state also led to reflections *on* family ties. Probing into such ties, people could take opponents to task for misreading or exceeding the proper application of examples. Hence Ng cites Mary Astell's *Reflections upon marriage* (and see Mack 1992: 408–409; Perry 1986), an almost instant response to Locke's *Two treatises of government* (1689–1690), which attacks any notional severance of family from the political realm. Where Locke had said one cannot argue from paternal authority to state authority, Astell restores the alignment: "If Absolute Sovereignty be not necessary in a State, how comes it to be so in a Family"? (quoted in Ng 2007: 226). While introducing "class distinctions to argue that a man cannot be superior to his wife if he is socially inferior to her," and calling "for erasing gender difference in the spiritual realm" (2007: 228, 229), overall hers was a conservative argument for recognizing state sovereignty. Ng follows others in suggesting that Locke's depoliticization of the family (containing the latter as a private space) had more effect as a rhetorical turn than as a reflection on current changes in familial organization. But there is interest precisely in the discourse being fashioned. One outcome was surely that his reconfiguring of the state as based on social contract could dispense with the family metaphor.[14] Family and state no longer circled around each other.

In her last substantive chapter, Ng points to an explicit area of the earlier family-state analogy in which friendship appears alongside kinship. It is intriguing evidence for the way values are kept in relation. This is a period when the language of friendship and kinship still ran together, and figures drawn from either were used to depict potential rivals to the state. Between them, the figures could act as alternatives for each other.

When in 1686 William Stout (whom we met in chapter 2) "realised that he wished to become a Quaker, he feared," in Tadmor's words (2001: 128, emphasis omitted), "that he would incur the displeasure of his relations, including 'my mother, brother, sister and other of my kindred.'"[15] (One hears a faint echo of the alienation expressed by some of Williamson's literary devotees.) The "plural usages" and the "diversity of the language of kinship" that she highlights (2001: 154) were open to the neologism that allowed kin of all kinds to be brought together under the rubric of (personal) relations, while relations in turn were augmented by a sphere of interpersonal connections, the circle of associates known as friends. It seems that the reach of friendship offered a mirror to the plurality of kinship usages, not in terminology ("friend" was a singleton) but in their scope: friend, too, "had a plurality of meanings" (2001: 167). Connoting the particularity of a personal tie, whether with kin, patrons, trading partners, or in freely chosen relationships of sentiment, as Tadmor's phrasing goes, friendship was in effect a moral and reciprocal relationship of services and favors, a mix of obligation and choice, at once instrumental and sentimental, contractual and spontaneous, public and private.[16] Discourses of kinship and of friendship each spilled over the bounds of (what latter-day moderns distinguish as) familial and non-familial, kin and non-kin.

Perhaps it is unsurprising that, to the extent to which relation was to divest kin of degree, friendship came to divest close ties of certain constraints. In Ng's account of Quaker usage, the appellation friend explicitly removed rank from interpersonal relations.[17] Among seventeenth-century English revolutionists, the early, not yet "quiet," Quakers magnified family-based metaphors, turning many of them into literal precepts to fashion their lives; thus marriage—the term evoked all kinds of unions—was in their eyes too spiritual a relationship to receive worldly sanction through civil or church procedures. Such stances signified the separateness of their community, at the time interpreted explicitly as a rival to the state, and provided grounds for challenging authority in general. Quakers had their own reason for the equalizing metaphor of brother and sister, for the father was cast not as a patriarch ruling a subordinate wife but as one of a pair of parents nursing their children. "Quakers called each other brother and sister or simply friend. Familial language allowed them to imagine closer, affective bonds with fellow Quakers" (Ng 2007: 201). Friend in turn widely became a salutation implying mutuality of respect or trust, drawing on usages in common circulation. The burgeoning of "the friends" of this or that society or association was one example, the original designation of the Quaker "Society of Friends" perhaps coming from an early self-description of Quaker associates as "Friends of Truth."

The distinction that blocked friend off from kin was still in the future. Possibly it was not until then that what had been in many respects alternatives began to acquire the status of metaphorical expression, in English understanding one term being carried to another that was *not* it. In the meanwhile, we have glimpsed the demise of something else. Evidence for the way values are kept in orbit also lies in the circumstances under which they cease to co-occur. Insofar as public discourse focused on relations of family and state in terms of explicit metaphorical expression, drawn in this way between things perceived as not one another, it also allowed for the eventuality that what emerged as the dominant term (here the state) would find other vehicles of expression. When the original equation unraveled, relations between family and the wider polity lost one of their expressions of notional equivalence.

Anthropology's Social Fields

From another historical terrain, a debate — retrospectively speaking — between mainstream twentieth-century anthropologists, I recover two perspectives from (the concept of) society. In some respects it is as though they came from different worlds. The protagonists have specific ethnographic backgrounds, West African and European Mediterranean, although each seeks conclusions of more general validity. Both put friendship and kinship into mutual dialogue. The first rests his case on a series of social distinctions; the second points to a quite other axis for social relations and their conditions of enactment. The first appears to adopt for his social description a metaphorical fusion of friendship and kinship of the kind we have been discussing; the second insists on an adjudication of similarities and dissimilarities that distributes the attributes of interpersonal sociality across two distinct spheres of social life. The latter thus mobilizes a divided field, of the kind that might also look like a doubling of halves; here the view from society becomes in effect the view from a relation between society and individual.

Often recalled in anthropological discussions of friendship is Pitt-Rivers's pithy observation on Fortes's phrase for the premise of prescriptive altruism in kin relations: his "axiom of amity." In Beer and Gardner's wording (2015: 428), Pitt-Rivers seized on the oddness of characterizing the heart of kinship through the language of friendship. "It appears, then, that Fortes has chosen to define the essence of kinship by appealing to the very concept of what it is not" (Pitt-Rivers 1973: 90). Fortes himself remarks on his choice of words, citing a passage from Aquinas's commentary on (Aristotle's) *Nicomachean ethics*. "The notion of 'amicitia,' here translated as 'friendship,' corresponds closely to what I mean by 'amity' in the kinship context" (1969: 239n19). He briefly observes that in feudal France the formula "kinsmen and friends" (*parens et amis*) regularly appears in documents relating to blood money. Fortes's axiom of amity, drawing on the Latin *amicitia* where Schwimmer drew on the Greek *philia*, was intended to characterize kinship anywhere; yet he thus chances upon a usage from premodern Europe where alignments of kin and friend were unexceptional.[18] "Recent studies suggest that kinship in the central Middle Ages . . . was primarily conceptualized as an extended network of living people connected by marriage alliances as well as by sibling and cousin relationships . . . [and] in the vernaculars these were often all indistinctively referred to as *amis* or *fründe*" (Teuscher 2013: 100, original italics).

Fortes recognizes amity across diverse social regimes, whether indistinguishable from social relations as such, or differentiating kin from strangers or consanguines from affines. As far as the West African Tallensi are concerned, amity is evident (for example) in the close bonds of mutuality formed between pairs of Tale clans or maximal lineages in order to strengthen ritual collaboration, as in the solidarity of joint sacrifice. The observation that "where amity is the rule in the relations of clans or tribes or communities, there kinship, or quasi-kinship . . . is invoked" (1969: 234) points to an evaluative contrast with relations between non-kin, which lie outside this range of prescriptive altruism. The Tale contrast is reinforced in the separation of "kinship" (consanguinity) from "affinity." At the same time, within the domestic or familial domain, amity encompasses bilateral kin linkages, embracing the collaborations entailed in intermarriage. However, there is nothing diffuse here. In Fortes's schema amity seems tied to the knowing exercise of specific relations: specification implies orders of obligation or prescription. "There is a fiduciary element in amity. We do not have to love our kinsfolk, but we expect to be able to trust them in ways that are not automatically possible with non-kinsfolk" (249). Amity belongs generally to the realm of moral in contraposition to jural values. The distinctions are (ideologically) radical, as in the "sharp contrast" Tallensi themselves make between immutable bonds of kinship and optional ones of friendship (63). This reminds us that Fortes's metaphor of amity does not come directly from Tale notions of friendship.

Pitt-Rivers transforms Fortes's term into another. Bringing together kinship and friendship within a common frame, he offers an overarching category, "amiable relations."[19] While all amiable relations encourage sentiments committing "the individual to actions of altruism . . . [and the] moral obligation . . . to forego self-interest in favour of another" (1973: 90), they may be polarized according to the emphasis put on rights and duties or on sentiment alone. There is "room for variants partaking in the properties of both, between the pole of kinship, inflexible, involuntary, immutable, established by birth and subject to the pressures of the 'the political-jural domain' (in Fortes' words) and the pole of friendship, pure and simple, which is its contrary in each of these ways" (90). Visualizing poles allows attributes to move along a continuum or sliding scale (my phrasing). "Amiable relations" thus glosses over the diversity that Fortes had brought into his analysis, as in differentiating domestic kinship from politico-jural relations. Rather, Pitt-Rivers's amiability is concerned with particular attitudes, notably the outward-going sentiment that renders both kin and friends as extensions of the self. It thus points to a distinctive tenor associated with people's interactions that would be compromised if it were too rule-bound. In short, amiability implies wariness about coercion or obligation, through the ideological (to use Miller's term) polarization of kin and friend that his new category embraces. The polarization *creates* the contradiction he finds in Fortes's account.

One aspect of Fortes's amity seemingly attractive to Pitt-Rivers is its appeal to solidarity and generosity, benign qualities true to amity's medieval European connotations. It is the obligations attendant on it that, among Pitt-Rivers's amiable relations, differentiate kin from friend. This brings us back to the larger narrative. The Enlightenment, so its own story goes, cultivated a public sphere (civility) where trust abounded without being tied to preexisting obligations, impersonal market relations freeing up friendship for the spontaneous expression of positive sentiment among people seeking out company for its own sake. An evident heir to such an aspiration was the twentieth-century idealization of "real" "Western middle-class friendship" through the kinds of intercourse it engendered, "untainted by the inequalities of patron-client relations, the constraints of kinship, [or] the pragmatism of certain forms of balanced exchange" (Bell and Coleman 1999: 10; and see Allan 1979: 36; Carrier 1999: 24, 27). This seems to be a story of amiability. An arena of civic (and civil) intercourse was purportedly complemented by circles of acquaintance based on fellow feeling. The diffuse qualities of amiable sentiment could be notionally detached from the trammels of specific relationships, insofar as these were constraining, and be reattributed to the beneficial effects of association and sociability as such. Here, kin might be regarded as nothing like friends or, where they overlapped, friends and kin could converge in the same personal network. Their polarization allowed almost any axis of dissimilarity to do boundary work; in other words, social boundaries could be drawn anywhere.

Amity lies in specifications that can hardly enroll the same quasi-spatial imagery: boundaries cannot be "drawn anywhere," for kin relationships are systematically organized, a premise Fortes traces back to Lewis Henry Morgan. By contrast with the polarization model of amiability, amity is not a product of proximity or degree of intimacy any more than the attributes of consanguines ("kin") and affines are. Thus in Fortes's Tallensi narrative, those outside the range of prescriptive altruism (amity) are at once marriageable and potentially hostile, likely to be engaged in warring or litigious interactions, and able to contract debts, all possibilities axiomatically debarred from kinship relations. When affines over time "become" kin, the relations have undergone the metamorphosis of a generational perspective; the two do not form poles of a continuum. Fortes's discussion is a provocative vehicle, then, for considering Pitt-Rivers's model of amiability as a social field.[20] Yet each endeavors to addresses fundamental issues of social formation: what joins them is the view from society.

No less than Fortes, Pitt-Rivers presumes the relational embeddedness of persons (the self is extended through its amiable relations).[21] For all that, the two anthropologists' premises summon quite divergent axes of sociality. Amity pinpoints moral sentiment as a relational value of kinship, springing from psycho-primordial experiences invested in kin ties, to be taken (under socially specifiable circumstances) to the limits of kin recognition. Amiability pinpoints the relational values of sentiment that overcome the distinction between kin and non-kin by drawing attention to the person as an individual self. Where the first supposes kin relations are subject to axioms, intrinsically part of an overall social structure, the second dwells on how the sentiments uncovered in friendship direct attention to a contrast between person as individual and person in society. Individual and society here become visible as the crucial tandem.

We can take this second position as an entailment of the polarization model. While a divide between the personal and impersonal gathers up kinship and friendship within the field of the personal, relations vary according to the degree of constraining convention (kinship) or open choice (friendship). On this scale, friends are closer to the ideal of amiability than kin are. In effect the one eclipses the other. Pitt-Rivers (1973: 101–102, transposed; original emphasis) observes that insofar as a relationship between friends remains "ideally, that is to say, conceptually, a *purely* moral one, untrammelled by the jural domain which regulates the affairs of the social family," it is attached not to "the social self" or to "the person in society," but to "the person in himself, the self as individual, the seat of the sentiments."

Not only in his materials but also in his analysis, Pitt-Rivers offers a glimpse into some of the Euro-American suppositions I have been calling vernacular, including what is judged to be of social import or otherwise.[22] As we shall further see, this view from society opens up what seems to lie beyond society.

Re-enchantment

Like any account, an anthropological one carries its own burden of inclusions and exclusions (Borneman 2001), such as a concern with how relations are modeled by people who would not use that phrase, and by others (anthropologists included) who would. With two kinds of absence in mind, values no longer held in orbit, and an arena of social action that may appear self-occluding, I circle once more around the friendship/kinship pair. Bringing it into view through pondering on what moderns (anthropologists included) sometimes find mysterious about personal relations also makes this a prelude to what subsequently might emerge as mystery at the heart of anthropological endeavor as such.[23]

Ng (2007: 7) notes that the persistent nature of the family-state analogy was not simply a mark of social conservatism, but "a sign of the politicization of literature." I infer she means the expansion of language as a vehicle for political argumentation, choice of figurative exposition making evident people's specific (political) standpoints. When it comes to discourse on nature, the historian of science Pickstone (2000: 43, original emphasis) argues that by "*pretending* that nature had meaning" devices such as allegory (and analogy as then understood) exposed what has been called its disenchantment. He is writing of certain seventeenth-century subcultures, largely of Protestant persuasion, where the concept of "natural history" prioritized, as he puts it, description over meaning. A new nature produced a new kind of (humanly inspired) literature. "Only to the extent that 'nature' was disenchanted [did not of itself offer meaning], could it be re-enchanted by language" (2000: 44, emphasis omitted).

This conception of enchantment pulls together certain threads from the preceding discussions that invite us to ponder on what is or is not made visible, or partly visible, through language. Think of those numerous occasions when I have referred to the neologism relation for kin. Perhaps language, in being invested with fresh meanings, is re-enchanted, too. Criticisms of patriarchy and patronage that were exposing many of the old ("public," "political") connotations of familial loyalty and kin positions in terms of the ("personal") interests that could be attributed to them—a repoliticization of kinship in terms of privilege and trust—could be thought of as disenchantment of a kind. Conversely, might a term that apparently encoded a thinning of direct kinship reference be re-enchanting the language of kinship itself? If so, the magic surely came from an associative and connective tenor in a universe of interpersonal relations side by side with the newly defined friend. Of Tadmor's (2001: 214) observation that friends were "extremely important in forming the social order . . . of early modern England," alongside the "sorts," "ranks," or "classes" on which accounts regularly dwell, I again remark the extent to which the discourse of friendship changed alongside that of kinship. Both made visible a (new) apprehension of connectivity.

We should not lose sight of possible entailments for other areas of reflection. When Locke addressed the (epistemic) relation in the abstract, bringing in the recognition of kinspersons in such a way it is hard to distinguish example from analogy, he was drawing on their connections for what they epitomized about properties of the mind and expressions of thought; kinship idioms assisted a metaphysical argument about human cognition. How Locke might have been received is equally of interest. Would his readers have made an association between an associative (epistemic, cognitive) faculty for making relations and appeals to the recognition of kin relations in their new, connective, guise?[24] Perhaps "association," as a mode of intentional and active relating, thereby became recognizable, an epistemological object in itself as we might detect in Hume's *Treatise*. What Hume certainly makes explicit, visible, is the very friendly nature of the (epistemic, cognitive) associations in which he delights.

The possibility of re-enchantment by language has particular resonance in reference to seventeenth-century experimentations with words, definitions, figures of speech, and the like, and (while knowing the Baroque can be reinvented) one would not want to leach it out from them. However, there are other threads that hint at partial visibility through language, as when terms or concepts are introduced with transcendental or fundamental import, sometimes openly, sometimes referring to something that seems half-concealed. Within the discussion of the view from society that evidently moved Fortes and Pitt-Rivers is another common concern bearing on interpersonal relations, less distinctly traced. This is glimpsed in the value each puts on the positive manner in which actors are bound up in other-oriented feelings for one another. It is almost as though something of a mystery were being made of it.[25] Would Pitt-Rivers concur with Paine, who writes that "on the basis of some cross-cultural evidence, it seems that ideal postulates *about human relations* are commonly put into the notion of friendship" ([1969] 1974b: 137, my emphasis)?[26] Speaking of the "irreducibility" of the principles and processes of kinship, Fortes springs upon the reader — briefly and then puts to one side — his supposition that "the axiom of amity reflects biological and psychological parameters of *human social existence*" (1969: 251, my emphasis). A curtain opened for a moment and then closed; like Paine's conclusion, this aside takes on a sense of the profound. The language of these appeals to human fundamentals suggests a search for some deeper meaning in interpersonal relations.[27]

Conserving a sense of mystery intimates a horizon beyond the disenchantment commentators purportedly take for granted in modern forms of relating, voided not just of (greater) meaning but also of former sources of (supernatural) power.[28] Anyone who has read Cannell's (2013) essay in *Vital relations* would correctly connect it to the present discussion. In citing Ng's account of the early English Quakers, I had in mind another Protestant community, the American Mormons, who for a while also defined their communal being through enacting a specific type of marriage.[29] Cannell follows Feeley-Harnik's emphasis (for example, 2001, 2013), based on historical materials from nineteenth-century America, concerning the role that religious sensibilities played in seemingly nonreligious aspects of scientific and political life. Mormon practices lead Cannell to surmise more generally that there is in contemporary anthropological discourses on Euro-American kinship, which from a certain perspective could be called Protestant kinship, a soul-shaped space for some of the senses in which people contemplate their relationships. In secular contexts, "kinship may be an acceptable locus for ineffable meaning when explicitly religious framings are not" (2013: 235).[30] "Religious kinship ideas [as of the Mormon kind] . . . may . . . reveal something truthful about the modern world that is otherwise difficult to see, precisely by evoking a world in which the domains of human experience are not fully divided from and against one another. In this sense, modern disenchantment may be partially transcended through a language and practice of kinship understood as ineffable" (238). Drawing particularly on Edwards's (2000) conversations about procreation in English Alltown, she dwells on the ineffable as moments of suspension or mystery in people's musing about how persons come into being. Such moments permit "the expression of feelings about kinship as [to] what is mysterious, yet intimate, in *the human condition*" (Cannell 2013: 234, my emphasis). She surmises that part of the mystery of the human condition lies in the (double) sense of connectedness to and yet separateness from others.[31]

And if mystery is of itself unutterable, there is an apt double entendre in Cannell's account, since such mystery is additionally rendered mute by the domaining away of religious language. Not only have religious aspects of kinship thinking become occluded, but it is also the case that secular approaches treat kinship as an institution apart from religion. From this comes further vernacular insight into the kinship/friendship duo.

The very separation between kin and friend, on which modernity has purportedly flourished, rested on a muteness of a kind. We know friend was dropped from the language of kinship. Attributing to Locke the development of the modern concept of "society" as an objective abstraction existing over and beyond the individual, Bray (2003: 213) suggests that Locke saw only anarchy in the old practices of intimacy that once fused kin and friend. One cannot, the latter stated (in the *Two treatises*), both be in the state of nature and be a member of civil society. In counterpoint, Bray was quoting from Immanuel Kant's considerably later assertion when he said that a rational ethics requires the moral basis of friendship to reside in an undifferentiated benevolence; then comes Kant's figure of speech, *as if* all were brothers under a universal father. Bringing friendship and brotherhood together surreptitiously reinstates or insinuates the appropriateness of the pairing. (Brotherhood is re-endorsed as equally undifferentiated.) Common though such analogies might be, they rise and fall, are voiced or muted, as concepts change.

This puts in fresh light those twentieth- and twenty-first-century crossovers in the way moderns talk of family and friends. Kinship and friendship: does not each enchant the other? It seems more than a matter of "meaningful" language. Perhaps the very separation of kin and friend, which creates the possibility for metaphorical usage, makes something of a mystery about their conjoining. For twentieth-century spouses to say that they are the best of friends might verbally echo sixteenth- or early seventeenth-century convention, but can hardly convey the same tension between the terms. In present-day parlance, there can be an unmistakably boundary-crossing frisson to it. Again, to regard a friend as one of the family is to put an emphasis on the crossover it would not have carried earlier. What cannot be said these days is that there might be a vital sense, in English-language understandings of relations, in which each is a form of the other. Yet such a sense sometimes seems on the verge of expression. Thus Edwards (2013: 288), writing of an emerging late modern figure, the donor-conceived sibling, talks "about the ways in which donor siblings imagine and bring into being their kinship connections in terms resonant of friendship."[32]

In that the one may add a sense of mystery to the other, each is thereby enlarged. What is bounded appears from another perspective unbounded. Perhaps it is indeed helpful to think of moderns' friendship and kinship as extensions or expansions of each other. McKinnon and Cannell (2013a: 34) recall Max Weber's surmise apropos altruistic fellow-feeling, namely that kinship sentiments can be generalized into other spheres. This begs the question of how to understand the vernacular conceptualization of sentiment itself as a quality of being that can be extended outward from some core expression. Extensions are cosmological in as much as they reproportion values that, unlike the confrontation of kin and friend in ideological terms, seem incontestable appeals to those "human" fundamentals. Consider Paine's ([1969] 1974b: 128) characterization of friendship in terms of its status as "a kind of institutionalized non-institution." Here kinship and friendship are not set over against each other as one might imagine (say) civil law and religion; with Pitt-Rivers, one is invited to think of them instead as exemplifications of an unbounded field of interpersonal relating (although, given their individual dimension in this cosmology, this means they are set over and against institutions).

Now the "shared, distinctive features" that Schneider (1968) found across kinship, nationality, and religion (cf. McKinnon and Cannell 2013a: 24) were unbounded, and implicitly expandable. To him it was frankly frustrating to realize that a core value of American kinship, diffuse and enduring solidarity, was also a core value in these other domains. Diffuseness as a value (in the vernacular) does not, of course, imply a diffuse analytic (that the value cannot be precisely defined), and the same goes for the "extensions" of kinship and friendship. When Bodenhorn (2013: 132) sums up contemporary approaches to kinship in terms of her own subject matter from Mexico, "this material emphasizes the importance of acknowledging that 'kinship' includes large universes of people whose relatedness may or may not have anything at all to do with notions of blood," we should listen to what she is saying. Carsten's original exposition of relatedness enables a precise delimitation of what in this or that context — in "this material," exactly — may not at first sight be apparent. Thus Bodenhorn's mutual bracketing of notions of blood and kinship shows up the potentially divergent extensions of each. "Languages of blood drive much more than kinship and . . . notions of kinship encompass much more than the reproduction of children" (2013: 132).[33] In turn, the conjoining of these concepts is given a fresh edge.

To discuss extension thus recalls the philosopher in chapter 4 who inspired two anthropologists to seriously extend a concept to its limits. Perhaps there is a sense in which today's kinship and friendship, if not exactly one another's shadows, are nonetheless one another's doubles. The sense lies in the very notion of limit, which at once supposes phenomena may also be limitless, and conceals limit itself when at the limit everything changes into something else. We arrive again at a view facing two ways: our kinship/friendship pair may simultaneously evoke the vernacular frisson of boundary-crossing and equally take away the apparent need for boundaries.[34] Schneider's fifty-year-old report on a vernacular articulation of diffuseness (shared, solidary) today might be translated as relationality. Maybe this is part of the Anglophone mystery of the two-sided nature of kinship/friendship.

Relationality

Extending the power of the wonder anthropologists often show toward their materials, Scott (2016: 478; see 2013) dwells on "what constitutes a wonder to others." For Euro-Americans—and for anthropologists when they are being Euro-American—an apprehension of the general power of relating suggests itself. Kinship/friendship offers in this regard a vernacular illustration.

Insofar as certain properties of the relation (such as the English-speaking stress on similarity, implying compatibility or likeness between phenomena) are being carried by ideas of kin and friend, these properties have an immanent status. It is, substantively, the compatibility and likeness immanent in the very relations of kinship and friendship that enable each to expand or extend the other. We have seen attempts to embrace the two through an overarching (underlying) concept for values held in common, as in Pitt-Rivers's amiability. "Interpersonal relations" is a taxonomically or categorically inclusive embrace of them both; from another perspective it also works as a common denominator of the kind that organizes (comparisons of) multitudinous similarities and dissimilarities. But for some writers there seems something beyond categorical inclusion. Anthropologists may at once embrace relations of kinship and friendship *and* evoke that embracing, encompassing move itself as an act of relating. Thus Miller suggested that, in conflating the study of each, they might well regard the pair as part of a more general manifestation of—and he gives the concept an abstract form—relationality. Where it may be seen, or where it is not-seen, relationality occupies its own space, distinct from that implied in conjoining the "missing halves" of either kinship or friendship.

Friends and relatives so easily seem part of the modern category of interpersonal relations, albeit with a personal as opposed to impersonal inflection, that the analytical temptation is to understand their conjoining in terms of broader or narrower classificatory schema. However, as Abbott's upsetting of segmentary delineations brings to mind, there is an inherent skewing to this. If kin relations are simply part of the larger category of interpersonal relations, one might find under the latter not only friends but, according to Beer and Gardner's triptych, many other subcategories, too. There is therefore, in their explicit pairing, an interesting internal limit or restriction to the combination of kinship *with* friendship. This would be true for my proposition: within the compass of kinship/friendship, when either set of relations is (together, separately) performed, then insofar as each is an extension of the other, each is also the other's restriction, too. Briefly, restriction is evident in the extent to which the interpersonal relations of kinship are referred to or delimited by those of

Kinship Unbound · 161

friendship, and vice versa. It would be too hasty to conclude that restriction is simply another term for the delimitative or constraining effect of categorization.

Translating "categorization" into "restriction" opens up the concept, makes a relation of it with respect to its negative, the unrestricted or lack of constraint, in a way English does not make immediately possible for the term "category."[35] So it is in respect of restriction that one can remark the extent to which interpersonal relations (ideas about how they are enacted) also assume an unrestricted relating. And here interpersonal relations drops its qualification: relations as such come into view. While lack of restriction appears to imply a largesse or expansiveness, the relation is infinite, having of itself neither size nor number. There may be times when what anthropologists call an otherwise ineffable relationality is none other than the minimal thing so-called (chapter 3), albeit in a hypothetically knowable or specifiable state. We have already seen what happens to the relation when it takes on its specifications, at once also but also much more than a matter of an abstraction given concrete form. Once manifest and specified, relations are everywhere, the relation manifest in the ubiquity of relations.

The term "relationality" seems apt for (a concept of) unconstrained relating. At the end of that third chapter, we arrived at unconstrained relationality by a particular analytical route. I hope I have now laid a more homely trail. It has meant trying to put my head inside that of a Euro-American of the modern or naturalist sort, not excluding anthropological types, in order to describe what seems a leaning or striving toward an ultimate goal of exposition. It is no surprise to find transcendent concepts in naturalist thought, and not least among knowledge-makers.[36] What is often articulated in terms of the human condition, in both anthropological and vernacular accounts, is reiterated in the desire for connection and in the transcendent status knowledge-makers do indeed accord the relation.

In their exposition of the relation's transformational potential, Holbraad and Pederson are explicit about treating it as transcendent, although they feel a need to link transcendence to divinity.[37] Let us see what happens, they say, "if one tries to align the concept of the relation with the concept of a transcendent [Christian] God" (2017: 265). Put into the context of Latour's ruminations on transcendence and immanence, they propose taking God's transcendence — his constitutive distantiation from humanity — seriously. This is less to enroll some kind of alterity than to point to the (salvational) promise of a potential that, for humanity, is not yet completely realized. Rendering "Latour's networks of relations God-like" (2017: 276) at once conserves and transforms the original, posing new questions about what relations might be. Similarly, in the figure of a Christian convert they present someone whose "self-relational individuality" turns prior social relationships into a new kind of relating. (The reduction-magnification to a single figure is almost in itself a transcending move.) While the gesture to Christianity is a fascinating commentary on anthropology's twenty-first-century recovery of religion as a source of transcendent thought, they are using other words to show at every step how the wonder of relating (wonder strictly after Scott) creates its own aura. Anthropological knowledge-makers these days, and not least these two authors, reflect on the very process by which relating is accomplished.[38] They themselves accede that the relation "was never meant to be a feature of ethnographic localities and societies in Mongolia, Melanesia or elsewhere, but above all — indeed strictly — an internal property of the way in which a particular mode of anthropological thinking conducts itself" (2017: 264). In other words, and this is for report, a cosmological sense of relationality (transcendent, aura-carrying, mysterious) accompanies the kind of exposition that is the ethnographic scope of the present work.

And for all the liberties taken on the way, in following the relation, more or less as an English-speaking Euro-American anthropologist, I hope to have shown something of what was there — in a few of its manifold guises — all along.

Coda to Part III

VISIBILITY

Differently staged dramas have been run side by side across these two chapters, a play between knowledge relations and interpersonal relations, and that between friendship and kinship. The relations are mine, and we are not in Mongolia or Melanesia. Rather, we are talking relations to (certain usages and imaginations of) relations.

A long time ago, it now seems, Latour ([1991] 1993: 112) referred to the uncontrollable proliferation of a certain type of modern being: "the object, constructor of the social, expelled from the social world, attributed to a transcendent world that is, however, not divine—a world that produces, in contrast, a floating subject, bearer of law and morality." He mentions the English air pump, first constructed in 1658–1659, among other apparatus, all of them "nonhumans [that] possess miraculous properties" because they are, invisibly, both social and asocial. (They form part of the miracle that inspires Westerners to see themselves apart from others.) He would, of course, be no stranger to the statement that it is "not immediately obvious that we can learn about the density and convection of huge volumes of air in the upper atmosphere, for example, by studying, as did Robert Boyle, the temperature and pressure of gases within small laboratory vessels" (McLeish 2019: 135). McLeish joins the assumption of physical uniformity required by seventeenth-century experimental science to the "hugely creative and non-intuitive" ability to work by analogy. Boyle's own self-conscious "literary technology" focused on construing knowledge as a public artifact. This technology "dramatized the social relations proper to a community of experimental philosophers," so Shapin and Schaffer's ([1985] 2011: 69) classic exposition of the air pump argues. In the deliberations to be found in Boyle's work are attempts to bring about a new world order as to what counts as knowledge through the parallel instrument of what was also brought about, an informed collectivity of persons bound by certain conventions of relating.[1] At least that seems visible in hindsight.

So what does Joseph Wright's *An experiment on a bird in the air pump* (1768) make visible? An often-reproduced icon of early modern science, my bringing it into sight intimates that much in the present book is meant to be recognizable, ethnographically familiar, English-speaking.[2] An eighteenth-century rehearsal of a seventeenth-century invention, this could be the scientific revolution domesticated. Boyle's air pump, and his demonstration (to show air had weight and pressure), had created space for further experimentation on objects placed in the jar (Shapin 1996: 98–99). Porter (2000: 350) argues that the subject of this painting is intended to excite compassion: "Sacrificed by an itinerant lecturer to demonstrate the vacuum, a breathless bird, trapped in a bell-jar, flutters."[3] The audience's reactions reveal a gamut of emotions, and indeed the painting would be nothing without the social circle. And who were they? Friends and relations perhaps.[4] However, relations do not stay within a single frame. The viewer is drawn in by the lecturer's gaze, to see both those (relations) already existing in the room, as between older and younger figures, and those created at that moment of attention or discovery.[5] The latter, of course, include knowledge relations. The demonstrator is no doubt expounding on the properties of air. But the viewer may well witness the relation between air and bird just as, in pointing to relations we might not at first see, Locke once gestured — "Take the air but a minute from the greatest part of living creatures, and they presently [immediately] lose sense, life, and motion."[6]

Conclusions

THE REINVENTION OF RELATION
AT MOMENTS OF KNOWLEDGE-MAKING

One's theoretical position is not supposed to be heterogeneous—theorizing is, after all, a clarifying and purifying exercise. Taking the contributions of anthropology as a whole, however, it is obvious that the discipline speaks in numerous, sometimes conflicting, registers. For the work of social criticism, such internal diversity may be an unexpected strength.

An academic consensus of sorts in today's world is that its inhabitants must more than ever understand the relations that compose it. Yet "relation" often seems hard won as a precept. There appears to be too little willingness to appreciate the interrelatedness and interdependence of phenomena, indeed to appreciate interrelatedness as intrinsic to a phenomenon's existence. That said, there need be no one road to arguing the point, and this may even give an edge to relation's portmanteau character, and to its diffuse and manifold applications. It goes without saying that there need be no one anthropological approach either. In that adopted here, the critical realization that putting a generic value on relating is already an imaginative exercise, cosmologically modernist and naturalist, helps elucidate the reach of its significance. Realization is not tantamount to a reason for wishing it away, for (say) querying relationality as a value in international discourse (although circumstances may give good reason to be wary of specific discourses). Rather, as stated at the outset, there is a strong argument for holding on to anthropologists' pervasive vocabulary of relations insofar as it joins the few languages spoken today, from the life sciences and elsewhere, for grasping some of the dimensions of the present ecological catastrophe.

Those who have acquired a new sense of the fragility of the world, as an ideo-bio-physical-social entity, articulate the new demand to grasp the interdependence of beings and entities of all kinds. It is just so that Barad (2007) may be heard when she argues that phenomena are always and infinitely the materializations of "intra-actions." An anthropologist might add there are still too many imagined worlds that ignore such realities, and there is much work of criticism still to be done. How can we not be reading, Skafish (2014: 30) implies apropos one academic dispute, but "in light of an ecological crisis demanding reinventing the relations between human and nonhuman"? And this is only the beginning of what requires reinventing. Thus it was suggested that the failure of a simple evocation of relations to dispatch the premise of similarity, a specter underlying many naturalist and modernist formulations, is highly germane to political action, anthropocenically speaking (Danowski and Viveiros de Castro [2014] 2017). Consider the analytical contexts laid out in part II that produce relations with this premise attached. These endorse prevailing Anglophone requirements of political action, namely that it proceed through demonstrating similarity or convergence of interests between whatever parties are being brought together. If the other side of this is that such requirements cannot deal with encounters based on the collective work of difference and division, what frequently slides into place is the prejudging (as in prejudice) of the dissimilar. At its extreme, disowning the dissimilar becomes a tenacious, too easily vicious, habit of mind.

Not to put too fine a point on it, then, but how do we bring relations within critical purview? Criticisms (subsuming critiques) anthropologists might bring to certain conceptualizations of relations lie side by side with the extent to which relations themselves do critical service. Exposition is clearly going to be complex, not least because relating inheres in its very practice. Nonetheless, there is a precedent for establishing a critical apparatus for what works as an apparatus. In the naturalist cosmology of English speakers, reflection (bringing to a point of knowing) is crucial to that kind of second-order understanding—knowing one knows—they call knowledge. This book has been following some of the roads these ideas have traveled in the recent past. We may broaden the question about reinvention to offer a general critical reflection: how the relation comes to be reinvented, or rediscovered, at moments of new knowledge-making.[1]

Reinvention happens over and again, trivially and monumentally, this or that juncture yielding insight into some of relation's own critical potential. New apprehensions in terms of the precarity of species existence, human included, is a starting point for reviewing some instances already encountered. Exposing a few of the heterogeneities of the positions being taken, it will gesture toward some alternative modes of criticism.

With a vocabulary that initially seemed novel to the social sciences, the opening years of the twenty-first century saw a surge of interest in delineating multispecies relations.[2] We might remind ourselves of earlier moments of new knowledge-making in Darwinism and, as the exceptional became embedded in general parlance, its vernacularization and repercussions for self-understanding. Take Marett's popular book on anthropology, for which its imprint, the Home University Library, envisaged a broad readership. These days an anthropologist is unlikely to imagine that Marett's observation, "all the forms of life in the world are related together," and apropos human life, "a fundamental kinship and continuity [lies] between all [its] forms" ([1912] 1936: 9, 11), implied anything more than reproducing for a general, if educated, audience a manner of speaking about relations with which his academic colleagues would have been long familiar. He was explicit about its evolutionary context in Darwinism as "the touch of nature that makes the whole world kin" (11).[3] In 1912 evolutionary anthropology was, as a school of thought, much embattled (Stocking 1995: 179), yet the findings had, so to speak, outlasted the argument. Several decades later, with the formation of genetic science generating self-consciously new moments, such as in the possibility of gene mapping, similar phrasing sounds quite fresh. As translated into English in 1998, a French Nobel Prize winner declared, "All living beings, from the most humble to the most complex, are related. The relationship is closer than we ever thought" (in Rabinow 2003: 104).

A hundred years after Marett, the kinship of *all* living beings is being described with a new literalism and a new basis in biology. An article on symbiosis outlines the essential interdependence of species entailed in the contribution of microbes to forming and sustaining life (Gilbert, Sapp, and Tauber 2012; cf. Gilbert 2017).[4] Given that its authors include historians and philosophers of biology, perhaps it is not surprising that they begin with reference to the early modern period in Europe and discuss concepts of individuality.[5] They argue (after Taylor) that the general notion of the autonomous individual agent, as understood then, framed the study of life forms later known as biology. Yet, they continue, as we now know "animals [among other organisms] . . . are composites of many species, living, developing, and evolving together" (2012: 326). And today "all classical conceptions of individuality are called into question by evidence of all-pervading symbiosis. . . . [So] our bodies must be understood as holobionts, whose anatomical, physiological, immunological and developmental functions evolved in shared relationships of different species" (327, 334).[6]

To shake off the constraining notions of individuality being criticized may need more inventiveness in thinking about relations as well. For, like the premise of similarity, relations (relationships) bring us to a point of political impasse. In their tracing of non-individual-based notions, from organic systems or ecologies to symbionts and holobionts, the authors draw both on behavioral concepts such as interaction or communication, and on a broader, more abstract conceptualization of relating. We now know there is a problem. In linguistic-conceptual form, if not in the authors' intentions, how relations are described may presuppose the very kind of already-existing entities to which they object. So when they talk of "inter-active relationships among species" (Gilbert, Sapp, and Tauber 2012: 326), the terms of the relation (diverse species) become, epistemically speaking, individualized, external to one another.[7] The concept of relation may turn out to be at once key for comprehending symbiosis and an impediment to describing it. The impasse is an expositional one.

This sounds like a descent from the supremely significant revisualization of interrelations to a quibble about linguistic usage and expositional practices in laying out arguments. Yet that would be a hasty verdict: it does not just underrate habits of thought and expression but also ignores the extent to which Anglophone relations have been molded by epistemic and interpersonal connotations alike. It is as though effort to dethrone the individual addressed the interpersonal, as we may imagine a modeling of interspecies relations, while ignoring the epistemic, the structuring of concepts.[8] The point is hardly insignificant for any attempt at redescription.

At that early modern moment when English ideas about kinship were being reconfigured once again, it was arguably becoming possible to conceive afresh, or with new force, of an individual person plus his or her relations in terms of an emergent social phenomenon, the conjugal family plus its connections. This entailed an enactment of external relations both in the way the individual or family (each with its own identity) was at once separate from such relations (that is, a network of kinsfolk) and "related" to them *and*—I surmised—in the way the substantive relation was itself becoming an object of wider reflection. Narrativizing the desirability of keeping up relations, or otherwise, may have thickened an appreciation of external relations operating between or among self-contained identities. Self-containment, held in place when one distinct thing is defined by its relation to another distinct thing, gives us entities with properties but without internal relations. Philosophers debate the extent to which, by contrast, all relations might be internal, that is, whether any relation can leave unaffected its terms or bearers (Johansson 2014). Yet, of course, and of course because it is so trite, in the two-way flow between vernacular and academic forms of expression, there are also significant blockages and modes of resistance. In this matter of internal relations, vernacular English conceptions appear largely and obstinately otherwise.

As for recourse to external relations, certain possibilities for reflection on new apprehensions of knowledge seem to have been long ago hidden from sight within that mundane concept of identity. Relations of an external kind, such as kept nature and culture in orbit with one another, would in turn be a correlate of that. And here one might remark on the influence of English modelings of kinship on the precursors of the life sciences that were developing in the nineteenth century. Kin ties became imaginatively based on the truth that biology made of their closeness and intimacy, bonding through natural inheritance. That formulation would turn again and again to what was known of nature as the yardstick for measuring modifications of a social or cultural kind. When it comes to interspecies relations, present reformulations that extend this truth to beyond the human are powerful and compelling—with a bid for a place in international discourse—in pointing to zoological continuities. But, as Franklin (2013a: 299) intimates, there will surely be contexts where naturalists and moderns need to also hold on to—as self-knowledge—the fact that this is what their models are doing. They are modeling nature from within a kinship matrix that takes foundational relations to be of nature and therefore to be modeled after it.

Locke offers some pertinent observations on what goes into all the elements of existence, and the habits of thought that conceal the relations implied. Thus he includes under what are often overlooked as "relative terms" those that, with "the form and appearance of signifying something absolute in the subject, do conceal a tacit, though less observable, relation" (1690: 2, 25, 3; 320); an example is the word "stores" (as a ship lays in stores), which has a relation to future use. And if bodies must be understood as holobionts, listen to Locke again on their surrounds. There are external relations nonetheless vital to an entity's character or a creature's survival, and he dwells vividly on both inanimate and animate bodies to mount his own criticism of popular perception. Thus inanimate bodies "owe so much of their present state to other bodies without [outside] them, that they would not be what they appear to be, were those bodies that environ them be removed" (1690: 4, 6, 11; 586). He talks of animate creatures in the same terms: "Those bodies on which they depend, are little taken notice of, and make no part of the complex ideas, we frame of those animals. Take the air but a minute from the greatest part of living creatures, and they presently [immediately] lose sense, life, and motion. . . . This is certain, things, however absolute and entire they seem in themselves are but retainers to other parts of nature. . . . Their observable qualities, actions, and powers, are owing to something without them; and there is not so complete and perfect a part, that we know, of nature, which does not owe the being it has, and the excellencies of it, to its neighbours" (1690: 4, 6, 11: 586–587). Locke could not be clearer in his criticism of the habits of thought by which we are "wont to consider the substances we meet with, each of them, as an entire thing by it self, having all its qualities in it self, and independent of other things" (1690: 4, 6, 11; 585). In short, we fail to notice how many of their features depend on their relations to such other things.

This last phrasing comes from the philosopher Stuart (2013: 32). In his opinion Locke barely attends to any theorization of relations, and it is Stuart who draws into Locke's earlier disquisition on relations and identity these criticisms from book four of his *Essay*. The context is a discussion about the certainty by which things or "substances" can be known. (At this point, in book four, given that he reserves the terminology of relations for ideational comparisons, Locke is dwelling on what he calls connections.)[9] While he externalizes "other" entities or bodies in furthering his objection to imagining that entities are independent of one another, and indeed deploys an environmental imagery, that externalization is but a moment in an argument. He continues, "And we must not confine our thoughts within the surface of any body, but look a great deal farther, to comprehend perfectly those qualities that are in it" (1690: 4, 6, 11; 587).

Another Locke?[10] What remains of enduring interest is how *little* impression this attention to (what we would call) interrelationship seemingly made on those classical conceptions of individuality, equally attributable to him, and still being called into question by present-day biology. Did it make his thinking appear too heterogeneous? If the issue is what is or is not picked up, then practices of exposition come to the fore.[11]

Actualized Alternatives

When (what looks like) attention to interrelations and mutual dependency is attributed to the concept-making formula of "internal relations," it may be signaling a particular line of thinking. One such was set in train by Leibniz, who—as Hume notes in an abstract of his own *Treatise*—was Locke's critic.[12] And Leibniz was no casual critic: he dealt with Locke's *Essay* argument by argument. Leibniz's concern with relations is encapsulated in his oft-quoted dictum (given in the introduction), a response to Locke, that there is no term so absolute or so detached that it does not involve relations.[13] Objects or entities in themselves invariably indicate other objects; thus space (to take a famous example) is "the order, or relationship, in which celestial bodies move in respect of each other" (Israel 2001: 521). According to Descombes ([1996] 2014: 207), Leibniz draws extrinsic and intrinsic relations together, "analyzing the relations of things and introducing the reality of relations into the reality of the subjects related." Internal relations is the point on which Ollman ([1971] 1976) sees Leibniz in Marx's theorizing, while Bowker's (2010) sense of himself as multiple rather than self-identical is contextualized through Deleuze's reading of the same seventeenth-century philosopher. This constellation of positions in debate is frequently presented as an alternative to purportedly establishment theorizing or mainstream suppositions in the vernacular.

The theorizing and suppositions in question may be more determinedly Anglophone. I would have saved myself a lot of expositional trouble had I paused longer not just on Stengers's fundamental hesitation with the concept of relations but also on Latour's lack of interest. A relation, in his view, is rather like an "intermediary," which "simply transports, transfers . . . is void in itself and can only be less faithful or more or less opaque" to the quasi-objects or agents he designates mediators; a mediator (by contrast) "is an original event; and creates what it translates as well as the entities between which it plays the mediating role" ([1991] 1993: 77–78). The now evident point is that mere intermediaries leave the pure forms of what is mediated intact.[14] Taking all that on board would have cut to the quick many of the entailments of "betweenness" with which we have been concerned. Yet, in English usage, relations are not straightforwardly equivalent to (Latourian) intermediaries. Whether or not they are deployed as mediators as well, the many ways in which they are used give them a thickness, filling up something of the void. It is just such a presence that I have been trying to convey. Ethnography is, to adapt a famous phrase, staying with the expositional trouble.

If anything shows this, it is the enduring imperative to go on being critical of those classical conceptions of individuality still being questioned, and the turn to interspecies anthropology is a pointed instance. Arguing about relational deficits acquires new impetus. Perhaps the connection to kinship might have been made more loudly within anthropology, too, yet when relations are principally thought of as external, the concept already shapes the study of non-Euro-American kin forms, not to speak of Euro-American. This is emphatically restated in Sahlins's synthesis of kinship studies, a veritable reinvention of relations.[15] "People who are intrinsic to one another's existence" (2013: 2), who "lead each other's lives and die each others' deaths" (2008: 49); the formulations perhaps hold a message from and for symbioticists, too. And whatever new vocabulary those who look to symbiogenesis find for what English speakers currently cast as relations, it might be helpful to be reminded of this concept's (relation's) early modern figuring. It is not nature versus culture, the body-mind split, or the separation of the substantial being from consciousness of the self that are only of interest. The silent absence of kinship from a tradition of learned discussion about the identity of either human beings or persons arguably has had consequences for biology and anthropology alike. Was there something about Euro-American kinship itself, apprehended as kinship/friendship or not, that had become auto-occluding?

However, this is getting ahead of the exposition. Let me first look back on parts of the preceding arguments in order to exemplify more generally both the need for criticism and what one might intend by calling for it.

Criticism and "Anti"-criticism

The six chapters forming the bulk of this volume have taken us through a limited if diversified range of analytical frameworks in order to yield some insight into the use of relations, at least as they occur in expositions mainly though not exclusively anthropological. (Both the work of relations in organizing those expositions and the variously conceived subjects of them are implied.) To the extent that these diverse contexts thus "produce" relations, they turn them (ethnographically) into objects of study and reflection. The analytical frameworks or contexts have themselves entailed some discussion, indeed it would be impossible to engage them otherwise, but by and large I have assumed the stance of an interpretative observer, including a speculative one from time to time. English usages have been the target. Needless to say, this is not the same as identifying them as exclusive or unique to English. Equally needless to say, where elements are marked as English-speaking—and the same goes for its avatars, Euro-American, naturalist, and such—they are but part of an overall exposition (the present work) that is also English-speaking. As objects of reflection, the relations emerging from this exposition may also to be put under critical scrutiny. This gives them reflexive purchase, and Hage helps make the point.[16]

Hage's (2012, 2015) contrast between the aims of alter-politics and anti-politics as stances in radical political thought turns on either providing an alternative to the present order or else aiming to defeat it on its own terms. Critical thinking may assist either aim, given its capacity to take the thinker out of him- or herself, and anthropology, he argues, does this in a distinctive way. With the discipline's ability "to continuously remind us of the actual possibilities of being other to ourselves" (2015: 59), he sees critical anthropology as a resource for articulating an alter-politics where critical sociology provides ammunition for an anti-politics. However, within the scope of critical anthropology, we might utilize something akin to the same contrast. Anthropologists move between developing positions to challenge the foundations of instituted phenomena through alternative formulations and acknowledging the effectiveness of broaching issues in the mode in which they are given. Adopting Hage's distinction for what it means to be critical in the course of scholarly exposition, I divide criticism into alter- and anti-manifestations. This affords a way of controlling (as in controlling analogical flow) heterogeneity among theoretical standpoints, not least in observing their crossovers. In one sense, there is nothing new here. It echoes what anthropologists do all the time — now being most ethnographically persuasive in applying their technical and exogenous terms of analysis, now being most ethnographically persuasive in synthesizing the language of their interlocutors. Each in turn can fold into the other (cf. Hage 2015: 59). However, in the present exercise, the alter/anti distinction is especially helpful in addressing the effects of an apparently hegemonic discourse among English speakers. A simple oppositional (anti) stance to how relations are used would be, in terms of exposition, grammatically and semantically fraught before it became impossible in other ways. Rather than an anti stance existing in isolation, it is actually *saved* by its counterpart, an alter stance, insofar as it is brought back to being one of a pair of critical possibilities.

Forms of alter-criticism dominate the chapters. That said, there is one "anti"-criticism (not countercritical but counter "alter") to be made explicit. Its potential political tenor evident, it voices a straightforward disquiet at what I see as certain implications of English-speaking formulations of relations.

Take the recurrent, apparently innocuous modeling of interpersonal relations in terms of the eighteenth-century vision of concentric rings. To amplify what has been presented in various registers, that vision is particularly associated with Smith.[17] The view that "human affection is oriented spatially around the self, and that it naturally weakens progressively as its object radiates outwards, further and further from the self" (Forman-Barzilai 2010: 120) has been said to owe its inception to Stoic philosophy. However (this is Forman-Barzilai's argument from political theory), the Scottish Enlightenment in the person of Smith changed the narrative. At the moment of making that knowledge afresh, he set relations to work in another way. Stoic cosmopolitanism was about collapsing "the natural concentric structure of our affections" (120), principally by diminishing self-interest (so we feel for ourselves as we feel for others), whereas Smith incorporated the Christian ethic that stressed increasing personal sensibility outward, by augmenting beneficence (we feel for others as we feel for ourselves).[18] For the latter, what is at issue is not the rejection of the familial in favor of becoming a citizen of the world, but a projection from the self in attendance on itself, and on its innermost intimate circle, to a periphery.[19] It was perceived as an alignment with nature, not a revolt from it. Thus Smith stops short of embracing the whole world. While goodwill has no boundary, the ability to act on it does: the "circumference of authentic sympathy" becomes adjusted to human finitude (150, quoting Peters 1995). Smith castigates Christian moralists who seemingly preoccupy themselves with too distant suffering.

The power of such thinking is in its transformative potential, in what is taken by others from it, in the assemblages it forms with other conceptualizations.[20] Thus the widespread notion that circles of affect demarcate the potential reach of social interaction naturalizes the extension *and restriction* of beneficence, rendering the self simultaneously source and arbiter. That such affect can be attached to any order of group, intensity decreasing in a sliding scale as one moves away from a center, further naturalizes the presumption that a boundary between us and them can be drawn anywhere.[21] This concept of social distance, whether in the vernacular or in (some) social science analysis, seems increasingly intensified in present times. The anthropologist Rio (2007: 22–25) puts the matter with great clarity. He offers a trenchant criticism of writers, following Alfred Schütz, who take for granted the specifically "Western ontology of social relations" that rests on we-they relationships. Parties in "we-relationships" think of themselves as sharing a community of time, a simultaneity of consciousness, each in the spatial proximity of companion others; in "they-relationships," people remain abstract and anonymous to one another. Indeed, a boundary that can be drawn anywhere. The issue is that it is enfolded within certain usages of relations. Those defining themselves as "us" base their community on the convergence of proximity and resemblance, on the similarities contained in the relations they recognize, where the intentions of strangers are suspect and where outsiders who cannot be ignored must be either assimilated or absolutely kept at bay.[22]

That premise of similarity: here is its political perniciousness. For indeed when it comes to defining people(s) in this concentric ("global") world, the boundary between the similar and dissimilar can also be drawn along any alignment. Politically speaking, dissimilarity is likely to close off rather than invite interest or curiosity, so what is beyond the pale can easily become a matter of apathy. All that matters is that people on the other side of the boundary — whatever draws its lines, race, poverty, religion, class, education — are not like "us." Not like us: that apparently obvious conceptualization is not all obvious. It requires dissimilarity to be linked to some kind of exclusion from the innermost heart of life that generates positive affect. Such unconcern for what is distant could not be further from the Stoic cultivation of unconcern toward the self. A centering of affect could not be further from those analogical relations where the boundaries, the divisions and differences, between "different kinds" (groups, kinships) of people presuppose that the one place where a boundary is not drawn is in how people think and feel.[23]

Two intimations of disquiet support the anti-criticism. First, it is recalled, Amin (chapter 2) was trying to reinvent a concept of the proximate stranger decentered from ideas of interpersonal or associational orientation. Second, to add here, Robbins's (2013: 458) response to what has been happening in anthropology over the last thirty years focuses on how the discipline has disposed of the peripheralizing effect trailed by certain connotations of dissimilarity (not his term), as in the "othering" of cultures, while he himself wishes to restore the critical purchase of being able to imagine circumstances that "challenge our own versions of the real."

Alter-criticism: Alternative Descriptions

These anti-critical comments target certain practices that English-speaking anthropologists find close to home. The targeting does not mean that their world is the only one where suspicion and hostility to outsiders (whoever outsiders are) is rife. Rather it is intended to point to a potent place *in that world* where such sentiments are fostered, and to one of their means in habitual conceptual forms. Appreciating the pervasiveness of such practices, and what else they might be doing, calls for something nearer alter-criticism. Given that this mode does indeed dominate my exposition, and the rest of this chapter, there is no need to offer more than brief exemplifications of where it has appeared.

The principal objects of alter-criticism, Anglophone and—where they apply—Euro-American and naturalist uses of relations, have been treated from two directions. One deployed alternative languages actualizable within existing anthropological discourse. This drew on a range of critical stances, many though certainly not all coalescing around critical theory and whatever antecedents one might wish to find for the ontological turn, as well as on diverse narrational forays. The other engaged with usages established in the hegemonic repertoire, generally in terms intelligible within the vernacular, while nonetheless being inventions upon it. It included the kinds of as-if scenarios presented in chapter 5, the could-have-been-otherwise.[24]

Under the first alter-critical mode, I would put the neologism (not mine) "expersonation"; in a discussion of comparison, I posed it as a counterpart to certain implications of the notion of self-consciousness, and then in a kind of back-translation to seventeenth- and eighteenth-century ideas of anonymous civility. A rather different expository suggestion lay in distinguishing "dissimilarity," redolent of a presumption of similarity, from "difference," singled out for its place in critical theory, more fully recalling the concept of disjunctive synthesis — or inclusive disjunction — in Viveiros de Castro's rendition (where difference, like relation, has no regular conceptual opposite).[25] Then the last chapter proposed filling in what seems missing from the social field of kinship, namely its other half, friendship, envisaging less an overarching category than something closer to the Yukaghir shadow or double. I dwell briefly on this last example. Drawing on the conceptual resources of the kind of anthropology sympathetic to the ontological turn, or to certain of its antecedents in Deleuzian thought, one can make a further case here for disjunctive synthesis: kinship and friendship each has the potential to become its other's other side.[26] Comparisons based on similarity and dissimilarity fall away. Rather than loss, deficit, or missing part, as vernacular apprehensions of an alternating form might have it, the stronger formulation denotes sides to a phenomenon in a relation of difference.

The phenomenon in question I dubbed "Euro-American kinship." This brings us to a place where I have deployed the second alter-critical mode. The discipline's present strengths include its interest in all kinds of situations where people are reinventing kinship for themselves. So perhaps this further mode responds to what moderns and naturalists have also been inventing, of which early modern antecedents offer a kind of alter-horizon.[27] I see the (disjunct) kinship/friendship duo not so much as a recovery of medieval kin and friend, the joining of *parens et amis*, than a creation of those years when friends were to be purified of kin and re-enchanted by associational solidarity and civil society. Arising from this is the equivocal positioning of "interpersonal relations." While in the vernacular there is often great insistence on the distinction between personal and impersonal relations, personal being the rubric under which kin and friends are usually put, I have preferred to leave open the ascription interpersonal. Initially proposed as a counter to logical or epistemic relations, I have been using "interpersonal" for generic moments when it is not necessary to specify whether personal or impersonal relations are at issue. That is registered as an order of engagement. The other side to expersonation, the more familiar impersonation, then becomes interesting. If the friend can also appear as an impersonation of interpersonal ties, unspecified, we are invited to reflect again on the positive kinship cast given these days to generalized humanity and to companionate nonhuman or beyond-the-human beings.

To have general purchase, either genre of alter-criticism may well need translating back into other expositional forms closer to the vernacular, including in this context regular anthropological usage. In redescribing certain of these issues, we begin with questioning in what possible sense "Euro-American kinship" can be imagined.

Making Euro-American Kinship

Naming English speakers and the English language at once summons a specification and is a stand-in for the concrete nature of any location or particularity of usage. To enlarge briefly on how one may arrive at a sense of specificity without implying that it requires characteristics exclusive or unique to it, we might recall that ancestry did this for the Australian activists we met in chapter 4, as nationhood does for many moderns. And where people gather up what gives a particularity to a sense of themselves, ethnographers often follow. Thus when it comes to early modern (another stand-in) developments in the way people managed their affairs with kin, some or much, though not all, of what applies to English speakers may apply equally to French or German or Dutch speakers, among many others, not forgetting European settlers in North America. As we have seen, the conceptual shift suggested by the English literalness of "relations" for kinsfolk at once apparently dovetailed with shifts in the organization of familial and familiar relations, *and* was not at all necessary to such changes, which were happening all over Europe.[28] To capture some of the equivocations here, I have throughout moved between "English" and a more embracing "Euro-American." It is time to make this second quasi-cultural designation carry a bit more freight, and make evident its place within a naturalist cosmology.[29]

Briefly, the world that knew itself as enlightened, and was afterward attributed among other things with a precursor in the scientific revolution, thought it was making new knowledge, remaking the already made-anew renaissance.[30] Although scholarship proclaimed this most conspicuously, it was we might say yet another reformation that was to leave little untouched. Transcendental axes of this cosmology — nature/culture, individual/society, object/subject, reason/emotion — drew on much older ideas about the nature of things, including curiosity in how anything is known. At the same time, at that particular moment of knowledge-making, "knowledge" itself acquired, yet again, fresh prominence as a second-order object of reflection. The consequences have been ubiquitous. For those who think or write about knowledge, everything is mediated by how it is known.[31] Indeed knowledge can acquire a transcendent value in the eyes of some, exactly as its English companion utility does. Simultaneously, naturalist cosmology embraces knowledge as immanent in everything that people subsequently make explicit to themselves, and thus as inhabiting particular ways of thinking and acting. Insofar as anthropology might put weight on particulars of time and place, a subsidiary designation is useful. The quasi-cultural designation "Euro-American" serves, "quasi" because "cultural" is not here evoking its cosmological counterpart, natural, but simply the immanence of values in certain social (cultural) forms.[32]

Separating culture and cosmology allows us to observe a relation between Euro-American practices, relevant to certain temporalities and geographies, and the naturalism inferred as their grounds or conditions of possibility. When making things known takes it for granted that entities have knowable attributes, a supposition is being made about the already-existing status of the entity as an individual. The same may be assumed of the agent of knowledge, when it is thought of as a person, the knower (excluding all that is "known" about tacit or embodied knowledge). Thus everything mediated by or filtered through how it is known can appear as also filtered through the identity of the individual knower as a conscious subject. Consciousness is frequently a sticking point in what can be made knowable.

A foray into the ethnography of naturalism (Candea and Alcayna-Stevens 2012) demonstrates some of the heterogeneous approaches through which Euro-Americans, in their practice as behavioral or environmental scientists, understand the worlds of those they study, and thus what they show of their own. Included is an anthropologist's attempt to account for apparent understandings in cross-species interaction. The anthropologist was struck by the keepers of a chimpanzee sanctuary who acted now as though it was obvious to know what a chimpanzee thinks and feels, now as though such knowing was quite impossible (Alcayna-Stevens 2012).[33] One is reminded of the kind of agnosticism to which Locke gave vent. The keepers were initially clear about their own and the chimpanzees' identity as distinct beings, yet between them lay a relation that evoked something else. Their being able to enact a relationship was in turn clear; specifying it in terms of the prior properties of this or that primate, through understanding how either thinks, feels, and anticipates, was not. Mutual communication of a kind seemed doable; mutual knowledge based on mindful (conscious) reflection was inconceivable.

The foray concludes with a short manifesto on mutuality, "Anthropology beyond the human" (Kohn 2012). Piqued by the question of how dogs dream, Kohn (2007) had recorded the dismay of an Amazonian Runa household when their dogs failed to divine their own imminent death. People pondered on this lapse of foreknowledge—if death was not knowable, nothing was! Runa hold that they know the meaning of dogs' dreams. How to understand dogs, and how dogs come to understand people, requires particular approaches to the life of selves, observes Kohn. He refers to Haraway's conviction that there is something about everyday engagement with other creatures "that can open new kinds of possibilities for relating and understanding" (2012: 137). Haraway's own (2003: 23) manifesto dwells on companion species in terms of conditions of engagement that do not require the frame of conscious knowledge: (simply) living lives that make other lives possible. Inviting me (the Strathern who writes about relations and kinship) into the dog kennel, as she puts it, this articulation of ecological understandings in present times has kinship in it. *The companion species manifesto* becomes "a kinship claim" (2003: 9). If we suspend an expectation of mutual comprehension, the kinship is other than Euro-American; if we expand the semantic range of mindedness, as Kohn (2013) has since done, we can speak of Euro-American transformed.[34]

It is a certain folding-in of kin relations with knowledge relations that I take to be at the heart of "Euro-American kinship." And it is with this that perhaps we glimpse its auto-occluding nature. Kin relations are bound up with knowledge of the world in such a way that "the world" comes to seem their (only, principal) horizon of reference.[35] The filter of this knowable world—its perceiver and cognizer—is the conscious knowing subject (Locke's "person" or self), and we have already encountered its claim to autonomy. Other things being equal, its reality is likely to assume precedence over anything else.

The Anglophone possibility of joining epistemic and interpersonal connotations of knowledge has a long history.[36] I recall the further twist that seems to have been particularly encouraged in modern times, early and late. Applied to persons, a (positive) role was and is given to knowledge in terms of recognition of mutuality. And that is not just repeated all over again but also magnified on its other side, friendship. Borneman (2001: 30–31) has criticized "the anthropology of kinship" for privileging regulative ideals where it should be analyzing diverse forms of intimacy and sociality, apropos care, for example. This parallels the criticism made all those years ago when Londoners brought friends into the anthropologists' questions about relatives. Relations make a ready appearance in the Euro-American vernacular; all one has to do is attend to families and relatives. Yet a dimension is missing: the (conscious, knowledge-making) individual is not seen clearly enough. It is in friendship between individuals, as we are told over and over again, that the positive value of relations lies, and purportedly appears in its ideal form. The notion of friend has long been suffused with personally expressed and positive moral sentiment, and this connotation occupies center stage. Now if friendship evinces a pure form of relationality, the purity derives from idealizing the outflowing (self-)expression of untrammeled individuals, and this mobilization of sentiment and feeling is—inadvertently or not—colloquially expressed in terms of the mind's workings:

friendship is nothing if it is not recognized. Recognition may move between background and foreground, as it does when people who take kin for granted suddenly become conscious of whom they are calling kin. In this regard, friend is a vernacular equivalent to kin, where (so to speak) self-consciousness has become everything. Friendship exists in being made known.

Perhaps recognition is so powerful because relating itself cannot be taken for granted. Perhaps, in turn, this underlines a particular Euro-American presentiment of otherness when it is given the epistemic value of being the unknown or unpredictable.[37] Haraway refers to relations as being about significant otherness at every scale, adding that knowledge is never done, and that in this sense "one cannot know the other or the self, but must ask in respect for all of time who and what are emerging in relationships" (2003: 50, emphasis omitted). Above all, dogs "are about the inescapable, contradictory story of relationships—co-constitutive relationships in which . . . the relating is never done once and for all" (12). I would suggest that the cross-species illumination can be turned back not just on (human) kinship in general but on a conceptual potential in Euro-American kinship thinking imagined as kinship/friendship.

For the uncertainty of that "never done" suggests an ongoing role for the ever-unfinished nature of the relating that keeps it (relating) in play. Hidden all along, so my speculation about Euro-American kinship goes, its other manifestation in friendship throws ideas about similarity of interest and purpose into the arena of interpersonal relations at large. What comes back, so to speak, if one brings friendship into the orbit of Euro-American kinship concepts, is a newly visible capacity for relating that allows for unpredictable alignments. It is inscribed among other ways in the vernacular's insistence on "choice" in friendship, coding for what is not (yet, fully) known. I have touched, all too fleetingly, on some uses of the idea of positive companionship, as in "living with" (for example, Kirksey and Helmreich 2010: 552) or "being alongside" (Latimer 2013), to suggest an arena of new knowledge—multispecies studies—that has conceivably reinvigorated the concept of friendship (kinship). But if what is in the flesh is in the syntax (paraphrasing Haraway 2003: 12), there is also hesitation here about what can be known. A vernacular coding for unpredictability sits alongside new perceptions of the needfulness of relating.

A Deferred Alter-criticism

Duplicating terms or phrases is a stylistic liberty, one I have taken at moments during the course of exposition with the concepts of culture and "culture" and relation and "relation." But I have also inserted other duplications as a commentary on other writers' practices, such as "understanding understanding" or "relating relations." These echo what is often taken as a grounding expositional issue: the reflexivity of knowledge conventionally expressed as knowing how one knows. The issue makes room for play, at least insofar as concept-duplication may or may not imply an identical or, to the contrary, a not-quite-identical pair. In any event, identity by distinction alone does not accomplish the specifying work entailed in concept-making. Thus when it appears crucial to distinguish "knowledge" from "information," distinction inevitably partners a domaining exercise, one that in this case would establish what is knowledge-like about knowledge, or information-like about information. The point is stimulated by Luhmann's (1990; and see 1982) late twentieth-century reanalysis of Western modernity.[38] One of his targets is the very notion of domains implying parts of a whole; he speaks instead of functional differentiation creating autopoetic, self-reproducing systems, each with an environment that can only be its own (one system cannot share an environment, any more than ancestors, with another). This formula implies in turn a constant rehearsal or duplication of identity within. Duplication accompanies the self-referencing, self-describing reasons for existence to which modern institutions appeal. Just as politics is embedded in an environment where it is feasible to take political action, so scholarly work must endorse an ethos and practice of scholarship, always able to find scholarly potential in the study of its surroundings. Hence it is possible to analyze those descriptions and performances that turn things into description and performance, or to analyze the relations that turn beings into evidence of relational selves. It all sounds, precisely, so self-evident.

It is with such a sense of identity that I have intended replications to convey (alter) criticism. Thus duplicating "understanding understanding" draws attention to the classic mode of Euro-American investigation that probes ever more into the identity of some object of knowledge, such as the nature of bureaucratic protocols, by questioning its own methods of objectification. More than that, my critical aim is to draw attention to a resonance between such epistemic exercises and the identitarian axis of Euro-American kinship ideas, those turning on (say) the fatherly qualities of fatherhood or the motherly ones of motherhood. Wagner's delineation of Euro-American kinship homologies echoes Luhmann's systems and subsystems that apprehend themselves through self-reference (organizations showing how organized they are; educational establishments meeting educational needs). This offers an interesting expository nexus in which to return briefly to the individuation of concepts, including that of the individual person.

Recall the contrasting emphases of amity and amiability in chapter 6. McKinnon (2013) suggests that while Fortes's (along with Evans-Pritchard's) theorization of social domains devolves from the classic nineteenth-century confrontation of kinship and territorial organization, it diverges in a subtle way from their predecessors' writing on the evolution of society.[39] For Fortes understands the development of distinct spheres of social life as the outcome of a process of increasing differentiation. "Rather than a progressive de-encompassment of the individual or more individuated forms of social relation from larger kin groups, Fortes and Evans-Pritchard reverse the sequence: they begin with individual dyadic relations in the natural bilateral family and gradually encompass those relations within successive layers of differentiated social domains" (2013: 48). McKinnon's contrast echoes that between Fortes (amity) and Pitt-Rivers (amiablity). To come analytically to a concept of an individual divested of relations, such as the friend freed from diverse restrictions, implies a different analytical strategy from starting out with an individualized entity, as Fortes and Evans-Pritchard start with "individual dyadic relations." The former strips the individual of relations (relationality, sociality) in order to bestow them again across the individual's personal networks and public associations; the latter begins with the person's elemental relations as the basis for further social complexity. To reiterate the last point, the positive gloss of amiability catches well the kind of expansive sociality that seems to be occluded by too restricted a focus on "kinship." It is the individual person who displays such expansiveness.

In addressing the scope of interpersonal relations, degrees of interest and disinterest are often brought in as explicit measures of sociality. Yet the polarization makes sense only if one conceptualizes individual selves stripped from relations. Articulated as we saw by writers of the Scottish Enlightenment, the personal interests of friends were to have no part in the indifferent (disinterested) sphere of the market although "self-interest" certainly did, while conversely the individual friend was "self-less" (disinterested) only to the extent of downplaying the self-interest invested in the interests of the very relationship as such.[40] It thus matters whether interest is attached to the person or the relation. Otherwise the concept of interest creates no end of ethical tangles; it also creates an incoherence of a larger sort. The incoherence is evident in what happens to kinship. The era when a "new concept of personal relations" (Silver 1990: 1492) was being formed left a lasting legacy of confusion about where kin relations belong in a universe split between the impersonal and personal. The alter critic might observe that families, the institution through which modern kinship relations are perceived, are as public as they are private, as much an impersonal statistic in the eyes of the state as molded by personal practices, a bureaucratic figment as well as a source of intimacies. Above all, in descriptions of familial life, any contrast between self-interest and disinterest degenerates into nonsense.

Moderns and naturalists imagine a historic moment when kin relations were shuffled to one side and ostensibly banished from the free associations of (male) civic life, along with the evils of patronage, nepotism, and the like.[41] The peculiar, if not nonexistent, place of kinship in the modern constitution remains a source of remark for anthropologists who live, conceptually speaking, with the imaginative consequences, including with a language weighted in the detachment of "individuals" (individual persons) from relations.[42] In this regard, the as-if drama in chapter 5 criticizes the direction of Hume's argument about relations as much as Locke's. Needless to say, that should not obscure these writers' own critical use of the general concept (relations) in order to cast doubt on the certainties of their time. Thus Hume challenges assumptions about the identity of things — in common parlance, in other philosophical schemes — by insisting that the workings of the mind depend on the association of ideas, one with one another. Yet the alter critic queries what Hume is doing when he adds to the abstract, ubiquitous notion of relations the affect of positive, interpersonal ties. As we have seen, his relations absorb familiarity and acquaintance, indeed at times conflate them, with a resulting language play on the ambiguities. (Political interests would determine whether this is a complaint or not.) We might conclude that much Euro-American anthropology has been trying to salvage what, out of such structurings of relations, can be used for the kind of knowledge they would make for broader purposes and more general inquiry.

In the eyes of those who seek to know it, the character of the relation necessarily includes the circumstances under which it is an object of, and a vehicle for, knowing. Concerning current vernacular English usage, a question was posed at the beginning: why it is assumed that kinship is about relations. Let us give the phrase a Viveiros de Castrian turn. Kinship (like friendship) is reflected on *as* relations. It thereby becomes a vehicle of knowledge, relating those who become known to one another and, through further specification as to what kind of relating is at issue, creating objects for reflection and scrutiny. Could-have-been-otherwise also reveals what is actualized: the particular contours of Euro-American kinship/friendship.

The Relation as an Object of Exposition

To describe naturalist cosmology it must be rendered describable, as I have hoped to do through observing certain Euro-American knowledge-making practices. Such practices have resonance insofar as the outcomes in turn seem cosmologically apt, that is, inspire through a sense of their degree of fit for the world at hand. Key to both is a throng of relations, an apparatus that becomes exaggerated in Anglophone usage. Knowledge is brought to consciousness through the explicitness with which people relate a multitude of things or uncover the vast extent of already-existing relations, whether in the face of an apparent deficit or not. Then again, that very pervasiveness propels simultaneous conviction and doubt (to use knowledge-words) about the primacy of relating that is sometimes expressed as though it emanated a transcendent or — to draw on Cannell — ineffable aura.

Contingency may re-enchant the act of description. Relation is not something that can be calculated, predicted, or secured, Gasché says (1999: 13); "to come into a relation is . . . also a matter of chance, of luck, as it were," and thus of "coming into an appropriate relationship to what is to be thought." The contingency that began this account, an apparently idiosyncratic use of the English language, might be apprehended thus. It is odd, to say the least, to think that English kin terms were not always about relatives and relations. The abundance of kinship's ties, links, bonds, rapports, friendships, correspondences, resemblances, and so forth, had never been short of expression, but the entailments of this new usage, an idiosyncrasy indeed, were flowing in other directions. They become caught up in those Euro-American traditions of thought — based on study, reflection, and scholarship — invested in making relations explicit, and indeed in stimulating that explicitness. Thus Kohn (2012: 138) affirms a kind of relational vitality in a context intended to transform how to think of thinking. To argue that "life is semiotic and semiosis is alive" is to change "how we think about relationality — arguably anthropology's fundamental concern and central analytic." Who knows what part this plays in the appearance of the relation at other moments understood as frontiers of or new challenges to knowledge-making? Campbell's (2009: 172) description of "the kinship resonances" detectable in people's defense of the British farming landscape, newly apprehended as less than a natural world, turns on a sense of more than human relatedness. From a view of novel reproductive interventions, Franklin (2013b: 293) reminds us of "the unbounded scope of potential interconnectedness" in bilateral kinship systems, a scope that always requires some other order of relatedness to curtail "the unlimited kin universe."[43] The entailments, like the person as a knowledge-maker, go well beyond the bounds of scholarship.

Anthropology itself has constantly made and remade its understanding of kinship as the most evidently relational of all institutions of meaning, including structuring it as the relations of relations to one another. In apposition to this (scholarly) expansiveness, the relation's restrictive effect on the kin universe — as Euro-Americans generally imagine and inhabit it — is arresting. I referred to it as self-occlusion: the occlusion of kin relations by the knowledge relations that are among its constituents, personified in the occlusion of kinspersons by the person as a knowledge-making subject (those moments when you see the person before the kinswoman). In short, relations obscure relations. Possible antecedents appear in certain early modern discourses; I have also tried to suggest as much, with respect to present-day moderns and naturalists, for the hypothetical arena of Euro-American kinship/friendship. That becomes self-occluding in another sense, that is, in the extent to which each set of relations appears to omit the other. The consequences are there for all to see: the values of an expansive sociality or relationality can be conceptualized apart from "kinship." This outcome seemingly joins the many purifications and domaining efforts of modern thinkers, politicians, and theorists who brought a social world ("society") into view. So it would be as part of that constantly renewed social world that we could have added scholarship, in the tradition of the scientific (*sensu lato*) enterprises and emergent disciplines of the Enlightenment, to Schneider's twentieth-century list of domains endorsing diffuse enduring solidarity. Needless to say, no one would have actually called it kinship.

Theoretical Heterogeneity

Theoretical heterogeneity is at once encompassed within English discourse and originates, so users often remark, beyond it (distant discourses, remote epochs). Heterogeneity, as in Navaro-Yashin's (2009) multiplicity of paradigms, is to be welcomed. Relations do their work under congruent and under conflicting circumstances alike. Neither the discordant voices of anthropologists, and examples have been introduced at several junctures, nor the scrutiny of the concept of relation, kept constantly in view, have made relations disappear. They are also sustained by what is equally under observation, the English vernacular. Overlap between anthropological and vernacular usage is a visible moment of contact that can work as a rallying point for divergent interests capable of addressing multifaceted causes.[44] For all its problems, common language saves us from having to have common understanding.

The analytical contexts conjured in order to focus on the relation as an object of exposition have been equally heterogeneous. The reader has been taken from Locke's oak tree, organ donation, and literary societies to Firth's musings on social anthropology, inhabitants of the Wahgi Valley, Merian's drawings of insects. Something like this heterogeneous list is offered by Mohácsi and Morita's (2015: 4) reflections on posthumanist trends in the discipline, and on how people act through innumerable nonhuman entities: cells, animals, plants, spirits, and concepts are on their list. They note that these items do not presuppose, in antithesis, an integrated human subject. This does not mean that such a subject cannot also be enacted. An expository dilemma that Nietzsche apparently posed to himself was that he could only describe his self through countless deferrals of metaphor (Gasché 1999: 45–47). This rendered the admonition "know thyself" useless, for that would imply someone other than as he was; to be-as-he-was had to take the form of action, a nonreflective resistance to self-consciousness, such as might be achieved through the repetitive activity of being. Again, the multidimensionality of selves supposed by certain late modern channels (of extraterrestrial consciousnesses) leads them to apprehend the present ecological crisis as the price to be paid for neglecting all the ways in which human beings are at the same time "other human and nonhuman beings" (Skafish 2017: 279). "Know thyselves!" becomes the admonition to take the action, develop the techniques, required to be in touch with one's own innumerable other lives. Now, the startling last item on Mohácsi and Morita's list is "concept." Rather than selves (and these two forms recall many such forms), if we pursued concepts—vital expersonations of self-conscious selves—what of enactment then? The two anthropologists give a lead. Ethnographic practice, Mohácsi and Morita (2015: 2) say, is a form of practice "where concepts cease to be pure analytical tools, and become actions in themselves." I have tried to activate the concept of relation, not least in terms of its multiplicity, and, in this limited sense, offer an ethnographic account.

That said, this exposition has trod a tightrope, bereft of so much that anthropology would seek to know through focusing on relations, and (for this author) uncomfortably so in the case of kinship. Yet it is through a focus on the ideas that (Euro-American) people have of relations that we discern how certain understandings of them mold their sense of how things exist. Anthropologists in turn may derive positive value less from the vernacular gloss of solidary connection or association than from relation's active, transpositional capacity. The openness of relation makes it a notion that English users can summon to transpose or convey certain realities beyond the scope of their language, as though bringing new concepts into view. The ensuing problem for exposition is a problematization in Rabinow's sense, an issue that demands thought because of one's relation to it. It lies in the recurrent activation of (all kinds of) relations in the recurrent nature of activity as such, and thus in their too easy repetition, in their excess or in the too-many of them.

A pair of relational modes, social/personal connection and epistemic/associative thinking, consistently recurs. The narrative has tried to make explicit some of the empirical effects of their (continuing) conflation. It has neither embarked from the distinctiveness of the two modes of relating, nor sought to arrive there as an end point. That would have obviated and thus got rid of what I trust has been laid out, which is how concepts are deployed, in this sense used, including the facilitations through which certain discourses encourage people to pass from one to the other. Thus do anthropologists present the practice of comparison, the basis at once of social discrimination and of cross-domain epistemology. When relations are discussed in the abstract, comparison may be put forward as an archetype, an index of an elemental relational operation. When it comes to usage, however, it obviously works not alone but as part of a conceptual package, where entities may be brought together with evaluative intent. So comparison comes with attendants, such as a premise of similarity and its implied negation (dissimilarity). To attribute certain usages of comparison to an English-based discourse is not to exclude usages elsewhere, but only to remark that *in this discourse* the premise of similarity has hegemonic weight; embedded or immanent in much else, it carries in its train a host of conceptual and social applications. My intention has been to capture not only the immanent standing of concepts, values, and taken-for-granted orientations in people's expression of thoughts and acts, but also dimensions of a cosmological order. Immanence is understood in relation to the transcendence that any of these expressions might also have, and here is a coincidence between scholarship and kinship. Both deploy much of the same range of assumptions that have allowed the anthropologist to recognize a force to exposition that goes beyond and thereby transcends any material in hand. Value placed on the expository force of knowledge indexes this. Perhaps a current meeting ground between vernacular and anthropological usage lies in understanding that force as a matter of relating.

Being Between

The force may be generated, in part at least, by an apparatus that works almost unseen. I return to a concept introduced at the beginning, drawn from another time and place than present-day anthropology and its concerns, although in some senses anterior to them. It is the sometime strangeness of relations existing "between" (relata).

Betweenness. Among many medieval professionals (philosophers and the like), such a conjunction was either unthinkable or else inadmissible. Deep matters of exposition, and thus of explicit knowledge-making, were involved.[45] For them relations could be debated only through the already-existing descriptions of entities and their qualities that initially made it difficult to propose that qualities, the category into which relations fell, could be shared between two entities. In retrospect, we would say that this description blocked other formulas: relations may indeed obscure relations. In retrospect, too, we might be drawn to an exceptional figure, Peter Aureoli, who argued otherwise (I depend on Henninger [1989] here). This early fourteenth-century scholastic formulated a way of expressing the idea that a relation connects, so that as a connecting idea it could appear as a connection — he used the Latin for medium or interval — between things.[46] (Kin relations sprang to his aid, fatherhood being referred to as a kind of medium connecting father with son.) His views might have been debated, but they did not gain general purchase, and in his circles the concept remained rather strange. So what conceptual spaces had to be made?[47] A retrospective view might ponder again on the inventions of those early modern thinkers for whom the notion that relations delineated a thing that could lie between things was to cease being odd and began to acquire its aura of power. Relations-between was to release what was then an expositional potential for refashioning the interconnectedness of the world.

Notes

INTRODUCTIONS: THE COMPULSION OF RELATIONS

1 See Hirsch and Strathern (2004). The late Dr. Kalinoe OBE became Papua New
   Guinea's secretary for justice and attorney general. (He granted me permission to
   quote from his remarks.)

2 Pondering an Amerindian concept of the concept, Viveiros de Castro (e.g., [2009]
   2014: 80) has challenged Euro-American anthropologists and philosophers in their
   endorsement of particular vectors of thought. We may wish to be aware how in this
   or that milieu concepts behave as, for instance, that of the imagined totality "society," for which Rio (2007: 2) finds a personified counterpart on the Melanesian
   island of Ambrym. The anthropomorphism (we know concepts are agents, but talk
   of behavior makes them sound like actors) implies some distance from the interests
   of those who postulate that concepts must be purified, defined, and given particular
   remits in order to aid investigation. The benefits of such precision are evident. Here
   the pursuit is after another kind of precision, namely attending to the circumstances
   under which concepts channel the course of exposition.

3 Duplex comes from a discussion (M. Strathern 2005) concerned with the persistence
   of divergent thinking summoned by relationality. There I dwelled on diverse modes,
   including "science's relation" (based on natural and cultural relations, as in the combination of discovery and invention) and "anthropology's relation" (epistemic and
   interpersonal relations, as combined in the concept of social relations), both usages
   belonging to what can be broadly called a naturalist cosmology.

4 Gell had already foreshortened the question to social relationships: "relationships between participants in social systems of various kinds" (1998: 4), with a strong sense
   of the social interactions implied. He had in mind extending the force of such relations in the form of "persons" to (the agency of) art objects. See Haraway ([1984]
   1989: 55): "The concept of social relations must include the entire complex of interactions among people; objects, including books, buildings, and rocks; and animals"
   (cited in Noble 2016: 93).

5 For a general anthropological commentary, see Allen (2000). While Aristotle spoke of similarities and resemblances, and deployed comparison and analogies (Lloyd 1966), apparently these moves did not involve the notion of a third entity to which two entities under comparison (say) are jointly attached, as would be implied by the "dyadic or two place property, *being-similar-to*" (Brower 2015: 2, original emphasis). On the contrary, their similitude is explained by a pair of monadic properties or accidents inhering in each entity.

6 Although in medieval times the prepositions "betwixt" and "between" were well used in the vernacular, and there are fifteenth- and sixteenth-century usages of both "relations between" and "comparisons between," their Latin counterpart was a rare novelty in scholastic philosophizing on relations (Henninger 1989). The discursive lift-off there — to borrow a phrase from Withington (2010) — of relations as relations-between-entities apparently came later. (Gasché [1999] expatiates on the trouble that the notion of "between" gave Martin Heidegger.) Locke sometimes talked of relations betwixt or between but generally deployed phrases that seem to the modern reader unnecessarily circumlocutionary (examples are given in M. Strathern 2016).

7 As the apogee of a naturalist cosmology (see below) where divisions between entities are presented as a matter of "spontaneous self-evidence" (Descola [2005] 2013: 199). Gasché (1999: 160) cites the role played by Leibniz in displacing pre-Enlightenment philosophizing on the very scope of exposition: when "the rule of a sovereign entity — God — is replaced by the rule of evident truth . . . [it is] the mind's representation of facts," rooted in the principle of sufficient reason, that comes into focus. Human knowledge becomes a principal problematic. Gasché is not here making an argument about relations, but perhaps allows us to. Is that displacement not accompanied by an investment in their expositional power? In her general account of the Enlightenment, the historian Outram (1995: 48) represents some of the questions of the time in terms of relational issues, such as "the relationship of man to nature."

8 All terms lead to other terms, he is saying, but relative terms show this explicitly (e.g., "weak" and "strong," each implying the other). Leibniz's overall argument was consonant with his objection to Isaac Newton's idea of space as something in itself, within which other objects move; for Leibniz, space was simply the "order" (a synonym at the time for "relation"), in which celestial bodies move in respect to one another.

9 Evans-Pritchard's (1962: 28) formal position explicitly drew on humanist, that is, pre-Enlightenment, notions of ordering. His declaration is worth remarking for the way it brings together the epistemic and interpersonal (see note 3): "Human societies . . . are seen as systems only because social life must have a pattern of some kind, inasmuch as man, being a reasonable creature, has to live in world in which his relations with those around him are ordered and intelligible."

10 Sahlins is paraphrasing Leenhardt ([1947] 1979), who was also drawn to comment on the notion of participation. Faubion (2001: 2, 11, emphasis omitted) gives this a kinship cast in referring to kinship's specific (though not unique) "constitution of intersubjectivity, of organized alterity," through which the self is "a subject through its relations to others . . . [just as] others identify the self through their relation to it."

11 "The relation is the irreducible minimum for all units in Marx's conception of social

reality"; thus "the relation between capital and labor is treated ... as a function of capital itself" — capital is a (social) relation (Ollman [1971] 1976: 14, 13). Ollman is noting Marx's dual usage: relation as internal to a factor (such as capital) and as a connection between factors.

12 It is not just that there is disagreement about the relative force of external or internal relations, but that a thinker's inclination on the matter colors the connotation of the terms. Those of an empiricist persuasion might speak of internal relations, as between "husband" and "wife," where each individual is seemingly dependent on the other. However, an internal relation in an idealist and/or holistic account implies a partition of a whole, as in the perception of marital partners as part of the whole entity "marriage." Descombes ([1996] 2014: 199) himself asserts that there can be no internal relation between individuals: "The very language in which we are invited to posit this internal relationship indicates that it is rather a connection that is exterior to the reality of both parties since it is, as we have just said, 'between them.'"

13 The full passage reads: "Multiplicity is a system defined by a modality of relational synthesis different from a connection or conjunction of terms. Deleuze calls it a disjunctive synthesis or inclusive disjunction, a relational mode that does not have similarity or identity as its (formal or final) cause, but divergence or distance; another name for this relational mode is 'becoming'" (Viveiros de Castro [2009] 2014: 112, emphasis omitted). Deleuze's specific debt to Leibniz is noted.

14 Arriving at a concept of relationships as the ground of infinite being (2013: 170), he suggests that the Iatmul person embodies a pair of brothers, "an internal relation that orients the process of one forever becoming the other brother" (202). The "other brother," he continues, is simultaneously external in a relational sense and the self-same brother with a similar internal configuration. (See further, chapter 4.)

15 As at moments in Locke's work, for instance, and Ollman's ([1971] 1976: 15).

16 See again Faubion (2001: 3): "The terms of kinship are inherently linking terms; ... they render the self in and through its relation to certain others." However, Radcliffe-Brown seems to have something more like external relations in mind (social structure as "actually existing relations" that "link together certain human beings" [(1940) 1952: 192]).

17 I am grateful to Debbora Battaglia for the relevance of these last two points here.

18 To offer one example, Frankenberg's (1957) focus on the politics of a Welsh village sprang from then-burgeoning interests in African village politics, a comparative agenda carried through in his proposing a social anthropology for Britain (1982).

19 As Descombes's ([1996] 2014: 157) discussion of Lévi-Strauss puts it, "Structural holism asks us to practice structural analysis as a form of holistic analysis, i.e., as a search for the relations that ground the system." His own account develops the proposition that no social interaction takes place without a third term, that is, the taken-for-granted, instituted meanings of collective life. In gift exchange, the whole is given before its parts in that a "gift" is already following the conventions of "gift giving."

20 In this work he is concerned to get rid of the misconception that there is any "relation" between "the material" and "the social world," because the very division of them is an artifact (Latour 2005: 75–76), an exercise that also redefines the connota-

tions of "the social" (108–109). That said, the whole "actor network" enterprise may be understood by Anglophone commentators as intensely relational (e.g., Candea et al. 2015b: 16; Jensen and Winthereik 2013: 29; Walford 2017: 66).

21 The oppositional mode of connection/disconnection is not at all the same as the disjunctive synthesis noted above, the significance of which will become apparent in due course.

22 Wagner (2011: 161). Explicitness about either present or absent relations can indicate relational thinking; however, an enacted relation (anthropologist-speaking) emptied of engagement or attachment may be rendered as a "non-relation" in the English vernacular.

23 Both volumes point to a wave of twenty-first-century arguments about the limits of the relation as an anthropological analytic. With shifts in the connotations of relation, the terms around it also shift. Thus the individual person, as a logical concept always relationally constructed with respect to other concepts, may be newly identified as a relational configuration socially speaking, in which individualism is a knowing strategy (see, e.g., Hastrup 2002).

24 And thus already differentiated. Rabinow is experimenting with a toolkit of concepts to advance inquiry in the human sciences, with attention to "the ways that information is given narrative and conceptual form, and how this knowledge fits into a conduct of life" (2003: 2). Under changing conditions of narration, concepts must be subject to constant rethinking.

25 Drawing from the manner in which synthetic biology can change the functionality of cells through changing their constituent medium, Rabinow and Bennett (2008, 2012) speak of remediation.

26 She objects generally to the vocabulary of mediation (Barad 2007: 231). "Intra-action" supersedes the conventional "interaction," which implies relations "between" preexisting entities.

27 "Knowing is a material practice, a specific engagement of the world where part of the world becomes differentially intelligible to another part of the world" (Barad 2007: 342). Difference is understood as meaningful, neither "meaning" nor "intelligibility" being human-based notions but matters of differential responsiveness (2007: 335). (Potential counterparts come to mind, such as Kohn 2013, but one could almost read this as a latter-day rewriting of Wagner 1986.)

28 In her view, the former would be a (representationalist) "reflection"; after Haraway, her preferred methodology is diffraction, a material entanglement (2007: 88) that she distances from analogy on the grounds that analogies presuppose already-differentiated elements. However, there are modes of anthropological cross-cultural comparison that deploy analogy precisely as a way of bringing diffraction into play: running sets of material-discursive practices through each other to produce differentials.

1. EXPERIMENTATIONS, ENGLISH AND OTHERWISE

1 See, for example, James (2003: 53–54), following Allen's (2000: 91–99) exposition of the philosopher Charles Renouvier (Émile Durkheim's "educator"). In Renouvier's list of basic categories of conceptual organization or understanding, as they were de-

volved from Aristotle, "relation" penetrated all the others. I emphasize the intervening notion of "knowledge" to draw attention to how the term "relation" is deployed
precisely in its categorical form when the task is how to understand understanding
(see chapter 3).

2 *Le rapport* works in French as a term for epistemic or logical relations, yet while it
can point to relations established (achieved) between persons, it does not—as far
as I know—designate them, that is, act in this context as a substantive. Apparently
la relation may designate persons, but acquaintances and associates excluding kin.
(In English, rapport [derived from the French] was in circulation in the seventeenth
century, connoting correspondence or conformity.) Stengers's emphasis on the effort
it takes to create rapport illuminates a point about relations made by Jensen and
Winthereik (2013: 200). They quote Latour's protest that, far from everything already being related, it is an act of power to achieve commensurability, to bring things
(actors) into relation. Perhaps it is with just this sense that Lévi-Strauss ([1958] 1963:
95–96) long ago wrote, "As soon as the various aspects of social life—economic, linguistic, etc.—are expressed as relationships [*comme des rapports*], anthropology will
become a general theory of relationships [*des rapports*]."

3 Carsten (2000b: 5) introduces the concept of relatedness in order to suspend certain
assumptions, and thereby bracket off a specific nexus of problems, which "kinship"
otherwise trails. Fortes's concept is abstract insofar as it may be isolated as a moral
principle, "a general and fundamental axiom which I call the axiom of prescriptive
altruism or . . . of amity" (1969: 251).

4 Apropos Schneider (e.g., 1972), "I take diffuse enduring solidarity and the like as the
corollary subjectivity of mutual being" (Sahlins 2011a: 12).

5 And tells "us," as observers of anthropologists, except at this moment I elide the two
positions.

6 A stance in direct debate with suppositions concerning innate principles or categories.

7 In his chapter on identity (written somewhat later), Locke was to make a distinction
between man and person, here seemingly conflated.

8 Mack (1992: 2–3) introduces her account of the complex character of seventeenth-
century Quaker visionaries with a counterpart nod to the numerous theoretical
lenses through which, at the end the twentieth century, they might have been depicted.

9 This summary of historical and anthropological material comes from an English literature specialist scrutinizing the preoccupation of novels of the time with women's
disinheritance. McLeish (2019: 151 ff.) explores the imaginative forms of (inferential,
inductive) writing that emerged, almost in concert, from experimental science and
from the novel alike.

10 Erickson's work is based on probate documents and records of lawsuits over marriage
settlements. In the late seventeenth and early eighteenth centuries, women were feeling the effects of the contraction of earlier provisions that had been in their favor
under the once-prevalent diversity of legal jurisdictions (five distinct bodies of law affecting property disposal). Thus the equal division of land and goods among children
and women's various property entitlements under ecclesiastical law was changing;
common law began limiting women's inheritance of land.

11 On the authority of the *Oxford English Dictionary*'s 1971 compact edition of the complete text. (This is not something Tadmor comments on.) Relation was used both for the connection, as "between persons arising out of the natural ties of blood or marriage," and for the person, "related to one by blood or marriage" (1971: 2478). The latter was special to kinsfolk, since the former (the connection itself) was deployed in a third usage, which referred to interpersonal relations in general. These are, of course, latter-day interpretations of seventeenth-century usage. Samuel Johnson's *Dictionary* of 1755 drew on both John Milton and John Dryden to illustrate relation defined as kindred or an alliance of kin.

12 The early modern period is appropriately styled, in Withington's view, insofar as many "modern" connotations took shape then. He comments on the "early modern obsession with ancient, 'hard,' and 'new' words" (2010: 108). (Describing Phillips's *The new world of words* [see below] as plagiaristic, he implies it was thus one among many.)

13 When, in Withington's words, a term moves from a period of assimilation to normative acceptance. Those in which he has especial interest — "society," "company," "modern" — were appropriated by humanist writers in the 1570s, but were to have discursive lift-off in the 1680s and 1690s (2010: 13, 234). Society in the sense of company or fellowship appeared in the early sixteenth century, though "company" itself was Norman-French and "fellowship" Anglo-Saxon (2010: 107).

14 This was a time when it was possible to fashion arguments about the separation of the society of the household from the body politic (Gobetti 1992; Zengotita 1984), even if to discern the transformation of one into the other (Schochet 1969).

15 Albeit diffuse in usage. I do not elaborate on the way in which terms for specific kin (e.g., "father") apparently contrasted with terms applied to all manner of kin ("uncle," "cousin"); specific terms were also *used* diffusely ("father" for "father-in-law").

16 The date is 1790, by which time the term had become sedimented in colloquial usage. Alberto Corsín Jiménez (pers. comm.) comments that if one thinks of the house as a "trap" for the relation, in having the interior space in which Mr. Wallace could be "found," it was also making room for the appearance of civil society.

17 If someone might be called "a relation" without the speaker having to specify the persons through whom the tie was traced, presumably there was an equivocation as to what the absence of specification implied. Either a link between known kinspersons was being expressed through a logical/epistemic term or else a kin-based sense of relation was inclusive of interpersonal connections of any kind. Like "society" and "company," "relation" applied to kin could carry overtones of affect. However (Tadmor's point), it is less the kind of relation than the fact of it that is immediately acknowledged.

18 When Shapin (1996: 28) quotes John Donne's famous lines, from 1611, on the decentering effect of post-Copernican investigations, "And New Philosophy calls all in doubt / . . . 'Tis all in pieces, all coherence gone; / All just supply, and all Relation," we surmise that "relation" was conveying the cosmology of an ordered or justly proportioned world.

19 Galileo would not have been using (cognates of) the term "relation" (with thanks to Jill Mann [pers. comm.]). Biagioli translates the comments of a Jesuit mathematician at the time (1610–1611) as follows: "Here in Rome we have seen them [the Medicean stars]. I will attach some diagrams at the end of this letter from which one can see most clearly that they are not fixed stars, but errant ones, as they change their position in relation to Jupiter" (2006: 111–112). I am grateful to Mario Biagioli for further elucidation: this latter phrase was literally conveyed as positions changing "among themselves."

20 He put them into a class of "wandering stars," though stars had never been seen orbiting other planets. The point was that "Galileo could construct a legitimate argument about the physical existence of the satellites of Jupiter by tabulating their periodical motions" (Biagioli 2006: 148). The same evidence also confirmed that what he saw was not simply an effect of imperfections in the instrument.

21 My thanks to John Dunn for subsequently pointing me to Dawson's (2007) salutary treatment of the problem of language in early modern philosophy, which examines Locke's own commentary on words.

22 There were also terms making their appearance in the sixteenth and seventeenth centuries, such as "attraction" and "sympathy," which from the outset seem to have applied to relations between natural phenomena and persons alike.

23 Thanks to Rob Wilson (2016) for making me clarify the point that the new in Locke's use was not the specific appeal to kin but what was happening to usages of relations at the time (see M. Strathern 2005: 64–65). I record my further appreciation for his sharing of materials, among them parts of his current work on relationality. Note that the concept of "kin" as such could be used of blood ties, family, common stock, groups of persons so connected, and also of a class or natural group or division of entities. Like "conceive," it contained the possibilities of epistemic as well as interpersonal application. The move I point to in the seventeenth century was in this sense a reinvention. ("Kin" and "kindred" were common long before; "kinship" is a nineteenth-century neologism.)

24 I am grateful to Carla Freccero, University of California, Santa Cruz, for pointing me to this work.

25 Such kinship "took a multiplicity of forms, created by promise as well as by blood, and by ritual and oath as well as by nature. It might spring from the love of parents and children, a brother or sister, or an uncle or aunt, nephew or niece—the love (in that once generic term) of a 'cousin.' But kinship might also be created directly, by human agency. Marriage was the most complete instrument of that agency . . . but marriage was not the only form in which kinship could be created by ritual or promise . . . '[S]worn brothers' . . . were another such, and they themselves are not a distinct and unique phenomenon. Their kinship overlapped both symbolically and actually with that created by a betrothal and with the 'spiritual' kinship created by baptism" (Bray 2003: 214). We should not overlook the intermingling of tropes either: Ng (2007: 29–30) gives early seventeenth-century examples of the trope of marriage being used interchangeability with those of brotherhood or of parent and child.

26 Tantalizingly, because I cannot pursue it here, as in today's French, "parent" was once used generically not only for parent in the modern sense but for those whom English speakers now call "relatives," such usage declining after the sixteenth century.

27 For a philosophical address to anthropological material, see the pertinent comments in Wilson (2016); among others he cites Stuart (2013), whose account of Locke's metaphysics indicates something of the range of discussion and interpretation that surrounds the vocabulary of identity, self, substance, man, person, and so forth.

28 As in the case of one of Locke's pupils, the third Earl of Shaftesbury, ruminating on the circumstances under which "I [may] indeed be said to be lost, or have lost my self" (Porter 2000: 166). Attending to its location in arguments of the time, Balibar ([1998] 2013) credits Locke with inventing the concept of consciousness.

29 Substance as a mass of matter has its own type of identity; here Locke is talking of the identity of an individual organism that has a typical and distinct form, and an individual life, or what we may gloss in the case of man as the "human individual" (Balibar [1998] 2013: 57). "Individual" was originally a term for an indivisible entity (an indivisible relational whole, Pálsson [1999] calls it); Balibar ([1998] 2013: 84) indicates this kind of restriction on Locke's usage of individual, as connoting a corporeal organization that gives a living being its permanence of form. However, it was also becoming used in the seventeenth century for separate entities, whether (as an adjective) for some thing distinguished from others by attributes of its own, or (as a noun) for an object determined by properties peculiar to itself, as well as for a single member of a natural class or group. (In this volume, I generally treat "the individual" as a precipitate of the ethos of "individualism," not of the "individuality" that Rapport [1997] elaborates.)

30 "This also shews wherein the identity of the same man [the human individual organism] consists; viz. in nothing but a participation of the same continued life, by constantly fleeting particles of matter, in succession vitally united to the same organized body" (Locke 1690: 2, 27, 6; 331–332). Where modern readers might look forward to a nature-culture dichotomy, over Locke's shoulder were contemporary debates on the resurrection and the Day of Judgment. The being accountable for his or her actions could not be the bodily enfolded and corruptible "man" but the moral "person," a bearer of rights and duties, a self with its enduring identity (Sandford 2013: xxi).

31 Apropos Locke's "invention of consciousness" (see note 28), Mack offers a glimpse into certain preexisting Protestant notions of mind. She writes of the (early to mid-) seventeenth-century Puritan and Anglican conviction that mental processes were defined in terms of physical processes, at least insofar as spirituality was concerned. The condition of the body was a sign of the condition of the soul: "The individual's spiritual state was reflected in the texture, moisture, and aroma of his or her own flesh" (1992: 22). For early Quakers, the "cravings of the intellect" were as transitory as those of the stomach or genitals: "The deepest, most hidden, most authentic aspect of the self was something akin to conscience, . . . a shard of universal truth, God's voice embedded in the self, which they called 'the light' or 'the seed'" (136–137). In fact, what they understood as "will" and "mind" were enemies of the soul. However, such Quakers differentiated themselves from other Puritans in the relative absence of

personal introspection, at least as shown in correspondence (160). Mack documents how this alters with the quietist Quakers of the later part of the century (when Locke was writing), where an "inner life and personal relationships" began emerging together from people's accounts (354), and bodily metaphors take on a quite different cast. Indeed the evolution of Quakerism, as Mack presents it, including the new domesticity of women, further illumines the tracery of changes I have so inexpertly touched upon.

32 In the introductory section on relation, a person ("Caius") is taken as a "positive being" who can be described either through attributes, such as gender or color, or else through a relative term such as "husband," which links him to some other person, or the comparative "whiter," which links him to some other thing. Thought is led beyond the initial subject, says Locke, and in this sense any idea may be the foundation of relation (2, 25, 1; 319). This is an instance of (affinal) kinship being used to exemplify a logical relation, that of comparison. Here the fact that the example is of a person brings kinship to mind as one among other possibilities: Caius is later imagined as compared to several persons, someone "being capable of as many relations, as there can be occasions of comparing him to other things" (2, 25, 7; 322).

33 With gratitude to Jeanette Edwards for pointing me to Johnson et al.'s (2013) collection, and for her specific observations "on the fading in and out of the significance of the idiom of blood" (Edwards 2014: 42). On lines in general, Bamford (2009: 170) notes that the botanist John Ray, credited with the first definition of "species," enunciated (in 1686) that however much variation there was among individual organisms of the same type, one species never springs from the seed of another.

34 Blood flowed between parents and children and, in a restricted sense, specifically between father and child. Thus sons might be conceived as "part of the bodies of fathers who pass on their glory to their sons," a point to be debated with the idea of nobility being instead "in the human soul" (Delille 2013: 127). In some formulations maternal blood was externalized by its circulating properties. Delille's discussion ranges from the latter half of the fifteenth century to the seventeenth century, by which time these ideas were consolidated, despite opposition to such theories from both church and state.

35 Flesh, like blood, had its own genealogy. When "flesh" depicted the (carnal) union of spouses, in Christian thought some of the virtues of "blood" were instead bound up with the blood of sacrifice and its analogy with baptismal water.

36 In this book, the term "naturalist" echoes their connotations. Reflecting semi-autobiographically on how to make an anthropology of "moderns" possible, Latour (2013a) refers to the frenzied users of a nature/culture schema by Descola's term "naturalists." (In practice, he adds, the users of this schema do not abide by it; the way ahead lies in discarding the smoke screen thrown up by notions of nature and an exterior material world. However, Descola is more interested in "naturalism," with its distinctions of subject and object, mind and matter, as itself a permutation of other ontological possibilities, so it is appropriate for his argument to keep certain established characterizations of nature/culture intact.) My usage of "naturalist" is obviously separate from vernacular English, where the adjective/noun devolved out of specific reference to students of physics or natural philosophy, as common seven-

teenth- and eighteenth-century definitions had it, and as the experimentalist Robert Boyle described himself (Shapin and Schaffer [1985] 2011: 307).

37 Following the arguments of Randolph Trumbauch, Perry (2004: 230–231) is comparing English eighteenth-century aristocratic and middle-class strategies in terms of the privatization of marriage. The English landed classes favored "marriage-of-incorporation," which conserved the "consanguineal family" by incorporating affines, while for an expanding "middling" class (at the wealthier end) "marriage by alliance" cemented relations between families, which made upward mobility possible. For an anthropological analysis of a broad range of issues that led to the rise and fall of close kin marriage in America, especially over the nineteenth century, see McKinnon (2013, 2018).

38 Not, Vilaça (2013: 364) adds, that she is making a novel correlation. I have interpolated human/nonhuman here, where her argument engages with the role of changing Christian conventions. The new concept of the individual thus implied is distinct from that found in "the modern western conception of the human" (Vaisman 2013: 106); see note 29.

39 Latour's (e.g., [1991] 1993) concept of purification has been widely taken up. Anthropologists have done remedial work here for a long time; for example, Pálsson (2013) addresses a theme dominant in Ingold's oeuvre: the mutual interpenetration of biological and social understandings in a larger understanding of life. It was in the seventeenth century that "nature as we know it" was invented (Descola [2005] 2013: 68).

40 The concepts of internal and external relations may be used recursively, as, for example, when they correspond to or evoke a notion of the inside and outside of things. Thus does Morita (2014) elucidate Lewis Mumford's machine that, in working, becomes a part of the connections surrounding it, embodying the connections in the design of its parts.

41 Insofar as they are occupied by discrete persons, then, the kinship positions do not control or govern each other as the terms to an internal relation do. What to naturalists is uncertain or inadequate knowledge can be held at bay in an analogic cosmology by rearranging the elements in question, for example, through omen and revelation. Naturalists do not "control" their natural world in this way. They can uncover it, exploit and change it, rescale and redescribe it, and in that sense reconfigure it, but insofar as each epistemic reordering is attributable to filling a gap in human knowledge, the reordering thus appears as human intervention or interpretation.

2. REGISTERS OF COMPARISON

1 Worldliness as also in worlding. "We can only identify figures to the extent that we can imagine worlds, that is, the systems of relationality through which figures appear" (Tsing 2010: 50).

2 From time to time I use "Euro-American" as a reminder of a wider discursive field. For a substantive delineation of Euro-American, not a term the indigenes use of themselves, see M. Strathern (2005: 163n1): "'American' here derives from North America, 'European' from Northern Europe, but Euro-American influence is neither confined to these parts nor uniform within them (it has global spread, is locally

patchy). I refer to a discourse not a people, although I personify the discourse in referring to its 'speakers' as Euro-Americans. The awkward term is meant to summon
those whose cosmologies were formed by the religious and rationalist upheavals of
the seventeenth and eighteenth centuries across Northern Europe, creating present-
day [North] America in their wake." Edwards's (2009: 6–8) related discussion is pertinent.

3 One participant summed up a Society event thus: "Nothing of any importance had
been said or done, no particular conclusions arrived at. . . . We had just enjoyed the
family occasion, basking in the pleasure of each other's company, reunited, for a few
short hours at least, with our Henry" (Reed 2011: 17).

4 Towns up and down Britain have versions of literary and philosophical, or as in the
case of the Alltown "Nat," natural history societies (Edwards 2000).

5 An image of "overlapping circles," with "the individual and close intimates at the
centre and acquaintances further out" is drawn vividly by Morgan for present-day
Britain (2009: 4). Running through many forms of acquaintance, he says, is a balance between closeness and distance; strangers "tend to be defined in negative terms,
as people who[m] we do not know or recognise" (3). I later note interviewees' ready
take-up of the idea of filling in concentric circles to show the distribution of kinsfolk, friends, and associates when sociologists Spencer and Pahl (2006: ch. 6) asked
them; here closeness and its converse is interpreted as a matter of intimacy, which
may or may not reflect propinquity. Tadmor (2001: 120) has a historian's comment
on the adequacy of this folk model for analysis; Carey (2017: 8) expresses an anthropologist's objection.

6 Conventional English usage means that it may have to be explicitly argued that "distance" is not a non-relation but a modality of relating, as Locke and Hume felt com-
pelled to do. (Both commented on the reflective work of the philosopher who has to
take words out of their ordinary circulation while at the same time remaining com-
prehensible to ordinary folk.)

7 Biagioli, who draws widely on Hunter (1981, 1989), notes that the Society did not
take ownership of the claims sent it, instead benefiting from the number of transactions: the more submissions it received, the more credit it generated for itself.

8 "Company" was used in many contexts, including domestic ones: "the various groupings of family, servants, apprentices and journeymen associated with a single working
household" (Withington 2010: 123). The purposefulness of such association might
have appealed to emerging functional understandings of social relations, as some
have argued are found in Locke's characterization of the "society" of the conjugal
unit, whose internal relations were constituted via several differentiated purposes
(Gobetti 1992).

9 Hunter (1981: 119) cautions against putting too much weight on the Royal Society's
specific innovation, only to point to it as part of a wider phenomenon: "This stylistic
change was connected with more general shifts in the intellectual climate of seventeenth century England, of which the growth of science was only one." Thus in 1661
Boyle made a plea for a style devoid of those rhetorical devices that darkened the
subject (Dawson 2007: 73).

10 Regular statistics are published by the NHS Blood and Transplant (NHSBT) service.

The procurement system is presently (2018–2019) under radical change, which will no doubt affect the categorization of donors.

11   See Nuffield Council on Bioethics (2011: 112). The division between directed and undirected donation does not match unambiguously onto existing relationships, and people may make friends in the course of donor-matching. An American anthropologist (Sharp 2014: 8) speaks of transplant surgeons who hoped they "might one day bypass altogether the capricious supply of those [organs] derived from altruistic strangers, kin, friends, coworkers, and acquaintances."

12   Articulated in an American situation where a woman gave a kidney to a "friend," rather than save it for her daughter who herself had only one; after all, the daughter had a reasonable expectation of such help from her children: "We're [all] like family" (Kaufman et al. 2009: 38).

13   Envisioning the relations that make epistemic communities, Amin (e.g., 2012: 50) talks of devices for coordination where strangers become collaborators but not friends, where integration is possible without appeals to common humanity, and where solidarities depend neither on interpersonal ties nor on group allegiances.

14   He uses the same phrase, although giving a clear warning against reading Enlightenment interpersonal relations off from those "prevailing in modern culture" (Silver 1990: 1496).

15   "The kinship that mattered was not the technicalities of precise genealogical relationship, but rather the kinship that made a difference in practice" (Smith 2005: 97). Smith observes how often sources refer to "friends and relatives" without differentiation ("relative" here as a modern gloss for kinsperson). Compare Tadmor (2001: 130) on a mid-seventeenth-century usage: friend was a category "applied particularly to those kin who were expected to be effective."

16   An exception is Firth's (Firth et al. 1969: 117) ethnographic note comparing the informality of North London friendships with the formalized bond-friendships he witnessed on the Pacific island of Tikopia.

17   The sociologist Allan (1979: 138) found that "kin and non-kin" relationships "occupy distinct and separate sectors of an individual's sociable life . . . [so] that in the normal run of events they do not often impinge upon one another." He is reporting on the results of social network studies. Elsewhere (1979: 140), however, he notes of sibling relationships maintained on the basis of compatibility that such "kin are friends in the full meaning of the term, and not simply kin"; conversely, "the more non-kin are thought of and labelled 'true friends,' the more the symbolism of kinship is used to describe them."

18   See above, note 5. In her classic study of transformations of gay kinship and friendship in 1980s San Francisco, Weston (1991: 73) refers to people editing their family trees "by arranging relatives along a continuum defined by poles of closeness and distance"; that applied no less as friends became special kinds of family. In any event, "it was not unusual for a gay man or lesbian to speak of another as family in one breath and friend in the next" (1991: 118).

19   The opposite has been argued apropos trade union collectivities in Argentina (Lazar 2018).

20   The positive value given to kinship and friendship *in the abstract* is an ethnographic

observation, although as Beer and Gardner add (2015: 426) there is no semantic impediment in contemporary English to a relative being considered either a close friend or a mortal enemy.

21 Beer and Gardner (2015) are quoting Desai and Gillick (2010) with respect to the "new kinship studies" grounded in perceptions of generalized relatedness (e.g., Carsten 2000b, 2004), "relatedness" potentially swallowing up anything distinctive about friendship.

22 Rezende had been studying friendship in London, a "relationship restricted to the private sphere, formed between people thought of as equals" (1999: 79), and was suddenly hearing her relatives in Rio de Janeiro speaking of their maids as "friends." They also speak of them as "family," a common usage in England a couple of centuries ago. Apropos contemporary Finland, Abrahams (1999: 155–156) remarks that "friends" include siblings and cousins as well as unrelated persons, while in the English-speaking village of Aughnaboy in 1960s Ireland, "friend" meant kinsman, "mate" or "chum" being used for non-kin friends (Leyton 1974b: 95). In China, by contrast, friends were described as co-villagers or co-workers. So "do we need to develop a concept that can encompass all friendship-like interactions?" (Smart 1999: 120).

23 The postcolonial formation of the elite friendships described by Werbner (2014: 143) was not a move from a universe of (rural) personal to (urban) impersonal relations, but "more a move from one universe of personal relations to another."

24 They lead to different philia systems, based, for example, on the kinds of modes of interaction described for Orokaiva. I add that Orokaiva have a term for the set of philia relations, but this is not the reason for Schwimmer's analytical decision and is not true of every system he considers. (In complete overlapping, either all persons designated as "friends" may be primarily classified as "kin" or all designated as "kin" may be primarily classified as "friends.")

25 It happens that Kuma men regard themselves as "exchanging sisters" when they marry (Reay 1959a), but exchange here refers to a systemic sense in which such unions are caught up in flows of persons, food, and wealth. The appropriateness of describing women in terms of men's relations with one another should not, of course, go unremarked.

26 See, for example, M. Strathern (1988), which is also the principal source of the assertions made in the following paragraph.

27 The brother-in-law relation is singled out for its prominence both in anthropological commentary and in much male Papua New Guinean discourse. (This is not quite fair to Orokaiva, since Schwimmer contrasts how Tangu men think of certain kinds of hereditary friends as "brothers-in-law" with the Orokaiva preference for thinking of similarly positioned persons as "brothers.") Several of the general points that follow are familiar to Melanesianists.

28 Robbins and Rumsey (2008) is the classic account of Melanesian inscrutability.

29 Through, Pickles adds, thinking about patterns and tactics. The exchanges in mind are especially wealth prestations between clans or other partners, not dissimilar from the kind that in Kuma (to continue with this example) would accompany cult performances or marriage and funeral payments.

30 Nonetheless, the distinction (inner and outer self) has been used with great effect in discussions of Melanesian and Amazonian selfhood under pressure from Christianization (e.g., Robbins et al. 2014), although I suspect its relevance has to be ethnographically and analytically argued. If one thinks of its web as the spider's brain, it makes no sense to talk of *a* spider *plus* its web (Almut Schneider, pers. comm.). That said, to imagine either (spider/web) as inside or outside the other could be useful in displacing that very image (a spider plus its web) through another imagistic device, such as figure/ground reversal.

31 A comparison that had long informed discussions of the nature of friendship (e.g., Bray 2003; Schwartz 2007). At a time when commerce was regarded as a civilizing impetus, the very concept of personal "interest" was also changing in its connotation, as Alberto Corsín Jiménez (pers. comm.) notes from Hirschman's discussion (1977).

32 Paine ([1969] 1974b: 123) advocates recognizing "interpersonal relations" as a field of inquiry in itself, in the first instance apropos (Euro-American) "middle-class culture" and more generally as a kind of "infra-structure" to other structurings.

CODA TO PART I: COMPARING PERSONS AGAIN

1 The English vernacular "pair" works for present purposes. I give it a twist from Ku Waru and Melpa speakers, neighbors of Kuma, for whom pairing is an autonomous mode of categorization that puts together socially particular beings (e.g., brother-clans with distinctive identities; specific creatures such as "marsupial-and-bird" or "dog-and-marsupial") where any convergence or divergence may be salient (Merlan and Rumsey 1991: 115; Lancy and A. Strathern 1981).

2 Lebner in effect describes the impact of the notion of individual identity on anthropologists' understanding of friendship in also describing her interlocutors' wariness of it. Migrants to the Brazilian city of Marabá speak of the impossibility of friendship between human beings as opposed to friendship with God. For them, the Christian "person is porous and its relationships are ultimately shaped and mediated by supernatural [including diabolic] agency. . . . If it is only 'individuals' with bounded interiorities, wills and sincere sentiments who have 'friends' . . . , a person enacting a supernaturalised life of uncertain presences and agencies has problems with human friendship" (2012: 505). Touching on the kind of friendship implied in the notion of friendship with God, Schwartz's (2007) discussion of Aquinas indicates just how much friendship and the love implied was an object of medieval debate.

3. EXPANSION AND CONTRACTION

1 Corsín Jiménez (2013: 3) sees in the present epoch a political economy that reinvents seventeenth-century baroque interests in the "deformalization" of forms. He is reporting on the turn to the neo-baroque articulated over the last twenty years in diverse critical commentaries on the modern culture industry, and on what appears as a routinely reflexive, "informationalized" world order.

2 The single viewpoint gives perspective, as in the artificial perspective system of Italian painters; Dutch composition presumed an aggregate of views made possible by a mobile eye over a wide vista, so an optical capacity was added to a perspectival one.

3 *Relazione* is from Davis's foreword to a special issue on the subject (Cohen and War-

kentin 2011). I am much obliged to her for the reference. One connotation of the Latin *relatio* was a deposition before a judge.

4   I say reconceived because Hoskin (1995; see also Corsín Jiménez 2013: 57–58) argues for earlier, preperspectival, models of a split self (through double-entry bookkeeping).

5   I am formalizing what I take to be implicit in practice; other values may be put explicitly on the relation here, such as experiments in "dialogical" or "symmetrical" anthropology.

6   In the professional's view, an activity that turns on fashioning representations; nearer to the anthropologist's might be Holbraad's (2008, 2009) inventive definitions or "infinitions," characteristic of Cuban diviners' pronouncements, imagined not as representations or claims about the world but as ontological interferences in it.

7   Lea (2008: 63) describes how "coordination" takes on a social life of its own, producing organizational complexes that succeed in the "unintended consequence of pinpointing the need for more effective coordination."

8   All the workshops, fact-finding missions, and health instruction programs that health officers bring to the local population rest on the conviction that "better quality and more accurate information will eventually become better self-understanding for the Aborigines" (Lea 2008: 121). The better that data are collected and analyzed, the nearer bureaucrats will be to implementing the helping state.

9   Added to anxiety about the health workers' own efforts to improve things is anxiety about intervention as such: health workers fear causing collateral damage to indigenous culture.

10   Faith in one's tools of work was the hopeful meeting ground of anthropologists and other professionals responding to the Japanese earthquake and tsunami of 2011 (Riles, Miyazaki, and Genda 2012). You do not abandon your tools; you reconstruct them according to changing situations. Such "retooling" is not to be (under)taken lightly, and in evoking a collaborative endpoint Riles (2013) lays out some of the interpersonal and epistemic complexities of this instance.

11   Hence Corsín Jiménez's (2013: 2) concern with how we grant epistemic status to objects, and thus with exploring the conditions of description when what "appears to be a description of an object is, on closer inspection, turned inside out into a description of epistemic awareness." He offers "conceptual interventions" as "an effort at 'trapping' the descriptive forms of late liberalism within their own culture of description" (28).

12   A reference to the titles of Locke's and Hume's treatises, although in the case of Locke, moderns should understand his "understanding" as closer to the concept of "cognition" (Nidditch [1975] 1979: viii) or (the faculty of) "reason" (John Hendry, pers. comm.; I add thanks to Hendry for sharing with me his historical sensitivity to word change and nuances). Hoskin (1995: 156), who also draws on Alpers, says that by introducing "the Self into the epistemological space where only the Other has been before . . . I see Smith as doing for epistemological space what the art of describing had done for pictorial space."

13   "Yanomami are not becoming the criollos we conceive of, nor are the Indians the state wants to reinstate the ones Yanomami take themselves to be" (Kelly 2011: 194).

"Yanomami are not becoming or seeking to become mestizo or to be assimilated with whites; on the contrary, the relation between Yanomami and [whites] must remain [different], for . . . people must be able to alternate from one meaningful position to another" (2011: 221, also 137). The point is relevant to the discussion in chapter 4.

14 From which background consanguines have to be purposively carved out (Kelly 2011: 95, quoting Viveiros de Castro 2001: 26).

15 Categories such as the sixteenth- and seventeenth-century *casta*, later overtaken by *raza*, Roberts argues, are part of an emerging biological understanding of human difference. That said, "To this day, *raza* is enacted through profession, language, and level of education" (2012: 19); children of the same family can be of different "race."

16 Roberts (2012: 76) observes that when "IVF patients with limited material resources go about financing and gathering assistance for their reproductive projects, they become whiter. Both reproductive dysfunction and attempts to alleviate that dysfunction are physiological and economic markers of whiteness."

17 Haciendas were landed estates allotted to Creoles, which for a long time controlled Indian labor; said to have been more widespread in Ecuador than in other Andean nations, they implemented labor policies to justify hierarchical structures, including programs "for whitening the national racial stock through mestizaje (mixture)" (Roberts 2012: 59).

18 The phrasing comes from Porter's (2000: 179) placing of Hume's *Treatise of human nature* (1739–1740) in the context of extensive philosophical interest in the "anatomy of the mind." He (2000: 156) quotes Hume's introduction to the effect that "all the sciences have a relation" to human nature. This is where Hume is advocating the application of Francis Bacon's—then century-old—experimental methods to moral philosophy, insofar as the way the mind works must underlie any exercise of the human faculties of reasoning, induction, and so forth. Thus sciences' pretension to knowledge was dependent (his term) on also (my phrase) understanding understanding.

19 Kelly further illuminates this well-rehearsed theoretical position. Consider the contrast between Amazonian consanguinity ("constructed") and affinity ("given"). Affinity points to relations based on difference, not identity, and "is the given because it is the ontological condition underlying all 'social' relations . . . [belonging] as such to the fabric of the universe" (Viveiros de Castro 2009: 259).

20 What appeared a single viewpoint ("no difference") from one angle could be divided between two, according to whether one took a view from nature or from society, and be brought together again in a simple contrast, as in the later eighteenth-century contrast between ties that were given ("family") and ties by choice (one of the uses of the term "connection").

21 With the long-standing double sense of "knowledge" in English, at once a matter of epistemology and of social recognition.

22 In her discussion of the concept of paradigm (or rapport) as an intervention, Stengers writes, "It is not enough . . . to find situations that resemble a model or confirm a theory. It is necessary for the appetite to be sharpened by the challenge . . . by an undulating landscape, rich with subtle differences that must be invented, where the term *recognize* does not refer to the observation of a resemblance but to the challenge of actualizing it" ([1993] 2000: 48, original emphasis). Compare Rabinow,

after Deleuze: "The pedagogic work of the concept . . . consists in conceptualization as an act of creation" (2011: 124).

23 Repeated in so many registers of anthropology, specification seems belittling (e.g., Ingold 1986, 2011; Rabinow and Stavrianakis 2016; Remne and Sillander 2017; Toren 2009, 2011). I do not mean to belittle the proposition itself.

24 Symbiosis, e.g., Helmreich (2009); Tsing (2015); collective, e.g., Descola ([2005] 2013); Latour (1999).

25 Description "intervenes," so to speak, insofar as it introduces its own order of exposition. Despite the epistemological lure of the idea of unraveling as an elucidating thing to do, we might wish to keep with that intransigence as a kind of saving inability. The inability to untie everything at once emerges as a form of comprehension that obviates the familiar onion-skin conundrum of stripping away what needs investigating. The three contexts introduced earlier (descriptions of medical-clinical settings) are appraisals of the knottiness of self-consciously interventionist activity, namely, health-care delivery.

26 By way of examples from one particular era, Battaglia (1990); Lederman (1986); LiPuma (1988); Mosko (1985).

27 Mirrored in faculty alignments, intellectual stances also imply social configurations, often experienced by practitioners as intra-departmental or cross-institutional conflicts and alliances.

28 The opposition mobilizes diverse distinctions that separate qualitative and quantitative approaches, including that already encountered, interpretivist versus positivist alignments (Abbott 2001: 60). Repeating a similar relation (without conflating the concepts [6 n1]), but on the qualitative side of the divide, Abbott also brings out a distinction between realism and constructionism. The fractal distinction is perhaps anticipated in Luhmann's (1982: 231) "internal disjunction" as subsystems reconstruct their relevant environments.

29 Peter Skafish (pers. comm.) points out that historically (in medieval and Renaissance Europe) the concept of analogy entailed the idea of participation in an ultimate category or being, such that relations of similarity or difference obtain between distinct things only because they also are parts of such a category. From this comes Descola's emphasis on hierarchies between beings; or the notion that identity—as in a dictionary definition—is only derivable through discriminating the marks of one entity by analogy with those of others. I hope it is clear that I am simply putting the two readings side by side, both rather drastically truncated. Thus Wagner elucidates the temporal processes, over the course of a narrative or otherwise enacted sequence, through which every innovative ("invented") relation/distinction recovers its original impetus in what is then seen, retroactively, as obviated. The original is now "counter-invented," which constitutes a continuing participation of sorts.

30 In the full passage, Descola captures the movement of this process: resemblance achieved through the operation of thought that brings together what was separate creates a new difference in the objects in question, "for they become alien to their earlier identity as soon as they intermingle in the mirror of correspondence and imitation" ([2005] 2013: 202).

31 Kelly drew on this argument apropos Yanomami-criollo aspirations. These assump-

tions turn on the manner in which differentiating or collectivizing "controls" on people's behavior may be taken for granted or require deliberate effort (Wagner 1975). The latter's concern is with polar (figure-ground) modes of a general perceptive faculty, not with categorical opposites. Thus, in this formulation, identity sets up the imperative for relating, and vice versa.

32 Keeping for the moment with the vocabulary of similarity and difference, we may note of analogical displacements over time that substitution "is not identity, because the thing that is substituted must be different from that which it replaces"; that is, similarity and difference alike are created by an act of substitution, which "changes, extends, and relocates [previously existing] . . . differences and similarities" (Wagner 1978: 37, 38).

33 "Pure relationships" is after the sociologist Giddens (e.g., 1991: 6; Beer and Gardner 2015: 429); the Late Modern Age is also his phrase.

34 As Corsín Jiménez implies is already the case with the digital commons.

4. THE DISSIMILAR AND THE DIFFERENT

1 A cultural disposition, we might say, analogous to the place of "trust" in much Euro-American social theory, as Carey (2017: 5) elucidates; he explicates that concept in terms of its negative salience elsewhere, as in social milieux where "mistrust" is the default disposition.

2 Under other circumstances, one might profitably open up a contrast between the same and the similar, where similar encodes difference (e.g., Weston 2018: 24), with its almost-but-not-quite connotations. However, I override this rhetorical distinction, that is, between "similarity" containing an overt reference to difference and "sameness," insofar as the latter also inevitably mobilizes (albeit covertly) reference to difference or "otherness" (see Argyrou 2002).

3 These remarks apply particularly to the imagining of "external" relations: "relating" discrete entities points to what lies "between" them. Part I gestured toward the agentive effect of making connections, as in recognizing the society one kept, so prevalent in eighteenth-century English; in that context I deployed "similarity" and "difference" in a plainly conventional manner. Now within the compass of "difference" all kinds of dualities, distinctions, oppositions, dichotomies, and so forth were explored in twentieth-century symbolic anthropology, not to speak of the privileging of difference in semiotics and structuralism, and its positive rather than oppositive status in Deleuzian thought (where its "opposite" if at all is "indifference" [Viveiros de Castro 2004b: 19]). Similarity carries none of this conceptualizing weight: regardless of all the contexts where making kin or sharing attributes are regularly described as mobilizing notions of sameness, its absence from social theory leads, for instance, to Boellstorff's (2016: 392) call for "an anthropology of similitude." This absence contrasts with the theoretical standing of "identity," to which "difference" is also colloquially joined in opposition. A notable exception to the apparent neglect also suggests a condition for it: Argyrou (2002: e.g., 92–93, 100) argues that there are good reasons why ethnographers place (aspects of) sameness beyond question when it comes to their relations with their interlocutors; at the same time, *proclaiming* sameness is a theoretical impossibility insofar as distinct identities are summoned as

soon as it (sameness) is articulated, that is, it comes into question. (It may be beyond question in other ways: Benson and O'Neill [2007: 32] quote Emmanuel Levinas's concern with "Western philosophy's systematic reduction of 'the other' . . . to 'the same,'" the latter embracing everything that [Western] thought can understand.)

4   In Anglophone parlance; other possibilities are afforded elsewhere, famously demonstrated by Jacques Derrida's deformation of the French *différence* (*différance*), which springs from the vernacular fusing of differentiation and deferral.

5   Deleuze's "disjunctive synthesis" is not resolvable into a conciliation of contraries (Stasch 2009: 16; Viveiros de Castro 2010: 224). Josephides (2015) draws disjunctive synthesis into an arresting series of tropes stimulated by Alain Badiou's conceptualization of "togetherness." As well as Badiou's own "anti-dialectical two," built on the Deleuzian disjunctive synthesis, she includes "oneself as another" (after Paul Ricoeur) and Heidegger's "being with others." This gives me the opportunity to comment that, within European philosophy, arguments about similarity and dissimilarity have frequently taken place in terms of interdigitations of Self and Other, a pair offering a range of critical and discriminating expositional possibilities not unlike some of those here expounded in other terms, while mobilizing its (the pair's) own concerns and subject matter.

6   This refers to its scope or register; there is nothing "weak" about the force of dissimilarity in English vernacular thinking, its negative potential taking many forms.

7   I was a member of the Working Group, an independent advisory committee that reported to the then UK Department for Culture, Media and Sport (DCMS); I confine my remarks to the published report.

8   I have inserted dissimilarity here, where the actors would have spoken of cultural difference. We see the power of this negative form of similarity in an otherwise humdrum decision-making process by which adjudications were being made by metropolitan institutions in the face of Indigenous Australian claims. Such a perception of relations contributes to the deafness that Povinelli vividly describes. In a recent reprise of an earlier land claims case (in Australia), she revisits "the demand on Indigenous people to couch their analytics of existence in the form of a cultural belief" (2016: 33). This was very evident in one desecration lawsuit: despite the court readily recognizing the existence of sacred sites, the case turned on the intentions of the mining company in question. It is precisely that recognition of certain land formations as sacred sites that allows lawyers and others to enjoy a sense of "authentic difference" and prejudge a site's character. For, she argues, such recognition gives no space to what *these* formations "desired or intended as a living or vital matter" (2016: 46). (Quite apart from the neoliberal assumption that beliefs may contradict one another while leaving other perceptions of the world intact, here the authentic seems an "oppositive" difference, that is, speaks to dissimilarity.)

9   The beginning of the report (DCMS 2003: 29) talks of "an irreconcilable conflict between 'scientists' and 'indigenous people,'" and of "polarized views," which meant that consensus would be difficult although it would be the group's achievement to show that some was possible. Polarization meant, among other things, that the voices of indigenous scientists were taken as some kind of compromise position between opposed camps.

10 Environment after Luhmann (1982: 81), where he talks not of domains or divisions of the same whole but, rather, of systems intersecting in terms of their functionality, such as relations between economics and politics or between politics and education.

11 "Incidentally, having read the offensive language used by the museum submission we must say it is little wonder there is an increasing lack of sympathy for scientific research of us as a people. We are not animals to be described as 'pure' or 'spoiled' by intermarriage" (DCMS 2003: 43; reply by the Tasmanian Aboriginal Centre to a collective letter from diverse museums in the United Kingdom).

12 This is what led him to experiment with an ethnographic account that did not overtly depend on the explication of social relations. "We might begin to imagine the semantic paradox of a social anthropology not mediated by 'social relationships.' . . . Angkaiyakmin have language neither for social relationships nor for the relationality anthropologists work with to 'put things in context' and to produce descriptions, analyses and interpretations. Participation of persons and things in each other is conceived without an idiom of 'relationality' . . . and is instead simply assumed" (Crook 2007: 28).

13 At the 2008 meeting of the European Society for Oceanists, brought up as a theme for the 2010 conference, from which the quotation comes. ECOPAS, drawing on universities in Fiji, Papua New Guinea, France, the Netherlands, Norway, and the United Kingdom, was convened under the aegis of the European Commission and advised the European Parliament on development strategy in the Pacific.

14 In international bureaucratese, "knowledge exchange" had replaced the old phrase "knowledge transfer"; it was not a Pacific Island neologism, although these Pacific Islanders seem to have given it a special emphasis. Over the last twenty-five years Pacific-based anthropologists have been concerned with knowledge exchanges in fields such as intellectual property rights, cultural property, heritage and repatriation, and the many situations where development aspirations have drawn on "indigenous knowledge." See the works cited by Leach and Davis (2012: 211).

15 Notably, through their "consent" (the basis of many institutional ethics protocols). The Working Group had been concerned about the brutal methods of extraction by which skeletal material often ended up in museum collections; in parallel lay museums' concerns to protect their holdings as required by UK law.

16 This "non-relational" is distinct from either that of Holbraad and Pedersen, mentioned in the introduction, or that of some philosophical usages, as Wilson (2016) describes. Apropos the latter, knowledge may be acquired relationally, but finding out facts about the intrinsic properties of things in this way does not make those facts relational: a comparison of people's relative heights can involve "non-relational" facts (what is intrinsic to each).

17 As it happens, the ethnographer's usage of "difference" conveys the strong sense I intend. The example provides less of a backward look to some preexisting cultural reality, in which either anthropologist or Pacific Islander (and all their crossovers in between) might be invested (see Rollason's [2014] criticism), than some insight into the way such difference may work as well "within" as "between" cultures. We may note that knowledge is not being treated as a matter of expertise that distinguishes

people, because (to paraphrase Viveiros de Castro [2003]) basically everyone has the same kind of knowledge, that is, their *own* knowledge.

18 "If kinship is about the production of persons, [then] relations focused on, and made possible by, the emergence of knowledge are the basis of kinship" (Leach 2009: 184).

19 A kinship calculus sets up the possibility of seeing things from another's placement (my relation to you and yours to mine). Exchange may also articulate the distinction between owners (of a place) and users (of its products), each of whom, as donor or recipient, also anticipates subsequently occupying the position of recipient or donor.

20 An unmistakably political dimension adheres to the Euro-American insistence that only certain kinds of knowledge make knowledge. For a recent analysis, see Bonifacio (2013) on the fate of Paraguayan shamans, and the insights drawn from Blaser (2010) on who gets to say what organization is.

21 Social science has long acknowledged that what is assumed here also requires work to achieve: "detachment" has to be created, just as labor is detached from human life as a commodity, or people involved in all kinds of relations are turned into commercially minded marketeers, not to speak of the indifference of bureaucrats or the nonchalance of surgeons.

22 Nombo had been meticulous to include only plants for which he could trace the people — and people's places — through whom he knew about them; he had deliberately left out the special formulae ("magic") that made knowledge locally efficacious.

23 It is a (globalized) world divided into ethnic or cultural "domains" that entails what she calls inter-ethnic logic (Carneiro da Cunha 2009: 69). The rights in question are rights to indigenous knowledge.

24 The properties of the world to which infinitions refer are already given, but have to be pulled into a basis for action. The Kuma clan asserting itself against its traditional enemies reinvents the "meaning" of the clan with *these* clan members at *this* time for *that* purpose — not as it was at the last ceremonial. The performance would become a baseline for the subsequent recognition of future flourishing, a judgment necessarily retrospective: the pig ceremonial has made the clan prosper.

25 A construct that is at once relational and self-same (Moutu 2013: 202).

26 Iatmul have thousands of proper names for things, features, events, and phenomena of all kinds, and these names come in pairs, elder and younger brother; they have always existed, and are taken as a matter of "necessity." This also illuminates his phrase "infinite being." "Iatmul names contain relationships and these are names derived from a realm of transcendence which is embodied in immanent human sociality" (Moutu 2013: 202).

27 The concept of customary law was initially created in the colonial need to find *some* similarities between what the state and what colonized peoples were doing (rendering the colonial project coherent thereby). Yet, Demian observes, in terms of vernacular practices, it is difference not similarity that people in general appear to seek out in maintaining their relations with neighbors, near and far. Demian (2014, 2015) makes it clear how, in the very concept of customary law, "law" has already encompassed or extracted from "custom" what it recognizes as similar to itself.

28 Among all the other reasons for impasse understood. Moutu continues: "If we choose to be different then we should also endeavour to find analytical methods that make us different" (2014: 5–6). He thus recasts the very concept of legal precedent in terms of something that appears to brook no comparison: the Iatmul marriage convention whereby alternating generations of men, aligned as elder and younger brother, find wives from the same clan, the clan of their paternal grandmothers. In this view, precedence entails a complementary but asymmetric relationship enacted over and again, the return of a prior moment in the present. (I am grateful for permission to quote from this unpublished paper.)

29 Its reality as an impasse is shown in the prolonged difficulty that Papua New Guinean lawyers have experienced over giving a foundational status to customary law (e.g., Zorn and Care 2002).

30 Although its adjectival form allows unrelated, irrelative, irrelevant, and so forth. To avoid misunderstanding, it should be stated that in the present context "non-relational" has nothing to do with the "individuality" of phenomena.

31 The self in self-reference behaves in complicated ways, as when "systems produce the elements that they interrelate by the elements that they interrelate," or when "self-simplifying devices . . . make it possible to use the system as a premise of its own operation" (Luhmann 1990: 145, 167). Autopoiesis in a communication system is summed up as "to continue to communicate" (14).

32 "Symbiosis means that . . . beings are related by common interests, but *common* does not mean having the same interest in common, only that the diverging interests now need each other"; such "connections" break indifference but bring no encompassing unity (Stengers 2011: 60–61, original emphasis).

33 I am indebted to Jill Mann for providing me with this account and her exegesis of it, as well as for other comments.

34 This last is my embellishment, a suggestion from the burial practices of sworn friends (noted in chapter 1); Bray (2003: 94) refers to a popular Latin version of the tale in which the sworn companions (here "brothers") "lie in death side by side." Mann simply mentions that Amis and Amiloun die on the same day and are buried in the same tomb.

35 As does Silver (1989: 281), who takes the tale to be celebrating identity and equality between friends, the triumph of trust over rivalry.

36 For other such allusions to blood, see Bildhauer (2013) and Delille (2013).

37 Schwartz (2007: 41), writing on Aquinas, emphasizes how love unites friends: "The lover aims to resemble (participate in the form of) the beloved." A lover is thus forever involved in a "movement towards" such resemblance.

38 See Gagné's (2019: 9) discussion of comparison as an outcome of analogical thought more generally apprehended, and indeed his caution about the "vast topography of analogical thought [that] is brushed aside as irrelevant in the search for the development of 'the comparative method' [where] . . . [t]oo many perspectives have to be occluded for one story to be told." The caution is particularly apposite apropos my selective usage of Descola's account of analogism, especially my omission of medieval concerns with notions concerning ultimate beings or categories and their placement in the order of things. To find resemblance in the way things are placed in (say)

an unfolding narration is likely to echo presumptions about the great chain of being (Descola [2005] 2013: 204–205).

CODA TO PART II: PREPARATION

1   I refer to "identity" along with its derivatives, "identical," "identify." Note that from this vernacular possibility we could draw a conclusion apparently contrary to common interpretation: that there is, in this context, "no difference" between the internal relations of self-identity and the external relations that differentiate one entity from another.

2   On the invention of identity entailing certain kinds of relations, the unit-with-its-relations, Foucault ([1966] 1970: 55) further observes that "discrimination imposes upon comparison the primary and fundamental investigation of difference: providing oneself by intuition with a distinct representation of things, and apprehending clearly the inevitable connection between one element in a series and that which immediately follows it."

3   Much is curtailed in this assertion; see, for example, Candea's (2019: 203) comment on Foucault's observations, and the pivotal role the former goes on to give identity across three clusters of concepts, of which the discussion here touches on but one.

5. ENLIGHTENMENT DRAMAS

1   Davis observes that Merian was not — like many still-life painters — striving for metaphor or allegory; rather, in awe of the manifestations of God's works, she "centered on interactions in nature and on transformative organic processes" (1995: 151).

2   I do not mean that abstract inference was an issue for her; on the contrary, tracking the timings of each stage in the life histories of individual insects (as from the extrusion of eggs to an emergent butterfly) surely offered a sufficient narrative framework. Rather, I mean that we should not take for granted her innovation in showing a sequence or connection where none had been inferred before.

3   From Smith's *Essays on philosophical subjects* (1795); Porter notes how reminiscent of Hume the formulation is. In "An inquiry concerning human understanding," Hume's section on the association of ideas begins, "It is evident that there is a principle of connection between the different thoughts and ideas of the mind." It continues: for even in the wildest of reveries imagination has turned on a "connection upheld among the different ideas which succeeded one another" (n.d. [1748]: 320), the connection being parsed in turn into three principles. Note the ease of the phrasing of "between" or "among" different ideas.

4   The role played by kinship rules ("customs") introduces Fortes's perspective on abstraction. "The one element that is constant and critical through all these vicissitudes of generic, specific, and optional activities is the relationship as such. It is always . . . identifiable by terminology and by norms, rules and customs," to which he appends a footnote: "That is why . . . kinship relations, like all social relations, can be referred to and discussed in abstraction from any actual situations in which they emerge" (1969: 62).

5   With respect to a usage of "relation" preceding the passage quoted above, the editors of Hume's *Treatise* comment, "Hume is discussing two kinds of relation: those

between individuals who are relatives or closely associated, and those between impressions and ideas. An experience of a person with whom we are closely associated always produces a double relation of impressions and ideas" (Norton and Norton 2000: 511). Hume's distinction between impressions (sensation) and ideas (thought), and the ensuing tandem "double relation," is briefly mentioned below.

6 Hume writes generally: "The farthest we can go towards a conception of external objects, when suppos'd specifically different from our perceptions, is to form a relative idea of them, without pretending to comprehend the related objects [themselves]. Generally speaking we do not suppose them specifically different; but only attribute to them different relations, connexions and durations" (1, 2, 6; 49, emphasis omitted). The supposition has already been encountered in Locke's writings: one can conceive of relations affecting things without otherwise knowing the identity of what is related.

7 The principle in question is the strength and liveliness of the idea people have of one another through long-standing association, as mentioned in the following section.

8 Hume's editors interpret his intention in another passage (2, 2, 9; 250) as indicating the special relationship we have with relatives (i.e., kinspersons) and acquaintances (Norton and Norton 2000: 511n5). Acquaintance is a long-standing term in English, having since the fourteenth century connoted both personal knowledge and the persons so acknowledged.

9 These passages have seemingly nothing to say about any valorization of "difference," which appears as the simple converse of an interest in degrees of similarity or likeness. Hume (1, 1, 5; 15) states as much: contemplating including "difference" with other relations (as Locke did with "diversity"), he instead considers it not as anything real or positive but "rather as a negation of relation."

10 It is hardly necessary to remind the reader that what referred to male persons did not refer to female persons, who were being conjugalized into family life. Porter (2000: 17) speaks of "Albion's polite and commercial people . . . [escaping] the iron cages of Calvinism, custom and kinship." (The references to family here cover both present-day connotations and the earlier connotations of household including non-kin.)

11 Identity in general was a notion with which Hume did considerable battle. It seemingly got in the way of the role he wished to give to relations as a facility of thought that produced strings of "related objects," albeit with the *illusion* of identity or continuity as commonly understood. (I return to this.)

12 "Self is that conscious thinking thing . . . which is sensible [of itself]" (Locke 1690: 2, 27, 17; 341). Strawson (2011: 35, and see 65) remarks of Hume's section on personal identity that "person" has here a "merely" mental reference, being deployed interchangeably with "mind" and "self." (That said, "person" as someone with the capacity of an agent seems to be of ancient usage in English, the term also connoting a bodily figure, selfhood, or personality, and so forth as Locke's and Hume's references to ordinary usage indicate.)

13 That is, apropos the passages with which I have been concerned; in some of his political writings Locke polemically separates kinship from politics (Zengotita 1984), or argues that the "first society," the family, was a precursor of the state (Schochet

1969: 87). The point is that no mention is made of kinship in the chapter on identity and diversity (ch. 27), which otherwise is filled with references to what we would call individual persons, named and generic. (Conversely, the refinement of man into "person" and "man" seems missing from the other chapters on relations.) Chapter 27 was inserted as an addition to the second edition of Locke's book; Nidditch's 1975 version is based on the fourth edition of 1700.

14 Fausto's (2012a: 36) observations draw attention to identity as a relation. Locke (1690: 2, 27, 1; 329) explicitly refers to both identity and diversity as "relations and ways of comparing." Sandford's comments on Balibar's discussion underline Locke's account on this very point, and its novelty by contrast with the formulations of René Descartes. "Thus the originality of the conception of consciousness in the *Essay* [Locke's] . . . lies in its *relation to* the conception of the person or the self," a reflexive relation that opens up "windows on the workings of the mind" (Sandford 2013: xx, xviii, original emphasis). The crucial relational move is between the self and (its) consciousness (of itself).

15 The extent to which these formulations of identity rehearse notions already embedded in Christian or monotheistic conceptions of self (Alan Strathern, pers. comm.) is a point that could be made at several junctures where a longer view would lead to different questions. The conclusion touches briefly on what one may call reinventions—even over the relatively short term, "innovations" get reinvented, too.

16 Indeed Locke almost said as much himself, albeit in a different register: Dawson (2007) reflects on his notion that language is a tie of society (company), and God has given us language to realize our sociable nature.

17 Locke specifically refers to "relation being the considering of one thing with another, which is extrinsical to it," relative terms—father, brother, king, husband, blacker, merrier—openly pointing to comparison between one thing and "something else separate, and exterior to the existence of that thing" (1690, 2, 25, 10; 323). Stuart (2013: 30–31) cautions that there is a specific inflection to Locke's concept of the extraneous, indicating that the act of comparison is an ideational one projected onto the world. It is not just that two entities being compared are extrinsic to each other, but that (as Descombes has it) as an act of comparison the relation is also extrinsic to the reality of either.

18 This is followed by a second example referring to the attribute of being white, drawn from long-standing debates about parts and wholes, unities and pluralities. (Note what seems a common usage of "person" here.)

19 Logically it is always "additional," it being irrelevant whether the circumstances of augmenting a person's relations (in this thinking) are positive or negative; here the state of marriage and the state of divorce are the same.

20 And one cannot overemphasize the (eventual) popular attraction of both philosophers; their works were to go into numerous editions, especially those produced for general readers.

21 Hume (1, 4, 6; 169) is equally explicit: "The understanding never observes any real connexion among objects"—it all resolves itself into a "customary association of ideas." (Here he gives a special inflection to connection.)

22 "The relation facilitates the transition of the mind from one object to another, and renders its passage as smooth *as if* it contemplated one continu'd object" (1, 4, 6; 166, my emphasis).

23 Including thought stimulated by psychoanalysis, not to speak of numerous counter-currents in art and literature.

24 The interchangeability of persons (my phrase) is evident in Hume's experiments concerning how people behave when confronted with various circumstances. "Let us suppose . . . that the person, along with whom I make all these experiments, is closely connected with me either by blood or friendship. He is, we shall suppose, my son or brother, or is united to me by a long and familiar acquaintance. Let us next suppose, that the cause of the passion [under study] acquires a double relation of impressions and ideas to this person; and let us see what the effects are of all these complicated attractions and relations," and so forth (2, 2, 2; 219).

25 People associate together according to their particular dispositions, not only "where they remark this resemblance betwixt themselves and others, but also by the natural course of the disposition, and by a certain sympathy, which always arises betwixt similar characters. . . . [As] love or affection arises from the resemblance, we may learn that a sympathy with others is agreeable only by giving an emotion to the spirits" (2, 2, 4; 229). Hume has just observed that resemblance converts a relation between ideas to an impression (a register of emotion and sentiment), through the vivacity given to the related ideas. I should add that scholars contrast Hume's formulation of sympathy, in effect a theory of contagion, with Adam Smith's (and others of the Scottish Enlightenment), whose imaginative projection (Weston 2018: 18) has been described as a procedural mechanism without intrinsic emotional content (Silver, quoted in Carey 2017: 50). Where emotion or feeling is involved, as in Hume's case, the formulation has been criticized in modern times (e.g., Hirschmann 2000: 181) for basing ideas of and knowledge about others on the individual subject's feelings, rather than the other way around (inferring feelings from that contact with others); this last would summon the transformative potential of interaction. In anthropology, interactive potential is highly relevant to Toren's (2011) and Pina-Cabral's (2017) notions of ontogeny, as well as to Laidlaw's (2014) conception of ethical self-fashioning, and thus of the self—not necessarily an individual person—modified through learning.

26 Herzfeld's ([1992] 1993) classic study of bureaucratic indifference reminds us of the metaphoric cast of state rationality. In any event, while bureaucracy may exemplify the public value of the impersonal, the value is played out under vastly diverse and changing circumstances (compare, e.g., Du Gay 2000).

27 Transformed thus, human organs are shorn of their previous social history, and what counts as far as medical transfer is concerned is their quality—how well they have been looked after (Lock 2002: 49; also see above, chapter 2).

28 Very different concerns have been described for Japan in the past (Lock 2002), so it is necessary to be specific. (Lock [2002: 226] quotes Yonemoto [1985], who states that in contrast to "Americans who think of organs as replaceable parts, . . . the Japanese tend to find in every part of a deceased's person's body a fragment of that person's mind and spirit.")

29 Jacob (2012) discusses the dovetailing of Israeli practices with both international (especially North American) conventions and people's own sense of cultural distinctiveness. The window of ethnographic opportunity described here opened her eyes to the relational figure missing from the hegemonic literature on transplant ethics, even though it took a striking local form.

30 She contrasts it with traditional understandings of "fictive kinship," as well as with "strategic naturalizing" in the United States where the reference point is biological relatedness. Apropos Israeli concepts, "it is unconvincing to see the pragmatic associations formed in the name of kinship as something other than kinship: since [people] claim kinship and impersonate it, their effects are indeed kinship effects and this kinship is at least as significant as blood or love relations in the understanding of transplantations" (Jacob 2012: 82).

31 My discussion is informed by Mol's critique of pluralism. Although it deals with what seems ever-expanding diversity, pluralism — which she takes as an almost intractable feature of the Euro-American thought — throws up an analogous relational deficit. Herself denying the plurality and individuation of units any primordial status, Mol redescribes this state of being: the distinctiveness of people's endeavors is in effect created by intersecting fields of practices that have a character she calls multiple. Her concept of the multiple implies forms of practices conjoined and disjunct from one another in overlapping, relationally complex ways that cannot be added up. Changing contexts render the world better understood as infinitely divisible (multiple).

32 Raffles (2010: 165) pursues Merian's afterlife in the ponderings of the nineteenth-century French historian and naturalist Jules Michelet. Refusing the idea that the butterfly is the fulfillment of the caterpillar, Michelet was struck instead by the impermanence of form.

33 Merian's paintings are widely reproduced. The one I have in mind, a watercolor made in Suriname between 1699 and 1701, is illustrated in Huxley (2003: 81, plate 68).

34 Sir John Hoskyns of the Royal Society wrote, in the 1670s, that new collection practices were making it easy to "find likenesse and unlikenesse of things upon a suddaine [unexpectedly]" (Hunter 1981: 67), that is, "similarities and differences [dissimilarities]," in today's parlance (Huxley 2003: 82).

6. KINSHIP UNBOUND

1 With the concept of estate, Gammage thereby extends the settler imaginary in order to reflect on it.

2 "Thick" and "thin" are meant to invoke an outside perception of the English relation, including Stengers's objection to its reduced connotations by contrast with *rapport*, and has nothing to do with thick/thin designations debated by some philosophers (e.g., Heil 2012: 13).

3 And with an interesting twist. "The trope of kinship and kin-based societies has formed the natural base and mythological origin point for [the narrative] . . . of progressive societies," that is, the narrative of how the modern world has transcended the constraints of small-scale, domestic, kin-focused relationships, and in defining kinship thus how this world has written kinship out of modernity (McKinnon 2013: 60; also 51).

4 This is despite much evidence to the contrary, not all of which can be put down to keeping alive modernity's "tradition." A "tall tale of modernity," Shryock (2018: 1) calls it, in a conversation with others ranging across Bolshevik-Stalinist political culture (Alexopoulos), national fervor in the Gulf States (Samin), Sufi adepts in the postsocialist Balkans (Henig), and the hypermodern realm of biosociality (Pálsson). Over and again, in these diverse locales, kinship (in its familial form) seems to have been treated with contempt only to reemerge with new resonances, whether in the stigma heaped upon children born to Soviet "enemies of the people" or the link between kinship and corruption exposed in the insider trading of corporations held up as principal actors in Western modernization theory. The perspective from which the initial denigration of kinship may be understood sounds familiar: the subordination of family to politics as an ultimate gesture of civic loyalty or the hostility of blood kinship to social solidarity. The conversation ends with comments on the pervasiveness and adaptability of kinship, and its crucial shaping of how "we relate to the planet, to other species, and to the larger networks of relation and constraint that make kinship itself possible for us, as humans" (2018: 5). Shryock himself asks how big or how small we want kinship to be.

5 Notable twenty-first-century collections include Carsten (2000a); Franklin and McKinnon (2001); Faubion (2001); Edwards and Salazar (2009); Bamford and Leach (2009); and McKinnon and Cannell (2013b).

6 On the kin one chooses (out of a field of kin), see chapter 2 for an old designation of friend. Writers make similar claims for "modernity." Thus Morgan (2009: 13) surmises that the term "acquaintance" must be relatively new for the way it dovetails with what he regards as the modernizing processes of urbanization and mobility (on its claim to antiquity, see chapter 5, note 8).

7 See Kapferer's (2016) following commentary. I am not investing "ordinary" with any special meaning, as might be derived from the debate on "ordinary ethics" that stimulated Robbins's article and is elaborated in commentaries that follow, notably by Das (2016; and see 2014) and Lambek (2016).

8 Or the world falls apart. For Euro-Americans the tension between the two tropes is replicable between elements within each. Writing of children's friending practices beyond a social media context, Winkler-Reid (2016: 167) deploys Lambek's (2013a) distinction between a mimetic, relational dimension of personhood continuous with other persons and a forensic one invoking notions of individual identity continuous over time, and how the breaking and making of friends co-implicates these two aspects of friendship. She quotes Torresan (2011), who identifies two strands in the anthropology of friendship: as an idiom of social relatedness or as mobilizing the notion of individual. I would ascribe a very similar duo to twentieth-century English kinship practice (M. Strathern 1992).

9 As Weston (1991) found for families of choice, where whatever lasts, as with immutable friendship relations, may be contrasted with blood ties that can be broken. The reference comes from Kantsa and Chalkidou (2014: 88).

10 By "analogy" Ng intends a relation of similarity (in some aspect or other), which is how the term was used at the time, her examples turning on specific metaphors. I keep to these English-speaking understandings here, at once a further contribution

to the previous discussion of analogy and a supplement to understanding what was reported of seventeenth-century concerns with word usage.

11 In the light of the previous chapter, we may comment that for the modern reader it indexes an interest in how ideas are carried from one locus to another.

12 A later distinction between vehicle (the term whose attributes are being transferred) and topic or tenor (to which the attributes are attached) has been part of extensive literary ruminations on the subject, as has emphasis on the relation between the terms. The carrying of ideas from one locus to another is found both in the kind of joining of ideas that Locke stressed in his understanding of relations as comparisons and in Hume's easy transition of ideas.

13 Emphasizing the importance of the analogy between husband and wife, Christ and church, Gouge wrote in 1622: "Because [the Apostle] propounded to husbands and wives the examples of Christ and the Church as patterns and motives to them, to doe their dutie, he applieth that which was first spoken of man and wife, unto Christ and his Church, to show that there being so fit a resemblance betwixt these two couples, the pattern propounded is the more pertinent to the purpose" (quoted by Ray 2002: 286).

14 That "Locke attacked the family-state analogy itself, breaking the analogy in order to make his argument for social contract and the natural freedom of men," as Ng (2007: 222) puts it, has been interpreted as a more fundamental break with analogizing (on the basis of appearances) itself. In discerning a functional analytic in Locke's description of paternal powers, Zengotita (1984: 25) proposes that he was trying to move away from analogical thought as such (and see Descola [2005] 2013: 204–205).

15 "Relations" is Tadmor's term at this juncture (Stout speaks of kindred), but she has already drawn attention to Stout's use of the former.

16 But not indiscriminately: it was restricted by the boundaries of idiosyncratic usage. Her account of eighteenth-century shopkeeper and diarist Thomas Turner shows that many neighbors and acquaintances were not recorded as "friends," an epithet he reserved for a special range of (kin and non-kin) connections. Feeley-Harnik (2017), also commenting on Tadmor's analysis, opens up another arena in considering the "spiritual" kinship that special friendships based on truth and trust created, as between nineteenth-century devotees of pigeon breeding.

17 "Quakerism began ... as a family and neighbourhood movement, one that drew on the ethics and emotions associated with kinship and friendship but divested them ... of patriarchy and clientage" (Mack 1992: 157). For early Quakers, friendship also had an apostolic and sacrificial cast, as well as that of messianic chivalry, all of which recall Bray's account.

18 It is customary, remarks Schwartz (2007: 2), for scholars to comment that both "Aristotlean *philia* and Thomist *amicitia* significantly differ from what we now understand as friendship," not least in their wide reach across all manner of people.

19 Pitt-Rivers was simply extending Fortes's term, but I find sufficient distinction in their approaches to convert it into the substantive "amiability." (Compare the overarching category of "sociable relationships" proposed by the sociologist Allan [1979: 2], which allows him to talk of the sociability [interactions] of friends and of kin.)

20 Many aspects of the latter's model echo the dimensions of vernacular comparison already described; it will be recalled that anthropology's traditional contribution was to add social-cultural specificity.

21 Pitt-Rivers explicitly objects to the system of thought based on notions of an individual motivated principally by self-interest; it cannot deal with situations where "the self is not the individual self alone, but includes . . . those with whom the self is conceived as solidary, in the first place, his kin" (1973: 90). I see here the Euro-American image of the (individual) self-and-its-relations (M. Strathern 2018). "Extensions of the self" is Pitt-Rivers's phrase. He remarks that "society imposes its rules, but imposes them, not on individuals as such, but on relationships. The individual is the same person throughout his life but in the course of the developmental cycle his status changes . . . [vis-à-vis] his relationship to others" (1973: 101).

22 Concomitantly, there was a moment in twentieth-century sociological studies of "British kinship" that stressed the diffuse nature of perceived obligations and their enactment among family members, who should simply emanate love and kindness, as being a matter of "poorly articulated norms." Drawing attention to Finch (1989) and to Finch and Mason (1993) in this regard, Patterson (1997: 2–3) pinpoints the combination (diffuse principles; positive affect) as itself a strongly articulated stance that may work against other specifications of support and reward.

23 Alongside Cannell's (2013) interest in the transcendent properties of religion (see below), we may put this proposition on magic: if one thinks of ontologies where relations between things are also bonds of magical influence, kinship *is* the magic of people's influences upon one another (Viveiros de Castro 2009: 249).

24 There is a parallel here with Schrempp's (2011: 111) surmise about attempts to account for the formation of categories of thought, where "we encounter images of kinship and the body that cannot but recall the former life of these images in the world of mythology." He provides a veritable cornucopia of metaphorical, as well as causative, relations in which kinship is often seen as a vehicle for cognition. This is a context for Durkheim's and Mauss's conclusion that logical relations are thus in a sense domestic relations. However, Schrempp's overall scope seems to take its cue from an Aristotelean categorization of relations, where "category" emerges as the more compelling phenomenon, rather than from an early modern one, which was extricating itself from an Aristotelean inflection (Henninger 1989).

25 This presages the later discussion of "relationality" (the term is a nineteenth-century neologism), chiming with one historian's sense — all grist to the ethnographic mill — that making a mystery of things is a penchant of anthropology in general (Alan Strathern, pers. comm.).

26 By contrast, Paine continues, with "other interpersonal relations such as acquaintanceships or partnerships" ([1969] 1974b: 137). There would be nothing remarkable about the formula if it sprang from his ethnographic base in Western middle-class culture (his terms), but he goes out of his way to make this a more general conclusion.

27 In certain scholarly discourses, the epithet "human" takes on a sense of the transcendent, as weaves through the interdisciplinary essays on cosmopolitanism edited by Josephides (2014); in twentieth-century anthropology it often announced a state-

ment intended to be universally applicable, and thus at the broadest horizon of inquiry.

28 Cannell (2013: 237) brings the two together with respect to Max Weber's "suggestion that in a disenchanted world the search for meaning and value—which, for many, could only with difficulty continue to be pursued in formal religious contexts—might be displaced onto a range of other settings," from which (she implies) kinship is usually absent.

29 "Communal" rather than "spiritual" being, since Cannell argues that today's Mormons (Latter-day Saints) place no special weight on the spiritual as opposed to the material/physical. Her own concern is the secularist assumptions that generations of anthropologists have brought to kinship, ignoring not only the religious formation of ideas about person but also the role played by Protestantism in the institutional formulation of the very features of American kinship (blood, law) that Schneider (1968) saw as intrinsic to it.

30 As an example of such framings, in Mormon teaching "kinship is recognition" (Cannell 2013: 229), but this works with a very particular inflection: the notion that Mormon children come from a heaven where everyone is already known. Procreation thus entails notions not available to other Americans, for instance, that children choose their families, actively recognizing connections already in existence.

31 Assisted no doubt (we may add) by the logic of similarity and dissimilarity.

32 Edwards (2015) suggests that while people regularly identify the donor sibling as a new kin entity, for the anthropologist illumination might come as much from understandings of friendship as of kinship. She adds that there is a sense in which new kinds of kin are "carved out" of friendship (see also Weston 1991).

33 For Euro-Americans, the issue of blood is not coincidental. Edwards (2009: 9–10) singles out the multivalency of blood, its powerful role in "constituting relatedness" not reducible to biological or genealogical determination, just as Franklin (2013b: 296–297) shows how the "geneticization" of consanguinity has become the "blooding" of the gene.

34 He may have been saying it tongue in cheek, but Scott (2016: 480) identifies "continuity" (relating across boundaries) as a source of wonder to the "Cartesian essentialist" who finds the world full of discontinuity (individual particulars). Schrempp (2011: 104–105) offers a description of frisson: the "strangeness" it evokes among moderns, for whom Nicolaus Copernicus symbolizes a world shifted from its anthropocentric axis, to find him (Copernicus) using kinship idioms to describe planets orbiting the sun. (Schrempp [2011: 105] could almost be describing Copernicus's solar myths as an earlier form of re-enchantment: "It is always possible to soften a scientific blow by—metaphorically if you will—reinvesting the world with an anthropocentric vision.")

35 A relational form is instead at hand in reduplication: categorization implies recategorization, the ever-renewable classification of phenomena (as in merographic relations). With the inevitable negative, lack of categorization can be seen in other lacks, such as (dis)order, (dis)organization, and the (un)differentiated, or in (un)categorized as what is not yet categorized.

36 Not just because of the long relationship with Christianity, but also insofar as the

conceptual pairing of immanence and transcendence is appropriate to the Euro-American/naturalist phenomena under discussion. Holbraad (2012: 145) sees the pairing "premised on an ontology of discontinuity whose cosmological expressions, in Christianity and beyond, include notions of rupture, paradox, mystery, miracle, and so forth." Transcendentalist regimes of thought encompass their opposite (immanentist regimes), but—needless to say—the reverse is not true; Alan Strathern's (2019) historical discussion is the source of this last point.

37 See, by way of instancing a discussion otherwise, Josephides (2014: 8).

38 After McLeish (2019: 150) we might say this includes a creative process: rare in the early modern period, he argues, *reflection* on "the creative process itself" came into its own in both nineteenth-century literary fiction and experimental science.

CODA TO PART III: VISIBILITY

1 For Shapin and Schaffer ([1985] 2011: 25), the "matter of fact" so produced is "both an epistemological and a social category," a formulation to be put alongside the turn to material semiotics anticipated in the delineation of entities as at once material and social (e.g., Law's [1994: 24] "relational materialism"). Shapin and Schaffer's subject can also be seen as an enactment of Wagner's early formulation (1978: 23) about the conventional order of Western culture: the idea "of collective responsibility for knowledge and human government, and of the 'innateness' of the individual and incidental, is characteristic largely of the rationalist movements that sponsor and emulate the culture of science." Sahlins (2008: 15) later calls this the "veritable [Western] metaphysics of order," traceable to the "deep antiquity" he includes in his broad historical sweep, through "the transformation of the oppugnancy of . . . individual elements into a stable collective, either by the constraining action of an external power holding the fractious elements in place, or by the elements themselves holding each other in check."

2 The painting is most appositely reproduced, I add, in the case of the first edition of Outram's (1990) *The enlightenment*.

3 Porter (2000: 350) further intimates (after Benedict Nicolson) that, symbolizing "the new separation of man and Nature," the cockatiel is no less than an icon of the Holy Ghost, trapped within an instrumental machine.

4 Commentators have suggested that the persons are generic types, not portraits, although they may have been modeled on Wright's acquaintances. Eric Evans (typescript, 1985, National Gallery) imagined they were possibly the Darwins and their friends the Sewards, who lived near one another at Lichfield. Under Erasmus Darwin's watchful eye (the time keeper), they include some of the scientifically minded members of the Lunar Society, such as the young but already married Richard Edgeworth flirting with Anna Seward, who was to become a literary notability; her father, Canon Seward, reassures one of his wards.

5 Not omitting, to continue the above note, the two who have discovered each other; we are told that the spontaneous attraction between Anna and Richard was open for all to see.

6 The context and reference is expanded in the conclusions that follow.

1 Susan McKinnon suggested that this phrase has a titular ring to it, hence it heads these conclusions. Indicating late modernity's divergence from the aspirations of the Enlightenment, some thirty years ago Giddens (1991: 20–21) emphasized the reflexivity that comes from chronic revisions to knowledge of all kinds, remarking that knowledge is not incidental to "modern institutions" but is constitutive of them. I am not sure we would write with such certainty today, but he has characterized an era formative to the present work.

2 For example, Kirksey and Helmreich (2010); Latimer and Miele (2013); Kirksey (2015); Tsing, Swanson, Gan, and Bubandt (2017); Swanson, Lien, and Ween (2018).

3 The Shakespearian phrase was being pressed into an analogy: if we can admit of the natural world that all is related, we can admit it among human beings, too.

4 The article was sent me by Donna Haraway, to whom manifold thanks.

5 Just to be clear in relation to other vocabularies, this is Rapport's (1997: 6) "individualism."

6 The developmental geneticist Gilbert (2017: M73) describes the holobiont, "an organism plus its persistent communities of symbionts," as "a radically new way of conceptualizing 'individuals.'" The term was originally invented by Margulis and Fester (1991).

7 "Multispecies" offers an alternative designation to interspecies. The wider problem has been taken up in numerous locations outside biology, by the informaticist Bowker (2010), for instance; in actor-network theory insofar as it "dispenses with any *a priori* delimitation of what can count as a relation" (Jensen and Winthereik 2013: 29); and among commentators on communication networks. Jensen and Winthereik (2013: 160) reflect on Deleuze's view that "the individual, so dear to liberal philosophy and politics, is washing away in a sea of data." And this is, of course, exactly the reason for Barad's reinvention of interaction as intra-action, the problem of assuming "that there are separate individual agencies that precede their interaction" (2007: 33), which has been taken to reaffirm the novel potential of relations (Noble 2016: 216). Finally, Stengers's ([1997] 2010a: 35, transposed) description of symbiosis as "an immanent process of 'reciprocal capture' . . . [, each entity interested in] the success of the other for its own reasons," requires a special reading of relations. She explicitly says that the co-invention of different identities "is without reference to an interest that would transcend its terms" (36).

8 As when description takes a human-centric focus to the way relations with "nonhumans" are imagined. This is not to detract from the work that has gone into the concomitant rewriting of the human, as Kirksey and Helmreich (2010: 553, 565) indicate, their examples including "messmates" (Haraway 2008) or "mixmates" (Franklin 2008), or human nature itself as an interspecies relationship (Tsing n.d.).

9 The exposition concerns "qualities" and "substances" or the substrate of things. As artifacts of knowledge-making, Locke distinguishes between "relations," especially through comparison, and "connections," arising from how the manifold qualities of substances, and what impinges on them, lead to complex ideas. The latter's "real constitutions" are hardly graspable, Locke is arguing, by the forms that the expres-

sion of thought conventionally takes (our distinct ideas of things). "We perceive not [the] connexion or dependence [of qualities] one on another. . . . For the chief part of our knowledge concerning substances is not, as in other things, barely of the relation of two ideas, that may exist separately; but is of the necessary connexion and co-existence of several distinct ideas in the same subject, or of their repugnancy so to co-exist" (1690: 4, 6, 10; 584). I am grateful both to Rabinow and Stavrianakis (2018) and to Peter Skafish (pers. comm.) for encouraging this elucidation.

10 With respect to chapter 5, I note that the connections referred to here impinge no more on his earlier argument about identity than relations do. I am not implying a contradiction on Locke's part (what he says supports an individual-plus-its-relations model), but rather pointing to what his exposition emphasizes at different junctures. Sahlins (1993: 24–25) draws on these observations to argue how the attributes of things can be known by what time does to them.

11 So while certain early modern thinkers (and I have focused on Locke and Hume) cannot on the face of it be responsible for the perpetuation of their views, they did bequeath a framework of description and argumentation — conventions of exposition — for holding them more or less intact.

12 For another line of thinking, see Heinich's (2016) note on Norbert Elias.

13 And it is specifically apropos Locke's discussion of "relation" in book two of his *Essay* that Leibniz makes this comment.

14 In wishing to rid himself of an autonomous definition of technique, Latour (e.g., 1999: 197; 2005: 39, 128) prefers "mediation" for the transformative and always specific work of "mediators," who operate as open-ended actants.

15 Sahlins explicitly says that the kinship relations through which "others become predicates of one's own existence" refer not to the "interchange of standpoints" that is a general feature of social interaction but "the integration of certain relationships, hence the participation of certain others in one's own being" (2008: 49).

16 Reflexive in the sense one might imagine works for an epistemic community drawing on such knowledge as an act of self-formation (Laidlaw 2014: 99, 104–105). Insofar as I aim for an ethnographic account of (an) anthropological practice, this is also an auto-ethnography, in which the author is expersonated through, distributed among, the tools of her trade.

17 Silver (1990: 1489) dwells on Francis Hutcheson's Newtonian metaphor of the gravitational pull of bodies, which decreases with distance: "Benevolence is by nature gradated."

18 Apropos the former, Josephides (2014: 3) refers to Charles-Louis Montesquieu's model of concentric circles, with the first loyalty given to the outermost, to humanity.

19 (My formulation.) Peters (1995: 664) draws these issues into Smith's spectatorial conception of self and other (see chapter 3).

20 My anti-criticism ignores many nuances in Smith's account, including his departures from Hume (and it is in Hume that I see antecedents to the affect-laden character of the English relation). Thus Smith is misunderstood, says Forman-Barzilai (2010: 137), if we read sympathy as an emotion rather than a social practice elicited in shared spaces. Germane to the present thesis about the force of expositional practice

going against the grain of an argument, she also notes that Smith was overtly critical of factionalism and nationalism (both corrupters of moral sentiment) as affection writ large.

21 And it is the vernacular we-they (self-other) paradigm that makes alterity as "difference" — in the sense used latterly in this volume — so hard to think.

22 Josephides (2014: 3) also describes two "historico-mythical moments" in Julia Kristeva's interpretation of the cosmopolitan person: where "the work of the Enlightenment upholds the universality of humankind," the foreigner is at once within and "absorbed and erased through marriage." While today's media have given proximity many new connotations, it has also proliferated boundary drawing.

23 Where persons are taken as all the same, not even but especially in situations where what people think and feel is largely left up to them (that you can't see into another's mind is a truism of everyone). At the same time as such universal agnosticism makes people potentially "other" to one another, it also draws them toward one another. Stasch (2009: 15), who has written on the opacity of minds widely reported in Melanesia (see chapter 2, note 28), dwells on "the relational, connective aspect of otherness," and the way Korowai people are moved by "difference."

24 When Hage (2015: 55) contrasts the potential of critical sociology with that of anthropology, he emphasizes the specific contribution of the latter's comparative facility, which "constantly exposes us to the possibility of being other than what we are . . . [indeed, invites us] to animate certain social forces and potentials that are lying dormant in our midst." My thanks to Peter Skafish (pers. comm.) for underlining this inflection to Hage's argument.

25 Or rather, to say its opposite is "indifference" is another way of sidestepping the whole vernacular discourse about similarity.

26 See Pedersen and Willerslev (2012), after Viveiros de Castro (2001).

27 At this point I have stretched Hage's original distinctions too far, for he sees causal antecedents (if such were to be claimed) as integral to the oppositional stance of a critical sociology, from which anthropology's alter stance is far removed (given its capacity to deal with societies and cultures ostensibly in no causal connection with the anthropologist's).

28 (Through other conceptual means.) Rather than getting into a debate about whether conceptual and social forms illuminate each other, I observe that any such conjunction or disjunction can also be an outcome of a particular order of information required for exposition. Drill down into other orders of information, and this or that relation no longer appears.

29 "Culture" has become a Euro-American self-descriptive, just as Caneiro da Cunha describes (chapter 4). In social science it may be used strategically for what is not otherwise specified. Thus at the time when the concept of culture rode high, Allan (1979) invoked it to make a generalizing comment beyond his analysis of friendship and kinship in Britain, with its detailed attention among other things to class differences. Abandoning that framework (he had been discussing innumerable differentiations), he could declare "friendship *in English culture* is not institutionalized" (1979: 39, my emphasis).

30 From a "restoration" of classical learning, through its "renovation" to its "revolu-

tionary" displacement (Dear 2001), with greater and lesser continuities and discontinuities. Mack's seventeenth-century Quakers, to whom I have alluded, spoke out against knowledge itself. "Not only was intellectual activity a dangerous pastime that encouraged the sin of pride and the idolatry of the Anglican priests; it was also simply irrelevant to the existential experience Quakers sought"; the activities of mind and heart alike resembled bodily drives, and "it was words — the seducers of the mind — not the flesh" that "proved to be the real whore" (1992: 143–144). "Feed not on knowledge!" was one exhortation (149).

31 The tautology is addressed below. However, addressing the political infrastructures of naturalism is beyond my frame; I note only the deliberateness of present-day attacks on knowledge, notably in the public media of the United Kingdom and the United States, especially knowledge marked as expert or professional. It is seen in the attention given on all sides to the evident interest — always self-interest — of public figures as against the content of what they say (I write in 2018). Any piece of apparent knowledge can be dismissed as an interested statement.

32 To the contrary, this usage of "culture" leaves unattended the vernacular sense of boundedness, a notion newly made impossible with respect to its frontier with nature (Salmon 2017: 41).

33 The words are those uttered by the keepers; the sanctuary's project was to resocialize primates, turning entertainment animals back into "chimpanzees," and keepers were caught between enactments of empathy with their charges and training them not to depend on interaction with human beings. "Keepers just as often act *as if* they can grasp the perspective of a chimpanzee, as they act *as if* they cannot" (Alcayna-Stevens 2012: 92, original emphasis).

34 "Semantic range" possibly includes what Lloyd (2012: ch. 4) intends by "semantic stretch," which dissolves the boundaries vernacular usage otherwise throws up between terms understood literally and metaphorically.

35 I have noted elsewhere (M. Strathern 2005: 40–45; 2014), of certain twentieth-century and twenty-first-century studies of mothers in England (North London, Miller [1997]; northern England, Degnen [2009]), the extent to which challenges to a woman's motherhood include her responsibility for the knowledge she has of the world.

36 An apparently ancient feature of English, by contrast with other Germanic and with Romance languages in Europe that separate propositional and personal knowledge; the different modalities of "knowing" in English (knowing something, knowing someone) are managed through use and contextualization. A separate matter is the changing connotations of terms, a remark prompted by conversations with John Hendry (pers. comm.) concerning the concept of "belief" and its early modern acquisition of a propositional sense in addition to that of reliance or trust on a person; Harrison (1990) delineates some of the profound religious implications of this.

37 These were the terms within which I described Kuma gender "conflict" (chapter 4), a description there contextualized within a knowledge discourse. "The other" as unknown or unpredictable (unknowable in this sense) may or may not overlap with the Euro-American figure of the other as dissimilar with regard to this or that attribute.

38 It follows the moment of new knowledge-making ushered in earlier in the twentieth

century by systems theory. "Supplanting" (Luhmann's term) the imaginary of parts and wholes was offered as a radical displacement of other theorizings through "a recasting of the general framework within which systems are conceived and analyzed" (Luhmann 1982: 229).

39 Social domain is a concept well embedded in British social anthropology (Dumont [1971] 2006).

40 Pitt-Rivers ([1999] 2016: 448), who discusses Hume's writing on the matter, summarizes some of the paradoxes of thinking in terms of self-interest and disinterest with regard to friends. Degree of fit may come to the rescue: Smith argued that friendship cannot be "truly" voluntary and disinterested (see the discussion in Carey [2017: 50]).

41 I comment here on the idealized exposition of selves and their friendships, insofar as corruption was supposedly dealt with by disappearing kinship, that is, excluding the idea of it from a defense of bureaucratic and market rationality. One might also wonder if the elevation of rationality then overrode the frequent kinship interests at play in the family-empires of the nineteenth century (e.g., Kuper 2009; and see Yanagisako [2013] apropos cosmopolitan qualifications for places in family firms).

42 Thus Reyna (2014: 176) criticizes Silver's distinction between utilitarian and non-utilitarian friendship; even if it were a good analytic for the West (he thinks otherwise), it "constructs a duality that implicitly denigrates utilitarian, non-Western, non-modern friendship."

43 Franklin (2013b: 293) adds to her observation that the "active selection and negotiation of kin definition and degrees of acknowledged proximity" are among the mechanisms. Other orders of relatedness may duplicate rather than curtail: Bestard (2009: 26–27) refers to genetic essentialism dissolving in the context of familial relationships into the "relativising" (in both senses) of the gene.

44 In recognition of an apparent contradiction, a more colloquial "English" formulation would read, "divergent interests *nonetheless* capable of addressing a multifaceted cause." I override that.

45 These in turn coloring their understanding of everyday categories. Thus, oft-quoted for his views on friendship, by the concept Aquinas "always means one's friendship towards the friend, that is, a relational property inhering in oneself" (Schwartz 2007: 8) rather than distributed between both. Thanks to Alberto Corsín Jiménez for drawing my attention to Schwartz.

46 For Aureoli, a relation "has the property of being 'in the middle' or 'connecting' two things; it is a disposition, condition, or something existing between two things" (*medians inter illa*) (Henninger 1989: 154). The formulation has to be understood with respect to Aureoli's then-minority view on such relations as existing in knowledge-making alone, and thus not independent of thought (Brower 2015).

47 Given, among other things, vernacular apprehensions of betweenness (see introductions, note 6). This does not mean that the issue has been tidied away to everyone's technical satisfaction. Heil (2012: 141, 149; and 2009) presents several objections: two, for example, being that the universe does not require relations for they add no being to it, and that the idea of a relation between things illogically invokes a kind of shadowy substance. The latter invocation is culturally fascinating: across diverse

discourses — as anthropologists have rendered them — relations can indeed appear substance-like, sources of vitality, entities on their own account. As a matter of report, I have suggested just such is implied in the English habit of making a direct comparison "between" entities as though their third term or ground were the relation itself.

References

Abbott, Andrew. 2001. *Chaos of disciplines*. Chicago: University of Chicago Press.

Abrahams, Ray. 1999. "Friends and networks as survival strategies in North-East Europe." In S. Bell and S. Coleman, eds., *The anthropology of friendship*, 155–168. Oxford: Berg.

Alcayna-Stevens, Lys. 2012. "Inalienable worlds: Inter-species relations, perspectives and 'doublethink' in a Catalonian Chimpanzee sanctuary." *Cambridge Anthropology* 30 (2): 82–100.

Allan, Graham. 1979. *A sociology of friendship and kinship*. London: George Allen and Unwin.

Allen, N. J. 2000. *Categories and classifications: Maussian reflections on the social*. Oxford: Berghahn.

Alpers, Svetlana. 1983. *The art of describing: Dutch art in the seventeenth century*. Chicago: University of Chicago Press.

Amin, Ash. 2012. *Land of strangers*. Cambridge: Polity.

Argyrou, Vassos. 2002. *Anthropology and the will to meaning: A postcolonial critique*. London: Pluto.

Balibar, Étienne. [1998] 2013. *Identity and difference: John Locke and the invention of consciousness*. Ed. Stella Sandford, trans. Warren Montag. London: Verso.

Bamford, Sandra. 2009. "'Family trees' among the Kamea of Papua New Guinea: A nongenealogical approach to imagining relatedness." In S. Bamford and J. Leach, eds., *Kinship and beyond: The genealogical model reconsidered*, 159–174. Oxford: Berghahn.

Bamford, Sandra, and James Leach, eds. 2009. *Kinship and beyond: The genealogical model reconsidered*. Oxford: Berghahn.

Barad, Karen. 2007. *Meeting the universe half-way: Quantum physics and the entanglement of matter and meaning*. Durham, NC: Duke University Press.

Bateson, Gregory. [1936] 1958. *Naven: A survey of the problems suggested by a composite picture of the culture of a New Guinea tribe drawn from three points of view*. 2nd edition. Stanford, CA: Stanford University Press.

Battaglia, Debbora. 1990. *On the bones of the serpent: Person, memory, and mortality among Sabarl Islanders of Papua New Guinea*. Chicago: University of Chicago Press.

Battaglia, Debbora. 1995. "On practical nostalgia: Self-prospecting among urban Trobrianders." In D. Battaglia, ed., *Rhetorics of self-making*, 77–96. Berkeley: University of California Press.

Battaglia, Debbora. 2005. "Insiders' voices in outer spaces." In D. Battaglia, ed., *E.T. culture: Anthropology in outerspaces*, 1–37. Durham, NC: Duke University Press.

Beer, Bettina, and Don Gardner. 2015. "Friendship, anthropology of." In J. D. Wright, ed., *International encyclopedia of the social and behavioral sciences*, 2nd edition, vol. 9, 425–431. Oxford: Elsevier.

Bell, Sandra, and Simon Coleman, eds. 1999. *The anthropology of friendship*. Oxford: Berg.

Benson, Peter, and Kevin O'Neill. 2007. "Facing risk: Levinas, ethnography and ethics." *Anthropology of Consciousness* 18 (2): 29–55.

Bessire, Lucas, and David Bond. 2014. "Ontological anthropology and the deferral of critique." *American Ethnologist* 41 (3): 440–456.

Bestard, Joan. 2009. "Knowing and relating: Kinship, assisted reproductive technologies and the new genetics." In J. Edwards and C. Salazar, eds., *European kinship in the age of biotechnology*, 19–28. New York: Berghahn.

Biagioli, Mario. 2006. *Galileo's instruments of credit: Telescopes, images, secrecy*. Chicago: University of Chicago Press.

Bildhauer, Bettina. 2013. "Medieval European conceptions of blood: Truth and human integrity." In J. Carsten, ed., "Blood will out: Essays on liquid transfers and flows," special issue, *Journal of the Royal Anthropological Institute*: S57–S76.

Blaser, Mario. 2010. *Storytelling globalization from the Chaco and beyond*. Durham, NC: Duke University Press.

Bodenhorn, Barbara. 2013. "On the road again: Movement, marriage, Mestizaje, and the race of kinship." In S. McKinnon and F. Cannell, eds., *Vital relations: Modernity and the persistent life of kinship*, 131–154. Santa Fe, NM: School for Advanced Research Press.

Boellstorff, Tom. 2016. "For whom the ontology turns: Theorizing the digital real." *Current Anthropology* 57 (4): 387–407.

Boissevain, Jeremy. 1974. *Friends of friends: Networks, manipulators and coalitions*. Oxford: Basil Blackwell.

Boissevain, Jeremy, and J. Clyde Mitchell, eds. 1973. *Network analysis: Studies in human interaction*. The Hague: Mouton & Co.

Bolter, Jay David, and Richard Grusin. 1999. *Remediation: Understanding new media*. Cambridge, MA: MIT Press.

Bonifacio, Valentina. 2013. "Building up the collective: A critical assessment of the relationship between indigenous organisations and international cooperation in the Paraguayan Chaco." *Social Anthropology* 21 (4): 510–522.

Borneman, John. 2001. "Caring and being cared for: Displacing marriage, kinship, gender, and sexuality." In J. D. Faubion, ed., *The ethics of kinship: Ethnographic inquiries*, 29–46. Lanham, MD: Rowman and Littlefield.

Bowker, Geoffrey C. 2010. "A plea for pleats." In C. Bruun Jensen and K. Rödje, eds., *Deleuzian intersections: Science, technology, anthropology*, 123–139. Oxford: Berghahn.

Brain, Robert. 1976. *Friends and lovers*. London: Hart-Davis, MacGibbon.

Bray, Alan. 2003. *The friend*. Chicago: University of Chicago Press.

Brightman, Marc, Carlos Fausto, and Vanessa Grotti. 2016. "Altering ownership in Amazonia." In M. Brightman, C. Fausto, and V. Grotti, eds., *Ownership and nurture: Studies in native Amazonian property relations*, 1–35. Oxford: Berghahn.

Brower, Jeffrey. 2015. "Medieval theories of relations" [revised]. In E. N. Zalta, ed., *The Stanford encyclopedia of philosophy*, online, http://plato.stanford.edu/entries/relations -medieval (accessed April 2, 2016).

Buci-Glucksmann, Christine. [1984] 1994. *Baroque reason: The aesthetics of modernity*. London: Sage.

Cadena, Marisol de la. 2010. "Indigenous cosmopolitics in the Andes: Conceptual reflections beyond 'politics.'" *Cultural Anthropology* 25 (2): 334–370.

Cadena, Marisol de la. 2015. *Earth beings: Ecologies of practice across Andean worlds*. Durham, NC: Duke University Press.

Camic, Charles, Neil Gross, and Michèle Lamont. 2011. "Introduction." In C. Camic, N. Gross, and M. Lamont, eds., *Social knowledge in the making*, 1–40. Chicago: University of Chicago Press.

Campbell, Ben. 2009. "Fields of post-human kinship." In J. Edwards and C. Salazar, eds., *European kinship in the age of biotechnology*, 162–178. New York: Berghahn.

Candea, Matei. 2019. *Comparison in anthropology: The impossible method*. Cambridge: Cambridge University Press.

Candea, M., and L. Alcayna-Stevens. 2012. "Internal others: Ethnographies of naturalism." *Cambridge Anthropology* 30 (2): 36–47.

Candea, Matei, Joanna Cook, Catherine Trundle, and Thomas Yarrow, eds. 2015a. *Detachment: Essays on the limits of relational thinking*. Manchester: Manchester University Press.

Candea, Matei, Joanna Cook, Catherine Trundle, and Thomas Yarrow. 2015b. "Introduction: Reconsidering detachment." In M. Candea, J. Cook, C. Trundle, and T. Yarrow, eds., *Detachment: Essays on the limits of relational thinking*, 1–31. Manchester: Manchester University Press.

Cannell, Fenella. 2013. "The re-enchantment of kinship." In S. McKinnon and F. Cannell, eds., *Vital relations: Modernity and the persistent life of kinship*, 217–240. Santa Fe, NM: School for Advanced Research Press.

Carey, Matthew. 2017. *Mistrust: An ethnographic theory*. Chicago: HAU Books.

Carneiro da Cunha, Manuela. 2009. *"Culture" and culture: Traditional knowledge and intellectual rights*. Chicago: Prickly Paradigm.

Carrier, James. 1999. "People who can be friends: Selves and social relationships." In S. Bell and S. Coleman, eds., *The anthropology of friendship*, 21–38. Oxford: Berg.

Carsten, Janet, ed. 2000a. *Cultures of relatedness: New approaches to the study of kinship*. Cambridge: Cambridge University Press.

Carsten, Janet. 2000b. "Introduction: Cultures of relatedness." In J. Carsten, ed., *Cultures of relatedness: New approaches to the study of kinship*, 1–36. Cambridge: Cambridge University Press.

Carsten, Janet. 2004. *After kinship*. Cambridge: Cambridge University Press.

Cohen, Thomas, and Germaine Warkentin. 2011. "Things not easily believed: Introducing the early modern relation." *Renaissance and Reformation / Renaissance et Réforme* 34 (1–2): 7–23.

Collier, Stephen J., and Aiwa Ong. 2005. "Global assemblages, anthropological problems." In A. Ong and S. J. Collier, eds., *Global assemblages: Technology, politics, and ethics as anthropological problems*, 3–21. Oxford: Blackwell.

Corsín Jiménez, Alberto. 2011. "Daribi kinship at perpendicular angles: A trompe l'oeil anthropology." *HAU: Journal of Ethnographic Theory* 1 (1): 141–157.

Corsín Jiménez, Alberto. 2013. *An anthropological trompe l'oeil for a common world: An essay on the economy of knowledge*. Oxford: Berghahn.

Corsín Jiménez, Alberto, and Rane Willerslev. 2007. "'An anthropological concept of the concept': Reversibility among the Siberian Yukaghirs." *Journal of the Royal Anthropological Institute* (n.s.) 13 (3): 527–544.

Costa, Luiz. 2017. *The owners of kinship: Asymmetrical relations in indigenous Amazonia*. Chicago: HAU Books.

Crook, Tony. 2007. *Exchanging skin: Anthropological knowledge, secrecy and Bolivip, Papua New Guinea*. Oxford: Oxford University Press for the British Academy.

Crook, Tony, and Peter Rudiak-Gould. 2018. *Pacific climate cultures: Living climate change in Oceania*. Berlin: de Gruyter.

Danowski, Déborah, and Eduardo Viveiros de Castro. [2014] 2017. *The ends of the world*. Trans. R. Nunes. Cambridge: Polity.

Das, Veena. 2014. "Action, expression, and everyday life: Recounting household events." In V. Das, M. Jackson, A. Kleinman, and B. Singh, eds., *The ground between: Anthropologists engage philosophy*, 279–305. Durham, NC: Duke University Press.

Das, Veena. 2016. "Comment on Joel Robbins, What is the matter with transcendence? On the place of religion in the new anthropology of ethics." *Journal of the Royal Anthropological Institute* (n.s.) 22 (4): 785–790.

Davidoff, Leonore. 2012. *Thicker than water: Siblings and their relations, 1780–1920*. Oxford: Oxford University Press.

Davis, Natalie Zemon. 1978. "Ghosts, kin, and progeny: Some features of family life in early modern France." In A. S. Rossi, J. Kagan, and T. K. Hareven, eds., *The family*, 87–114. New York: W. W. Norton.

Davis, Natalie Zemon. 1986. "Boundaries and the sense of self in sixteenth-century France." In T. C. Heller, M. Sosna, and D. E. Wellerby, eds., *Reconstructing individualism: Autonomy, individuality, and the self in Western thought*, 53–63. Stanford, CA: Stanford University Press.

Davis, Natalie Zemon. 1995. *Women on the margins: Three seventeenth-century lives*. Cambridge, MA: Harvard University Press.

Dawson, Hannah. 2007. *Locke, language and early-modern philosophy*. Cambridge: Cambridge University Press.

DCMS. 2003. *The report of the Working Group on Human Remains*. London: Department for Culture, Media and Sport.

Dear, Peter. 2001. *Revolutionizing the sciences: European knowledge and its ambitions, 1500–1700*. Houndmills, Hants, UK: Palgrave.

Degnen, Cathrine. 2009. "Eating genes and raising people: Kinship thinking and genetically modified food in the north of England." In J. Edwards and C. Salazar, eds., *European kinship in the age of biotechnology*, 45–63. New York: Berghahn.

DeLanda, Manuel. 2006. *A new philosophy of society: Assemblage theory and social complexity*. New York: Continuum.

Delille, Gérard. 2013. "The shed blood of Christ: From blood as metaphor to blood as bearer of identity." In C. Johnson, B. Jussen, D. Sabean, and S. Teuscher, eds., *Blood and kinship: Matter for metaphor from ancient Rome to the present*, 125–143. Oxford: Berghahn.

Demian, Melissa. 2014. "On the repugnance of customary law." *Comparative Studies in Society and History* 56 (2): 508–536.

Demian, Melissa. 2015. "Dislocating custom." In M. Demian, ed., "Symposium on internationalizing custom and localizing law," *PoLAR: Political and Legal Anthropology Review* 38 (1): 91–107.

Desai, Amit, and Evan Killick, eds. 2010. *The ways of friendship: Anthropological perspectives*. Oxford: Berghahn.

Descola, Philippe. 2001. "The genres of gender: Local models and global paradigms in the comparison of Amazonia and Melanesia." In T. Gregor and D. Tuzin, eds., *Gender in Amazonia and Melanesia: An exploration of the comparative method*, 91–114. Berkeley: University of California Press.

Descola, Philippe. [2005] 2013. *Beyond nature and culture*. Trans. Janet Lloyd. Chicago: University of Chicago Press.

Descombes, Vincent. [1996] 2014. *The institutions of meaning: A defense of anthropological holism*. Trans. Stephen Adam Schwartz. Cambridge, MA: Harvard University Press.

Douglas, Mary. 1970. "Introduction." In M. Douglas, ed., *Witchcraft confessions and accusations*, xiii–xxxviii. London: Tavistock.

Du Gay, Paul. 2000. *In praise of bureaucracy: Weber, organization, ethics*. London: Sage.

Duhamelle, Christophe. 2007. "The making of stability: Kinship, church, and power among the Rhenish imperial knighthood, seventeenth and eighteenth centuries." In D. Sabean, S. Teuscher, and J. Mathieu, eds., *Kinship in Europe: Approaches to long-term development (1300–1900)*, 125–144. Oxford: Berghahn.

Dumont, Louis. [1971] 2006. *Introduction to two theories of social anthropology: Descent groups and marriage alliance*. Ed. and trans. R. Parkin. Oxford: Berghahn.

Dunn, John. 1969. *The political thought of John Locke: An historical account of the argument of the "Two treatises of government."* Cambridge: Cambridge University Press.

Edwards, Jeanette. 2000. *Born and bred: Idioms of kinship and new reproductive technologies in England*. Oxford: Oxford University Press.

Edwards, Jeanette. 2009. "The matter in kinship." In J. Edwards and C. Salazar, eds., *European kinship in the age of biotechnology*, 1–18. New York: Berghahn.

Edwards, Jeanette. 2013. "Donor siblings: Participating in each other's conception." *HAU: Journal of Ethnographic Theory* 3 (2): 285–292.

Edwards, Jeanette. 2014. "Tugging on a thread (of thought): A comment on Marilyn Strathern's 'Anthropological reasoning.'" *HAU: Journal of Ethnographic Theory* 4 (3): 39–44.

Edwards, Jeanette. 2015. "Donor conception and (dis)closure in the UK: Siblingship, friendship and kinship." *Sociologus: Journal for Empirical Anthropology* 65 (1): 101–122.

Edwards, Jeanette, and Carles Salazar, eds. 2009. *European kinship in the age of biotechnology*. New York: Berghahn.

Erickson, Amy Louise. 1993. *Women and property in early modern England*. London: Routledge.

Evans-Pritchard, E. E. [1937] 1950. *Witchcraft, oracles and magic among the Azande*. Oxford: Clarendon.

Evans-Pritchard, E. E. [1950] 1962. "Social anthropology: Past and present." In E. E. Evans-Pritchard, *Essays in social anthropology*, 13–28. London: Faber and Faber.

Faubion, James D. 2001. "Introduction: Toward an anthropology of the ethics of kinship." In J. D. Faubion, ed., *The ethics of kinship: Ethnographic inquiries*, 1–28. Lanham, MD: Rowman and Littlefield.

Fausto, Carlos. 2012a. "Too many owners: Mastery and ownership in Amazonia." In M. Brightman, V. Grotti, and O. Ulturgasheva, eds., *Animism in rainforest and tundra: Personhood, animals, plants and things in contemporary Amazonia and Siberia*, 29–48. Oxford: Berghahn.

Fausto, Carlos. [2001] 2012b. *Warfare and shamanism in Amazonia*. Trans. D. Rodgers. Cambridge: Cambridge University Press.

Feeley-Harnik, Gillian. 2001. "The ethnography of creation: Lewis Henry Morgan and the American beaver." In S. Franklin and S. McKinnon, eds., *Relative values: Reconfiguring kinship studies*. Durham, NC: Duke University Press.

Feeley-Harnik, Gillian. 2013. "Placing the dead: Kinship, slavery, and free labour in pre– and post–Civil War America." In S. McKinnon and F. Cannell, eds., *Vital relations: Modernity and the persistent life of kinship*, 179–216. Santa Fe, NM: School for Advanced Research Press.

Feeley-Harnik, Gillian. 2017. "Spiritual kinship in an age of dissent: Pigeon fanciers in Darwin's England." In A. Malik, T. Thomas, and R. Wellman, eds., *New directions in spiritual kinship: Sacred ties across the Abrahamic religions*, 51–83. New York: Palgrave Macmillan.

Feldman, Gregory. 2011. "If ethnography is more than participant observation, then relations are more than connections: The case for non-local ethnography in a world of apparatuses." *Anthropological Theory* 11 (4): 375–395.

Finch, Janet. 1989. *Family obligations and social change*. Cambridge: Polity.

Finch, Janet, and Jennifer Mason. 1993. *Negotiating family responsibilities*. London: Routledge.

Firth, Raymond. [1936] 1957. *We, the Tikopia: A sociological study of kinship in primitive Polynesia*. London: George Allen & Unwin.

Firth, Raymond. [1951] 1961. *Elements of social organization*. London: Watts & Co.

Firth, Raymond, Jane Hubert, and Anthony Forge. 1969. *Families and their relatives: Kinship in a middle-class sector of London*. London: Routledge and Kegan Paul.

Forman-Barzilai, Fonna. 2010. *Adam Smith and the circles of sympathy: Cosmopolitanism and moral theory*. Cambridge: Cambridge University Press.

Fortes, Meyer. 1969. *Kinship and the social order: The legacy of Lewis Henry Morgan*. Chicago: Aldine.

Foucault, Michel. [1966] 1970. *The order of things: An archaeology of the human sciences*. Trans. Anon. London: Tavistock.

Frankenberg, Ronald. 1957. *Village on the border: A social study of religion, politics and football in a North Wales community.* London: Cohen and West.

Frankenberg, Ronald. 1982. "A social anthropology for Britain." In R. Frankenberg, ed., *Custom and conflict in British society*, 1–35. Manchester: Manchester University Press.

Franklin, Sarah. 2008. "Future mix." Paper presented to 107th Annual Meeting of the American Anthropological Association, San Francisco, CA, November 19–23.

Franklin, Sarah. 2013a. *Biological relatives: IVF, stem cells, and the future of kinship.* Durham, NC: Duke University Press.

Franklin, Sarah. 2013b. "From blood to genes? Rethinking consanguinity in the context of geneticization." In C. Johnson, B. Jussen, D. Sabean, and S. Teuscher, eds., *Blood and kinship: Matter for metaphor from ancient Rome to the present*, 285–306. Oxford: Berghahn.

Franklin, Sarah, and Susan McKinnon, eds. 2001. *Relative values: Reconfiguring kinship studies.* Durham, NC: Duke University Press.

Gagné, Renaud. 2018. "Regimes of comparatism." In R. Gagné, S. Goldhill, and G. E. R. Lloyd, eds., *Regimes of comparatism: Frameworks of comparison in history, religion and anthropology*, 1–17. Leiden: Brill.

Gammage, Bill. 2011. *The biggest estate on earth: How Aborigines made Australia.* Sydney: Allen and Unwin.

Gasché, Rodolphe. 1999. *Of minimal things: Studies on the notion of relation.* Stanford, CA: Stanford University Press.

Gell, Alfred. 1998. *Art and agency: An anthropological theory.* Oxford: Clarendon.

Gershon, Ilana. 2010. *The breakup 2.0: Disconnecting over new media.* Ithaca, NY: Cornell University Press.

Giddens, Anthony. 1991. *Modernity and self-identity: Self and society in the late modern age.* Cambridge: Polity.

Gilbert, Scott. 2017. "Holobiont by birth: Multilineage individuals as the concretion of cooperative processes." In A. Tsing, H. Swanson, E. Gan, and N. Bubandt, eds., *Arts of living on a damaged planet*, M73–M89. Minneapolis: University of Minnesota Press.

Gilbert, Scott F., Jan Sapp, and Alfred I. Tauber. 2012. "A symbiotic view of life: We have never been individuals." *Quarterly Review of Biology* 87 (4): 325–341.

Gingrich, André, and Richard Fox, eds. 2002. *Anthropology, by comparison.* London: Routledge.

Gobetti, Daniela. 1992. *Private and public: Individuals, households, and body politic in Locke and Hutcheson.* London: Routledge.

Goody, Jack. 1962. *Death, property and the ancestors: A study of the mortuary customs of the Lodagaa of West Africa.* London: Tavistock.

Goody, Jack. 1983. *The development of the family and marriage in Europe.* Cambridge: Cambridge University Press.

Green, Sarah. 2005. *Notes from the Balkans: Locating marginality and ambiguity on the Greek-Albanian border.* Princeton, NJ: Princeton University Press.

Green, Sarah. 2014. "Anthropological knots: Conditions of possibilities and interventions." *HAU: Journal of Ethnographic Theory* 4 (3): 1–21.

Guichard, Martine, Tilo Grätz, and Youssouf Diallo, eds. 2014. *Friendship, descent and alliance in Africa: Anthropological perspectives.* Oxford: Berghahn.

Hage, Ghassan. 2012. "Critical anthropological thought and the radical political imaginary today." *Critique of Anthropology* 32 (3): 285–308.

Hage, Ghassan. 2015. *Alter-politics: Critical anthropology and the radical imagination.* Melbourne: Melbourne University Press.

Haraway, Donna. [1984] 1989. "Teddy bear patriarchy: Taxidermy in the Garden of Eden, New York City, 1908–1936." In Donna Haraway, *Primate visions: Gender, race, and nature in the world of modern science*, 26–58. New York: Routledge.

Haraway, Donna. [1985] 1991. "A cyborg manifesto: Science, technology, and socialist-feminism in the late twentieth century." In Donna Haraway, *Simians, cyborgs, and women: The reinvention of nature*, 149–181. London: Free Association Books.

Haraway, Donna. 1997. "Modest_Witness@Second_Millennium.FemaleMan©_meets Oncomouse™." In Donna Haraway, *Modest_Witness@Second_Millennium.FemaleMan©_meets Oncomouse™: Feminism and technoscience*, 21–121. New York: Routledge.

Haraway, Donna. 2003. *The companion species manifesto: Dogs, people, and significant otherness.* Chicago: Prickly Paradigm.

Haraway, Donna. 2008. *When species meet.* Minneapolis: University of Minnesota Press.

Harrison, Peter. 1990. *"Religion" and the religions in the English Enlightenment.* Cambridge: Cambridge University Press.

Harvey, Penny, and Hannah Knox. 2010. "Abstraction, materiality and the 'science of the concrete' in engineering practice." In T. Bennett and P. Joyce, eds., *Material powers: Cultural studies, history and the material turn*, 124–142. London: Routledge.

Hastrup, Kirsten. 2002. "Anthropology's comparative consciousness: The case of human rights." In A. Gingrich and R. Fox, eds., *Anthropology, by comparison*, 27–43. London: Routledge.

Hawthorn, Geoffrey. 1991. *Plausible worlds: Possibility and understanding in history and the social sciences.* Cambridge: Cambridge University Press.

Heil, John. 2009. "Relations." In R. Le Poidevin and R. Cameron, eds., *Routledge companion to metaphysics*, 310–321. London: Routledge.

Heil, John. 2012. *The universe as we find it.* Oxford: Clarendon.

Heinich, Nathalie. 2016. "De l'objet à la relation: Une révolution copernicienne [From object to relation: A Copernican revolution]." *Revue du MAUSS* 47 (1): 30–31.

Helmreich, Stefan. 2009. *Alien ocean: Anthropological voyages in microbial seas.* Berkeley: University of California Press.

Henninger, Mark G., SJ. 1989. *Relations: Medieval theories 1250–1325.* Oxford: Clarendon.

Herman, Arthur. 2001. *The Scottish Enlightenment: The Scots' invention of the modern world.* London: Harper Perennial.

Herzfeld, Michael. [1992] 1993. *The social production of indifference: Exploring the symbolic roots of Western bureaucracy.* Chicago: University of Chicago Press.

Hirsch, Eric, and Marilyn Strathern, eds. 2004. *Transactions and creations: Property debates and the stimulus of Melanesia.* Oxford: Berghahn.

Hirschman, Albert O. 1977. *The passions and the interests: Political arguments for capitalism before its triumph.* Princeton, NJ: Princeton University Press.

Hirschmann, Nancy J. 2000. "Sympathy, empathy and obligation: A feminist re-reading." In A. J. Jacobson, ed., *Feminist interpretations of David Hume*, 174–193. University Park: Pennsylvania State University Press.

Holbraad, Martin. 2008. "Definitive evidence, from Cuban gods." In M. Engelke, ed., "The objects of evidence: Anthropological approaches to the production of knowledge," special issue, *Journal of the Royal Anthropological Institute*: S93–S109.

Holbraad, Martin. 2009. "Ontography and alterity: Defining anthropological truth." In C. Toren and J. de Pina-Cabral, eds., "What is happening to epistemology?," special issue, *Social Analysis* 53 (2): 80–93.

Holbraad, Martin. 2012. *Truth in motion: The recursive anthropology of Cuban divination*. Chicago: University of Chicago Press.

Holbraad, Martin. 2017. "The contingency of concepts: Transcendental deduction and ethnographic expression in anthropological thinking." In P. Charbonnier, G. Salmon, and P. Skafish, eds., *Comparative metaphysics: Ontology after anthropology*, 133–158. London: Rowman and Littlefield.

Holbraad, Martin, and Morten Axel Pedersen. 2017. *The ontological turn: An anthropological exposition*. Cambridge: Cambridge University Press.

Hoskin, Keith. 1995. "The viewing self and the world we view: Beyond the perspectival illusion." *Organization* 2 (1): 141–162.

Hoskin, Keith. 1996. "The 'awful idea of accountability': Inscribing people into the measurement of objects." In R. Munro and J. Mouritsen, eds., *Accountability: Power, ethos and the technologies of managing*, 265–282. London: International Thomson Business Press.

Hume, David. N.d. [1748]. "An inquiry concerning human understanding." In *Essays, literary, moral, and political*. London: Ward, Lock, & Co.

Hume, David. [1739–1740] 2000. *A treatise of human nature*. Ed. David Norton and Mary Norton, with other material by D. F. and M. J. Norton. Oxford: Oxford University Press.

Hunter, Michael. 1981. *Science and society in Restoration England*. Cambridge: Cambridge University Press.

Hunter, Michael. 1989. *Establishing the new science: The experience of the early Royal Society*. Woodbridge, UK: Boydell.

Huxley, Robert. 2003. "Natural history collectors and their collections: 'Simpling macaronis' and instruments of empire." In K. Sloan, with A. Burnett, eds., *Enlightenment: Discovering the world in the eighteenth century*, 80–91. London: British Museum Press.

Ingold, Tim. 1986. "What is a social relationship?" In T. Ingold, *Evolution and social life*, 222–292. Cambridge: Cambridge University Press.

Ingold, Tim. 2011. *Being alive: Essays on movement, knowledge and description*. London: Routledge.

Ingold, Tim. 2013. "Dreaming of dragons: On the imagination of real life." *Journal of the Royal Anthropological Institute* (n.s.) 19 (4): 734–752.

Israel, Jonathan I. 2001. *Radical enlightenment: Philosophy and the making of modernity, 1650–1750*. Oxford: Oxford University Press.

Jacob, Marie-Andrée. 2012. *Matching organs with donors: Legality and kinship in transplants*. Philadelphia: University of Pennsylvania Press.

James, Wendy. 2003. *The ceremonial animal: A new portrait of anthropology*. Oxford: Oxford University Press.

Jay, Martin. 1988. "Scopic regimes of modernity." In H. Foster, ed., *Vision and visuality*. Seattle, WA: Bay Press.

Jensen, Casper Bruun. 2012. "Proposing the motion: 'The task of anthropology is to invent relations.'" *Critique of Anthropology* 32 (1): 47–53.

Jensen, Casper Bruun, and Brit Winthereik. 2013. *Monitoring movements in development aid: Recursive partnerships and infrastructures*. Cambridge, MA: MIT Press.

Johansson, Ingvar. 2014. "All relations are internal: The new version." In A. Reboul, ed., *Mind, values, and metaphysics*, 225–240. New York: Springer.

Johnson, Christopher H., Bernard Jussen, David W. Sabean, and Simon Teuscher, eds. 2013. *Blood and kinship: Matter for metaphor from ancient Rome to the present*. Oxford: Berghahn.

Josephides, Lisette. 2014. "Introduction: Framing the debate." In L. Josephides and A. Hall, *We the cosmopolitans: Moral and existential conditions of being human*, 1–28. Oxford: Berghahn.

Josephides, Lisette. 2015. "Together we are two: The disjunctive synthesis in affirmative mode." In L. Josephides, ed., *Knowledge and ethics in anthropology: Obligations and requirements*, 31–59. London: Bloomsbury Academic.

Kantsa, Venetia, and Aspa Chalkidou. 2014. "Doing family 'in the space between laws': Notes on lesbian motherhood in Greece." *Lambda Nordica* (19) 3–4: 86–108.

Kapferer, Bruce. 2013. "How anthropologists think: Configurations of the exotic." *Journal of the Royal Anthropological Institute* (n.s.) 19 (4): 813–836.

Kapferer, Bruce. 2016. "Comment on Joel Robbins, What is the matter with transcendence? On the place of religion in the new anthropology of ethics." *Journal of the Royal Anthropological Institute* (n.s.) 22 (4): 790–795.

Kaufman, Sharon R., Ann J. Russ, and Janet K. Shim. 2009. "Aged bodies and kinship matters: The ethical field of kidney transplant." In H. Lambert and M. McDonald, eds., *Social bodies*, 17–46. New York: Berghahn.

Kelly, José. 2011. *State healthcare and Yanomami transformations*. Tucson: University of Arizona Press.

Kirksey, Eben. 2015. *Emergent ecologies*. Durham, NC: Duke University Press.

Kirksey, Eben, and Stefan Helmreich. 2010. "The emergence of multispecies ethnography." *Cultural Anthropology* 25 (4): 545–576.

Kohn, Eduardo. 2007. "How dogs dream: Amazonian natures and the politics of transspecies engagement." *American Ethnologist* 34 (1): 3–24.

Kohn, Eduardo. 2012. "Anthropology beyond the human." *Cambridge Anthropology* 30 (2): 136–140.

Kohn, Eduardo. 2013. *How forests think: Toward an anthropology beyond the human*. Berkeley: University of California Press.

Kuper, Adam. 2009. *Incest and influence: The private life of bourgeois England*. Cambridge, MA: Harvard University Press.

Laidlaw, James. 2014. *The subject of virtue: An anthropology of ethics and freedom*. Cambridge: Cambridge University Press.

Lambek, Michael. 2013a. "The continuous and discontinuous person: Two dimensions of ethical life." *Journal of the Royal Anthropological Institute* (n.s.) 19 (4): 837–858.

Lambek, Michael. 2013b. "Kinship, modernity, and the immodern." In S. McKinnon and

F. Cannell, eds., *Vital relations: Modernity and the persistent life of kinship*, 241–260. Santa Fe, NM: School for Advanced Research Press.

Lambek, Michael. 2016. "Comment on Joel Robbins, What is the matter with transcendence? On the place of religion in the new anthropology of ethics." *Journal of the Royal Anthropological Institute* (n.s.) 22 (4): 781–785.

Lancy, David, and Andrew Strathern. 1981. "'Making twos': Pairing as an alternative to the taxonomic mode of representation." *American Anthropologist* 83: 773–795.

Latimer, Joanna. 2013. "Being alongside: Rethinking relations amongst different kinds." *Theory, Culture and Society* 30 (7/8): 77–104.

Latimer, Joanna, and Maria Miele, eds. 2013. "Naturecultures: Science, affect and the non-human." Special issue, *Theory, Culture and Society* 30 (7/8): 5–198.

Latour, Bruno. [1991] 1993. *We have never been modern*. Trans. C. Porter. Cambridge, MA: Harvard University Press.

Latour, Bruno. 1999. *Pandora's hope: Essays on the reality of science studies*. Cambridge, MA: Harvard University Press.

Latour, Bruno. 2005. *Reassembling the social: An introduction to Actor-Network-Theory*. Oxford: Oxford University Press.

Latour, Bruno. 2013a. "Biography of an enquiry: On a book about modes of existence." *Social Studies of Science* 43 (2): 287–301.

Latour, Bruno. 2013b. *An inquiry into modes of existence: An anthropology of the moderns*. Trans. C. Porter. Cambridge, MA: Harvard University Press.

Law, John. 1994. *Organizing modernity*. Oxford: Blackwell.

Law, John. 2004. *After method: Mess in social science research*. London: Routledge.

Lazar, Sian. 2012. "Disjunctive comparison: Citizenship and trade unionism in Bolivia and Argentina." *Journal of the Royal Anthropological Institute* (n.s.) 18 (2): 349–368.

Lazar, Sian. 2018. "A 'kinship anthropology of politics'? Interest, the collective self, and kinship in Argentina." *Journal of the Royal Anthropological Institute* (n.s.) 24 (2): 256–274.

Lea, Tess. 2008. *Bureaucrats and bleeding hearts: Indigenous health in Northern Australia*. Sydney: UNSW Press.

Leach, James. 2009. "Knowledge as kinship: Mutable essence and the significance of transmission on the Rai Coast of Papua New Guinea." In S. Bamford and J. Leach, eds., *Kinship and beyond: The genealogical model reconsidered*, 175–192. Oxford: Berghahn.

Leach, James. 2012. "Leaving the magic out: Knowledge and effect in different places." *Anthropological Forum* 22 (3): 251–270.

Leach, James, and Richard Davis. 2012. "Recognising and translating knowledge: Navigating the political, epistemological, legal and ontological." *Anthropological Forum* 22 (3): 209–223.

Lebner, Ashley. 2012. "A Christian politics of friendship on a Brazilian frontier." *Ethnos* 77 (4): 496–517.

Lederman, Rena. 1986. *What gifts engender: Social relations and politics in Mendi, Highland Papua New Guinea*. Cambridge: Cambridge University Press.

Lederman, Rena. 2005. "Unchosen grounds: Cultivating cross-subfield accents for a public voice." In D. Segal and S. Yanagisako, eds., *Unwrapping the sacred bundle: Reflections on the disciplining of anthropology*. Durham, NC: Duke University Press.

Leenhardt, Maurice. [1947] 1979. *"Do kamo": Person and myth in the Melanesian world*. Trans. B. M. Gulati. Chicago: University of Chicago Press.

Lévi-Strauss, Claude. [1958] 1963. *Structural anthropology, volume I*. Trans. C. Jacobson and B. G. Schoepf. New York: Basic Books.

Lévi-Strauss, Claude. [1973] 1978. "Reflections on the atom of kinship." In *Structural anthropology, volume II*, 82–112. Trans. M. Layton. Harmondsworth, UK: Penguin.

Leyton, Elliott, ed. 1974a. *The compact: Selected dimension of friendship*. Newfoundland Social and Economic Papers no. 3. Institute of Social and Economic Research, Memorial University of Newfoundland, Canada.

Leyton, Elliott. 1974b. "Irish friends and 'friends': The nexus of friendship, kinship and class in Aughnaboy, Ireland." In E. Leyton, ed., *The compact: Selected dimensions of friendship*, 93–104. Institute of Social and Economic Research, Memorial University of Newfoundland, Canada.

LiPuma, Edward. 1988. *The gift of kinship: Structure and practice in Maring social organisation*. Cambridge: Cambridge University Press.

Lloyd, G. E. R. 1966. *Polarity and analogy: Two types of argumentation in early Greek thought*. Cambridge: Cambridge University Press.

Lloyd, G. E. R. 2012. *Being, humanity and understanding: Studies in ancient and modern societies*. Oxford: Oxford University Press.

Lloyd, G. E. R. 2015. *Analogical investigations: Historical and cross-cultural perspectives on human reasoning*. Cambridge: Cambridge University Press.

Lock, Margaret. 2002. *Twice dead: Organ transplants and the reinvention of death*. Berkeley: University of California Press.

Locke, John. [1690] 1975. *An essay concerning human understanding*. Ed. Peter H. Nidditch. Oxford: Clarendon.

Locke, John. [1689–1690] 1988. *Two treatises of government*. Ed. Peter Laslett. Cambridge: Cambridge University Press.

Luhmann, Niklas. 1982. *The differentiation of society*. Trans. S. Holmes and C. Larmore. New York: Columbia University Press.

Luhmann, Niklas. 1990. *Essays on self-reference*. New York: Columbia University Press.

Mack, Phyllis. 1992. *Visionary women: Ecstatic prophecy in seventeenth-century England*. Berkeley: University of California Press.

Mann, Jill. 2008. "Messianic chivalry in 'Amis and Amiloun.'" *New Medieval Literatures* 10: 137–159.

Marett, R. R. [1912] 1936. *Anthropology*. Home University Library. London: Thornton Butterworth.

Margulis, Lynn, and René Fester. 1991. *Symbiosis as a source of evolutionary innovation: Speciation and morphogenesis*. Cambridge, MA: MIT Press.

Marshall, Duncan, ed. 1967. *The autobiography of William Stout of Lancaster, 1665–1752*. Manchester: Manchester University Press.

McKinnon, Susan. 2013. "Kinship within and beyond the 'movement of progressive societies.'" In S. McKinnon and F. Cannell, eds., *Vital relations: Modernity and the persistent life of kinship*, 39–62. Santa Fe, NM: School for Advanced Research Press.

McKinnon, Susan. 2018. "Cousin marriage, hierarchy, and heredity: Contestations over domestic and national body politics in nineteenth-century America." 2018 Radcliffe-Brown Lecture. London: British Academy.

McKinnon, Susan, and Fenella Cannell. 2013a. "The difference kinship makes." In S. McKinnon and F. Cannell, eds., *Vital relations: Modernity and the persistent life of kinship*, 3–38. Santa Fe, NM: School for Advanced Research Press.

McKinnon, Susan, and Fenella Cannell, eds. 2013b. *Vital relations: Modernity and the persistent life of kinship*. Santa Fe, NM: School for Advanced Research Press.

McLeish, Tom. 2019. *The poetry and music of science: Comparing creativity in science and art*. Oxford: Oxford University Press.

Merlan, Francesca, and Alan Rumsey. 1991. *Ku Waru: Language and segmentary politics in the western Nebilyer Valley, Papua New Guinea*. Cambridge: Cambridge University Press.

Miller, Daniel. 1997. "How infants grow mothers in North London." *Theory, Culture and Society* 14: 67–88.

Miller, Daniel. 2016. *Social media in an English village*. London: UCL Press.

Miller, Daniel. 2017. "The ideology of friendship in the era of Facebook." *HAU: Journal of Ethnographic Theory* 7 (1): 377–395.

Miller, Daniel, Elisabetta Costa, Nell Haynes, Tom McDonald, Razvan Nicolescu, Jolynna Sinanan, Juliano Spyer, Shriram Ventkatraman, and Xinyan Wang. 2016. *How the world changed social media*. London: UCL Press.

Mohácsi, Gergely, and Atsuro Morita, eds. 2015. "Introduction." In "Acting with non-human entities," special issue, *Natureculture* 03: 1–6.

Mol, Annemarie. 2002. *The body multiple: Ontology in medical practice*. Durham, NC: Duke University Press.

Morgan, David. 2009. *Acquaintances: The space between intimates and strangers*. Maidenhead, UK: Open University Press.

Morita, Atsuro. 2014. "The ethnographic machine: Experimenting with context and comparison in Strathernian ethnography." *Science, Technology & Human Values* 39 (2): 214–235.

Mosko, Mark. 1985. *Quadripartite structures: Categories, relations and homologies in Bush Mekeo culture*. Cambridge: Cambridge University Press.

Moutu, Andrew. 2013. *Names are thicker than blood: Kinship and ownership amongst the Iatmul*. Oxford: Oxford University Press for the British Academy.

Moutu, Andrew. 2014. "The tyranny of analogy in legal precedent." Unpublished paper given to Underlying Law Seminar Series, Port Moresby, Papua New Guinea, October 2014.

Munn, Nancy. 1990. "Constructing regional worlds in experience: Kula exchange, witchcraft and Gawan local events." *Man* (n.s.) 25 (1): 1–17.

Navaro-Yashin, Yael. 2009. "Affective spaces, melancholic objects: Ruination and the production of anthropological knowledge." *Journal of the Royal Anthropological Institute* (n.s.) 15 (1): 1–18.

Ng, Su Fang. 2007. *Literature and the politics of family in seventeenth-century England*. Cambridge: Cambridge University Press.

Nidditch, Peter. [1975] 1979. Foreword. In John Locke, *An essay concerning human understanding*, vi–xxvi. Oxford: Clarendon.

Noble, Brian. 2016. *Articulating dinosaurs: A political anthropology*. Toronto: University of Toronto Press.

Nombo, Porer, and James Leach. 2010. *Reite plants: An ethnobotanical study in Tok Pisin and English*. Canberra: Australian National University e-Press.

Norton, David, and Mary Norton. 2000. "Annotations to the *Treatise*." In D. F. Norton and M. J. Norton, eds., *Hume's A treatise of human nature*, 423–566. Oxford: Oxford University Press.

Nuffield Council on Bioethics. 2011. *Human bodies: Donation for medicine and research*. London: Nuffield Council on Bioethics.

Ollman, Bertell. [1971] 1976. *Alienation: Marx's conception of man in capitalist society*. Cambridge: Cambridge University Press.

Outram, Dorinda. 1995. *The Enlightenment*. Cambridge: Cambridge University Press.

Paine, Robert. 1974a. "Anthropological approaches to friendship." In E. Leyton, ed., *The compact: Selected dimensions of friendship*, 1–14. Institute of Social and Economic Research, Memorial University of Newfoundland, Canada.

Paine, Robert. [1969] 1974b. "An exploratory analysis in 'middle-class' culture." In E. Leyton, ed., *The compact: Selected dimensions of friendship*, 117–137. Institute of Social and Economic Research, Memorial University of Newfoundland, Canada.

Paine, Robert. 1999. "Friendship: The hazards of an ideal relationship." In S. Bell and S. Coleman, eds., *The anthropology of friendship*, 39–58. Oxford: Berg.

Pálsson, Gísli. 1999. "Commentary on Nurit Bird-David's '"Animism" revisited: Personhood, environment, and relational epistemology.'" *Current Anthropology* 40 (Suppl.): 83–84.

Pálsson, Gísli. 2013. "Ensembles of biosocial relations." In T. Ingold and G. Pálsson, eds., *Biosocial becomings: Integrating social and biological anthropology*, 22–42. Cambridge: Cambridge University Press.

Patterson, Nerys Thomas. 1997. "Conflicting norms in modern British kinship: Case studies of domestic violence and competition for care in North Wales, 1920–1996." *History of the Family* 2 (1): 1–19.

Pedersen, Morten Axel, and Rane Willerslev. 2012. "'The soul of the body is the soul': Rethinking the concept of the soul through North Asian ethnography." *Common Knowledge* 18 (3): 464–486.

Perry, Ruth. 1986. *The celebrated Mary Astell: An early English feminist*. Chicago: University of Chicago Press.

Perry, Ruth. 2004. *Novel relations: The transformation of kinship in English literature and culture, 1748–1818*. Cambridge: Cambridge University Press.

Peters, John. 1995. "Publicity and pain: Self-abstraction in Adam Smith's 'Theory of moral sentiments.'" *Public Culture* 3: 657–675.

Phillips, Edward. 1658. *The new world of English words: or, a general dictionary: containing the interpretations of such hard words as are derived from other languages*. London.

Phillips, Edward. 1696. *The new world of words: or, a universal English dictionary. Containing the proper significations and derivations of all words from other languages*. London.

Pickles, Anthony. 2014. "'*Bom* bombed *kwin*': How two card games model *kula, moka*, and Goroka." *Oceania* 84 (3): 272–288.

Pickstone, John. 2000. *Ways of knowing: A new history of science, technology and medicine.* Manchester: Manchester University Press.

Pina-Cabral, João de. 2017. *World: An anthropological examination.* Chicago: HAU Books.

Pitt-Rivers, Julian. 1968. "Pseudo-kinship." In *International encyclopedia of the social sciences*, 408–413. London / New York: Macmillan / Free Press.

Pitt-Rivers, Julian. 1973. "The kith and the kin." In J. Goody, ed., *The character of kinship*, 89–105. Cambridge: Cambridge University Press.

Pitt-Rivers, Julian. [1999] 2016. "The paradox of friendship." Trans. M. Carey. *HAU: Journal of Ethnographic Theory* 6 (3): 443–452.

Porter, Roy. 2000. *Enlightenment: Britain and the creation of the modern world.* London: Allen Lane.

Povinelli, Elizabeth. 2002. *The cunning of recognition: Alterities and the making of Australian multiculturalism.* Durham, NC: Duke University Press.

Povinelli, Elizabeth. 2016. *Geontologies: A requiem to late liberalism.* Durham, NC: Duke University Press.

Pratt, Mary Louise. 1992. *Imperial eyes: Travel writing and transculturation.* London: Routledge.

Rabinow, Paul. 2003. *Anthropos today: Reflections on modern equipment.* Princeton, NJ: Princeton University Press.

Rabinow, Paul. 2011. *The accompaniment: Assembling the contemporary.* Chicago: University of Chicago Press.

Rabinow, Paul, and Gaymon Bennett. 2008. *Ars synthetica: Designs for human practice.* Rice University, Connexions, no longer available online, http://cnx.prg/content/col10612/1.2/ (accessed December 29, 2009).

Rabinow, Paul, and Gaymon Bennett. 2012. *Designing human practices: An experiment with synthetic biology.* Chicago: University of Chicago Press.

Rabinow, Paul, and Anthony Stavrianakis. 2016. "Movement space: Putting anthropological theory, concepts, and cases to the test." *HAU: Journal of Ethnographic Theory* 6 (1): 403–431.

Rabinow, Paul, and Anthony Stavrianakis. 2018. *Inquiry after modernism.* Online, snafu .dog (accessed August 20, 2018).

Radcliffe-Brown, A. R. [1940] 1952. "On social structure." In *Structure and function in primitive society*, 188–204. London: Cohen and West.

Raffles, Hugh. 2010. *Insectopedia.* New York: Pantheon.

Rapport, Nigel. 1997. *Transcendent individual: Towards a literary and liberal anthropology.* London: Routledge.

Ray, Sid. 2002. "'Those whom God hath joined together': Bondage metaphor and marital advice in early modern England." In K. B. McBride, ed., *Domestic arrangements in early modern England*. Pittsburgh, PA: Duquesne University Press.

Reay, Marie. 1959a. *The Kuma: Freedom and conformity in the New Guinea Highlands.* Carlton, Victoria: Melbourne University Press.

Reay, Marie. 1959b. "Two kinds of ritual conflict." *Oceania* 29: 290–296.

Reed, Adam. 2011. *Literature and agency in English fiction reading: A study of the Henry Williamson Society.* Manchester: Manchester University Press.

Remne, Jon Henrik Ziegler, and Kenneth Sillander, eds. 2017. *Human nature and social life: Perspectives on extended sociality*. Cambridge: Cambridge University Press.

Reyna, Stephen. 2014. "Afterword: Friendship in a world of force and power." In M. Guichard, T. Grätz, and Y. Diallo, eds., *Friendship, descent and alliance in Africa: Anthropological perspectives*, 161–179. Oxford: Berghahn.

Rezende, Claudia Barcellos. 1999. "Building affinity through friendship." In S. Bell and S. Coleman, eds., *The anthropology of friendship*, 79–97. Oxford: Berg.

Riles, Annelise. 2000. *The network inside out*. Ann Arbor: University of Michigan Press.

Riles, Annelise, ed. 2006. *Documents: Artifacts of modern knowledge*. Ann Arbor: University of Michigan Press.

Riles, Annelise. 2013. "Market collaboration: Finance, culture, and ethnography after neoliberalism." *American Anthropologist* 115 (4): 555–569.

Riles, Annelise, Hirozaku Miyazaki, and Yuji Genda. 2012. *Re-tooling: Techniques for an uncertain world*. Trans. C. Watanabe. Ithaca, NY: Cornell University Law School.

Rio, Knut. 2007. *The power of perspective: Social ontology and agency on Ambrym Island, Vanuatu*. Oxford: Berghahn.

Robbins, Joel. 2004. *Becoming sinners: Christianity and moral torment in a Papua New Guinea society*. Berkeley: University of California Press.

Robbins, Joel. 2013. "Beyond the suffering subject: Toward an anthropology of the good." *Journal of the Royal Anthropological Institute* (n.s.) 19 (3): 447–462.

Robbins, Joel. 2016. "What is the matter with transcendence? On the place of religion in the new anthropology of ethics." *Journal of the Royal Anthropological Institute* (n.s.) 22 (4): 767–808.

Robbins, Joel, and Alan Rumsey. 2008. "Introduction: Cultural and linguistic anthropology and the opacity of other minds." *Anthropological Quarterly* 81 (2): 407–420.

Robbins, Joel, Bambi Schieffelin, and Aparacida Vilaça. 2014. "Evangelical conversion and the transformation of the self in Amazonia and Melanesia: Christianity and the revival of anthropological comparison." *Comparative Studies in Society and History* 56 (3): 559–590.

Roberts, Elizabeth. 2012. *God's laboratory: Assisted reproduction in the Andes*. Berkeley: University of California Press.

Roberts, Elizabeth. 2013. "Assisted existence: An ethnography of being in Ecuador." *Journal of the Royal Anthropological Institute* (n.s.) 19 (3): 562–580.

Rollason, Will, ed. 2014. *Pacific futures: Projects, politics and interests*. Oxford: Berghahn.

Sabean, David. 2007. "Outline and summaries." In D. W. Sabean, S. Teuscher, and J. Mathieu, eds., *Kinship in Europe: Approaches to long-term development (1300–1900)*, 51–57, 187–193. Oxford: Berghahn.

Sabean, David W. 2013. "Descent and alliance: Cultural meanings of blood in the Baroque." In C. Johnson, B. Jussen, D. Sabean, and S. Teuscher, eds., *Blood and kinship: Matter for metaphor from ancient Rome to the present*, 144–175. Oxford: Berghahn.

Sabean, David W., and Simon Teuscher. 2007. "Kinship in Europe: A new approach to long-term development." In D. W. Sabean, S. Teuscher, and J. Mathieu, eds., *Kinship in Europe: Approaches to long-term development (1300–1900)*, 1–32. Oxford: Berghahn.

Sahlins, Marshall. 1993. "Goodbye to *Tristes Tropes*: Ethnography in the context of modern world history." *Journal of Modern History* 65 (1): 1–25.

Sahlins, Marshall. 2008. *The western illusion of human nature: With reflections on the long history of hierarchy, equality, and the sublimation of anarchy in the West, and comparative notes on other conceptions of the human condition.* Chicago: Prickly Paradigm.

Sahlins, Marshall. 2011a. "What kinship is (part one)." *Journal of the Royal Anthropological Institute* (n.s.) 17 (1): 2–19.

Sahlins, Marshall. 2011b. "What kinship is (part two)." *Journal of the Royal Anthropological Institute* (n.s.) 17 (2): 227–242.

Sahlins, Marshall. 2013. *What kinship is—and is not.* Chicago: University of Chicago Press.

Salmon, Gildas. 2017. "On ontological delegation: The birth of neoclassical anthropology." Trans. N. Carter. In P. Charbonnier, G. Salmon, and P. Skafish, eds., *Comparative metaphysics: Ontology after anthropology*, 41–60. London: Rowman and Littlefield.

Sanders, Valerie. 2001. *The brother-sister culture in nineteenth-century literature: From Austen to Woolf.* Basingstoke, UK: Palgrave.

Sandford, Stella. 2013. "The incomplete Locke: Balibar, Locke and the philosophy of the subject." In E. Balibar, *Identity and difference: John Locke and the invention of consciousness*, xi–xlvi. Trans. W. Montag. London: Verso.

Schneider, David. 1968. *American kinship: A cultural account.* Englewood Cliffs, NJ: Prentice-Hall.

Schneider, D. M. 1972. "What is kinship all about?" In P. Reining, ed., *Kinship studies in the Morgan Centennial Year*, 32–63. Washington, DC: Anthropological Society of Washington, DC.

Schochet, Gordon. 1969. "The family and the origins of the state in Locke's political philosophy." In J. Yolton, ed., *John Locke: Problems and perspectives*, 81–98. Cambridge: Cambridge University Press.

Schram, Ryan. 2015. "A society divided: Death, personhood, and Christianity in Auhelawa, Papua New Guinea." *HAU: Journal of Ethnographic Theory* 5 (1): 317–337.

Schrempp, Gregory. 2011. "Copernican kinship: An origin myth for the category." *HAU: Journal of Ethnographic Theory* 1 (1): 103–139.

Schwartz, Daniel. 2007. *Aquinas on friendship.* Oxford: Clarendon.

Schwimmer, Eric. 1974. "Friendship and kinship: An attempt to relate two anthropological concepts." In E. Leyton, ed., *The compact: Selected dimensions of friendship*, 49–70. Institute of Social and Economic Research, Memorial University of Newfoundland, Canada.

Scott, Michael. 2007. "The severed snake." In *Matrilineages, making place, and a Melanesian Christianity in Southeast Solomon Islands.* Durham, NC: Carolina Academic Press.

Scott, Michael. 2013. "The anthropology of ontology (religious science?)." *Journal of the Royal Anthropological Institute* (n.s.) 19 (4): 859–872.

Scott, Michael. 2016. "To be Makiran is to see like Mr. Parrot: The anthropology of wonder in Solomon Islands." *Journal of the Royal Anthropological Institute* (n.s.) 22 (3): 474–495.

Shapin, Steven. 1994. *A social history of truth: Civility and science in seventeenth-century England.* Chicago: University of Chicago Press.

Shapin, Steven. 1996. *The scientific revolution.* Chicago: University of Chicago Press.

Shapin, Steven, and Simon Schaffer. [1985] 2011. *Leviathan and the air-pump: Hobbes, Boyle, and the experimental life.* Princeton, NJ: Princeton University Press.

Sharp, Lesley. 2006. *Strange harvest: Organ transplants, denatured bodies, and the transformed self.* Berkeley: University of California Press.

Sharp, Lesley. 2014. *The transplant imaginary: Mechanical hearts, animal parts, and moral thinking in highly experimental science.* Berkeley: University of California Press.

Shryock, Andrew. 2018. "Making kinship bigger: Andrew Shryock in conversation with Golfo Alexopoulos, Nadav Samin, David Henig, and Gísli Pálsson." *Comparative Studies in Society and History*, http://cssh.lsa.umich.edu/2018/04/01/making-kinship-bigger (accessed June 27, 2018).

Silver, Allan. 1989. "Friendship and trust as moral ideals: An historical approach." *European Journal of Sociology* 30: 274–297.

Silver, Allan. 1990. "Friendship in commercial society: Eighteenth-century social theory and modern sociology." *American Journal of Sociology* 95 (6): 1474–1504.

Skafish, Peter. 2014. "Introduction." In E. Viveiros de Castro, *Cannibal metaphysics for a post-structural anthropology*, 9–33. Minneapolis, MN: Univocal Publishing.

Skafish, Peter. 2017. "Metamorphosis of consciousness: Concept, system and anthropology in American channels." In P. Charbonnier, G. Salmon, and P. Skafish, eds., *Comparative metaphysics: Ontology after anthropology*, 275–299. London: Rowman and Littlefield.

Sloan, Kim. 2003. "'Aimed at universality and belonging to the nation': The Enlightenment and the British Museum." In K. Sloan, with A. Burnett, ed., *Enlightenment: Discovering the world in the eighteenth century*, 12–25. London: British Museum Press.

Smart, Alan. 1999. "Expressions of interest: Friendship and *guanxi* in Chinese societies." In S. Bell and S. Coleman, eds., *The anthropology of friendship*, 119–136. Oxford: Berg.

Smith, Julia M. H. 2005. *Europe after Rome: A new cultural history, 500–1000.* Oxford: Oxford University Press.

Spencer, Liz, and Ray Pahl. 2006. *Rethinking friendship: Hidden solidarities today.* Princeton, NJ: Princeton University Press.

Stasch, Rupert. 2009. *Society of others: Kinship and mourning in a West Papuan place.* Berkeley: University of California Press.

Steedman, Carolyn. 2009. *Labours lost: Domestic service and the making of modern England.* Cambridge: Cambridge University Press.

Stengers, Isabelle. [1993] 2000. *The invention of modern science.* Trans. D. Smith. Minneapolis: University of Minnesota Press.

Stengers, Isabelle. [1997] 2010a. *Cosmopolitics I.* Trans. R. Bononno. Minneapolis: University of Minnesota Press.

Stengers, Isabelle. [1997] 2010b. *Cosmopolitics II.* Trans. R. Bononno. Minneapolis: University of Minnesota Press.

Stengers, Isabelle. 2011. "Comparison as a matter of concern." *Common Knowledge* 17 (1): 48–63.

Stocking, George. 1995. *After Tylor: British social anthropology 1888–1951.* Madison: University of Wisconsin Press.

Strathern, Alan. 2019. *Unearthly powers: Religious and political thought in world history.* Cambridge: Cambridge University Press.

Strathern, Marilyn. 1988. *The gender of the gift: Problems with women and problems with society in Melanesia.* Berkeley: University of California Press.

Strathern, Marilyn. 1992. *After nature: English kinship in the late twentieth century.* Cambridge: Cambridge University Press.

Strathern, Marilyn. 2005. *Kinship, law and the unexpected: Relatives are always a surprise.* Cambridge: Cambridge University Press.

Strathern, Marilyn. 2014. "Kinship as a relation." *L'Homme* 210: 43–61.

Strathern, Marilyn. 2016. "Divergences and crossovers: Response to Robert Wilson's 'Thinking about relations.'" *Anthropological Theory* 16 (4): 350–358.

Strathern, Marilyn. 2018. "Persons and partible persons." In M. Candea, ed., *Schools and styles of anthropological theory*, 236–246. London: Routledge.

Strawson, Galen. 2011. *The evident connexion: Hume on personal identity.* Oxford: Oxford University Press.

Stuart, Matthew. 2013. *Locke's metaphysics.* Oxford: Clarendon.

Swanson, Heather, Marianne Lien, and Gro Ween, eds. 2018. *Domestication gone wild: Politics and practices of multispecies relations.* Durham, NC: Duke University Press.

Tadmor, Naomi. 2001. *Family and friends in eighteenth-century England: Household, kinship, and patronage.* Cambridge: Cambridge University Press.

Taylor, Charles. 1989. *Sources of the self: The making of modern identity.* Cambridge, MA: Harvard University Press.

Teuscher, Simon. 2013. "Flesh and blood in the treatises on the *Arbor consanguinitatis* (thirteenth to sixteenth centuries)." In C. Johnson, B. Jussen, D. Sabean, and S. Teuscher, eds., *Blood and kinship: Matter for metaphor from ancient Rome to the present*, 83–104. Oxford: Berghahn.

Toren, Christina. 1990. *Making sense of hierarchy: Cognition as social process in Fiji.* London: Athlone.

Toren, Christina. 2009. "Intersubjectivity as epistemology." *Social Analysis* 53 (2): 130–146.

Toren, Christina. 2011. "Imagining the world that warrants our imagination: The revelation of ontogeny." *Cambridge Anthropology* 30 (1): 64–79.

Torresan, Angela. 2011. "Strange bedfellows: Brazilian immigrants negotiating friendship in Lisbon." *Ethnos: Journal of Anthropology* 76: 233–253.

Tsing, Anna. N.d. "Unruly edges: Mushrooms as companion species." Unpublished ms, Department of Anthropology, University of California, Santa Cruz.

Tsing, Anna. 2010. "Worlding the Matsutake diaspora: Or, can actor-network theory experiment with holism?" In T. Otto and N. Bubandt, eds., *Experiments in holism: Theory and practice in anthropology*, 47–66. Oxford: Wiley-Blackwell.

Tsing, Anna. 2012. "On nonscalability: The living world is not amenable to precision-nested scales." *Common Knowledge* 18 (3): 505–524.

Tsing, Anna. 2015. *The mushroom at the end of the world: On the possibility of life in capitalist ruins.* Princeton, NJ: Princeton University Press.

Tsing, Anna, Heather Swanson, Elaine Gan, and Nils Bubandt, eds. 2017. *Arts of living on a damaged planet: Monsters of the Anthropocene.* Minneapolis: University of Minnesota Press.

Vaisman, Noa. 2013. "Shedding ourselves: Perspectivism, the bounded subject and the nature-culture divide." In T. Ingold and G. Pálsson, eds., *Biosocial becomings: Integrating social and biological anthropology*, 106–122. Cambridge: Cambridge University Press.

Verran, Helen. 1998. "Re-imagining land ownership in Australia." *Postcolonial Studies* 1: 237–254.

Vilaça, Aparecida. 2013. "Reconfiguring humanity in Amazonia: Christianity and change." In J. Boddy and M. Lambek, eds., *A companion to the anthropology of religion*, 363–386. Malden, MA: Wiley-Blackwell.

Vilaça, Aparecida. 2016. *Praying and preying: Christianity in indigenous Amazonia.* Berkeley: University of California Press.

Viveiros de Castro, Eduardo. 2001. "GUT feelings about Amazonia: Potential affinity." In L. Rival and N. Whitehead, eds., *Beyond the visible and the material: The Amerindianization of society in the work of Peter Rivière*, 19–43. Oxford: Oxford University Press.

Viveiros de Castro, Eduardo. 2003. *And.* Manchester Papers in Social Anthropology 7. Manchester: Department of Social Anthropology.

Viveiros de Castro, Eduardo. 2004a. "Exchanging perspectives: The transformation of objects into subjects in Amerindian ontologies." *Common Knowledge* 10 (3): 463–484.

Viveiros de Castro, Eduardo. 2004b. "Perspectival anthropology and the method of controlled equivocation." *Tipití* 2 (1): 3–22.

Viveiros de Castro, Eduardo. 2009. "The gift and the given: Three nano-essays on kinship and magic." In S. Bamford and J. Leach, eds., *Kinship and beyond: The genealogical model reconsidered*, 237–268. New York: Berghahn.

Viveiros de Castro, Eduardo. 2010. "Intensive filiation and demonic alliance." In C. Bruun Jensen and K. Rödje, eds., *Deleuzian intersections: Science, technology, anthropology*, 219–253. Oxford: Berghahn.

Viveiros de Castro, Eduardo. [2009] 2014. *Cannibal metaphysics for a post-structural anthropology.* Trans. and ed. P. Skafish. Minneapolis, MN: Univocal Publishing.

Viveiros de Castro, Eduardo. 2015. *The relative native: Essays on indigenous conceptual worlds.* Chicago: HAU Books.

Wagner, Roy. 1975. *The invention of culture.* Englewood Cliffs, NJ: Prentice-Hall.

Wagner, Roy. 1977. "Analogic kinship: A Daribi example." *American Ethnologist* 4 (4): 623–642.

Wagner, Roy. 1978. *Lethal speech: Daribi myth as symbolic obviation.* Ithaca, NY: Cornell University Press.

Wagner, Roy. 1986. *Symbols that stand for themselves.* Chicago: University of Chicago Press.

Wagner, Roy. 2001. *An anthropology of the subject: Holographic worldview in New Guinea and its meaning and significance for the world of anthropology.* Berkeley: University of California Press.

Wagner, Roy. 2011. "Vújà de and the quintessentialists' guild." *Common Knowledge* 17 (1): 155–162.

Wagner, Roy. 2012. "'Luck in the double focus': Ritualized hospitality in Melanesia." In M. Candea and G. da Col, eds., "The return to hospitality: Strangers, guests and ambiguous encounters," special issue, *Journal of the Royal Anthropological Institute*: S161–S174.

Waldby, Catherine, and Robert Mitchell. 2006. *Tissue economies: Blood, organs, and cell lines in late capitalism*. Durham, NC: Duke University Press.

Walford, Antonia. 2017. "Raw data: Making relations matter." *Social Analysis* 61 (2): 65–80.

Wallman, Sandra. 1974. "Kinship, a-kinship, anti-kinship: Variations in the logic of kinship situations." In E. Leyton, ed., *The compact: Selected dimensions of friendship*, 105–116. Institute of Social and Economic Research, Memorial University of Newfoundland, Canada.

Warms, Richard. 2014. "Friendship and kinship among merchants and veterans in Mali." In M. Guichard, T. Grätz, and Y. Diallo, eds., *Friendship, descent and alliance in Africa: Anthropological perspectives*, 119–132. Oxford: Berghahn.

Weiner, James. 2006. "Eliciting customary law." *Asia Pacific Journal of Anthropology* 7 (1): 15–25.

Werbner, Richard. 2014. "'Down to earth': Friendship and a national elite circle." In M. Guichard, T. Grätz, and Y. Diallo, eds., *Friendship, descent and alliance in Africa: Anthropological perspectives*, 133–144. Oxford: Berghahn.

Weston, Kath. 1991. *Families we choose: Lesbians, gays, kinship*. New York: Columbia University Press.

Weston, Kath. 2018. "The ethnographer's magic as sympathetic magic." *Social Anthropology / Anthropologie Sociale* 26 (1): 15–29.

Whitfield, Nicholas. 2013. "Who is my stranger? Origins of the gift in wartime London, 1939–45." In J. Carsten, ed., "Blood will out: Essays on liquid transfer and flows," special issue, *Journal of the Royal Anthropological Institute*: S95–S117.

Wilson, Robert. 2016. "Thinking about relations: Strathern, Sahlins, and Locke on anthropological knowledge." *Anthropological Theory* 16 (4): 327–349.

Winkler-Reid, Sarah. 2016. "Friendship, bitching, and the making of ethical selves: What it means to be a good friend among girls in a London school." *Journal of the Royal Anthropological Institute* (n.s.) 22 (1): 166–182.

Withington, Phil. 2010. *Society in early modern England: The vernacular origins of some powerful ideas*. Cambridge: Polity.

Yanagisako, Sylvia. 2013. "Transnational family capitalism: Producing 'made in Italy' in China." In S. McKinnon and F. Cannell, eds., *Vital relations: Modernity and the persistent life of kinship*, 63–84. Santa Fe, NM: School for Advanced Research Press.

Yonemoto, Shōhei. 1985. *Baioesshikusu* [Bioethics]. Tokyo: Kodansha, Gendai Shinsho.

Zengotita, Thomas de. 1984. "The functional reduction of kinship in the social thought of John Locke." In G. W. Stocking, ed., *Functionalism historicized: Essays on British social anthropology*, 10–30. Madison: University of Wisconsin Press.

Zorn, Jean, and Jennifer Corrin Care. 2002. "Everything old is new again: The Underlying Law Act of Papua New Guinea." *Lawasia Journal*: 61–97.

Index of Names and Places

Abbott, Andrew, 90, 161
Abrahams, Ray, 59, 203n22
Africa and Africans, 58, 123, 140, 193n18. *See also* Botswana; Cameroon; Ghana; Lesotho; Mali; West Africa
Albion (Britain), 214n10
Alcayna-Stevens, Lys, 180
Allan, Graham, 154, 202n17, 219n19, 225n29
Allen, Nicholas, 194n1
Alltown, England, 158, 201n4
Alpers, Svetlana, 73, 205n12
Amazonia, 43–44, 79, 88, 108–109, 204n30. *See also* Runa people; Yanomami people
Ambrym Island, Vanuatu, 191n2
America. *See* North America and Americans; South America
Amin, Ash, 52, 177
Amsterdam, 122–123, 141
Andes, 79. *See also* Ecuador, Andean
Angkaiyakmin people, Papua New Guinea, 69, 210n12
Anglo-Saxon, 36, 131, 196n13
Aquinas, Thomas, 61, 152, 204n2, 212n37, 219n18, 227n45
Arawak people, Suriname, 123
Argentina, 202n19
Argyrou, Vassos, 208n3
Aristotle, 4, 61–62, 152, 194n1. *See also* Aristotelian thought [Index of Subjects]
Astell, Mary, 150
Aughnaboy, Ireland, 203n22

Aureoli, Peter, 190
Australia, 99–101, 143–144; health management in, 77–78; Indigenous activists from, 98–101, 179, 209n8; Northern Territory of, 77–78; settlers of, 143–44; Tasmanian Aboriginal Centre and, 210n11
Azande, central Africa, 6

Bacon, Francis, 122, 206n18
Badiou, Alain, 209n5
Balibar, Étienne, 35, 198nn28–29, 215n14
Bamford, Sandra, 104, 199n33
Bangwa people, Cameroon, 61
Barad, Karen, 17–18, 223n7
Bateson, Gregory, 9, 13
Battaglia, Debbora, 8, 144
Beer, Bettina, 51, 58, 62, 68, 152, 161, 203n20
Bell, Sandra, 57, 154
Bennett, Gaymon, 194n25
Bessire, Lucas, 13
Bestard, Joan, 227n43
Biagioli, Mario, 34, 48–50
Bildhauer, Bettina, 212n36
Blaser, Mario, 211n20
Bodenhorn, Barbara, 160
Boellstorff, Tom, 208n3
Bohr, Niels, 17
Boissevain, Jeremy, 56, 147
Bolter, Jay, 15
Bond, David, 13

Bonifacio, Valentina, 211n20
Borneman, John, 156, 181
Botswana, 59
Bowker, Geoffrey, 173, 223n7
Boyle, Robert, 165–166, 200n36, 201n9
Brain, Robert, 61–62, 114
Bray, Alan, 36–37, 53, 159, 204n31, 212n34, 219n17
Brazil, 58, 108, 204n2
Brightman, Marc, 87
Britain, 201n5
Brower, Jeffrey, 4–5, 227n46
Buci-Glucksmann, Christine, 73

Cameroon, Bangwa, 61
Camic, Charles, 88–89
Campbell, Ben, 186
Canada, 137
Candea, Matei, xiii, 13, 50, 86, 118, 180
Cannell, Fenella, 147, 158–160, 186, 220n23
Care, Jennifer Corrin, 212n29
Carey, Matthew, 201n5, 208n1, 227n40
Caribbean, 139. See also Arawak people; Cuba
Carneiro da Cunha, Manuela, 105–106, 109, 225n29
Carrier, James, 58, 154
Carsten, Janet, 27, 121, 128, 144, 160, 203n21
China, 58
Christ, 114, 149
Cohen, Thomas, 75
Coleman, Simon, 57, 154
Collier, Stephen J., 15
Cook, Joanna, 13, 86
Copernicus, Nicolaus, 221n34
Corsín Jiménez, Alberto, 7, 73, 93–95, 111–112, 196n16, 204n31, 205n11
Costa, Luiz, 87
Crook, Tony, 25, 69, 100–101
Cuba, 205n6

Danowski, Déborah, 168
Daribi people, Papua New Guinea, 93
Darwin, Erasmus, x, 222n4
Das, Veena, 218n7
Davidoff, Leonore, 42
Davis, Natalie Zemon, 21, 39, 122–124, 141
Davis, Richard, 210n14

Dawson, Hannah, 149, 197n21, 201n9, 215n16
Dear, Peter, 50, 141, 225n30
Degnen, Cathrine, 226n35
de la Cadena, Marisol, 101
DeLanda, Manuel, 15
Deleuze, Gilles, and Deleuzian thought, 7, 178, 193n13, 207n22, 208n3, 209n5, 223n7
Delille, Gérard, 39–40, 212n36
Demian, Melissa, 110, 211n27
Derrida, Jacques, 85, 209n4
Desai, Amit, 203n21
Descartes, René, 75, 215n14, 221n34
Descola, Philippe, 7, 20, 40–41, 50, 92, 192n7, 200n39, 212n38, 219n14
Descombes, Vincent, 5–7, 133, 173, 193n19, 215n17
Donne, John, 196n18
Douglas, Mary, 9
Dryden, John, 196n11
Du Gay, Paul, 216n26
Duhamelle, Christophe, 39
Dumont, Louis, 227n39
Dunn, John, 35
Durkheim, Émile, 194n1, 220n24

Ecuador, Amazonian. See Runa people
Ecuador, Andean, 79, 81–83, 206n17
Edgeworth, Richard, 222nn4–5
Edwards, Jeanette, 158–159, 199n33, 201n2, 201n4, 221n33
Elias, Norbert, 224n12
England, 30, 38–39, 58, 226n35. See also Britain; United Kingdom
English: Middle, 113; Old, 53
English language. See Anglophone usage [Index of Subjects]; English language usage [Index of Subjects]
Erickson, Amy, 30, 39
Euro-Americans. See Euro-American thought/practices [Index of Subjects]
Europe and Europeans, 38–41, 53, 59, 122–123, 127, 137, 147, 153, 201n2, 207n29; languages, 226n36; scholars, 102–103; settlers, 139–140, 143, 179
European Mediterranean, 152
Evans, Eric, x, 222n4
Evans-Pritchard, E. E., 6–7, 183–184

Faubion, James, 192n10, 193n16
Fausto, Carlos, 87
Feeley-Harnik, Gillian, 158, 219n16
Feldman, Gregory, 8, 14
Fester, René, 223n6
Fiji, 210n13
Finch, Janet, 220n22
Finland, 59, 203n22
Firth, Raymond, 55–57, 60, 68, 122, 125–126, 135, 187
Forge, Anthony, 55–57
Forman-Barzilai, Fonna, 175, 224n20
Fortes, Meyer, 27, 61, 126–127, 129, 135, 152–155, 157, 183–184, 213n4
Foucault, Michel, 117
Fox, Richard, 10
France and French, 152, 169, 179, 210n13, 217n32; New, 75. *See also* French language usage [Index of Subjects]
Frankenberg, Ronald, 193n18
Franklin, Sarah, 171, 186, 221n33, 223n7

Gaborone city, Botswana, 59
Gagné, Renaud, 212n38
Galilei, Galileo, 34, 36, 48–50, 54
Gammage, Bill, 143–144
Gardner, Don, 51, 58, 62, 68, 152, 161, 203n20
Gasché, Rodolphe, 84–87, 186, 188, 192nn6-7
Gawthern, Abigail, 32
Gell, Alfred, 1, 191n4
Germany and Germans, 39, 121, 179
Gershon, Ilana, 15
Ghana, 153. *See also* Tallensi people
Giddens, Anthony, 208n33, 223n1
Gilbert, Scott, 169–170, 223n6
Gingrich, André, 10
Gobetti, Daniela, 196n14, 201n8
Goody, Jack, 9, 128
Goroka town, Papua New Guinea, 66
Gouge, William, 149
Greek language, 61–62, 152
Green, Sarah, 77, 86, 143
Gross, Neil, 88–89
Grotti, Vanessa, 87
Grusin, Richard, 15
Guichard, Martine, 57–58

Hage, Ghassan, 13, 174–175, 225n24, 225n27
Haraway, Donna, 12–13, 34, 112–113, 180–182, 191n4, 223n7
Harrison, Peter, 226n36
Harvey, Penny, 140
Hastrup, Kirsten, 194n23
Hawthorn, Geoffrey, 129
Heidegger, Martin, 85, 192n6, 209n5
Heil, John, 227n46
Heinich, Nathalie, 224n12
Helmreich, Stefan, 182, 223n7
Hendry, John, 205n12, 226n36
Henninger, Mark G., 190, 192n6, 220n24, 227n46
Herman, Arthur, 124
Herzfeld, Michael, 216n26
Hirschman, Albert, 204n31
Hirschmann, Nancy, 216n25
Hobbes, Thomas, 76, 82
Holbraad, Martin, 13–14, 88, 106, 162–163, 205n6, 210n16, 222n36
Hoskin, Keith, 76, 136, 205n4, 205n12
Hoskyns, John, 217n34
Hubert, Jane, 55–57
Hume, David, 20, 76, 82, 122, 124–132, 134, 136, 141–142, 143, 145, 157, 172, 185, 205n12, 206n18, 219n12, 226n20, 227n40. *See also* Hume, David [Index of Subjects]
Hunter, Michael, 201n7, 201n9, 217n34
Hutcheson, Francis, 224n17
Huxley, Robert, 217nn33–34

Iatmul people, Sepik River, Papua New Guinea, 8, 108–110, 146, 211n26, 212n28
Ingold, Tim, 125, 200n39
Ireland, 203n22
Israel, 138–139, 217n29
Israel, Jonathan, 173
Italy, 39; Florence and Padua, 48

Jacob, Marie-Andrée, 136–139
James, Wendy, 194n1
Japan and Japanese, 205n10, 216n28
Jay, Martin, 73
Jensen, Casper Bruun, 42, 195n2, 223n7
Johansson, Ingvar, 170
Johnson, Christopher, 39

Johnson, Samuel, 196n11
Josephides, Lisette, 209n5, 220n27, 222n37, 224n18, 225n22

Kalinoe, Lawrence, 1
Kant, Immanuel, 159
Kapferer, Bruce, 88, 218n7
Kaufman, Sharon, 137, 202n12
Kelly, José, 79–81, 88, 207n31
Kepler, Johannes, 48, 50
Killick, Evan, 203n20
Kirksey, Eben, 182, 223n8
Knox, Hannah, 140
Kohn, Eduardo, 180–181, 186, 194n27
Korowai people, West Papua, 67, 225n23
Kristeva, Julia, 225n22
Kuma people, Wahgi Valley, Papua New Guinea, 61–63, 106–107, 109, 113, 115, 204n1, 226n37
Kuper, Adam, 41–42, 227n41
Ku Waru people, Papua New Guinea, 204n1

Laidlaw, James, 15, 216n25, 224n16
Lambek, Michael, 143, 218nn7–8
Lamont, Michèle, 88–89
Lancy, David, 204n1
Latimer, Joanna, 182
Latin, 4, 152, 190
Latour, Bruno, 10, 162, 165, 173, 195n2, 200n39
Law, John, 41, 78, 101
Lazar, Sian, 10, 202n19
Lea, Tess, 77–78
Leach, James, 103–105, 210n14
Lebner, Ashley, 204n2
Lederman, Rena, 89–90
Leenhardt, Maurice, 17, 192n10
Leibniz, Gottfried, 5–6, 172–173, 192nn7–8, 193n13
Lesotho, 59
Levinas, Emmanuel, 209n3
Lévi-Strauss, Claude, 10, 195n2
Lévy-Bruhl, Lucien, 6
Leyton, Elliott, 57, 203n22
Lichfield, England, 222n4
Lloyd, G. E. R., 50, 115, 226n34
Lock, Margaret, 216nn27–28
Locke, John, 5, 10, 20, 28–30, 37–38, 84, 118, 122, 132–135, 141–142, 148, 150, 157, 159, 166,

171–172, 180–181, 185, 187, 205n12, 219n12, 219n14. *See also* Locke, John [Index of Subjects]
London, 100; North, 55–56, 60, 68, 181, 226n35
Luhmann, Niklas, 112, 183, 207n28, 212n31

Mack, Phyllis, 150, 195n8, 198n31, 219n17, 226n30
Madang Province, Papua New Guinea. *See* Reite people; Tangu people
Mali, 59
Mann, Jill, 113–115
Marabá city, Brazil, 204n2
Marett, R. R., 26, 169
Margulis, Lynn, 223n6
Marshall, Duncan, 54
Marx, Karl, 6, 173
Mason, Jennifer, 220n20
Mauss, Marcel, 220n24
McKinnon, Susan, 42, 144, 147, 159–160, 183–184, 200n37, 223n1
McLeish, Tom, 165, 195n9, 222n38
Medici family, 34, 48–49
Melanesia, 8, 63, 66–67, 69, 88, 108, 163, 165, 203n27, 204n30, 225n23. *See also* Ambrym Island; New Caledonia; Papua New Guinea
Melpa speakers, Mt. Hagen, Papua New Guinea, 204n1
Merian, Maria Sibylla, 21, 121–124, 140–142, 187
Merlan, Francesca, 204n1
Mexico, 160
Michelet, Jules, 217n32
Middle English language, 113
Miller, Daniel, 145–146, 154, 161, 226n35
Milton, John, 149, 196n11
Mitchell, J. Clyde, 56
Mitchell, Robert, 137
Mohácsi, Gergely, 187–188
Mol, Annemarie, 140
Mongolia, 163, 165
Montesquieu, Charles-Louis, 224n18
Morgan, David, 52, 201n5, 218n6
Morgan, Lewis Henry, 154
Morita, Atsuro, 42, 187–188
Moutu, Andrew, 8, 108–110
Mumford, Lewis, 22n40
Munn, Nancy, 122

Navaro-Yashin, Yael, ix, 187
Neo-Melanesian (Pidgin), 104
Netherlands, 210n13. *See also* Amsterdam;
   Dutch colony [Index of Subjects]; Dutch
   speakers [Index of Subjects]
New Caledonia, 17
New France, 75
Newton, Isaac, 26–28, 34, 36, 122, 192n8
New Zealand, 99
Ng, Su Fang, 148–151, 156, 158, 197n25
Nicolson, Benedict, 222n3
Nidditch, Peter, 215n13
Nietzsche, Friedrich, 85, 188
Noble, Brian, 223n7
Nombo, Porer, 104–105, 205n12
North America and Americans, 42, 88, 99, 144,
   147, 158, 179, 200n2, 202n12, 216n28, 217n29
Norton, David, and Mary Norton, 125, 214n5,
   214n8
Norway, 210n13

Oceania, 59–60, 101. *See also* Pacific Islands and
   Islanders
Ollman, Bertell, 6, 173
Ong, Aihwa, 15
Orokaiva people, Papua New Guinea, 62, 65, 67
Outram, Dorinda , 222n1

Pacific Islands and Islanders, 101–104, 107,
   202n16, 210nn13–14
Pahl, Ray, 56, 201n5
Paine, Robert, 58–61, 68, 157, 160, 204n32
Pálsson, Gísli, 200n39
Papua New Guinea (PNG), 1–2, 61–63, 106,
   210n13; constitution, 109; independence,
   109–110; lawyers, 212n29. *See also* Angkaiyak-
   min people; Iatmul people; Kuma people;
   Orokaiva people; Reite people; Tangu people
Paraguay, 211n20
Patterson, Nerys Thomas, 220n22
Pedersen, Morten Axel, 13–14, 162–163, 210n16
Perry, Ruth, 30, 41, 150
Peters, John, 176, 224n19
Phillips, Edward, 34
Pickles, Anthony, 66
Pickstone, John, 156
Pina-Cabral, João de, 8, 11, 28–30, 216n25

Pitt-Rivers, Julian, 60, 152–155, 157, 161, 184,
   227n40
Porter, Roy, 37, 124, 166, 206n18, 214n10
Povinelli, Elizabeth, 100, 209n8
Prague, 48
Pratt, Mary Louise, 123
Puttenham, George, 150

Rabinow, Paul, 15, 27, 139, 169, 188, 194n25,
   206n22, 224n9
Radcliffe-Brown, A. R., 9–10
Raffles, Hugh, 217n32
Rapport, Nigel, 223n5
Ray, John, 199n33
Ray, Sid, 149–150
Reay, Marie, 61, 106–107
Reed, Adam, 46–47
Reite people, Papua New Guinea, 103–105, 111
Renouvier, Charles, 194n1
Reyna, Stephen, 227n42
Rezende, Claudia Barcellos, 58
Ricoeur, Paul, 209n5
Riles, Annelise, 16, 148, 205n10
Rio, Knut, 176, 191n2
Rio de Janeiro, 203n22
Rivers, W. H. R., 26
Robbins, Joel, 88, 146, 177, 203n22, 204n30
Roberts, Elizabeth, 79, 81–82
Rollason, Will, 66, 210n17
Rudiak-Gould, Peter, 101
Rumsey, Alan, 203n22, 204n1
Runa people, Amazonian Ecuador, 180
Russ, Ann J., 137, 202n12
Russia and Russians, 111

Sabean, David, 38–41, 134
Sahlins, Marshall, 6, 27–28, 61, 173, 222n1,
   224n10
Salmon, Gildas, 16, 88, 226n32
Sanders, Valerie, 41
Sandford, Stella, 198n30, 215n14
Sapp, Jan, 169–170
Schaffer, Simon, 50, 165, 22n36
Schneider, Almut, 204n30
Schneider, David, 27, 44, 160, 187, 221n29
Schochet, Gordon, 196n14, 214n13
Schram, Ryan, 88

Schrempp, Gregory, 220n24, 221n34
Schütz, Alfred, 176
Schwartz, Daniel, 204nn31–32, 212n37, 219n18, 227n45
Schwimmer, Eric, 59–62, 65, 68, 74, 146, 152
Scotland and Scots, 67. *See also* Scottish Enlightenment [Index of Subjects]
Scott, Michael, 87, 161, 163, 221n34
Seward, Anna, 222n4
Seward, Canon, 222nn4–5
Shaftesbury, Earl of, 28, 198
Shapin, Steven, 34, 50, 141, 165–166, 196n18, 200n36
Sharp, Lesley, 137, 202n11
Shim, Janet, 137, 202n12
Shryock, Andrew, 218n4
Siberia. *See* Yukaghir
Sicily, 147
Silver, Allan, 52–53, 67–68, 146, 184, 212n35, 216n25, 224n17, 227n42
Simmel, Georg, 52
Skafish, Peter, 2, 168, 188, 207n29, 224n9
Sloan, Kim, 141
Smart, Alan, 58
Smith, Adam, 76, 124, 175–176, 205n12, 216n25, 227n40
Smith, Julia, 53
South America, 79, 123. *See also* Amazonia; Andes; Argentina; Caribbean; Paraguay
South Pacific, 101, 210n13
Spain and Spanish, 111
Spencer, Liz, 56, 201n5
Stasch, Rupert, 65, 67, 88, 225n23
Stavrianakis, Anthony, 207n23, 224n9
Steedman, Carolyn, 31, 123
Stengers, Isabelle, 26–28, 34, 102–103, 110, 113, 173, 206n22, 217n2, 223n7
Stocking, George, 169
Stout, William, 54, 150
Strathern, Alan, 215n15, 220n25, 222n36
Strathern, Andrew, 204n1
Strawson, Galen, 214n12
Stuart, Matthew, 172, 198n27, 215n17
Suriname, 122–123, 141, 217n33

Tadmor, Naomi, 30–33, 36, 53–54, 150–151, 157, 201n5, 202n15
Tallensi people, Ghana, 153–154

Tangu people, Papua New Guinea, 203n27
Tasmania, 210n11
Tauber, Alfred, 169–170
Taylor, Charles, 37–38, 169
Teuscher, Simon, 38–41, 134, 153
Tikopia Island, 122, 202n16
Tok Pisin (Neo-Melanesian) language, 104
Toren, Christina, 136, 216n25
Torresan, Angela, 218n8
Trías, Eugenio, 111–112
Trumbauch, Randolph, 200n37
Trundle, Catherine, 13, 86
Tsing, Anna, 139–140, 142, 200n1, 223n7
Turner, Thomas, 219n16

United Kingdom, 98–99, 101, 210n11, 210n15, 226n30
United States, 58, 89, 137, 217n30, 226n30

Vaisman, Noa, 200n38
Venetian, 75
Venezuelan Amazon. *See* Yanomami people
Verran, Helen, 101
Vilaça, Aparecida, 42, 88, 101
Viveiros de Castro, Eduardo, x, 3, 7, 43–44, 84, 88, 108, 168, 178, 185, 191n2, 206n19, 208n3, 211n17, 220n23

Wagner, Roy, 9, 66–67, 74, 91–95, 117, 183, 194n27, 207n29, 222n1
Wahgi Valley, Papua New Guinea highlands, 61, 187. *See also* Kuma people
Waldby, Catherine, 137
Wallace, Mr., 32
Wallman, Sandra, 59
Warkentin, Germaine, 75
Warms, Richard, 59
Weber, Max, 159, 221n28
Weiner, James, 100
Werbner, Richard, 59
West Africa, 9–10, 152–153
Weston, Kath, 46, 100, 202n18, 208n2, 216n25, 218n9, 221n32
West Papua, 67
Whitfield, Nicholas, 50
Willerslev, Rane, 7, 111–112
Williamson, Henry, 46–47, 151

Wilson, Robert, 35, 198n27, 210n16
Winkler-Reid, Sarah, 218n8
Winthereik, Brit, 195n2, 223n7
Withington, Phil, 31–33, 36, 50, 201n8
Wright, Joseph, x, 166

Yanagisako, Sylvia, 227n41
Yanomami people, Venezuela, 79–83, 207n31

Yarrow, Thomas, 13, 86
Yonemoto, Shōhei, 216n28
Yukaghir, Siberia, 111–113, 178

Zande. *See* Azande
Zengotita, Thomas de, 196n14, 214n13, 219n14
Zorn, Jean, 212n29

Index of Subjects

absence, of relation, 84, 110, 132–135, 143

absolute and relative terms, 4; concealment in, 5, 171–172. *See also* relative

abstract: persons, 121, 176; principle, 124; relation/relationality, 1, 25, 121, 132, 161; terms, and positive tenor of, 25, 27, 202n20

abstraction, 33, 66, 122–125; concreteness and, 113, 125–129, 132

abundance (proliferation): of relations, 1, 42, 84, 91, 135, 145, 185–186; of similarity, 110

acknowledgment. *See* recognition

acquaintance, 47, 52, 54, 127–128; modernization myth of, 218n6; relation (kin) and, 128, 130, 214n8, 216n24

actor network theory, 194n20, 223n7

affect, 127–128, 153–154; centered, 177; in friendship, 36, 58; graded, 128, 175–176; intensity of, 131; in kinship, 56, 127–128, 196n17; terms laden by, 129, 224n20

affinity, as resemblance or agreement, 26–27, 34, 83, 155; change in meaning of, 34–35, 83, 131; English derivation of, 83

affinity, in kin relations, 10, 40–41, 128; Amazonian, 43–44, 80, 83, 108–109; English-speaking, 55, 83; friendship and, 62–63; Papua New Guinean, 63, 104. *See also* brother and brother-in-law

aftereffect, 20, 129, 132–135

agential realism, 17

agreement. *See* correspondence; *rapport*

air pump, 69–70. See also *Experiment on a bird in the air pump* (Wright)

allegory, 149, 156, 213n1

alliance, 10; cooperative (Orokaiva), 64–65; family, 38–41, 83, 134, 196n11; military (Kuma), 61–62; personal, 147

alterity, 118, 142, 162; alter-ship and, 87; of anthropological language, 76, 87; between brothers (Iatmul), 109; Yanomami, 80–81, 83

"alter lineage," in European thought, 5–6, 140, 172–173

alternative actualized. *See* "alter lineage"

altruism, 138, 184; in interpersonal relations, 153, 159; mystery of, 157; in organ donation, 51; prescriptive (*see* amity)

amiability, in interpersonal relations, 154–155, 161, 183–184

"amiable relations," 153–154

amicitia (Latin, "friendship"), 152, 219n18

amis (French, "friends"), in medieval usage, 153

"Amis and Amiloun," 114–116

amity, axiom of, 153–155, 183–184, 195n3

anachronism, 123, 141

analogic cosmology (analogism), 92, 200n41, 212n38

analogic flow, 92–93, 175

analogic kinship, 91–92, 146

analogy: analytical, 69, 91–95, 111–112, 118, 177; Aristotelean, 192n5; comparison and, 69, 92,

analogy (*continued*)
113–118, 212n38; defined in English, 115–116;
based on dissimilarity, 194n29, 219n14; negative, 115, 118; in political debate, 148–150,
156; in science, 165; unrestricted, 92–93
"analytical context," 18–19, 168, 187
ancestors: Australian, 98–101, 179; Kuma, 107;
(English) measuring degree, 30, 127
Anglomania, eighteenth-century, 122
Anglophone anthropology, 16, 39, 55, 135
Anglophone thought, 11, 16, 108, 128, 143, 173,
177, 181
Anglophone usage, 3, 11, 25, 27, 43, 55, 60, 87,
128, 135, 173, 177, 186, 194n20, 209n4
Anthropocene, 168
anthropology, 3, 9, 11, 58–59, 77, 136, 147, 161,
163; Anglophone, 16, 39, 55, 135; "anthropology's relation" and, 19, 191n3; dialogi-
cal/symmetrical, 205n5; divisions within,
60, 88–90; of kinship, 181; social, 146,
187; sociocultural, 3; symbolic, 208n3; as
theory of relations, 1, 195n2. *See also* British
School of Social Anthropology; "Carsten's
question"
anti-criticism, and alter-criticism, 174–178,
182–185
anti-politics, and alter-politics, 13–14, 174
apparatus, concept of, 16–18, 168
appearance: of civil society, 196n16; elicited,
107. *See also* visibility
"appearance appearing," 73, 78, 124
Aristotelian thought, 192n5, 219n18; on categories, 220n24. See also *Nicomachean ethics*
Art of describing (Alpers), 73
assemblage, 15, 176
assisted conception, 81–83
association, 8, 49, 108, 128, 184, 214n7; benign
qualities of, 154; between chemical elements,
27; ethos of, 46–49, 53, 128, 178; of Friends
(Quaker), 151; of ideas, 124, 135, 157, 185,
215n21; literary, 46–48; purposeful, 33–34,
49–50, 156, 201n2; voluntary, 59
attachment: and detachment, 13, 49, 54–56,
104, 128; reattachment and, 104–105; of relations, 86–87
attraction, 27, 117, 127, 129, 197n22
attributes: distributed, 57–58, 64, 152–153; as
properties of things, 43, 93, 180

audit, self-scrutiny and, 76–78, 205n4
authenticity, 146, 176, 209n8
authority: authorial, 75; paternalistic, 149–151.
See also trust: in science
auto-occluding. *See* occlusion
autopoietic system, 112, 183, 212n31

Baroque sensibility, 73, 124, 157
becoming, 7, 79, 193n13; Iatmul, 108–109, 146;
Yukaghir, 111
benevolence: gradated, 224n17; undifferentiated, 37, 159
betrothal, 36
"between," 4–5, 7, 9–10, 70, 103, 173, 189–190,
193n12, 194n26, 227n47; in English vernacular, 192n6, 213n3. *See also* "*inter-*" *terms* (e.g.,
interaction; interchangeability)
Beyond nature and culture (Descola), 40
bilateral kin reckoning, 30, 127, 153, 184, 186
bioethics, 136–139
biology, 139, 169, 171–174; compatibility
through, 136–137; substance of, 9, 137; synthetic, 15, 194n25; ties of, 42, 52, 94, 206n15,
217n30
blood, sacrificial, 114, 199n35
blood brotherhood, 114
blood money, 152
blood relations (in European kinship), 55, 30,
39–40, 114, 127–129, 131, 160, 218n9, 221n33
body, 171–172, 216n28; changing/making of,
79–84; etiquette, 49; intimacy, 36; substitutability, 135–140. *See also* holobiont
boundaries: crossing of, 89–90, 159–160; drawing of, 103, 154, 176–177, 186, 225n22. *See
also* inclusion and exclusion
breeding, deliberate, 42
British Museum, 141
British School of Social Anthropology, 8, 146,
227n39
brother(hood), 30, 127, 159; sister and, 30, 42,
44, 151; sworn, 36, 114–116, 197n25, 212n34
brother and brother-in-law, 61–62, 64–65,
203n27; Amazonian, 43–44, 108–109;
Bangwa, 61; Iatmul, 108–109, 146; Kuma,
61–63, 115; Orokaiva, 62, 65, 67
bureaucratic ethos, 68
bureaucratic projects, 58, 77–78, 136, 227n41

burial: of friends, 36, 114; other mortuary practices and, 9–10, 64

card playing, 66
"carrying" ideas, 149–150, 173, 219nn11–12. *See also* association
"Carsten's question," 121, 128, 144
category, 6, 54–56, 161; Aristotelian, 4, 220n24; categorization and, 60, 84–85, 161, 221n35; delineation of, 93; of knowledge, 117; of thought, 25, 212n38
causality, 6, 32, 35, 127, 141. *See also* third term
ceremonial exchange, 66, 104
ceremonial performance, 106–108
chain of being, 213n38
chimpanzee sanctuary, 180
choice: of family, 202n18, 223n30; versus given attributes, 56, 58, 68, 145, 206n20; liberal, 145–146, 182
Christianity, 13, 17, 108–109, 112, 162–163, 204n30, 204n2, 215n15, 222n36; Calvinist, 214n10; ethics in, 175–176; Eucharist in, 114; tract writers of, 149–150. *See also* Mormon (Latter-day Saints) church; Puritan thought; Quaker society
church (Christian), 57; and state, 149, 151
circles: of acquaintances, 154, 201n5; of family and friends, 67, 127, 166; of sympathy, 176. *See also* concentric rings
civilizing mission, 79–80
civil society, 33, 52, 101, 154, 159, 177–178, 185, 218n4; appearance of, 196n16
clanship: Papua New Guinea Highlands, 105–108, 116, 211n24; Tallensi, 153
class, social, 41, 54–55, 59, 82–83, 134, 150, 157, 176, 200n37, 225n29
classification, based on attributes, 40, 64; by pairing, 113–116; of persons, 131; schemas of, 41, 123–124, 141–142, 161
climate change, 101
closeness and distance, 13, 47–50, 127–128, 176, 201n5, 202n19; in kin relations, 56, 128; in marriage, 41–42, 44. *See also* "sliding scale"
colonial plantations, 122–123, 139–140
colonial settlement, 143–44
commercial society, 52, 67–68, 211n21, 214n10
common ground, 116, 161. *See also* third term

commons: digital, 208n34; knowledge, 93–94
communication, 8, 15, 86, 112–113, 180; generic, 49–50. *See also* social media
community: of discourse, 149; ideology of, 176
companion concepts, 139
companion species, 140, 180–182
Companion species manifesto (Haraway), 181
"company," 49, 196n13, 201n8; of others, 86, 129; for own sake, 154
comparatio (Latin, "bringing together, comparison"), 10, 118
comparative method, 3–4, 10, 14, 58–59, 64, 74, 194n28, 212n38; impeded, 86
"comparing comparisons," 47–50, 57–63, 69
comparison, 4–5, 19, 27, 46, 53, 74, 98, 100, 107–108, 114, 199n32; analogy and, 69, 89, 91–93, 113–118; anthropological, 10, 60, 63, 91; classification and, 117, 142; contrast and, 45; disjunctive, 10; in English vernacular, 56–57, 60, 64, 91; of ideas (Hume), 128; of ideas (Locke), 5, 29, 133–134; leaving out third term, 109, 116, 228n47; of legal systems, 109–110; of persons, 53–57, 111–112; of relations, 6–7, 10, 64–68; through relations, 5, 133–134, 189; restricted and unrestricted, 91; based on similarity and dissimilarity, 19, 60, 91, 99, 142, 178, 215n14; of social media, 5, 145. *See also* friendship and kinship
concentric rings, 47, 56, 87, 103, 175–177, 201n5. *See also* circles
concept, x, 2, 17–18, 113, 194n24; activated, 130, 188; of a concept, 191n2; formation of, 34, 85–86, 183; Yukaghir analogy to, 110–111
conception, assisted, 81–82
conceptual and interpersonal relations. *See* "duplex"
concreteness, and abstraction, 113, 125–129, 132
conjugal family, 30, 41–42; and natal kin, 64; as unit plus connections, 134, 170
conjugal relations, 107, 133–134, 201n8, 219n13
connecting: cause, 127; event, 113; principle, 124; transplant organ as, 137
connection, 8, 55, 108, 113, 124, 128; affect and, 127–128; choice and, 206n20; cultivated, 82–83, 134; disconnection and, 13, 97, 194n21; expansion of term, 32, 35, 40–41, 83; generic, 128; between households, 31; of ideas, 124, 126–128, 130, 135; as interdepen-

connection (*continued*)

dence, 32, 124, 224n10; in Merian, 123–125; principle of (Hume), 213n3; "real" (Locke), 172, 215n21, 224n10; reckoning through, 127, 130; similarity and, 83; value of, 53–54, 70, 83, 156–157, 162. *See also* causality

"connection," for intimates including kin, 32, 41, 53, 83

consanguinity, 55, 127–128, 206n14; affinity and, 83, 128, 153, 154; geneticization and, 221n33

consciousness/self-consciousness, 34, 57, 60, 123, 134, 136; analysis/method of, 60, 64–68, 74, 76; class, 41; expersonation and, 66–69, 177, 188; knowing subject and, 18, 86, 110–111, 180–182, 186; Locke's invention of, 37–38, 132–135, 198n28, 198n31, 214n12, 215n14; shared, 46–47

constrained and unconstrained: as analytic, 88–91, 93–95, 161–162; attributes, 58, 146, 155. *See also* restricted/unrestricted relations

contagion, theory of, 216n25

context. *See* "analytical context"

contingency, 8, 138, 186

continuity and discontinuity, 132–133, 135, 141–142, 222n36

contrast, 45, 56, 115; analogy and, 118; of viewpoints, 99

control: analogical, 93, 200n41; analytical, 19; on behavior, 208n31; comparative, 55; of knowledge, 103–105

correlation, 10, 18, 26, 34, 104, 171; correlative and, 134

correspondence, 91, 114, 127, 150

cosmology: analogic (analogism), 92, 200n41, 212n38; identified, 40, 180; import of, in friendship and kinship, 146; naturalism as, 40, 44, 185, 192n7

cosmopolitanism, 175–176, 220n27, 225n22

cosmopolitics, 101

counterfactual, 121–122, 129, 140, 177, 185; in being other to ourselves, 174, 225n24; question, 132

cousin, 54–55, 62, 127, 203n22; marriage to, 41–42

credibility. *See* trust

criollo (Spanish, "nonindigenous people, whites"), 79–82, 206n17

critical approach to relations, 16, 168

critical sociology and anthropology, 174, 225n24, 225n27

critical theory, 52, 85, 177

criticism, 26–29, 148–150; alter-, 175, 177–179, 182–185; anthropological, 3, 6, 11–12, 13–16, 60, 168, 174; anti-, 174–177; by Hume, 135; by Leibniz, 5, 172; by Locke, 171–172; social, 14, 135, 167

culture(s): in comparative analysis, 64; concept of, xiii, 4, 10, 26, 179, 205n9, 225n29; and cosmology, 180; "culture" and, 105–106, 182; equivalence of, 98–99, 105, 109; in neoliberalism, 98. *See also* nature: society/culture and

culture, American, 90

custom, 125–126, 129, 213n4, 214n10, 215n21; Papua New Guinean, 109–110, 211n27

cyborg, myth of, 112

"cyborg manifesto" (Haraway), 112–113

Darwinism, 169

DCMS (Department for Media, Culture and Sport, UK Government), 98–99, 209n7

deficit: of knowledge, 89, 140; relational, 135–136, 139, 143–144, 173, 178

degree, 129–132; of connection/relation, 30, 32, 47, 55–56, 64, 125, 127; of fit, 57, 60, 64, 185, 227n4; of interest and disinterest, 184; of similarity and dissimilarity, 80–81, 91, 130; taxonomic, 117; unspecified, 32, 54–55. *See also* closeness and distance

delegation, from study to subject of study, 16, 88

dependence: devalued, 167–168, 226n33; valued, 81–82, 171. *See also* interdependence

description: as intervention, 77, 80, 207n25; as object of knowledge, 3, 34, 73, 205n11; re-, 28, 79, 111–112, 170, 179. *See also* exposition

detachment, 86–87, 104, 123; achievement of, 211n21; of analogy from comparison, 115; of difference from dissimilarity, 97–98; of information from knowledge, 104; of kinship from friendship, 146; of law from custom, 211n27. *See also* attachment; dissociation

difference, 7, 20, 83, 97–98, 101–103, 111, 113, 208n2, 212n28; concealed, 101–102; as divergence, 103; diversity and, 214n9; strong sense of, 168, 177–178, 210n17, 225n23. *See also* dissimilarity; divergence; division; indifference

difference, "none between": affinity and consanguinity, 83; expansion and contraction, 84; friend and relative, 51; kin and acquaintance, 94, 129–130

"diffuse and enduring solidarity," 27, 160, 187

diffuseness, 1, 3, 19, 25, 28, 50, 95, 160, 167; in amiability, 154; in kinship, 220n22

disciplinarity: claims for, 136; inter-, 87, 89; order of exposition and, ix, 87–91

disease relations, 140

disenchantment, 156, 158

disjunctive: comparison, 10; synthesis, 7, 98, 178, 194n21, 209n5

displacement, 27, 111–113, 115; analogic, 92, 208n32; of perceptual space, 92

dissimilarity: between cultures, 99, 106; and difference, 20, 97–98, 113–116, 121, 177–178; logic of, 109, 168; oppositive, 209n8. *See also* similarity; similarity and dissimilarity

dissociation, 135; of individual persons and relations, 135, 184; of kinship and friendship, 36–37, 114, 146; of land and claims, 140; of organs and social history, 137, 216n27; of persons and bodies, 137; of phenomena and relations, 142. *See also* detachment

distance, as a relation, 127, 201n6. *See also* closeness and distance

divergence, 90, 103–104; non-relational, 102–103, 110; radical, 98, 102, 106; of worlds, 101

division, 87, 168; within culture, 105; multiplicity and, 84, 217n31; of persons, 104, 106, 115, 177; in relations, 88, 104; of whole, 210n10. *See also* fractal distinction

domain: concept of, 42, 52, 103, 112–113, 153, 160, 210n10, 211n23; critique of, 112–113, 183–184; politico-jural, 153–154

donation, 211n19; organ, 50–51, 137–139; ova, 82

donor sibling, 159

doubleness, 76; as figure seen twice, 148; in figures of speech, 150; of ideas and impressions, 125, 129, 214n5, 216n25. *See also* duplication; pairing; shadow (double)

dramatization: for bureaucratic effect, 77, 136–138; of conflict, 106–107; of impersonal relations, 138–139; of scholarly debate, 20–21, 122, 132–135; of social relations, 165

"duplex," of concepts (epistemic, conceptual, logical, associative *alongside* social, personal, interpersonal), 3, 8, 19, 100, 108, 133, 166, 170, 178, 188, 191n3, 197n23

duplication: of consciousness, 46, 84; of terms/concepts, xiii, 73, 78, 182–183

Dutch colony, 122

Dutch speakers, 179

duty: and affect, 145, 219n13; family, 138; in "natural" relations, 30

early modern epoch, 30, 37, 57, 169, 170, 178, 196n12; use of "relation" for kin during, 31–33, 53; science of, 166

East India Company, 50

ecology: crisis of, 12, 167; "of practices," 103; understanding of, 123, 182

ECOPAS (European Consortium for Pacific Studies), 101–102, 105, 210n13

effect: of difference/divergence, 101–102, 110; of God's presence, 82, 204n2; as measure of relations, 64–66, 83–84, 211n24; unknown, 106–107

elder brother/younger brother, Iatmul, 8, 108–110, 146, 211n26

Elements of social organization (Firth), 125

empathy, 100, 226n33. *See also* sympathy

enchantment. *See* disenchantment; re-enchantment

endogamy, familial, 39, 41, 134

English language usage, 2–3, 11, 16, 19, 25, 27, 34, 36, 47, 52, 54, 61, 69, 83, 91, 97, 104, 113, 115–116, 121–122, 128, 136, 149–150, 173–175, 179, 198n26, 206n21, 226n36, 227n44

Enlightenment, European, 29, 75, 81, 122, 124, 131, 192n7, 223n1; Dutch sources of, 141; pre-, 82, 192n9; proto-, 139. *See also* Scottish Enlightenment

entity, "with relations attached," 38–40, 67, 69, 94, 134, 170, 172, 220n21, 224n10

environment, 112, 123, 210n10; conceptual, 113, 172, 183

epistemic relations, 33, 100, 108, 157, 170; interpersonal relations and (*see* "duplex")

epistolary relations, 49–50

Essay concerning human understanding (Locke), 133

estate, 143

ethics, 102, 128, 210n15; Christian, 175–176; rational, 159; self and, 76, 216n25; transplant, 217n29

ethnography, ix, 86, 88, 123, 173–174; anthropological exposition of, 86–87, 173, 175, 180, 188, 224n16; European, 59; in monograph form, 66; object of, 16, 18; of relations, 2, 18–19, 163, 174. *See also* "analytical context"

etiquette/protocol, 49–50, 65, 148

"Euro-American kinship," 21, 144–148, 158, 178–182

Euro-American metaphysics, 86–87, 93, 99, 155, 217n31

Euro-American thought/practices, 44, 45, 74, 79–80, 102, 161, 173–174, 177, 180, 186–187; defined, 200n2

event, 173; non-happening of, 122, 129, 132–135; in science, 141

evolutionary anthropology, 169, 184

evolutionary thought, 109

exchange: of benefits, 60–63, 184; competitive, 62, 66; of information, 99, 104–105; marriage, 61, 64–65, 203n25; partners, 63–64; of perspectives, 64; pragmatism of, 154; relations, 93; sharing and, 99, 111

exclusion. *See* inclusion and exclusion

"excess." *See* abundance (proliferation)

exogamy: clan, 115; familial, 115

exotic, 88, 91, 101

expansion: contraction and, 84, 87, 91; industrial, 139–140; of relations, 159–160, 186; without transformation, 140. *See also* connection

experiment: as method, 75–76, 124, 139; with relations, 34–35; scientific, 26–28, 49, 165, 206n18, 222n38; thought, 131, 216n24; with words, 35

Experiment on a bird in the air pump (Wright), x, 166

"expersonation" and impersonation, 66–68, 177–178, 188, 217n30, 224n16

expertise, 98–99, 137, 210n17, 226n31

exposition, 2–3, 19, 29, 63, 73, 85, 126, 145, 173–174, 187; defined, 4, 224n11; as drama, 133, 146, 162, 170; practice of, x, 8, 14, 16, 26, 63, 66, 78, 90, 104, 112–113, 118, 133, 209n5; relation as object of, 185–190; routes to, 146, 182. *See also* narrative; twisting

external, as mutual outsides, 148

external object, 15, 214n6

external relations, 6, 10, 38–40, 133–134, 170–172, 208n3, 215n17. *See also* internal relations

extraterrestrial perspective, 8, 188

Facebook, 145. *See also* social media

factory production, 140

familiarity, 93–94, 129–131, 135

family: alliances, 39–41, 134; analogy for state, 148–151, 214n13; chosen, 218n9; depoliticized, 149, 219n14; early modern, 30–32, 38–39; friends and, 46, 51, 55–56, 202n18; of modern kinship, 184; positive affect in, 12; privatization of, 30, 41, 150; relatives and, 147; resemblance, 89; ties as bondage, 131. *See also* conjugal family

farming landscape, British, 186

father(hood), 28, 30, 130. *See also* mother and father; patriarchy

fellowship, 36, 154

fertility: ceremonial, 106; clinical, 81–82

fictive friendship, 145

fictive kinship, 217n30

field: conceptual, 7–11; social, 47, 88, 91, 147, 152–155

figure of speech: in early modern debate, 148–152, 156; rhetorical, 159, 201n9. *See also* analogy; metaphor

flesh. *See* procreation

flow: of analogy, 93; overflow and, 91–95; of relations, 95; of sentiment, 42, 127

form: formlessness and, 91, 93; impermanence of, 217n32; material, 141–142. *See also* Baroque sensibility

formal and informal attributes, 58, 65

formal and informal relations, 65–66

fractal distinction, 90–92, 146; relational character of, 90

Francophone, 60

French language usage, 34, 195n2, 196n13, 198n26

freond (Old English, used for "kin"), 53

friend, 35–37, 48, 50, 202n12, 219n16; being counted as, 55–56, 65; Facebook, 145–146; as generic term, 36; Quaker use of, 151; spouse and, 36–37, 114–116

"friend(s)": "and relatives," 51, 55, 202n17; used of kin, 53; used of kin and non-kin, 31, 36, 114

friendship: "amiable," 152–154, 155, 184; as *amicitia*, 152; as brotherhood, 159; choice in, 56, 145, 182; in civil society, 50, 52, 128; disinterested, 52, 184; fictive, 145; generic, 31–32; with God, 204n2; hereditary, 65, 203n27; ideology of, 145–146, 155; impersonal connotation of, 145; impersonation and, 178; instrumental and otherwise, 151, 227n42; middle-class (Western), 154; non-kin, 31, 33, 61–62, 151; plurality of, 151; purified of kin, 178; re-enchanted, 178; and self-consciousness, 181–182; urban, 59

friendship and kinship: in anthropological dialogue, 144–148, 152–156, 220n21; comparison and contrast of, 45, 50–51, 53–57, 91; degrees of intimacy in, 155; idealized, 146; mystery of conjoining, 159–161; paired, 146, 148, 150, 161; polarized, 154–155; as rivals to the state, 150; separation of, 146, 151, 158–159; and social boundaries, 154. *See also* "Euro-American kinship"

fründe (German, "friend"), in medieval usage, 153

function, 15, 25; differentiation by, 183; understanding of, 4, 201n8

future: effects, 66, 107, 122; knowledge of, 180. *See also* infinition

gender relations, 4, 30, 34, 49, 61, 63, 106–107, 131, 150–151, 167, 214n10

genealogical thinking, 9

generic terms, 27, 31, 54; interpersonal ties and, 83, 128, 130; such as "connection," 32, 54; such as "friend," 32; such as "kin, kindred," 31, 131; such as "relation," 28, 31–33, 35, 53–55, 143. *See also* communication: generic

genetics, 169, 221n33, 227n43

gift exchange, 63, 65, 87, 104

global: idiom, 57, 145; process, 8

God (Christian), 82, 149, 192n7, 198n31, 215n16; friendship with, 204n2; transcendent, 162; works of, 213n1

ground of comparison/connection. *See* third term

growth: as biological process, 139; misconstrued, 139, 149; as social process, 12

habit and habituation, 129, 171–172, 177

health professionals, 77–82, 136–139

Henry Williamson Society, 46

heterogeneity: "controlled," 175; relational, 89, 103; theoretical, 12–13, 167–168, 172, 187

hierarchy, 82–83, 207n2; of analogies, 117. *See also* patronage

holism, 113; structural, 193n12, 193n19. *See also* part and whole

holobiont, 169–170, 171, 223n6

homology, 93–94, 183

hospitality, 65–66

household: composition of, 30–31; connections between, 31; government of, 149

human: "beyond the," 171, 178, 180, 186; flourishing of, 127; as humanity, 94, 162, 178; as interspecies relation, 223n8; not divine, 136, 162; "other-than-," 11, 86, 168; as transcendent category, 92, 157–158, 220n27

human being. *See* "man" (Locke's individual human being)

"human condition," 29, 158, 162

human nature, 51, 78, 83, 86, 124, 129–131, 136, 157, 206n18

Hume, David: on acquaintance, 128; on association of ideas, 124–128, 130, 213n3; on identity, 135, 214n11; on impressions, 124, 130, 214n5; kinship examples in, 127–131; Leibniz and, 172; Locke and, 122, 125, 132, 135; on "love of relations," 129–131; on particular and general ideas, 124; on the person, 127, 130; popularity of, 134–135; on self, 132; on sympathy, 127; thought experiment and, 131. *See also* Hume, David [Index of Names and Places]; *Treatise of human nature*

husband, 44, 134. *See also* conjugal family; spouse

idealization: of friendship, 58, 68, 94, 155, 181, 227n41; of friendship and kinship, 146

ideas, association of. *See* Hume, David

identification, 7–8, 40, 93; and differentiation, 62, 93, 97, 103, 116 identity, 7, 11, 37–40, 42, 92, 117–118, 141–142, 198n30, 207n29, 218n8; challenged, 180, 183; concealing relations/kinship, 133, 174; duplication through, 183; familial, 39; illusion of, 135, 171–172; invention of, 19, 37, 198n28; personal, 132–135; as a relation, 133, 215n14; through relations, 81–83

ideology: of friendship versus kinship, 145–146, 154, 159; in social media, 15

image: perceptual, 92; of thought, x. *See also* painting; visibility

imagination, role of, 124–126, 171, 213n3

immanence, 162, 179–180, 189, 211n26, 222n36

"immanent transcendence," 28, 211n26

impersonal, 52, 136, 139; personal relations and, 53–54, 68, 155, 178, 184; relations of modernity, 68, 136–137, 184

impersonation. *See* "expersonation" and impersonation

incest, 42, 126

inclusion and exclusion, 39, 53–55, 56, 65, 175–177

indeterminacy, of relations, 59–60, 106–107, 139, 182; openness and, 15, 28, 188

indifference, 52–53, 67, 116, 184; bureaucratic, 136, 211n21, 216n26; as opposite of difference, 208n3, 225n25

individual (self), with relations attached. *See* entity

individual entity, 5, 7, 170, 180, 193n12, 217n31; divested of relations, 52, 184–185; organism (human being), 132–135; person, 9, 13, 39, 42, 67, 94, 133, 183–184, 194n23, 198n29, 220n21; society and, 135, 152, 155. *See also* person

individuality, 169–170, 181, 198n29, 212n30

individuation, 184, 217n31

industrial interchangeability, 139–140

ineffable aura, 158–159, 186

ineffable relationality, 162

"infinite being" (relationship), 8, 109

infinition ("inventive definition"), 106–107, 205n6

information, 183; assumed, 98–100; circulated, 49, 104; versus entitlement, 99; free-floating, 104–105, 123

inheritance, 30, 39, 54

innate/invented relations, 92, 208n31

inside/outside: machines, 200n40; networks,

148; persons, 67, 86, 173. *See also* inclusion and exclusion

intentionality, 86, 170

interaction, 28–29, 62, 170. *See also* intra-action

interchangeability, 52, 135–140; of animate forms, 139–142; of persons, 136–137; of relations, 114–115

interdependence, 12, 27, 32; in Orokaiva, 62; of phenomena, 17, 124, 167–168; of species, 169, 172

interest: common/joint, 12, 130, 212n32; and disinterest, 52, 67–68, 96, 184, 227n40; material, 63; and other-interest, 51; and self-interest, 51–52, 67–68, 175, 184, 220n21, 226n31. *See also* altruism

interethnic logic, 105–106

intermediary, as opposed to mediator, 173

"internal disjunction," 207n28

internal relations, 6, 7, 9, 170, 172–173, 193n12; external relations and, 6, 42, 84, 171–172. *See also* external relations

interpersonal and conceptual relations. *See* "duplex"

interpersonal relations, 11, 21, 32, 47, 49, 68, 94, 102, 130, 133, 161, 175, 177; deeper meaning of, 158; as field of inquiry, 147, 204n32; generic use of, 49, 128, 178; intimacy in, 137; networks of, 147, 156–157; and positive affect, 154, 185; unbounded, 94, 160, 162

intersection, 113, 217n31

interspecies anthropology. *See* multispecies (interspecies) relations

intersubjectivity, 133, 136, 192n10

intervention, 17–18; convention and, 80; descriptive, 20, 63, 77–84, 97, 205n11, 206n22; divine, 82; social, 83–84

intimacy, 36, 46–48, 54, 60, 67, 84, 107, 159, 201n5

intra-action, 17–18, 168, 223n7. *See also* interaction

invention, 167–190; of consciousness, 37–38, 132–135; of identity, 19, 37, 213n2; of kinship, 138–139; of nature, 200n39. *See also* twisting

in vitro fertilization (IVF). *See* assisted conception

Jesuit missionaries, 75

Jupiter's satellites, 34, 48, 197n19

kin: denied as "not relations," 110; differentiation of, 62; Hume on, 127–131; Locke on, 29–30, 35; making, 20, 80; marriage of (American/English), 41–42, 200n37; and non-kin, 202n18; as persons, 44, 94; relations of, 12, 131, 213n4; as stranger, 46–47, 52

"kin"/ "kindred," as generic terms, 31, 33, 53, 131, 150, 196n11, 197n23

kind: of persons, 100, 103, 107; social or natural, 93–94, 131

kinship, 16; absence of, 132–135, 174; of all phenomena, 136, 117; Amazonian, 43, 87; American, 44, 147, 160, 200n37; anthropological focus on, 58, 146–147; as attraction, 117; Australian, 99–100; authentic, 146; British, 220n22; bureaucratic, 137–139; as constraint, 145, 153, 155, 214n10; contingent, 138; as corrupting, 227n41; English, 30, 38, 55–56; European, 38–41, 134, 179; expansion and contraction of, 147; Melanesian (see Index of Names and Places: Angkaiyakmin people; Iatmul people; Kuma people; Orokaiva people; Reite people; Tangu people); metaphors of, 148–152; as missing something, 144, 148, 161, 178; in modernity, 143; mutuality in, 27, 51; naturalist, 44; as natural order, 41; as personal, 147, 156; politicized, 148, 156; Protestant, 158; rules, 126, 213n4; as a tool, 138. See also deficit; "Euro-American kinship"; family

kinship and friendship. See friendship and kinship

kin terms and terminology, 9, 30, 43–44, 54, 121, 196n15

knots, relational, 85–86, 207n25

"knowing how one knows," 168, 183

knowledge: attacks on, 226nn30–31; close and distant, 48–50; enhancing, 99; exchange of, 101–104, 210n14; flowing, 91–93; fore-, 180; formless, 93; increasing/decreasing, 47, 94; "indigenous," 210n4; kinship and, 54, 104, 181–182; lost, 99; mutual, 51, 181; obscuring effect of, 181; observational, 122–123, 125; one's "own," 99, 105, 211n17; positive aura of, 26; as property, 93; public, 49, 166; relations as, 29, 166; of relations not terms, 28–30; responsibility for, 105; as second-order understanding, 179, 185; social, 47, 88–89, 91;

transcendent, 179; on trust, 48–49. See also consciousness/self-consciousness; "Euro-American kinship"; recognition

knowledge commons, 93–94

knowledge experiments, 34

knowledge-making, 20, 60, 78, 163; new moments of, 169, 175, 179, 182, 223n6, 226n38

"know thyself," 188

land and landscape, 103–104, 140; in Australia, 101, 143, 209n8; as an estate, 143

language, self-consciousness of, 31–32; re-enchantment by, 156; as tie of society, 215n16. See also English language usage; figure of speech; twisting; vernacular

Latin and English, 31–32, 212n34

law: customary, 109–110; forbidding certain unions, 37; of nature, 42; transplant protocols and, 138

life: continuity of, 38, 132–133, 141; and death, 109; forms of, 141–142, 169; of individual, 220n21; as semiotic, 186; social, 4, 9, 74, 195n2; as source of identity, 38, 132. See also oak tree

life cycle, 122–124, 141–142, 213n2

life form, 123

life sciences, 12, 167, 169, 171

likeness, 19, 83, 98, 115, 116, 128; and unlikeness, 142, 176, 217n34. See also resemblance; similarity

limit: of a concept, 111–112, 160; of relational possibility, 84, 110, 194n23. See also restricted/unrestricted relations

lineage (kinship), European emergence of, 30, 39, 134

literal: and figurative, 91–92; and mystical, 149

literary fiction, 130, 195n9, 122n38. See also Henry Williamson Society

literary reflection, 85, 148–150, 156, 219n12

Locke, John: ambiguity over, 35; on comparison/relation, 5, 29, 84, 133–134; on consciousness, 37–38, 132–135; Hume and, 122, 125, 132, 135; on identity, 37–38, 118, 132–135; on interdependency, 171; on kinship, 29–30, 35, 122, 150; Leibniz and, 5, 172; on personhood, 37–38, 129–134, 181; popularity of, 134–135; on society, 159; Stuart on, 172; on substance and sameness, 132, 141–142;

Locke, John (*continued*)
on workings of mind, 29, 171–172. See also
Essay concerning human understanding;
Locke, John [Index of Names and Places];
"man" (Locke's individual human being);
Two treatises of government
love: of acquaintances, 128; and connections,
127; of friends, 61, 212n4; of kin, 127, 153; of
relations, 129–130. See also *philia*
Lunar Society, 222n4

macrocosm, 92
magic: for efficacy, 211n22; of interpersonal
relations, 156; of kinship, 220n23; of re-
enchantment, 156
"man" (Locke's individual human being), 30,
38, 132–133, 198nn29–30; distinguished from
person, 132
management. *See* bureaucratic projects
market, 67–68, 184, 211n21, 227n41. *See also*
commercial society
marriage: alliances through, 41–42, 59, 153;
cousin, 41–42; friendship and, 36, 113–
114, 197n25; as metaphor, 149; pattern of
(Bangwa), 61; pattern of (Kuma), 61–63;
pattern of (Tallensi), 154–155; prohibitions,
37, 128; as special (Mormon), 158; as special
(Quaker), 151. *See also* endogamy; exogamy
matchmaker, in organ donation, 138–139. *See*
also intermediary
measure: of performance, 77; of relations, 63;
of sociality, 35, 66, 128, 171, 184. *See also*
audit; degree
mediation: concept of, 14, 180, 194n26, 224n14;
and immediacy, 13–15; social, 13–14. *See also*
intermediary; social media
"Medicean stars." *See* Jupiter's satellites
medieval Europe, 38, 153
medieval philosophy, 4, 12, 19, 85, 189–190,
192n6
men, in kinship roles. *See* brother and brother-
in-law; father(hood); gender; parent; spouse
Merian, Maria Sibylla, innovations of, 122–124,
141–142, 217n32. *See also* Merian, Maria Sibylla [Index of Names and Places]
"merographic relations," 6, 221n35
metamorphosis, 123, 140–142; in kin relations,
155

Metamorphosis of the insects of Suriname
(Merian), 123
metaphor, 146, 149–150, 159, 213n1; and
analogy, 92; vernacular model of, 66, 88, 114.
See also figure of speech
method, 76–77, 125, 205n10. *See also* "analytical
context"; experiment
microcosm, 92
middle class, 41, 82–83; "culture" of, 59, 154,
204n32
millenarianism, 101
mind, 28, 180–181; inscrutability of, 66, 225n23;
philosophers on, 29, 117, 124, 185, 198n31,
206n18; and self, 214n12. *See also* conscious-
ness/self-consciousness; subject
minimal relation, 20, 84–86, 92; and irreducibility, 91; "thing," 85–86, 162
miracle: of machines, 165; in naturalism, 82,
222n36; of rebirth, 114; of similarity, 116
"missing side" (of kinship), 148, 161, 178
modernity, 68, 127, 145, 196n12; disenchanted,
158; of family, 30; myths of, 59, 143, 185,
217n3, 218n4; scopic regimes of, 73; and self-
consciousness, 66–67, 69; Western, 183. *See*
also early modern epoch
moderns, 21, 56–57, 66–67, 79, 156, 179,
199n36; and modernization, 79, 81, 144,
218n6; and "naturalists," 40, 118, 140, 171,
178, 185
monarchy, 149, 150
monograph, anthropological, 6, 66
Montagu House, London, 141
moral authority, 102
morality: in interpersonal relations, 61, 129, 153;
versus jural relations, 153, 155; of persons, 55,
127, 136
Mormon (Latter-day Saints) church, 158,
221n30
mother(hood), 30, 36–37, 122
mother and father: analogically conceived,
93–94; paired (Quaker), 151; in thought experiment, 131
multiplicity, 187; in Deleuze, 7, 193n13; in Mol,
217n31
multispecies (interspecies) relations, 141, 168–
170, 173, 180–181, 223n8
museum: collections of, 141; retention of remains in, 98–100, 104. *See also* British Mu-

seum; Working Group on Human Remains in Museum Collections (London)

Museum of Natural History, London, 100

mutuality: in kinship, 27–28, 36, 43, 173, 181; in logical connections, 97; in personal relations, 13, 47, 51, 60

mystery: in anthropology, 156; of friendship, 47; of personal relations, 156–158, 220n25; in transcendental thought, 222n38

names, Iatmul, 211n26

narrative, 4, 74, 154, 170, 175; indigenous Australian, 99, 101; inventing kin through, 138–139; Merian's strategy of, 123–124, 141; philosophical, 129; in Reite, 103; relation as, 4, 11, 75. See also exposition; report

nation and nationhood, 81, 179

natural history, 156

naturalism, 20, 40–44, 162, 168, 179–180; categories of, translated, 93; as cosmology, 40, 44, 185, 192n7; as self-evidential, 183, 192n7

"naturalists": and moderns, 40, 118, 140, 171, 178, 185, 199n36; old sense of, 122

natural kind, 93–94, 131

natural philosophy, 48–49, 75, 124, 129

"natural relations," 30

nature, 26, 34, 40, 175–176; affinity analogous to, 80; disenchanted, 156; principles of, 124; re-enchanted, 156; society/culture and, 40, 42, 78–83, 93, 98, 171, 174, 199n36, 226n32. See also human nature

necessity, in relations, 108–109, 211nn26–27

neighbors, 129, 143, 211n27, 219n16. See also affinity

neoliberal (regime), 77, 98, 100, 145, 209n8

neologism. See "expersonation" and impersonation; philia; "relation/relative"; twisting

network: analysis of, 9–10, 57, 202n17; familial, 56, 134; God-like, 162; inside-out, 147–148; in medieval kinship, 153; organizational, 148; personal, 33, 56, 148, 154; social, 50, 56–57

Newtonianism, 224n17. See also Newton, Isaac [Index of Names and Places]

Nicomachean ethics (Aristotle), 61–62, 152

non-relation, 13, 52, 103, 110–113, 194n22, 201n6, 212n30

nurture of relations, 104

oak tree, example of: in Hume, 135, 141–142; in Locke, 132, 141–142

object, ethnographic, 16, 18; of knowledge/reflection, 101, 174, 179, 183; of study, 4, 10, 25, 83, 174

obligation, 65; in amiability, 153–154; in amity, 153; versus intimacy, 145; in kin relations (duty), 30, 56, 138, 145, 220n22; on part of researchers, 102

observation: inference and, 125–126, 135; of nature, 123, 141; verifiable, 141

occlusion: auto-, 147, 156, 174, 181; between friend and kin, 145, 147–148; of kin relations, 187; obviational, 92; of relational thinking, 133, 144; of religious expression, 158; of sociality, 184

ontogeny, personal, 28, 136, 216n25

ontology and ontological, 43, 79, 102, 113, 176; "no difference" between types of relations, 83, 128; ontological transformation, 81; ontological turn, 177; of relationships, 8, 17, 108

Opticks (Newton), 26

order, 4, 41, 124, 149; of and as relation, 149, 172, 196n18; social, 157; Western metaphysics of, 222n1; world, 165

organ, donation and transplantation of, 50–51, 137–140, 144

organization, 38, 46, 89; in anthropological practice, 9, 18, 60, 79–84, 85, 88; bureaucratic, 77–78, 205n7; and disorganization, 79; in exposition, 74, 79–84; of plantations, 139–140; social (Firth), 125, 135

"organizing organization," 77

otherness: in Amazonia, 80–81; of cultures, 177; in Euro-American thought, 78, 86, 209n3, 229n24; Iatmul "other brother," 8, 108; as unknown, 181–182. See also alterity; "self-other" relation

ownership, 87, 211n19; Amerindian, 43; of knowledge, 93, 103–105, 210n14

painting: Dutch, 73; Italian, 204n3; of still life, 213n1. See also Merian, Maria Sibylla; Wright, Joseph [Index of Names and Places]

pairing, 12, 70, 148, 159, 175, 183; of brothers (Iatmul), 108–109, 193n14; of friends, 113–116; kinship/friendship, 146, 148, 150,

pairing (*continued*)
161; of relation and acquaintance, 128; in Yukaghir, 111
paradigm, ix, 81, 187, 206n22
parens et amis (archaic French, "kinsmen and
friends"), 152, 178
parent: and child, 30–31, 54, 127, 131, 145, 151;
solicitude of, 93
"parent," as generic, 198n26
parenté (French, "kinship"), 117
part and whole, relations of, 6, 10, 59, 112,
193n19, 215n18
participation, 6, 92, 207n29, 212n37, 224n15
paternal filiation. *See* father(hood)
patriarchy, 149–150, 156, 219n17
patronage, 49, 58, 154, 156, 185, 219n17; of
Galileo, 34, 48–49; in medical care, 81–82
person: in anthropology, 9, 85–86, 180; in
Euro-American kin relations, 44, 94;
Hume's use of, 127, 130; individuated, 94,
155, 121; Locke's use of, 37–38, 129–134; in
Radcliffe-Brown, 9; with rights, 121; social,
10. *See also* entity; "man" (Locke's individual
human being)
personal, impersonal relations and, 53–54, 68,
155, 178, 184
personal ontogeny, 28, 136
"personal relations," 45, 53, 148, 154–155; mystery of, 156; new concept of, 184; nonspecific, 35. *See also* interpersonal relations
personhood, Amazonian, 44. *See also* Amazonia [Index of Names and Places]
perspective, 12, 46, 66–67, 73, 76, 152, 204n2,
205n4; exchange of, 64–65; as other than
perspectivism, 43
phenomenon, concept of, 17–18
philia (Greek, "friendship, love"): in anthropology, 61–63, 152, 219n18; universe, 62, 65,
68, 203n24
Philosophical transactions (Royal Society), 75
placement, 33, 64, 116, 211n34; in landscape,
103–104, 211n22 ; and place-change, 27,
114–116, 211n19. *See also* displacement
plantation, sugar, 122–123, 139–140
pluralism, concept of, 140
polarization: as continuum, 153–155; and dissimilarity, 154
pole, of perceptual mediation, 20, 91–92

politics: as action, 12, 99, 102, 148, 168; alter-
and anti-, 14, 174–175; concealed, 104–105;
of "culture," 105–106; as ends, 13; of detachment, 105; of knowledge ownership, 101–
105; of language, 156, 175. *See also* neoliberal
(regime)
popularity, of Hume and Locke, 134–135. *See
also* Anglomania
positive tenor: of abstract terms, 25, 27; of
friendship, 154–155, 181; of kinship, 12,
202n20, 220n6; of knowledge, 26, 181; of mutuality, 181; of relations, 12–13, 25, 37, 127–130
positivism, versus interpretivism, 89, 91
postcolonial legal system, 109–110
predation, Amazonian, 87
premise of similarity. *See* similarity
privacy: in friendship, 53, 60, 68; as a sphere,
203n22
problematization, in exposition, 16, 188
procreation: by blood or flesh, 39, 199n35; conversations on, 158, 221n30; elicitation of, 63.
See also assisted conception
property, 121; as "accident," 4; cultural, 210n14;
as intrinsic, 43; personal, women's rights in,
30, 39, 195n10
proportion: expositional, ix; relation as, 128,
196n18; and values, 159. *See also* degree
Protestant, 158, 198n31. *See also* Puritan
thought; Quaker society
proximity, 47, 201n5, 225n22; contiguity and,
127–128; degree of, 47, 227n43; effect of,
176. *See also* "sliding scale"
public sphere. *See* civil society; commons
"pure" relationships of modernity, 94, 181; purification and, 39, 187
Puritan thought, 149, 198n31

Quaker society: families of, 41, 150–151, 158;
against knowledge, 198n31, 226n30; Society
of Friends, 151; visionaries, 195n8, 219n17
quantitative-qualitative divide, in social science, 90

rank, 151, 157
rapport (French, "association, attraction, agreement, affinity"), 26–28, 34, 195n2, 206n22,
217n2

real: Locke's connection, 215n21; "unreal" (mental) and, 4–5, 12

real friends/kin, 56, 137, 154. *See also* "true" friend/relative

reasoning, 75, 130, 148

recognition: of friends, 51–55, 181; of kin, 32–33, 211n31; and materialization, 63; of persons, 28, 54–55, 84, 206n21; politics of (Australia), 100, 209n8; of relations/connections, 28, 63, 103, 131, 157, 182; in Stengers, 206n22

re-enchantment: by anthropocentrism, 221n34; by contingency, 186; by language, 156–158; by relations, 157–160

Reflections upon marriage (Astell), 150

reflective practice, 65, 76, 157, 163, 171, 174, 179, 186, 222n38; reflexivity and, 29, 66, 76, 174, 223n1, 224n16. *See also* consciousness/self-consciousness

reinvention, of concepts, 19, 168–184

relata (scholastic Latin, "whatever are being related"), 84–85

relatedness, 27, 130, 160, 186, 203n21, 227n43; interrelatedness and, 169, 172, 186

relating, 9, 83, 95, 167, 169; always unfinished, 182; as formless disposition, 91; power of, 161–163; transcendent, 8, 186; unconstrained/unrestricted, 95, 161–162

"relating relations," 75–79, 111, 183

relatio (scholastic Latin, "disposition toward something, comparison"), 4, 10, 205n3

relation (French, "connection, acquaintance"), 195n2

relation: connection and, 8, 32, 35; non-, 110–113; "relations" and, 105–108, 182; relationship and, 8, 108–110

"relation/relative," for kinsperson, 12, 31–33, 53–54, 122, 143, 156–157, 186; North London usage of, 55–56

relational: non-relational analysis and, 13, 103, 110–113, 210n16; post-, 13

relational deficit, 135–136, 139, 143–144, 173, 178, 217n31

relationality, 11, 121–122, 167, 169, 181, 184, 186; anthropology of, 145, 210n12; everyday sense of, 121, 128, 136; immanent, 103; transcendent, 161–163; unconstrained, 94; worlds of, 200n1

relational pointers, 43

relative: idea, 214n5; term, 5, 29, 134, 171–172, 199n32. *See also* absolute; "relation/relative"

relazione (Italian, "report, narrative"), 75

religion: displaced, 158, 160, 192n7; in secular life, 158; state and, 6, 149, 151. *See also* Christianity

remediation, 16

Renaissance Europe, 179, 207n9

repatriation, 98–101, 104, 210n14

repetition: in fractal distinctions, 90–92, 207n28; and self-consciousness, 84, 188. *See also* duplication

report, to Royal Society, 49, 141. See also *relazione*

representation, lure of, 78, 205n6

researcher: anthropological, 101–105; scientific, 98–101

resemblance, 8, 35, 83, 108, 115, 117–118, 127–131, 141, 192n5, 207n30, 212n37, 216n25. *See also* similarity

restricted/unrestricted relations, 87–94, 161–162; and negation, 97; through specification, 87–89, 139

resurrection, 114, 198n30

reversibility, 109, 111, 113

Rhenish imperial knighthood, 39

ritual conflict (Kuma), 106–107, 169

ritual moieties (Iatmul), 108

Royal Society (London), 48–50, 54, 75, 141, 201n9, 217n34

Russian sponsors, of Yukaghir, 111

sacrifice, 166, 219n17; between friends, 114. *See also* altruism

same(ness), 38, 83, 132, 135, 141–142, 198n30; among conspecifics, 43; similar and, 116, 208n4. *See also* self-same state

scalability/nonscalability, 139–140, 142

scale. *See* degree; "sliding scale"

scholasticism. *See* medieval philosophy

science, 124; behavioral, 180; humanities and, 89; interests of, 34, 98–100; life, 12, 167, 169, 171; natural, 85, 89–90, 169; "science's relation" and, 191n3; scientific association, 33; scientific credibility, 34, 48–50, 53, 123, 141; scientific-feminist history, 34, 112; scientific revolution, 5, 48, 121, 124, 141; social, 90,

science (*continued*)
145, 176, 211n21, 225n29; uniformity in, 165. *See also* natural history; Royal Society
Scottish Enlightenment, 52, 67, 121, 124, 129, 141, 136, 175, 184, 216n25
secular anthropology, 158
self: ethical, 76; and individual, 155; and inner life, 199n31; instability of, 37, 198n28; multi-dimensionality of, 188; nonreflexive form of, 84; and person (Locke), 38, 129–132, 181; postmodern, 112; self-description, 77–78, 151, 183; self-identity, 11–12, 37–38, 69, 132–135; self-interest (*see* interest); self-knowledge, 188 (*see also* consciousness); self-occlusion, 147, 156, 174, 181; self-reference, 44, 92, 112, 133, 183; self-relation, 13, 76, 163, 183; self-scrutiny, 76–78; social, 58, 155; split, 76, 205n4
self-evident phenomena, 4, 94, 183, 192n7
"self-other" relation, 47, 76, 84, 205n12, 209n5; cosmological import of, 86–87; as we/they, 176–177
self-same state, 37, 83, 141, 211n25
sentiment, 44, 51, 94; nonspecific, 129–131, 151, 159; among those related, 127–128, 155; un-constrained, 58. *See also* affect; solicitude
separation, of persons, 86–87, 106–107. *See also* brother and brother-in-law; detachment
servant, 31, 123, 203n22
shadow (double): kinship and friendship as each other's, 160; philosophy of, 111; Yuka-ghir, 111–112, 178
sibling, 42–43, 62, 65, 126, 153, 202n17, 203n22. *See also* brother(hood); sister(hood)
side. *See* "missing side" (of kinship)
similarity, xiii, 109, 141–142, 192n5, 208n3; abundance of, 110, 115–116; and affinity, 83; in analogy, 92; concealed, 116; connection and, 83, 97; degrees of, 130, 136, 142, 214n9; premise of, 12, 19, 98–101, 110, 128, 142, 168, 178, 189; and sameness, 116, 208n3
similarity and difference, 43, 60, 64–65, 89–90, 92, 95, 97–98, 117–118, 141, 178, 208n32, 208n3, 217n34
similarity and dissimilarity, 20, 98–101, 109, 113–116, 118, 128, 130, 136, 142, 152, 177–178
sister(hood), brother and, 30, 42, 44, 151; as

brotherhood, 112; transformed in marriage, 30, 36–37, 61–63
slave, 123, 140
"sliding scale," 47, 74, 154–155; benevolence of, 175–176, 224n17; kin relations in, 55
sociability, 154, 215n16, 219n19. *See also* association
social analysis, 58, 112
social change, 66
social criticism, 14, 135, 167
social field, 47, 88, 91, 147, 152–155
sociality, 20; divergent axes of, 147; Euro-American, 147; immanent, 211n26; relations and, 85–86
social knowledge, 47, 88–89, 91
social life, 4, 9, 74, 195n2
social media, 13–15, 145–146
social mediation, 13–14
social person, 10
social relations, 2, 8–11, 13, 67, 85, 125–126, 140, 163, 191n4, 210n12; "Western" ontology of, 176
social self, 58, 155
social structure, 9, 58, 60, 68, 125, 147, 155
society, 10, 26; in comparative analysis, 4, 64; and culture, 4, 10, 59; making of, 79–80, 187; and person/individual, 58, 155; relations as building blocks of, 125, 129; of strangers, 52, 137; structured, 126, 146–147. *See also* nature: society/culture and
"society": as an association, 33, 130; as companionship, 36, 49, 185; early modern conno-tations of, 33–34, 49–50, 196n13; Friends (Quaker) of, 151; natural history, 201n4. *See also* civil society; "company"; Henry Williamson Society; Lunar Society; Royal Society
sociology and history, distinctions between, 90
solicitude: of kin or friends, 94; maternal or paternal, 93
species interdependence. *See* multispecies (interspecies) relations
specification, 14, 84–87, 91, 154, 179; and obli-gation, 153; of relations, 25, 162
spirit beings, 17, 111
spouse: as friend, 36–37, 114, 159; as sibling, 42, 64. *See also* conjugal family
state: and church/religion, 6, 149, 151; family

analogy and, 148–152; family relations and, 150; the helping, 205n8; precursor of, 214n13; rationality of, 216n26; welfare, 138

Stoic cosmopolitanism, 175–176

strabismic optics, 73, 76, 144

stranger(s): company of, 129; in intimate publics, 51–52, 137; kin/friend as, 46–47, 52; in organ donation, 50–51, 137; socially distant, 176; society of, 52, 137. See also exotic

structuralism, French, 60. See also social structure

subject: knowing, 18, 110–111, 180–182, 186; as modern subjectivity, 86; and object, 84, 165

substance: Amerindian, 43; identity and, 37, 43, 132–135, 172, 198n29; knowledge as, 10

substitutability: medical, 51, 137–139; of persons, 115; as surrogacy, 115; in symbolic process, 208n32. See also interchangeability

sworn brother/friend, 36, 114–116, 197n25, 212n34

symbiosis, 86, 113, 169–170, 173, 212n32; symbiogenesis and, 173; symbionts and, 170

sympathy, 46, 83, 131, 197n22; authentic, 176; in Hume, 127, 129, 216n25; in Smith, 216n25, 224n20

system, 113, 117, 126, 146, 212n31; requirements of, 59–60, 227n38

tautology. See duplication

taxonomy, 116–117, 161

technical terms, in philosophy, 132, 201n6. See also vernacular

terms: absolute and relative, 4–5, 134, 171–172; to a relation, 7, 9–10, 41, 133–134; tension between, 91, 159. See also third term

terra nullius (Latin, "land belonging to no-one"), 140

"thick"/"thin," 29, 37, 69, 127, 131, 143–144, 156, 170, 173, 217n2

third party, 14, 131

third term, as ground of comparison/connection, 5, 30, 67, 108–109, 116, 127, 133, 193n19, 228n47

traders, Dutch, 123

trade union, 57

transcendence, 165, 179–180, 189, 220n23; divine, 162–163; in interpersonal relations, 8, 11, 17, 28, 108; of relation/relating, 162–163, 186; of society, 147; of values, 146. See also "immanent transcendence"

transformation, 122–123; industrial, 140, 216n27; of particulars, 116; relational, 11, 109, 139, 162, 176, 216n25, 224n14. See also metamorphosis

transmission, of knowledge, 103–104

transplant: professionals in, 138–139; relatedness, 138; slave as, 140. See also organ

Treatise of human nature (Hume), 124, 172, 206n18

"true" friend/relative, 56, 202n17; "true" friendship, 58. See also "pure" relationships of modernity

trust, 151, 208n11, 212n35, 219n16; between affines, 61; between kin, 153; in science, 48–50, 53, 75. See also science: scientific credibility

twin: of hunter, 111; through identical forms, 115

twisting, of language, 61–63, 66–68, 74, 204n1

Two treatises of government (Locke), 150, 159

Underlying Law Act (PNG), 110

understanding, 181; Locke's sense of, 205n12

"understanding understanding," 78, 124, 182, 206n18

undifferentiated benevolence, 37, 159

union, image of, 149–150

unit. See entity

unity: clan, 106–107, 115; global, 123; and plurality, 140

unpredictability. See indeterminacy

usage, 2, 29, 58; immanent, 179–180; of relations, 16, 174; of terms/concepts, 109, 188–189, 219n10. See also English language usage; vernacular

"us-them" (we-they) boundary, 176–177

utility, 179

values: in anthropological practice, 12, 58; in common, 161; distributed, 49, 57, 65; in relation/tension, 90, 146, 149, 150; transcendent, 146

vernacular, 148–152, 187; and analytical usage, 74, 170–171, 188; anthropologists' use of, 57, 60, 145, 162. See also English language usage visibility: and invisibility, 101, 106, 116, 118, 124, 156, 165–166, 171; in kinship and friendship, 144, 148; in networks, 148; reversible, 111; of society, 187; too big to see, 143–144, 148; of women, 21. *See also* appearance; occlusion

Vital relations (McKinnon and Cannell), 147

We, the Tikopia (Firth), 122

wealth: exchange of, 63–64, 104, 203n29; as property, 30, 39

"Western" thought, 11, 58, 209n3

"we-they." *See* "self-other" relation; "us-them" (we-they) boundary

"what never happened," 20–21, 122, 132–135

"white": becoming, 79–83, 205n13; as national project (Ecuador), 81, 206n15, 206n17

wife, 30, 36–37, 44, 63–65, 114–115, 134

witchcraft, 6–7, 10, 61

women: bonds between, 65; capacity for action, 63; as daughters and sisters, 30, 36–37; disinheritance of, 30, 39, 195nn9–10; as mother (Merian) and daughter, 122; as mothers and wives, 30, 36–37; patronage and, 81–82; occlusion in public life, 21, 34, 39; as sisters and wives, 63–65, 115

women and men. *See* conjugal family; gender relations; parent

wonder: anthropological, 161, 221n34; of relating, 163

words: new world of, 33–34, 156–157, 196n12; as seducer, 226n30; word play, 35, 185. *See also* figure of speech; twisting; usage

Working Group on Human Remains in Museum Collections (London), 98–100, 102, 210n15

working practices, academic, 88

xenophobia, 176